Clark Bryan

A new book of Berkshire, which gives the history of the past

Clark Bryan

A new book of Berkshire, which gives the history of the past

ISBN/EAN: 9783337175207

Printed in Europe, USA, Canada, Australia, Japan

Cover: Foto ©ninafisch / pixelio.de

More available books at **www.hansebooks.com**

NEW BOOK OF BERKSHIRE.

GREYLOCK—(FROM THE NORTH.)

A NEW BOOK OF BERKSHIRE,

Which gives the history of the past, and forecasts the bright and glowing future of Berkshire's Hills and Homes,

Telling where they are and how to find them; what they are, and why they are what they are—at once the most charming and desirable Summer Homes in the world.

CLARK W. BRYAN & CO., PUBLISHERS,
SPRINGFIELD, MASS.

Dome of the Taconics—(Mount Washington.)

Copyright, 1890.
All Rights Reserved.

PREFATORY.

THE outcome of a thorough revision and re-writing of The Book of Berkshire, originally published in 1886, is A New Book of Berkshire for 1890. The words of introduction used on the occasion of the first issue of the book are as pertinent and proper now as then, and were these :—

Berkshire, by common consent, is not only a good place to be born in, but a good place to live in, and a good place to die in, as well. It is also prominently recognized as a good place to go out from, and equally a good place to come back to. Its traditions are marvelously full, rich and interesting. Its history is replete with story, song and incident—with mention of good deeds, of patriotism, valor, chivalry and refinement; of enviable record and renown, and "last, but not least,"—so to speak—it is big with promise for the future ; that is to say, To-Day sees rising from the embers of its altars and its fires of Yesterday, a wealth of golden wreaths around the brows of fame and fortune, with which to gloriously perpetuate its To-Morrow.

The record which Berkshire has made, both at home and abroad, is one to be proudly recited and to be read of admiringly and profitably. Its beauties of form, its favorable features of landscape, and its pictures of loveliness, in combination, are unsurpassed, however broad the comparison may be made.

A Berkshire birth is something to be proud of, a Berkshire sojourn a delight, a rest, a recreation, a circumstance of pleasant memory, ever after, and a Berkshire residence a rich and enjoyable life experience, far beyond that of "the common lot of humanity," as scattered broadcast over the earth.

To illustrate and describe—all too briefly, however,—what God and man have done for this region among the hills; to picture its beauties and glories, and to forecast the possibilities and the probabilities of Berkshire as it may be, is the object of the issue of this little book. The work of its preparation has been a labor of love, albeit that labor has been exacting, perplexing and sometimes discouraging. But it has had the pleasant thought and careful consideration of several years, the best efforts of our head, heart, hands and feet for many months, and these would have fallen far short of what has been accomplished, but for the valuable assistance and aid which have been so freely accorded to the enterprise.

Our Book, as the public will readily discover, is prepared in a spirit of much enthusiasm regarding the subject matter in hand. Should the reader feel that there is, as the late Artemas Ward, once said, "Too Mutch" in this vein, and incline to the opinion that it savors somewhat of "gush," by comparing our own writing with those from the "outside world," from whose eminent and conservative pens we have made quotations, it will be seen that we are in good company in making up our estimate of the Berkshire Hills and Homes.

With this much of remark we close this ceremony of introduction with the simple announcement that whether THE BOOK OF BERKSHIRE is good or bad, perfect or imperfect, valuable or valueless, worthy or unworthy of regard and patronage, it is peculiarly its own, and strong in individuality, if in nothing else. It is not a History, nor is it a hastily prepared Guide Book, alone, but it is THE BOOK OF BERKSHIRE, now A NEW BOOK OF BERKSHIRE.

THE PUBLISHERS.

BERKSHIRE.

BERKSHIRE, among all the summer resorts of the United States, is the solitary representative of its kind. There is no other such combination of the wild and the beautiful in nature—of perfect harmony in variety. Another region may be found conspicuous for imposing wildness, another that is pretty, possibly beautiful; others may be healthful and invigorating, pleasant places for summer sojourn and interesting in their surroundings, where guests may find agreeable provision for their comfort and enjoyment; but there is not another region with which Berkshire must divide the honor of having all these at once—certainly, none possessing them all in the same high degree. Though the sublime work of nature may be found here, it is subservient to extraordinary beauty in the general effect upon the visitor. In the quality of this beauty Berkshire admits no rival; if duplicates of its other claims may be found scattered elsewhere, the beauty of its scenery is unique and unrivaled. It seems as if, walled in from outside contamination and set apart from the spoiling hand of manufacture and traffic, here had been assembled the choicest touches of the Creator's handiwork.

In most mountainous regions there is a tiresome similarity among the mountains, the hills, the forests, the valleys, the streams and the landscape, but this is not so in Berkshire. Here, not only has no other region been patterned from, but the mountains and hills, on every hand, are fashioned in the most varied styles, the valleys are no two alike, and the scenery everywhere passes before the eye of the traveler in the richest and most lavish profusion of dissimilar characteristics.

Amid all this, not an inharmonious effect is perceptible; but, more than this, there is a marvelous blending of masterpieces of natural beauty, of the wild and the picturesque. Though there is civilization, somehow a wilderness is not out of place, and though the surface of the earth be ruffled and rugged, often forest-covered and untillable, yet it impresses one as the fittest dwelling-place of the highest civilization, above and removed from the toil and trouble, the money getting struggle of business and professional life.

The effect of the environment upon the visitor from cities, upon the hard worker who would seek refuge from the cares of life and a tiresome noise and bustle, is of a most soothing character. Not only are the nerves rested from an irritating tension, but there is something about the scenery that imparts a quietude, a repose, a freedom from distraction, a healing with the balm of Dame Nature. The unequaled harmony of the surroundings exhales an influence that enraptures the beholder, and creates within him an inward form of the external.

The hills and mountains of Berkshire are now gentle and sloping in their lines, now wild and broken, sheltering well watered, thoroughly cultivated valleys, where towns and villages, famous for their beauty, hide among the trees; a region of lakes, mountain torrents, glens, lovers' lanes, rocks, and echoes; a region, too, where one may spend the summer and not die of *ennui* from lack of good and congenial society.

People who go to mountain resorts expect to suffer more or less discomfort, to step out of civilization and enter primitive communities, to whom the world is strange, if not unknown. Berkshire, of all of them, is alone the place where this expectation is disappointed. One may leave a civilization to come here, but he enters another; he may abandon a pleasant home, but he finds a new one of unalloyed charms. He escapes from a world that is in many respects uncongenial, and discovers in its neighborhood, yet separated from it, a region of the best civilized institutions, thriving in their own soil, and at the same time deriving nourishment from foreign soils.

Here his ideas and feelings will be as cosmopolitan as in New York or Boston, and the comforts of living, all things considered, many fold enhanced, unless during the winter, and even then there are pleasures unknown to city life. The daily morning newspapers of Springfield and Albany are received by nine o'clock or earlier; New York and Boston morning papers arrive before noon; evening papers are received on the same date; numerous mails are in daily receipt, including Sunday. The facilities for telegraphing and telephoning are ample in every part of the county, and a dozen excellent local newspapers collect and spread the news. Local tradesmen are provided with an abundance and a large variety of the goods, the wares and the merchandise of the world. The central part of the county being but 110 miles from salt water, the food that is brought therefrom is always fresh and abundant. There is nothing in the way of nutriment, either for body or mind, that is not common in Berkshire and may not be had easily and cheaply.

A journey from New York city to the southern half of the county, which is the portion of this famous region most sought, requires but four hours and a half in drawing-room cars or in first class passenger cars that are the tidiest and best furnished and finished ones in the United States. The distance is about 150 miles. From Boston the time is less than five hours, the distance being a little over 150 miles. Three lines of railway cross the region, and a line of railways extends up and down. At the north end is the Hoosac Tunnel route of the Fitchburg road; in the center the Boston & Albany; at the south end the Central New England and Western road, from Hartford to and across the Poughkeepsie bridge. From the center of the county, at Pittsfield, to the north end runs the Pittsfield & North Adams railroad, and towards the south runs the Housatonic road to Bridgeport, where connection is had with the New York, New Haven & Hartford road. These railway lines afford accommodations for travel to and from the region that make it easily accessible, and that make the return to the city an easy and short matter.

No railroad in the country has taken greater pains to accommodate people who go to summer resorts than have been taken by the Housatonic road. Through cars on express trains are run to and from New York in about four hours and a half, and, if the traveler does not care to take the drawing-room car, he can ride in a car that almost seems like one, with its brussels carpet, toilet-room, fine upholstery and cabinet finish. He can leave New York in the morning and eat a noon dinner in Berkshire, or leave near the close of business hours and eat a late dinner or supper here. The facilities for return are equally good, for he can leave Berkshire at several convenient times, the last one being about 5 p. m., when an express train leaves, to arrive in New York about nine. Several express trains run both ways, and for Monday morning return a special one arrives in New York about 11.45 a. m. Within five hours of this region, over these railroads and connecting lines, there are about ten millions of people, the most intellectual, the most cultivated, the most wealthy on the continent, and possessing the highest social development, and from these people are contributed those who resort to Berkshire and can appreciate its offerings.

The Berkshire region has been referred to as a summer resort, but it is more than this. It is the only autumn resort in the United States, taking no account of mere sportsmen's resorts. The seaside resorts are not frequented in autumn, because of the raw winds and the dreary outlook; inland resorts, away from mountains, lose their attractiveness with the loss of hot weather, and the visitor is no longer able to keep up his indulgences with comfort; and in the mountainous regions, generally there is no autumn, except in name, and the passage from summer to wintry weather is rapid. But in Berkshire there is an autumn of surpassing loveliness. The air may get a frosty keenness and there may be some cold waves, but these are only the cheap price of ruddy cheeks and elastic muscles, a clear brain and bountiful flow of spirits.

In place of the dreary time that comes upon most resorts by the middle of September, Berkshire often gets a climate that is quite mild up to the middle of November, and now and then a month later. As September passes, the foliage begins to turn from green to brilliant and varied hues. It is said by travelers to be true that nowhere else in the world are such wonderful effects in autumn foliage coloring seen as here. As the leaves lose their green, the reds, scarlets, cardinals, yellows, purples, in a dozen shades, interspersed with evergreens, all in infinite arrangements, confront the beholder on every hand with their amazing spectacles. Every mountain is a huge bouquet, chameleon like under the changing sunlight. In October the leaves fall, coloring the very breezes into brilliance as they float along in irregular buoyancy, and making vast carpets, woven with a gigantic hand, from the richest colors. Toward the close of this, an eastern wind and rain will obliterate the last vestiges of the delaying leaves on the trees, and in a night the genii of the storm will transform the illuminated forest into bare limbs and twigs.

But the scenery is by no means spoiled. The hazy-bluish browns and greens alternate with darker shades, and the winter snow and sleet at last whiten the limbs or clothe them with diamonds. A driving wind will so place the snow upon the limbs that it seems at a distance as if some great spirit had blown his breath upon the forest and it had frozen there. The most striking effect of all is caused by a rain, that freezes as it falls; then an icy coat is put about everything, and among the curious and strange results, the long, slim, white birches are bowed to earth, and every part of every tree is bent into graceful curves, making pictures that few city people ever saw, except in engravings, which, however, could never express the wonderful beauty of the rainbow colors made from the sunbeams by the refracting ice.

Until such a time of the year Berkshire entertains guests, not only those who come to enjoy the country in good health, but those who come to find a sanitarium. Among the latter is a gentleman who has lived in the far South many years, where he had a home that he has abandoned for a home in Berkshire, declaring that his best health is realized here. An extract from a New York *Herald* editorial article expresses the dictum of hygienic science : "People in search of health are very eager to get to the mountains in summer, but ignore the hygienic properties of high level air in winter. Many invalids who cannot go to seaside winter resorts, and conclude that they must languish throughout the cold weather in their city homes, might do surprisingly well to try the beneficial effects of a winter sojourn on some of the moderate elevations of our Atlantic highlands."

There is another point applicable alone to this region. One goes to other resorts to find himself a foreigner, as it were, and after the "season" is over, an intruder ; but he comes to Berkshire to a home. If he does not own a place here, still he can obtain the best of keeping at any time at highly attractive hotels. The making of an autumn season in Berkshire is due to the people who come to Lenox. In the waning of the summer they leave Newport and other places and take possession of their Berkshire homes or find entertainment at hotels. Until this was done it was not known by any but the permanent residents that the autumn season here was enjoyable ; and now the discovery of winter's beauties is keeping people later and later, even to the middle of January. So, Berkshire has become dear to a great many of the people who come here, because here they have established homes, built fine houses, and bought real landscape views, the paintings of which, in their wealth of beauty, would be worth thousands of dollars. One may withstand the allurements of all other resorts, but he capitulates to Berkshire as the only place choice enough for his country home.

A New York *Tribune* correspondent, in 1885, wrote : "Nature certainly made one of her most successful efforts when this secluded and restful region in Western Massachusetts was planned and brought forth. Nowhere else do little hamlets, with their white church spires pointing skyward, seem to nestle so cozily and contentedly among the hills ; nowhere else do the lakes and rivers hold such flattering mirrors for the mountains, and nowhere else does Nature get from Jack Frost so fine a cloth of gold as she throws over the bosom of these hills."

Again, it may be claimed solely for Berkshire that no other region offers such varied inducements to visitors, guests and new residents. They range from simple farm-house accommodations to hotels that are as delightfully agreeable homes as hotels can be, and where the fare is high class ; the temporary society is from that of people of quite limited means, who come to stay two weeks, for instance, to the *élite* of fashion and wealth, who have their homes here with all luxurious accessories. Old people can find seclusion and quiet ; children, isolation, where they will be tolerated ; brain workers, rest and recreation ; the man or woman of society and fashion, congenial surroundings ; houses can be hired for family use ; it is the place for the tourist as well as the resident—for the wheelman, the pedestrian, the horseback rider and tourists in carriages ; while it is much sought for camping out locations. One can find village life, with many villages to select from, or he can enjoy farm life ; he may pick from hotels or from private families ; he may keep house or board ; and he may live upon mountains and hills or in valleys.

The roads of Berkshire have for years been known for their excellence. The drift gravel that is found in abundance has been freely used where the roads were naturally heavy with mud or sand, and the consequence is that everywhere—upon mountains as well as along valleys—the roads are smooth and hard, free from cobble stones, ruts and mud holes, and upon the main lines of travel as good as the roads in any park in the country. For this reason wheelmen are numerous, and carriage driving general. Within a few years several towns have utilized stone-crushing machines, for further highway improvement. Pittsfield alone has laid over 20,000 square yards of macadam during the past four years.

The manufacturing establishments that are in Berkshire are so situated as to be in no wise offensive ; the typical factory village is nowhere to be found, but, on the contrary, the work-people generally live in neat homes. Mills are situated in narrow, deep valleys, where they are hidden from view. In paper manufacture Berkshire has been famous for nearly 100 years; wood pulp was first used successfully in paper-making in Lee ; the quality of the correspondence papers made at Dalton and South Lee, and of the record papers made at Dalton and Adams, is hardly equaled anywhere in the world, for reasons that are peculiar to the location.

The excellent advanced schools that are in Berkshire afford such opportunities for education, that homes, permanent and temporary, are sought here by many people who have young children. In Great Barrington is a well taught High School, the Sedgwick Institute for boys, and the Housatonic Hall School for girls ; in Stockbridge, the Williams Academy and Prof. Hoffman's School for young men ; in Lee, Pittsfield, Adams, North Adams and Williamstown, excellent High Schools—in the last named and beautiful historic town, are located Williams College, and Glen Seminary for young ladies; in South Williamstown, Greylock Institute; Chickering's Commercial College, Prof. J. E. Peirson's School, for boys fitting for college, and Miss Saulsbury's School, for young ladies, in Pittsfield; in North Adams, Drury Academy; and the Robbins School, in Norfolk, Ct. Besides good schooling for children, for wealthy people who are the victims of municipal extravagance and thievery in cities, Berkshire has many towns where taxes are light and the rate low.

In freedom from contagious diseases Berkshire has always been fortunate ; though it is almost a suburb of dense populations, yet it has a seclusion and a situation off the main lines of travel, so that the introduction of disease from without is not easy. Cholera never penetrated the region, though it came to the outskirts. Within the region the germs of disease do not thrive, partly on account of the altitude and the dry air, and partly because the sanitary conditions are high and the precautions prompt and prescient. Every town has a board of health, and several villages have sewage systems. The people understand that filth furnishes nourishment for disease germs, and are careful to remove it to harmless places. The climate is dry, cool and bracing ; the elevation of the country has the effect of stimulation, it accelerates the breathing and the circulation, and gives tone to the nervous system. The disease most benefited is consumption, and the registration reports show that the mortality from this disease is less in Berkshire than in any other county of the state, being little more than half what it is in some of the maritime counties. For children the air is extremely favorable ; cholera infantum, the summer scourge of cities, is rarely seen, and other summer diseases are comparatively rare and mild. The temperature is two to six degrees lower than it is in the lower country on the east and west.

The drinking water is every where of extreme purity ; the principal villages get their water in pipes from mountainous springs, and where this is not done each family gets water from a spring or excellent well. The drinking water is never a source of disease.

Within a very few years Berkshire has been getting a reputation for architecture. A large portion of the houses, of course, are in the usual style of country architecture, but scattered among them are many beautiful buildings that will surprise city people, accustomed as they are to square, monotonous, roofless houses. Mrs. Mark Hopkins's million dollar house in Great Barrington will rank among the finest in the United States ; the Congregational Church there is a beauty, and contains the best organ on the continent, and the parsonage adjoining is excelled hardly anywhere. In Stockbridge, St. Paul's Church is one of the

1.—Lake Garfield   2.—Congregational Church, Lenox.   3.—Ancient House, South Egremont.   4.—Sage's Ravine, Mount Washington.   5.—Plantain Pond, Mount Washington.

choicest ones in the country, and among notable dwelling houses are those of Joseph H. Choate, the Rev. Dr. Henry M. Field, the late Henry Ivison, Lucius Tuckerman, Charles E. Butler, C. F. Southmayd, the Town Offices, and others. In Lenox beautiful and superb dwellings lie on every hand, in locations commanding charming views; only a few of these houses can be mentioned—those of Charles Lanier, the houses of W. D. Sloane, Dr. R. C. Greenleaf, F. A. Schermerhorn, John E. Parsons, William R. Robeson, William B. Shattuck, D. W. Bishop, George Westinghouse, Jr., ex-Secretary Frelinghuysen, C. G. Havens, and many others. Of late years the old colonial style has become very much in vogue. The new Trinity Church in Lenox is notable. Dwelling house architecture in Pittsfield has fine representatives in W. R. Allen's house, W. F. Milton's house, the residence of E. Pope Sampson, and many new cottages of unique and pretty design for successful young business men have sprung up within a few years. Architect H. Neil Wilson has been instrumental in bringing about many changes in this regard in the Athenæum, in Mrs. Pollock's house, and many others. Governor Weston's house, Hon. Zenas Crane's house, and the handsome new Congregational Church, in Dalton, James Renfrew's house in Adams, the new Morgan building, the Clarke building and the Hopkins memorial building at Williams College, are among the notable buildings, all of which would be given distinction anywhere.

The geological formation of Berkshire has been the subject of much controversy for many years, and has long brought to the region the best geologists of the country and enlisted those who lived here—Prof. Amos Eaton, Dr. Chester Dewey, Prof. Ebenezer Emmons, Prof. Edward Hitchcock and Prof. James D. Dana. Prof. Dana began to study the rocks in 1871, and continued with assiduity up to 1885, and he embodied a condensed account of his conclusions in a paper read before the Berkshire Historical and Scientific Society, published in the *Berkshire Courier* of February 11, 1885. He sustains Prof. Emmons in these conclusions: "That this non-fossiliferous Taconic series was older than those Hudson river slates; older than the lowest fossil bearing rocks of New York; older than the oldest known rock of the New York Silurian, the Potsdam sandstone; therefore a distinct system of rocks, the Taconic System. In the geological series, the system, in his opinion, came in between the Adirondack rocks, or Archæan, and the Potsdam sandstone, the rock directly overlying the Archæan in Northern New York. Thus the name of the Taconic Mountains became of wide importance in geological science, for geologists abroad, as well as at home."

Besides numerous literary, social and village improvement associations in the towns, there are several county societies, to which it would be an honor to belong. The Historical and Scientific Society has done and is doing better work than any other county society of the kind in the country has done. There are three agricultural societies, one of them the second best in the state, and the old Berkshire, begun in 1807, is the pioneer in the country. The Berkshire County Bible Society was organized in 1817, nearly the first in the country; the Berkshire and Columbia Missionary Society, established in 1798, was probably the earliest missionary society organized in this country. The Berkshire Branch of the Woman's Board of Missions has about 1,700 members; and there is a Berkshire County Sunday School Union. The Clericus Club, organized by Rev. W. W. Newton of Pittsfield, and the Congregational Club, are among the newest county societies.

While Berkshire has no dense population, on the other hand it is not so sparsely populated as to suffer from paucity of numbers. The population of the county in 1885 was 74,000, and that of the principal towns, and those in which the visitor is interested, varies from about 14,500 to 160. The sojourner has a choice among villages varying in size from hamlets to cities, and among more rural places that descend in population, from village suburbs to an isolated farm-house in remote regions.

The model villages of the American continent are in Berkshire: Stockbridge, Lenox, Great Barrington, Sheffield, Williamstown, Pittsfield— where can the like of these be found anywhere in the New World, and all within 45 miles of each other? Indeed, some of these villages are absolutely unique; there is only one Stockbridge, no other Lenox,—none like Pittsfield, and but a single Williamstown. Each have attractions peculiarly its own, and yet each possessing traits in common with their sister villages. Amid the glory of these hills and valleys, villages have grown that lead a vast nation in beauty, in neatness, in picturesqueness, and in social composition.

As Prof. Hitchcock writes, "Where does the traveler meet in any part of our land with lovelier spots than Pittsfield, Lenox, Lee, Stockbridge and Great Barrington?"

Unlike other resorts where a man finds his surroundings agreeable wherever he is able to pay for his keeping, Berkshire is composed of many distinctive communities where he who enters may find himself a sad misfit. One seeking the quiet of Stockbridge, would be out of place in fashionable Lenox, and if he should mistake Lenox for Mount Washington, Cheshire or Tyringham, he would be in a pitiable situation. Some idea of the peculiarities of each place is meant to be conveyed in this book, but after all, one may have to live here to know where he likes it best. He cannot toss a cent for choice among Berkshire's varieties.

The guest will find Berkshire's hotel life most perfect—that is, where summer and autumn visitors are in the habit of going. There is no landlord here, with a vast building, bragging of its 500 or 1,500 rooms and who rarely comes in contact with his guests; there is no place where the guests jostle each other as strangers and where they shift for themselves, as in large hotels. But, on the contrary, fellow guests become acquaintances, associates and friends; the landlord, with perhaps an assistant, gives personal attention to their wants, and in every way they are made to feel at home, and as it were, members of one large family. Hotel keeping is an art that has reached a high development in Berkshire.

The native people of Berkshire compare very favorably, indeed, with those of any region or city in the United States. Under good schools, reading habits; leisure for study and thought, in the winter at any rate; well developed electric, railway and postal communication; and under frequent traveling, these people, as a whole, are up with the times; they know what is going on in the world, they are abreast with the thought of the age, they live at least in comfort and often in luxury. The average well-to-do and wealthy people of the cities who come here, expecting to find a native population of country bumpkins, will be surprised in finding a large portion of the people as cosmopolitan as themselves and many who are decidedly more intelligent. If the people act slower than city people do, the latter will be taught a lesson that if life is worth living, it is more worth the living when one takes time to derive the most happiness on the way. The city people who have acquired homes here have learned this lesson.

The nature of the inhabitants of this region and its fitness for the residence of literary and of intellectual and cultivated people is attested by the famous people who were natives or who were nurtured here, and by the distinguished people who have found here a congenial atmosphere. In the early days of Lenox as a resort, there came Nathaniel Hawthorne, Frances Anne Kemble, Henry Ward Beecher; John Morell left this town eventually to become Chief Justice of the Michigan Supreme Court. In Stockbridge, were Jonathan Edwards; Rev. Dr. H. M., David Dudley, Stephen D., and Cyrus W. Field; G. P. R. James; Theodore Sedgwick, Mrs. Charles Sedgwick and Catherine Sedgwick; here the Rev. Dr. Mark Hopkins was born. In Great Barrington, there were notably William Cullen Bryant, the Rev. Samuel Hopkins and other members of the Hopkins family, from one of whom descended the Rev. Dr. Mark Hopkins, ex-president of Williams College, president of the American Board of Foreign Missions for over thirty years and a vigorous writer on religious subjects. Sheffield is known as the native town of the Rev. Dr. Orville Dewey, of his sister Miss Jerusha Dewey, of his daughter Miss Mary E. Dewey; of President Frederick A. P. Barnard and of his brother Major General John G. Barnard; of Bishop Janes of the Methodist church; Prof. George F. Root of Chicago, the musician; Judge Daniel Dewey of the Supreme Court; of Daniel Dewey Barnard, who was Minister to Prussia from 1849 to 1853. In New Marlboro, lived that stout defender of Calvinism, the Rev. Jacob Catlin. From Egremont went Grosvenor P. Lowrey, the New York lawyer. In Pittsfield were Herman Melville, Oliver Wendell Holmes; the Rev. William Allen, a native, afterwards president of Bowdoin College; Pittsfield is the home of Senator Dawes and has been the home of many distinguished politicians, judges and lawyers, among them Governor Briggs, Judges Julius Rockwell, James D. Colt, James M. Barker and Congressman Francis W. Rockwell. Governor E. D. Morgan of New York was a native of Washington. The Rev. Dr. Barnas Sears was a native of Sandisfield, and was for ten years president of Brown University; "Josh Billings" lived and died in Lanesboro. Mrs. D. H. R. Goodale lived on Mount Washington, where the childhood of her daughters, the poets, Elaine and Dora R., were passed. In Hinsdale were born Governor F. E. Warren, of Wyoming Territory; R. H. White, the Boston merchant; A. D. Matthews, Brooklyn's oldest merchant; President William E. Merriam, of Ripton College; the Rev. Dr. John W. Yeomans, once president of La Fayette College. North Adams was for some time the home of the Rev. T. T. Munger. Col. T. J. Skinner, in Williamstown, was for many years Chief Justice of the Court of Common Pleas; Daniel N. Dewey was long a Probate Judge, and Charles A. Dewey, both from Sheffield stock, was a Judge of the Supreme Court. The mountain town of Peru has sent out two judges, four missionaries, besides one college president.

The mention of these names, that come most readily to mind out of many more that have been or are distinguished, shows what kind of stock the permanent resident population of Berkshire is and some of the distinguished people who have found it a congenial home. Under each town, reference will be found made to well-known people who have summer and autumn homes here.

A great gathering of the sons and daughters of Berkshire, who had gone into every part of the Union, was held at Pittsfield in 1844, when there came to the meeting in person and in spirit a multitude of Berkshire people, of whom, in many ways, the nation has time and again had abundant reasons for being proud. Governor Briggs was president; the Rev. Dr. Mark Hopkins preached a sermon; poems were composed by Frances Anne Kemble, Mrs. Lydia H. Sigourney, Oliver Wendell Holmes, William Pitt Palmer and the Rev. Dr. William Allen. The oration was delivered by the Hon. Joshua A. Spencer of Oneida County, N. Y.; and speeches and sentiments were given by Drake Mills, New York; Judge Charles A. Dewey, Northampton; Thomas Allen, St. Louis; Theodore Sedgwick, New York; the tragedian, Macready; the Rev. Dr. Heman Humphrey, president of Amherst College; the Rev. Dr. Orville Dewey, New York; Prof. Chester A. Dewey, Rochester, N. Y.,; Josiah Quincy, New Hampshire; David Dudley Field, and others. The assemblage was made up of a large number of people who were born in Berkshire or had spent a considerable portion of their lives here, among them being many distinguished people.

It need not be surprising, then, that the county abounds in literary and social clubs, in village improvement associations and in public and private libraries. The face of nature here is a stimulus to thought, to the imagination, to the higher feelings and emotions. If Berkshire renews the vitality of the tired worker who seeks recreation, so it creates and strengthens genius, talent and proficiency. In other resorts there is nothing beneath the outward show to hold the visitor after the effect becomes monotonous; but beneath the forms of beauty and majesty and harmony, of which one here never tires, there is something that constitutes an abiding place, a Promised Land, a fixed country home,

> "For Childhood's opening bloom,
> For sportive Youth to stray in,
> For Manhood to enjoy its strength,
> And Age to wear away in."

THE FUTURE OF BERKSHIRE.

The future of no part of the country is more apparent than that of Berkshire. While other resorts see only a horde of sight-seers, a stream of humanity that hurries along as if in a public street, Berkshire, while entertaining transients, will be the great country home of the wealthy and cultivated people of New York, Philadelphia, Boston, Albany, Hartford, New Haven and the East. The tendency this way has been apparent for many years, but never so much as lately. The price of land for agricultural purposes is worth on the average hardly $50 an acre; but where the site commands a fine view or has a social value, the price has already gone up to hundreds of dollars an acre, and the time will come when thousands will be the measure of value outside of villages, as it is now within them. Within the distance of a day's ride on a railway, the 10,000,000 people of the present day, who will probably double their number in thirty years, are sending here increasing numbers of country home seekers every year, while the visitors of a transient character are coming more than ever before to stay a short time in one place or to make a tour of the region. Those now living may not live to see the time, but that time is surely coming when the sides and tops of every hill and mountain here and the best valley locations will all be taken up with the houses of the people to whom reference has been made. With the influx of this population comes the development of the æsthetic emotions in the beauty that is purchased by wealth and the sentiments that arise from it, and a development of the region itself, in making its treasures more accessible and in converting it into a vast inhabited park, charming the senses, invigorating the health, prompting thought and imagination, a retiring place for the weary and a pleasure ground for appreciative thousands. Every year marks an increase in the summer home-making of the city cousin in the grand old Hills of Berkshire.

LENOX.

IT is a conspicuous feature of Berkshire towns that though they all owe a kinship to Berkshire characteristics, yet they have differentiated into individualities. Lenox, Stockbridge, Great Barrington, Williamstown, Pittsfield, Lee, Sheffield, Mount Washington, New Marlboro and Egremont will bear as strong contrasts among each other in nature and in society as each will bear with the world external to Berkshire, and yet all are distinctively Berkshire towns in their composition. This unlikeness of parts in a general union of underlying constitution entitles Berkshire to great distinction as a resort, for the peculiarity is not to be found elsewhere. The lavish hand of nature has accomplished this singularity for the aspect of the country; and a strong local feeling, fostered by town government and a high spirit of freedom and independence, and the inborn talent and capability of the inhabitants, have been the means of differentiating the social characteristics. In this general movement Lenox bears the impress of an external hand more than any other town. It is now owned and regulated principally by people who migrate to it for a portion of the year; the native influence has not been extinguished, perhaps, but it is all subservient to the new comers. Hence Lenox has been moulded into one of the most singular of the Berkshire towns, and it has grown into a resort that is quite fittingly termed "The Inland Newport." People of wealth and fashion flock to it in the summer, and their numbers increase in the autumn, beginning about the 1st of September, when the Newport season wanes and when many of the people who have been there in the summer travel this way with their costly turnouts to take possession of their Berkshire homes in Lenox or find entertainment at Curtis's Hotel. But Lenox never can attain a social character that will in the least obscure the work of nature. Here, as in neighboring towns, the beautiful and the picturesque, after types of their own, admit no rivals. The lap of earth spreads out in an original phase of Berkshire's common beauty, and provokes the profoundest admiration that never tires.

The Early Visitors.

No civilized people can behold Lenox without coveting an incessant inspiration of the spirit of its landscape. It lay in the nature of things that man could not once behold it without renewing the acquaintance, until frequency must end in possession. So Lenox has come to be the chief country home resort of the continent, and is rapidly developing in the same tendency. Though the town never lay on any great thoroughfare, yet, being the shire town from 1787 to 1871, it was early the destination of many people who came from a distance beyond the county. Here came the judges of the State courts and many distinguished lawyers and some witnesses and litigants from all over New England and New York, so that the town, let it once be noised about as a thing of beauty and worthy of resort, would be called to mind by many people scattered over the East as fulfilling all that was said in its praise. An influential part of the public was thus made familiar with the town and prepared to elevate it to renown, if not to visit it for pleasure.

The discoverer of Lenox was Charles Sedgwick; that is, he was the first discoverer to make his discovery known. Through his culture he appreciated the natural aspects of the town, and through his wide acquaintance he made them known to many people of taste and intelligence, who in turn noised abroad the delightful character of the region. Mr. Sedgwick moved to Lenox in 1821, a time that marks the first coming of visitors; yet it is doubtful that the very first visitors came through his influence. As near as memory serves the oldest inhabitants, the first people to come and stay during the summer were the widow and children of the Rev. Samuel Munson, who was pastor of the Congregational church from 1770 to 1793. They were here, it is thought, somewhere between 1820 and 1825. About that time, also, the Misses Merritt, of New York, came to stay during the summer; they were amateur artists, and, as they remained season after season, they made many sketches of scenery, which they took to New York—so many that one room in their house there was called "Lenox," where their friends were enthusiastically shown pictures of scenes in their summer home.

But Charles Sedgwick soon brought greater numbers of people this way, and before long coöperating causes brought this charming town to the notice of the whole country. The Lenox Academy, incorporated in

1803, graduated pupils that returned in after years; Mrs. Charles Sedgwick established a school for girls that brought many noted people to town; and the residence of Catherine M. Sedgwick, begun in 1831, gave an immense impetus to the movement.

INFLUENCE OF THE LENOX ACADEMY.

The Lenox Academy has been a very famous institution. It has had many excellent principals, among them being Matthew H. Buckham, president of the University of Vermont; and among the many men of distinction who have been pupils here were the Rev. Dr. Mark Hopkins, Judge Henry W. Bishop, the Rev. Dr. Henry M. Field, Prof. Chas. A Joy, Anson Jones, once president of Texas, Charles Sedgwick, Samuel R· Betts, who was a United States district court judge, and a long list of others. Sometime in the '70's the school was suspended, but in September, 1880, Prof. H. H. Ballard, an accomplished scholar, was the principal. In 1875 he organized here a school scientific society for the study of natural history, in connection with the Lenox High School. This was given the name of the Agassiz Association in 1880, and an invitation from Prof. Ballard was published in the *St. Nicholas Magazine* to young people to organize branches on the same plan as the parent society. The idea spread rapidly and took with both young and old, so that within a short time (1886) there were classes in nearly every State and Territory in the Union, embracing many thousands of members. Three new branches are organizing every week, on the average. Of this association, *Science* says, editorially : "The conductors of these enterprises have done something permanent and effectual towards spreading a taste for self-culture in an almost new sense." A hand-book of this association may be got from Prof. Ballard, now the librarian of the Pittsfield Athenæum. It is to this academy, now eighty-three years old, and its pupils, that Lenox owes much of the fame that has gone abroad. The school is now of the past, however, and the old academy building on the Main street is an interesting though now tenantless land-mark of the town, and always attractive to the eye of visitors—a connecting link of golden memories between the past and present.

THE INFLUENCE OF CATHERINE M. SEDGWICK.

The residence of Catherine M. Sedgwick in Lenox at once made the town known to all the reading, literary, and leading people of the day. Here Harriet Martineau visited her several times, the last time being in 1835. The social features of Lenox under the reign of Miss Sedgwick are feelingly expressed by Fanny Kemble, "*Our* Fanny," as Miss Sedgwick has called her: "Of the society which gathered summer after summer to the pleasant hill region, the seat of her family home, attracted thither even more by the delightful intercourse of its various gifted members than by the pure air and fine scenery of Berkshire, Miss Sedgwick was the center and soul, dispensing the most graceful hospitality and doing the honors of her beautiful hills and valleys to her visitors with an unwearied kindliness and courtesy that must forever have combined in their memories the most delightful social intercourse with the most charming natural scenery." The last time that Miss Sedgwick was in Lenox was in the spring of 1863.

In Lenox, Miss Sedgwick wrote the last of her works: "Live and Let Live;" "Home;" "The Morals of Manners;" "The Boy of Mount Rhigi," the scene of which lies on the mountain in the northwestern part of Salisbury, Ct.; and "Married or Single."

Miss Sedgwick took unbounded pride in the preëminent beauty of Berkshire. Referring to this, the Editor's Easy Chair of *Harper's Magazine* for October, 1867, says: "If some lover of the coast, some devotee of the ocean, looked doubtingly upon the pine sheeted hillsides as too rigid and monotonous, she knew where to take him to silence his scepticism by one wide and sufficing glimpse of inland splendor. Nor were her pride and confidence misplaced. Returning, haply, after the lapse of years, the lover of the sea, who had been unjust to the real charms of the superb Berkshire landscape, recanted wholly as he stood looking from the heights of Lenox southward over the lovely lake [Mahkeenac] to Monument Mountain, and the soft smooth outline of Taconic in the delicate heaven further away. There was no sense of imprisonment in the hills, no feeling of oppression, and as his eye turned northward to the tranquil dignity of Greylock, it was only to confess that neither Bryant, nor Hawthorne, nor Miss Sedgwick, nor Herman Melville, all of whom had made their homes in Berkshire, had too warmly praised the beauty or described the character of its landscape." Miss Sedgwick's remains were entombed in the earthly paradise she loved so well—in a portion of it set apart for a cemetery, in Stockbridge. The house occupied by Miss Sedgwick, and Charles Sedgwick, who owned it, is on Kemble street, and is owned by Mrs. Elizabeth Sedgwick Rackemann, who, with her family, is to occupy it in the future, after letting it for several years. The influence of Miss Sedgwick upon Lenox is incalculable; she brought hither many of the first people of the land, and founded here a literary headquarters that endured for many years.

INFLUENCE OF MRS. CHARLES SEDGWICK'S SCHOOL.

Another source of Lenox's fame was Mrs. Charles Sedgwick's school. She was of the Northampton Dwight family, and was a highly cultured woman with a wide and distinguished acquaintance. In 1828 she received into her house a few pupils to educate with her own, and this was the beginning of the celebrated school that closed only with her life in 1864. She wrote several books for children, among them "The Beatitudes," and she contributed to periodical publications. Her school was regarded as one of the best, if not the best, in the United States for years for the education of girls and young women; and her pupils were accordingly drawn from the wealthy and cultivated people of the day. Among the few early pupils that are remembered were Charlotte Cushman, Harriet G. Hosmer, Lucy Marcy, daughter of Governor Marcy, the wife of Chief Justice Brigham, of the Superior Court, Lydia Saltonstall, of Salem; Maria Cummings, author of "The Lamplighter;" a daughter of John Van Buren; daughters of Weyman Crow, of St. Louis; Hattie Bellows, of Bellows Falls, Vt.; Alice Delano, Carrie White, Carrie Train. There were eighteen or twenty pupils in all, and their parents, relatives and friends often came to the town to visit them, to find that the town itself was so rich in natural charms that it must be revisited again and again. So came Governor Marcy, John Van Buren and other distinguished men. Lady Churchill, wife of the late secretary for India, was formerly one of Mrs. Sedgwick's pupils as Miss Jerome, of New York.

THE RESIDENCE OF FANNY KEMBLE.

Miss Sedgwick had not long been living in Lenox after 1833, the time when Frances Anne Kemble first came to this country, before she induced her to come to Lenox. The great actress has said that she found Miss Sedgwick her first *friend* in this country. Mrs. Kemble came, she saw, she was conquered. She worshiped the matchless, outspread, lavish beauties of nature that she saw here, and annually came to revel in their delights. For years she stayed at Curtis's Hotel, but finally bought a house that she called "The Perch," situated on Kemble street. To have Mrs. Kemble at any place in those days was to distinguish it above all others in the United States; where she went, the wealth and culture of the country must also go, and when it was known that she had found a charming summer country home in Lenox, the town got its first decided start as a summer resort. Here Mrs. Kemble came off and on for about thirty years. She is spoken of by Miss Sedgwick in a letter of

November 16, 1861, as knitting garments for soldiers. Finally Mrs. Kemble sold her house, the one now owned by Mrs. Thomson, and after living at the Kneeland place, "Fairlawn," which she hired, and boarding at the hotel for several years, she returned to England. Recent reports have been to the effect that she had talked of returning to this country, to pass the remainder of her days, but these lack verification. If she were to be buried in the village graveyard, she once said, "I will not rise to trouble any one if they will let me sleep there. I will ask only to be permitted once in a while to raise my head and look out upon this glorious scene." Mrs. Kemble's cultivated imagination was in harmony in Lenox with its natural and social environment, and it is no wonder that her enthusiasm over the town should have endured so long.

Mrs. Kemble thus writes of the views from her house: "Immediately sloping before me, the green hillside, on the summit of which stands the house I am inhabiting, sinks softly down to a small valley, filled with thick rich wood, in the center of which a jewel-like lake lies gleaming. Beyond this valley the hills lie, one above another to the horizon, where they scoop the sky with a broken, irregular outline that the eye dwells upon with ever new delight as its colors glow and vary with the ascending and descending sunlight, and all the shadowy procession of the clouds. In one direction this undulating line of distance is over-topped by a considerable mountain with a fine, jagged crest, and ever since early morning troops of clouds and wandering showers of rain and the all-prevailing sunbeams have chased each other over the wooded slopes and down into the dark hollow where the lake lies sleeping, making a pageant far finer than the one Prospero raised for Ferdinand and Miranda on his desert island."

Again Mrs. Kemble describes a scene: "The day is bright and breezy and full of shifting lights and shadows playing over a landscape that combines every variety of beauty—valleys, in the hollows of which lie small lakes glittering like sapphires; uplands, clothed with grain fields and orchards, and studded with farm houses, each the center of its own free domain; hills, clothed from base to brow with every variety of forest tree; the woods, some wild, some tangled and all but impenetrable, others clear of underbrush, shady, moss carpeted and sun checkered; noble masses of granite rock, great shafts of marble, clear mountain brooks; and a full, free, flowing, sparkling river;—all this under a cloud varied sky, such as generally canopies mountain districts, the sunset glories of which are often magnificent." Mrs. Kemble has published three volumes of autobiography and recollections, and a volume of poems, among which may be found "Lines Addressed to Young Gentlemen Leaving Lenox Academy," and the poem read at the Berkshire Jubilee in 1844. The village clock in the tower of the Congregational church, on the hill, was a gift of Miss Kemble, and is the more prized on that account as the years it ticks away pass by.

RESIDENCE OF HENRY WARD BEECHER.

The late Rev. Henry Ward Beecher came here about 1853, and bought a house and several acres on a hill towards Lee, since called Beecher Hill. General John F. Rathbone now owns the place, and the old house has been moved to another site and is now occupied by his farmer. The effect of such a region as Berkshire upon Mr. Beecher's imagination and feeling can well be imagined. His whole soul went into his adoration, and his enthusiasm was boundless. Berkshire was too fine a place to be absent from an unnecessary moment, and so often did Mr. Beecher come here that his congregation in Brooklyn stood in actual fear that he would abandon his church and pass the remainder of his life in Lenox. The members of his church bestirred themselves, and at last prevailed upon him to accept a country home in Peekskill after he had spent a few seasons here. Mr. Beecher's Berkshire inspiration found expression in several of his letters, republished as "Star Papers." He speaks of Lenox as "known for the singular purity and exhilarating effects of its air and for the beauty of its scenery." "The endless variety of such a country never ceases to astonish and please. At every ten steps the aspect changes; every variation of the atmosphere, and therefore every hour of the day, produces new effects. It is everlasting company to you." He wrote in admiration of the trees of Lenox, of which there are 175 to 200 kinds; of the restful effect of the surroundings, and of the ministering influence of nature here toward happiness.

"This is perfect rest," he wrote. "The air is full of birds' notes, of insects' hum, of the barn-yard clack of hens and peeping chickens; the eye is full of noble outlined hills, of meadow growing trees; of grass glancing with light shot from a million dew drops, and of the great heavenly arch, unstained with cloud, from side to side without a mote or film, filled with silent, golden ether, which surely descends on such a morning as this from the very hills of heaven."

Again Mr. Beecher wrote of a morning: "On such a glorious morning of a perfect day as this, when all the smoky haze has gone from the horizon, when the sun comes up fresh and clear and will go down unreddened by vapor, the mountains come back from their hiding, and I wander forth, wondering how there should be sorrow in the world. * * * Each hour is a perfect hour, clear, full and unsated. It is the joy of being alive. * * * Such days are let down from heaven."

NATHANIEL HAWTHORNE.

Here, too, came Nathaniel Hawthorne, in 1850, and occupied a house on the slope north of Lake Mahkeenac, in the edge of Stockbridge, now owned by W. A. Tappan and generally known as the Hawthorne place. Herman Melville came down from Pittsfield, his frequent visitor. G. P. R. James came occasionally from Stockbridge, and Fanny Kemble was often at the house. She was a daring horsewoman, and it is said that she once rode a horse to the very summit of Monument Mountain, a most courageous feat. Julian Hawthorne, then a small boy, calls to mind a day when she rode to the house in the saddle, and, holding him before her, gave him a gallop up and down the road.

Mr. Hawthorne came here to get from Berkshire what all weary and over-worked men can have for the coming after — recuperation. The great novelist was soon able to work, and one of his greatest efforts, after his "Scarlet Letter," was written in this little red house—"The House of the Seven Gables." Mrs. Hawthorne, in describing the surroundings, uses this language: "Sit down upon the couch, and you will see such a landscape out of the window as will charm perpetually; for the motion of light and shadow among the mountains and on the lake varies the scene all the time.

The effect of living here upon Hawthorne is told in his own words: "After such a winter and spring as I have passed, of tranquil and complete joy, with mountain air and outlines to live upon."

Hawthorne left Lenox late in the autumn of 1851, after writing "The Wonder Book," many of the events in which had a reality in Lenox, and planning and preparing his materials for "The Blithedale Romance." In commenting on the literary work in Lenox, Julian Hawthorne writes: "Lenox was one of those places where a man might be supposed to write because the beauty around him moved him to expression." The old desk on which much of his writing in Lenox was penned, is now in the Pittsfield Berkshire Athenæum Museum.

CURTIS's HOTEL AND ITS GUESTS.

An important feature of Lenox for many years has been Curtis's Hotel. The front portion of the building was erected in 1829 and called the Berkshire Coffee House, designed for the accommodation of judges, lawyers and others coming to court. In 1833 William O. Curtis came from a farm in Stockbridge to Lenox, and after some time was engaged in staging between here and Pittsfield and in the livery business till 1853, when he bought this hotel. At the time Lenox was already a popular resort for people who were choice in their preference, and under Mr. Curtis's management the house, in the course of time, gained a reputation and a character of the very highest order. In short, such entertainment here has long been famous, and many are the people, who know what the best public house entertainment throughout the world is, who can indorse the fact. Mr. Curtis's son, William D. Curtis, has for several years been associated with him, and, indeed, has borne the principal duties of management, besides constantly looking after the renting of the many cottages in town for the owners, and being a general agent for doing all sorts of business transactions for people who do not reside in town all the time. William O. Curtis has many interesting reminiscences of the noted people who have been at his house or lived elsewhere in town during the fifty-three years of his residence here. He taught many of the pupils of Mrs. Charles Sedgwick's school how to ride horseback when he was a young man, and accompanied them many a mile over the delightful roads of Lenox and vicinity. He tells of the innocent frolics of school girls, since distinguished, and calls to mind numerous recollections of Fanny Kemble. He spent days and days with the great actress in driving around the country or in fishing. Indeed, a volume would be required to specify all that Mr. Curtis can call to mind about his noted guests. But, after all, the best informed person in Lenox about Lenox affairs and traditions is William D. Curtis, who has stowed away a vast amount of information in orderly fashion about the inhabitants of the town, past and present, the drives for many miles around, and everything that pertains to the town.

The old hotel had long been too small for the demands that were made upon its space, until, in 1884, extensive additions and repairs were made, and the whole house was put in the best condition. There was built a brick addition, double the size of the original hotel, three stories high, with attic and cellar. The dining-room is the best lighted and most cheerful one to be found in a hotel, with a seating capacity of about 225. The heat in cool weather comes from fire-places, of which there are many in the house, or from steam; the lighting is done with gas; and an electric bell system extends through the whole house. Each floor is provided with several Brighton water closets in a room perfectly secluded from other rooms, and all the plumbing of the house is of fine and intelligent workmanship. There are three stairways between floors. There are several private parlors; and many of the other rooms are so made as to be used *en suite*, if so desired. All walls are of brick, the floors are double, and hot and cold water comes to one place on each floor, from which place it is carried to rooms. No sewer pipes run into living rooms. The ventilation of the house on every floor is faultless.

In one respect, the rooms become better as one ascends to the upper floor, and that is in the views of the beauties of nature with which Lenox has been so bountifully supplied by a prodigal hand. The most charming views are obtained from the attic story; the range of vision extends as far as the Dome on the south, the West Stockbridge mountains on the west, Greylock on the north, and the distant mountain tops where begins the eastern slope of the valley. The emotional and imaginative soul can revel in the perception of cottages, lakes and woodland, mountain, valley, glade and hill, that make Lenox and her surroundings such a paradise. In the past few years this plan of "cottaging" has come to be quite popular in Lenox. The gentleman hires a cottage—practically a large house already furnished—in the village, and the family therein enjoy all the privacy and comfort of their own home. Their meals are taken at the hotel. By this means they have the advantage of the society of friends whom they may meet at the hotel, while at the same time they are relieved of all the care of an establishment of their own—the worry over details of house management and servants. During the past season a larger number of people enjoyed this phase of Lenox life than ever before in the history of the famous resort.

The table of Curtis's Hotel has long been famous for its excellence, and the attendance throughout the house is the most painstaking. The Messrs. Curtis have about 250 guests at the height of the season—October 1st. The hotel is supplied with vegetables from Mr. Curtis's three-acre vegetable garden on his large farm, not far from the village, and with milk, cream and butter from the choicest dairy. The proprietors own a large livery stable, in which sixty to seventy horses and many vehicles of all kinds are kept for the uses of the guests and the public in general as well.

The hotel has had so many guests of more than common note that probably twenty-five pages of this book could not contain their names. If, as is maintained by some scientists, the actinic rays of the sun impress our photographs, though unseen, upon the surfaces to which the rays are reflected from our faces and forms, what a remarkable array of invisible pictures must be spread out upon the walls of the old hotel,—

the pictures of the chief justices and judges of the supreme and superior courts for many years, the talented lawyers from all parts of the country who practiced before them, Chief Justice Shaw, Governor Andrew, John Van Buren, Governor Marcy, of New York, Fanny Kemble, Charlotte Cushman, Henry Ward Beecher, Nathaniel Hawthorne, Catherine Sedgwick, Horace Greeley, Dr. Channing, and all the others.

The registers of the hotel are a treasure of autograph signatures of noted people who have been here, most of them as visitors of the town. In the register of 1857 are the names of Edwards Pierrepont, Fanny Kemble; Captain, later Commodore, Inman, of the United States navy; Harriet G. Hosmer; Horace Gray, Jr., now a judge of the United States supreme court; Cassius M. Clay, John Jacob Astor; George S. Boutwell, President Grant's Secretary of the Treasury; Chief Justice Shaw, and, most conspicuous of all, the name of James Fiske, Jr., whose frequent signatures for several years were made with his dashing pen when he stayed here while meeting his various peddlers. During the few subsequent years are the names of Mr. and Mrs. James Ticknor Fields; the Rev. Dr. George P. Fisher, professor in Yale College; Parke Godwin, Horace E. Scudder, Bret Harte, John A. Andrew; C.B. Dahlgren, of the United States navy; Mrs. Ledyard, mother of the African traveler, and so on, with many more. About 1836 Judge David Davis studied law with Judge Bishop, and subsequently married a daughter of Judge Walker, of this town.

To this hotel have been Joseph Pulitzer, editor of the New York *World;* the late Frederick T. Frelinghuysen, Secretary of the Treasury; General McClellan, Millard Fillmore, Jenny Lind, James Russell Lowell, Epes Sargent, Mrs. Mowatt, the actress. The Rev. Dr. W. E. Channing delivered an address in town on August 1, 1842, anniversary of the West Indian emancipation, his last public address; and the day before he left town he had a long ride to Mount Washington, with William O. Curtis for driver. On his way to Vermont, where he died a few days thereafter, Mr. Curtis drove the team that took him as far as Williamstown. Dr. Channing came here for his health, and, in endeavoring to get it, he saw so much of the country that he wrote to a friend: "We enjoy our life here greatly. The country is inexhaustible in pleasant excursions." Mr. Curtis calls to mind a memorable time when Kossuth came to his hotel, drawn to town by the Sedgwicks. He was then the lion of the nation, and that he should come here was reason for thinking that Lenox must be a remarkable place. And so it is! One evening there was dancing at the hotel in honor of Kossuth, and in the distinguished company were Catherine M. Sedgwick, Charles Sedgwick, Judge Bishop, and Fanny Kemble. While a guest at this hotel, Charles Sumner courted his wife, the widow Hooper, who was living in a neighboring house. Sir Edward Thornton, once British minister, has been here, and in 1883 here came Sir Sidney and Lady Waterlow, Lord Carrington, and the Earl of Cork and Orrery.

A good idea of who the guests are that now come to Curtis's Hotel may be formed by the stranger from these names of people who have been here within recent years: Sir Lionel Sackville West, British minister; Horace Helyar and family, British legation; Th. Roustan, French minister; B. Lovenorn, Danish minister; M. Reuterskiold, Swedish minister; A. Iswolsky, Russian legation; Count Gyldenstolpe, German legation; ex-President Chester A. Arthur; Admiral Jouett, United States navy. Among the many well-known families represented are the following in New York: Schermerhorn, Astor, Webb, Leavitt, Winthrop, Iselin, Roosevelt, Frelinghuysen, Tompkins, Jones, Barclay, Kane, Crocker, Potter, Aspinwall, Goelet, Brown, Thorne, Stuyvesant, Van Nest, Folsom, Harriman, Godkin, Parsons, Newbold, Lanier, Barnes, Sands, Bradford, Lawrence, Ingraham, Ledyard, Rives, Harper, Pulitzer, Dehon, Bartlett, Tailer, Draper, Chapin, Livermore, Trevor, Egleston, Delafield, Sloane, Marié, Johnson, Kneeland, Moller, Van Auken, Collier, Haven, Warren, Bouvier, Carey, Livingston, Vanderbilt, Westinghouse, Mrs. ex-President Cleveland. In Boston: Shaw, Hunniwell, Perkins, Sargent, Brooks, Meyer, Lee, Brimmer, Higginson, Wharton, Otis, Appleton, Saltonstall, Endicott, Armory, Winthrop, Minot, Sears, Lawrence, Curtis, Thayer, Silsbee, Gray, Rotch, Adams, Kuhn, Beebe, Chadwick, etc. In Philadelphia: Rogers, Biddle, Mason, Meigs, Struthers, Devereux, Adams, etc. In Troy: Green, Griswold, Ogden, Warren, Burden, etc.

The First Country Homes for City People.

In the establishment of country homes in Lenox of people from cities, the pioneer is thought to have been Mrs. Sarah G. Lee, of New Orleans, who bought a home here about 1837; John Brown came and built the house subsequently bought by Fanny Kemble, in 1840. Within a few years, before 1850, came at brief intervals Samuel G. Ward about 1843, Wickham Hoffmann, Ogden Haggerty in 1845, E. J. Woolsey and William H. Aspinwall, all of New York, and Russell S. Cook, of Boston. Edwards Pierrepont, who had been here for many seasons, finally bought property, and so did his father-in-law, Mr. Willoughby. William A. Tappan, of Boston, was also one of the early comers to buy a home.

As long ago as 1844, Barber's history of Massachusetts towns thus refers to Lenox: "The refined state of society in this place, the fine mountain air and scenery, and the superior accommodations at the hotel, all render Lenox a most desirable place of resort during the warm season." But earlier than this, in the first quarter of the century, Prof. Silliman, in his tour from Hartford to Quebec, speaks of Lenox as "a town of uncommon beauty. Lenox has fine mountain air, and has equally fine mountain scenery. Indeed, it is one of the prettiest of our inland towns, and, even in the view of an European traveler, it would appear like a gem among the mountains."

FULL LIST OF HOMES.

The many homes of the people who have sought Lenox for its beauties and society, will now be briefly mentioned and located as well as can be by taking them in order, beginning at the center of the village and going out on each of the various streets that radiate therefrom.

The Egleston house, opposite the hotel, was built about 1790 by the grandfather of the present owner for the former's father-in-law, General Paterson. It has had the successive ownership of Judge Bishop, Edwards Pierrepont, and Thomas Egleston, and is now owned by a son of the last named, Thomas Egleston, who spends the season here. The house has been considerably repaired and overhauled.

Next beyond, the house that Mrs. Lee, the pioneer, built, is now owned by Mrs. Charles Kneeland, of New York, entirely remodeled, and called "Fairlawn."

Continuing down West street, on the same side we come to the "Cushman Villa," built about 1860 by Mrs. F. R. Beck, of New York, who owned and occupied it till her death. It was bought, about 1875, by Charlotte Cushman, who died soon after. It was then sold to Emma Stebbins, the sculptor, and after her death it passed into the hands of her sisters, Mrs. Garland and Mrs. Fleming, both of New York, and Mrs. F. R. Tilton, whose husband is an artist in Rome. It is occupied at various times by the owners.

The Judge Bishop house, on the West street corner, opposite the Egleston house, built about 1855, is owned by his son, H. W. Bishop, of Chicago, and is now occupied by J. L. Barclay, of New York. Mr. Bishop has just built a summer home at Pittsfield.

The house beyond, owned by Miss Helen Parish, of New York, and lately remodeled by her, was built about 1860 by the late county treasurer, George J. Tucker. Miss Parish comes here every summer.

The Hooper house, built about 1865 by Miss Alice Hooper, of Boston, is now owned by her sister, Mrs. T. K. Lothrop, of Boston, and is rented for several years to John T. Williams, of New York.

"The Elms," on the south side of West street, owned by W. R. Robeson, from Boston, was obtained from Prof. Salisbury, of Yale College, who bought it from William Ellery Sedgwick, the builder of the house about 1855, and a permanent resident while he lived here. Mr. Robeson lives in town about half the year, and has a taxable residence here.

The house of William B. Shattuck, of New York, is an exceedingly fine one, on the south side of West street. The first house built on the place dates early in the century. The property was bought about 1865 by Dr. E. J. Dunning, of New York, who sold to Mr. Shattuck in 1883. The present owner, who is a season resident, spent about $50,000 on the place in 1885 in building a fine new house, and in providing such belongings as a bowling alley, tennis court, and so on.

We now come to houses at the farther end of West street and around the north end of Lake Mahkeenac. Here Henry A. Barclay, of New York, has his "Bonnie Brae," where he built a fine house in 1885. His stable is considered the best in town. From this house and the others in this part of the town the outlook is most enchanting.

Miss Cecile Bristed, of New York, who had often been to Lenox, built a pretty cottage at the base of Bald Head Mountain in 1885, and called the place "The Orchard." Miss Bristed is now Mrs. S. W. Griffeth.

"Lakeside," on Lake Mahkeenac, was owned by Charles Astor Bristed, and, since his death, by his widow. The house was burned in 1885.

Samuel G. Ward, of New York, owns "Oakswood," where he built a house about 1878, after being absent from town for several years. It is a beautiful place, with a fine oak grove back of the house.

George Higginson, Jr., from Boston, who is a permanent resident and lives here nearly all the year, owns a place with an enchanting outlook, which he bought about 1860. His land extends down to Lake Mahkeenac.

The "Tanglewood" of the late Mrs. Caroline Tappan, of Boston, is near the Hawthorne House. She came here before 1850. The property is now the summer home of Miss Mary Tappan.

Across the way is a little red house, formerly occupied by Hawthorne, and now owned by William A. Tappan, from Boston, who came to Lenox before 1850, and who lives here throughout the whole year. Stockbridge people are very particular to have it known that the house is in their town; however, it is a Lenox house in everything but the accident of a town boundary. Few visitors are allowed to inspect the cottage.

Near the lake, William S. Bullard, of Boston, has his "Highwood," which he bought from S. G. Ward about 1860.

We return to the hotel now, and proceed along hilly South street. S. Parkman Shaw, from Boston, several years ago built a house, which he occupied for some time. It is now, by lease, the summer home of Prof. Horsford, of Cambridge, and of chemical fame.

Mrs. F. W. Rackemann comes to town every season, and occupies the place for some time leased to Mrs. Burton N. Harrison, the well-known dramatic writer.

Alfred Devereux, of Philadelphia, a few years ago bought a house half a mile south of the center, and repaired it for summer and autumn residence.

Alfred Gilmore, from Scranton, Pa., is now a permanent resident here on his "Lithgow Farm," which he bought from Edwards Pierrepont about 1870.

A handsome house and extensive grounds, bought several years ago from J. F. D. Lanier, are the summer and autumn home of Mrs. Joseph White, of New York, opposite to the house next mentioned.

The "Allen Winden" (pronounced "Allah Vandah") of Charles Lanier, of New York, is one of the most sightly places in town, on top of a high hill. The views from this and other houses on this hill are truly ravishing. The house is a costly one, built in 1882.

On the Judge Walker place, called "Yokun Farm," live Richard Goodman, who has been here many years, and his son, Richard Goodman, Jr. The old house is a fine relic of the olden time, from which modern architects have drawn ideas. The Messrs. Goodman take great interest in town affairs, and Mr. Goodman, the junior, is a constant writer on agriculture, cattle breeding, and many other topics. Both have long been permanent residents.

The "Interlaken" (between the lakes) of D. W. Bishop, Jr., of New York, on the east side of the road, was bought by him about 1875. Three lakes are visible from it: Laurel Lake on the southwest, and nearly to the west, Lily Pond and Lake Mahkeenac. Within the past two years this handsome villa has been extensively remodeled and enlarged, the grounds tastefully laid out by the deft hand of the landscape gardener. The view from the east piazzas of "Interlaken" are said to be among the finest in all Berkshire.

On the west side of the road, is one of the finest houses in Berkshire, that of W. D. Sloane, of New York. It is an exceedingly large house, 160 feet by 100, and costing a good fortune. The grounds were laid out by Frederick Law Olmstead, sanitary and drainage matters were looked after by Col. George E. Waring, of Newport, and the furnishings are by Davenport, of Boston. Eight miles of tile are used in drainage. A system of water supply has been made for Mr. Sloane and Mr. Goodman ; water is forced from Lily Pond, a distance of 2,000 feet, to an elevation of 300 feet to a large stone reservoir. Mr. Sloane paid $500 an acre here for 100 acres. This is one of the most striking residences in Lenox, and all that wealth, and architectural and engineering skill can devise, has been availed of. During the year 1889 an elegant music room, said to be the finest in the country, was built. The house is said to have cost over half a million dollars, and some of the most noted receptions and musical gatherings in this town have been held within the walls of "Elm Court." Mr. Sloane's summer residence is among the most notable in Lenox, and during the season is the center of attraction of the social life of the village.

Towards half a mile south of this house, on the east side of the Stockbridge road, is the house of Philip J. Sands, of New York, who has spent the summer here at "Glad Hill," for the three years during which the house has been in existence. The view toward Laurel Lake is a masterpiece.

On the opposite side of the road is the "Merrywood" of Charles Bullard, from Boston, who has lived here since 1883, before which time he lived with his father, W. S. Bullard, whose home has been mentioned.

Taking the cross-road that leads from the Stockbridge road to Lenox Dale, the first place is the "Larchmont" of Mrs. Madeline Schenck, from New York, who built here about 1881. Some two or three years ago, George Westinghouse, Jr., of Pittsburg, Pa., a gentleman whose name and fame are widely known by the "air brake," and also one of the famous electrical inventors in the country, became possessed of this estate, and later began operations for the erection of a mansion which promises to eclipse all others in this section, and which is to be occupied during the present season (1890). It is of marble, quarried on his own premises near the house, and in its appointments is said to have few equals in all Berkshire. The house and grounds when completed will cost upwards of a million dollars.

Near by is the "Norwood" of R. S. Chapin, of New York, who bought the premises in 1885, after having hired houses in town for several seasons. He paid $18,000 for thirty acres.

Opposite "Norwood" is the late F. W. Rackemann's place, which was rented to Dr. William H. Draper, of New York, for several seasons. It is a pretty cottage, built in 1880, and is now the summer home of John Struthers of Philadelphia.

Between this road and Laurel Lake a fine stock farm of 150 acres is owned by Robert and Ogden Goelet, of New York, who spent every summer and autumn at Curtis's Hotel for many years. This estate was bought about 1875. Fine horses are reared here for their own stables, and there is also a good herd of Jersey cattle.

At the junction of this cross-road with the Lee road is the "Laurel Lake Farm" of John O. Sargent, of New York, which he bought a few years ago.

Beginning at the upper end of Kemble street, the first house beyond Trinity church on the left is the house owned by the Rev. Dr. A. J. Lyman, of Brooklyn, a native of Lenox, whose father was a teacher in the Academy. It is to be the home of Rev. Wm. M. Grosvenor, of Brooklyn, the new rector of Trinity church.

Directly opposite Trinity church, on the right hand side of the road, is the handsome residence of the late ex-Secretary Frelinghuysen, and one of the most charming locations in Lenox; having a sweep of view down the valley to the west unsurpassed in many respects. The house is of old colonial style, and is among the first of that style of architecture in the village, of the later day adoption of that sort of home. It is a striking house, handsome, roomy, and yet unpretentious. The acre and a little more comprising this site, cost about $13,000. Ex-President Arthur was a guest of the Frelinghuysen's soon after his retirement from the presidential chair.

On the right-hand side of the street is the Sedgwick place, now owned by Mrs. Elizabeth Sedgwick Rackemann, who, with her family, will hereafter occupy it, after having rented it for several years.

On this same street, and built only two years ago, is the handsome residence of C. G. Haven, of New York. It is one of the most attractive homes in Lenox. This, too, is of the old colonial style of architecture, and has a beautiful view to the west. Mr. Haven and family are so charmed with Lenox that they are loth to leave it, even in the late autumn, and have spent some of their winters here, making occasional trips to the city when they desired a few days "recreation," as he terms it. Mr. Haven and family are capital entertainers, and his coaching parties are looked forward to with great anticipation.

Further down the street, on the right, is "The Perch" of Mrs. Ellen L. Thompson, of New York. It was Fanny Kemble's old place, built by John Brown in 1840; she gave it to her daughter, the wife of Dr. Wister, of Philadelphia, who sold it to the present owner. The house was the home of one of the first Lenox home-seekers, and has been much improved since it was built. Its history makes it always an interesting place.

Taking up Walker street, the house at the east corner of Walker and Church streets is that of D. W. Bishop, of New York, which is to be rented. He paid $21,000 for it in 1885.

Opposite this is the house of Mrs. E. S. Jones of New York, who bought it of John Struthers. The latter built it in 1882.

East of the Club house, a house was built for Mrs. M. E. Rogers, of Philadelphia, in 1885. It is now rented to John E. Burrell.

The second house beyond is that of Mrs. Robert Shaw Oliver, of Albany, who has lived in it, but who rents now to Peter Moller, Jr., a former extensive sugar refiner, a permanent resident. The house was owned by Mrs. Ogden Hoffman, of New York, several years ago.

The next house is General F. C. Barlow's, which was built for him several years ago. He has a fine view northward, including Greylock.

On the opposite side is "Ventfort," which Secretary of the Navy William C. Whitney held under a five-year lease. It is the Haggerty place, one of the early country homes in the town, now owned by Mrs. Ogden Haggerty. It has some of the finest trees and one of the best lawns in town.

The coming and stay of the Whitneys in Lenox was the occasion of a great deal of social life, and some of the finest receptions ever planned and carried out in this town were those at "Ventfort." Here, last season (1889), Mrs. Grover Cleveland was a guest, and the hospitality and social life of Lenox in connection with the Whitneys will long be remembered with pleasure in this village.

A very fine home is the "Pine Croft" of F. Augustus Schermerhorn, of New York, on the south side of the road. The house, built by his mother, is large, and the grounds are extensive, including a heavy forest. He owns 400 acres, some of them comprising a farm, on which he breeds the best horses for his stable.

The new residence of David Lydig, old colonial, and with a fine music room and other accessories, will be occupied this season (1890) for the first time.

On the Lee road, Captain John S. Barnes, United States navy, of New York, has his "Coldbrook Farm." He built the house in 1882, and added thereto in 1885.

On Beecher Hill, General John F. Rathbone, of Albany, has a house for summer residence, which was built about 1865. Mr. Beecher's house has been moved down into the valley, and is now occupied by General Rathbone's farmer. The place, formerly known as "Blossom Farm," is now called "Wyndhurst."

The Dorr place, "Highlawn," on top of the hill, one-half mile from Lenox Furnace, was built by Russell Cook, of Boston, near 1842, who was one of the early men to get a country home here, on one of the finest hills in Berkshire. The lawn is one of the best in Lenox, and has the best specimens of foreign and native trees in town. The heirs of George and Francis Dorr own the property and rent it.

On East road, which runs north and south about a mile east of the village, is the "Sunswick Farm," that Edward Delafield bought about 1875. His widow owns it and occupies it summers.

On the same road, south of the road to Lenox Station, is the home of R. S. Dana, of New York, who built the house about 1875. He has a fine stable of fast horses.

On Yokun avenue, which runs from West street north, is the house of Miss Clementina Furniss, of New York, at "Edgecomb," built about 1880. The house is noted about town for its beautiful furnishings. From the houses on this avenue the views south and west are superb.

Next to this is the "Gusty Gables" of Miss DeP. Carey, of New York, built for her about 1880. This attractive cottage was occupied by Morris K. Jesup, of New York, in the season of 1885, while the owner was in Europe.

George W. Folsom, of New York, has a beautiful place on this avenue, at "Sunny Ridge," which he occupies in the summer and autumn; the house was built in 1884.

John E. Parsons, of New York, came to Lenox a long time ago, and in 1875, on the west side of Yokun avenue, built a house, to which he made extensive additions in 1885. The place is called, "Stonover."

On the same side of the avenue, north, is the house of Henri M. Braem, of New York, the Danish consul, which he built about 1875. His famous Jersey herds are among the most valuable in the county.

Still farther along is one of the notable houses of the town, at "Windy Side," that of Dr. R. C. Greenleaf, from Boston, who now makes Lenox his permanent home. This house, built about 1875, has a very large music room, with a Roosevelt organ and an enormous fire-place; the whole house is furnished in exquisite taste.

Cliffwood street, or the Lebanon road, as it is also called, affords a beautiful outlook toward the southwest. Beginning at Main street, Prof. J. S. Schanck, of Princeton College, occupies a house on the left, built 75 years ago or more.

"Hope Cottage" has been rented to Mrs. Henry P. Egleston, of New York, for a term of years

Mrs. S. Parkman Shaw and family have a handsome cottage on this avenue, which has recently been extensively remodeled.

On this avenue Dr. Barnard McKay, of New York, built a house about 1880, which he occupies summers.

On the north side of this street is the pretty new cottage, old colonial style, of E. McA. Livingston, of New York, who will occupy it largely as a permanent home for summer and winter residence.

Winchell cottage has been rented to Mrs. Hartman Kuhn, of New York, for a term of years.

On Cliffwood avenue, also, Mrs. J. W. Biddle, of Philadelphia, bought a summer home about 1880, and is a summer resident.

A queer house on the south side of this avenue was owned until 1889 by Mrs Charles F. McKim; it was built for her and her sister, Mrs. George Von L. Meyer, in 1885. On the death of Mrs. McKim the property was purchased by Anson Phelps Stokes, who has also purchased several acres of land from adjoining farmers and is converting the same into an extensive country seat. A large music room is being built, and will be completed this season. It is said to be one of the finest music rooms in the country.

The next below is the new residence of W. B. Bacon, who has built a house of the old colonial style, finished in 1889, and is one of the attractive places of Lenox.

Directly opposite is the new summer home of J. W. Burden of Troy, for many years a summer resident of Lenox.

Still further is the new residence of Dr. F. P. Kinnicut, and a cozy, permanent home.

Returning to Main street and going north, the first houses above the hotel are the "Elm Cottages," one occupied by W. C. Schermerhorn and the other by Buchanan Winthrop, both houses built about 1880.

The Bennett cottage is rented to Henry S. Leavitt, of New York, for a term of years.

The Platner house is rented for a term of years to Mrs. William C. Wharton, of Boston.

The Wright cottage is let to Miss Carey for a term of years.

The Tucker cottage will be rented for 1890, as also the Cook cottage.

Ambrose C. Kingsland, of New York, has built recently a fine cottage at the junction of Main and Northwood streets, and known as the Elezur Williams corner.

Miss May Tucker, of New York, occupies her cottage on "Chestnut Hill," which she built in 1884.

The house at "Hillside" was established about 1870 by Mrs. Grace M. Kuhn, of Boston, and it is occupied by Mrs. Cruger of New York.

The Loring house, owned by Mrs. R. S. Dana, of New York, at the head of Main street, is rented every year.

Opposite the Loring house is a handsome villa occupied by the owner, Mrs. Hartman Kuhn.

The Newton cottage, built in 1883, was occupied by Mrs. Marshall O. Roberts, of New York, in 1885, and is rented every year.

The extensive estate of "Cliffwood" is owned by Mrs. E. J. Woolsey, of Astoria, L. I. The house was built by E. J. Woolsey and William H. Aspinwall many years ago. The estate is a natural park of 500 acres, taking in the whole of a ridge of woods running from the Congregational church to West Mountain. The drives are eight miles in length, and there are three main entrances. The house may be seen from the lower end of the county and from adjacent Connecticut.

Following up the Pittsfield road is the home of Henry Naylor, of New York, which he built in 1883, and is occupied by his family for a short season every summer.

Mrs. Lucinda Morgan has built a summer home for herself and family, called "Cliffwood," on the Pittsfield road, a short distance north of the church, on the right hand side. It is surrounded by a large stone wall with massive posts and caps.

William H. Bradford, of New York, has an estate that embraces five farms, bought in 1882. His land has a mile of street frontage. The name of this home is "Wayside."

Col. R. T. Auchmuty, from New York, is a permanent resident at "The Dormers," and is a leading man in town affairs. He came here many years ago and bought three farms. He has been very active in promoting the welfare of the town, in the construction of the sewer system, in getting water for public and private use; he has been a selectman several times, is a member of the school committee, he was one of the prime movers in organizing the Lenox Club, and he was chairman of the building committee of Trinity church. Lenox owes a great deal to the public spirit of Col. Auchmuty.

The cottage on Walker street, run as a boarding house by Mrs. Flint, has been leased for a term of years by Henri Matthieu, formerly chef for Mr. W. D. Sloane, who will run the place as a hotel. He has named the house "Bellevue," and opens it this season (1890).

LAND PRICES AND PURCHASES.

Real estate prices in Lenox have gone up to astonishing figures for a country place. The average price per acre for all the land sold in 1885 was $933, not including house values enough to materially affect the figures. Applications for land purchase are constantly coming in from those who want to establish homes here. The increase in land prices has been enormous.. About 1853, Judge Bishop sold the Egleston place for $3,000, because the assessors taxed it to that amount, and he thought that he was getting a high price. In 1885, this property sold for $25,000, and the place is worth at least $30,000. Location governs price. No matter how fabulous the figures for a lot rightly located, it will find a purchaser, and he who pays the highest price for the smallest lot is the king of the Lenox realm. Latest fashionable prices, $25,000 an acre.

In 1890 the number of homes that people from cities own in Lenox and occupy to the exclusion of other homes, or for a season every year, or nearly so, is about 80. A few of these are rented now and then a year, because of the absence of the owner in Europe, perhaps, or elsewhere; including these and the houses that are regularly let every year, the total number of rented cottages in 1886 was 60.

There are half a dozen boarding-houses in the village, where guests are taken. Besides these, six or eight coachmen's boarding-houses may be found, a kind of accommodation peculiar to Lenox.

DRIVES AND WALKS.

The drives and walks in and around Lenox are incomparably lovely. A large list of the drives, with distances appended, will be found elsewhere in this volume. To characterize the peculiar charms of each one would take many pages. Whichever way one turns, the variety will be found inexhaustible and the beauty exquisite. Eight roads radiate from the village, connecting with a network of roads without, so that every drive out has a return by some other way. The roads of the town and of the towns up and down the great valley are most of them in perfect condition, and all are better roads than can be found in any other country region in the Union. An interesting drive or walk may be made to Lenox Furnace, two and a half miles distant, to see the process of glass making.

A few walks may here be specified by way of introduction. The most attractive ones, perhaps, are through the Woolsey estate, where a half-dozen walks may be had from one and a half to six miles in length out from the village and back. The "Ledge" is a favorite spot, three-quarters of a mile out.

The "Pinnacle," one mile out, on W. O. Curtis's "Pinnacle Farm," affords pretty views from its wooded top.

Walks are made to Tucker Hill, one-half mile out east of the Congregational church.

Through the Schermerhorn woods, one-half mile distant, the walk is very refreshing on a hot day, through the dark aisles of the giant pines.

Lily Pond, through the Lanier woods, is another resort, a mile and a half distant.

To the top of Bald Head Mountain, two and a half miles out, is a walk that will always leave an impression. The view is one of the best in Berkshire.

On the North Lenox Mountain, four miles distant, the scene is very fine. Near this, four and a half miles distant, is Yokun's Seat, 2,080 feet high, the highest mountain in town, with extensive view.

Several walks are made to the Housatonic River, two and a half miles off, to Laurel Lake, three miles away, and to the head of Lake Mahkeenac, two miles distant, all exceedingly beautiful.

SOCIAL FEATURES.

The favorite game among the younger people is tennis, which is played at many private courts and at the court of the Lenox Club, than which there is no finer. The annual tennis tournament is held in October and lasts three days. The best players in the country and many from abroad have participated in the tournaments. The last day's games are played on the club courts, and the prizes which are given by the club are presented then. The scenes at these tournaments are always brilliant and interesting. Archery is indulged in to some extent.

The entertainments given by those who live in cottages consist of lawn parties, archery meets, tennis matches, breakfasts, dinners, dancing, and musicales, the last mostly at the Ladies' Club or the Lenox Club. The social features of Lenox long ago attained a character and a reputation that have become so well known as to need but a few words here in the way of calling up some of the doings of the season of 1885. Among society people Lenox is a continuation of Newport, from which place people come about the 1st of September. Ex-President Arthur was the social lion of the town for several weeks, and was frequently at the dinner and tea parties that are a prominent feature of the town. He became such an admirer of Lenox that he prolonged his stay beyond the time originally contemplated. Secretary of the Navy Whitney entertained many friends, among them being William C. Endicott, Secretary of War.

At Curtis's Hotel were the family of the late Frederick T. Frelinghuysen, Secretary of State ; Minister Th. de Bounder, from Belgium ; Sir Arthur and Lady Aylmer; Sir Arthur Guest; John A. Kasson, ex-minister to Germany and Austria; Frank Thompson, president of the Pennsylvania Railroad; Admiral and Mrs. Upshur, and Captain Carter, U. S. N. Several elaborate weddings were the excitement of their time. Coaching parties were frequent, one going on a trip to Richfield Springs and Cazenovia, and another being made by some of the members of the New York Coaching Club, who rode from New Hamburg, on the Hudson, and were the guests of their associate, F. A. Schermerhorn, for a few days. One day there was a "tub parade," in which fourteen carts participated, all lavishly decorated with autumn leaves, flowers, ribbons, and drapery of various sorts. After a parade through the principal streets, the participants and their friends were entertained by Miss Furniss at her beautiful house on Yokun avenue. This has now come to be a regular thing, and the annual "tub" parade draws visitors to Lenox in great numbers. A ladies' fair was held for a charitable object; and the Lenox Club had its annual reception and ball; and its races were held on Lee Pleasure Park. One million dollars' worth of diamonds is said to have been displayed at an evening reception. One lady is reported to have received sixty calls in one day. The great social event of one week was that given in honor of a tennis tournament at Sedgwick Hall. Everybody was there, the costumes of the ladies were beautiful, flowers, palms and ferns decked the rooms, and an army of waiters from New York attended to the guests. There is unremitting gayety, and a constant round of elegant balls, tea parties, dinners, lawn parties, and so on, sometimes several at the same time, during every season.

Another annual event of great interest is the Lenox Club races held at the Lee Pleasure Park. The races are attended by "all Lenox" and the enjoyment of the contests is genuine.

The Clubs.

The Clubs of Lenox are natural to its social life. The Lenox Club, for gentlemen, was organized about 1865 by Ogden Goelet, William Ellery Sedgwick, Richard Goodman, Sr., George B. Warren, and the late Edward M. Rogers. About 1874 the club was incorporated and buildings were erected, at a cost of $10,000, containing a billiard room, bowling alley, and other club belongings. In 1885, at an expense of $10,000, several rooms were added, and a fine tennis court. There is a reading room, and a library has been started. So many members live in the town in

OLD COURT HOUSE—NOW SEDGWICK HALL.

the winter that the club house is heated and kept open and occupied throughout the entire year. The club has over 100 stockholders and 115 members. Ladies are admitted to the premises on such public occasions as musicales and tennis contests. In some years the ladies were given the use of the tennis court. In 1889 a large piece of property adjoining the grounds was purchased by the club, and here new tennis courts are to be laid out.

Sedgwick Hall was the old court house, and was bought for $6,000 in 1871 by Mrs. Adaline E. Schermerhorn and given to trustees for the use of the town. She established the Charles Sedgwick Library and Reading Room, which the trustees maintain. The Library has towards 6,000 volumes. The Hall has been used for dancing. The children of Mrs. Schermerhorn have repaired the building at a cost of $10,000. In 1889, the "Schermerhorn Annex" to Sedgwick hall was built by F. A. Schermerhorn at a cost of $25,000. It is a large brick building, standing in the rear of the old hall, and contains the already famous assembly room. Here it was that Mrs. Whitney gave a ball in honor of Mrs. Cleveland in the fall of 1889, one of the most brilliant events ever given in Lenox.

The appearance of Lenox village is that of the most exacting neatness and beauty. Not a blemish offends the eye. Tasteful homes, smooth lawns, flowers, graceful trees, the coming and going of handsome equipages and many harmonizing accessories please the sight constantly. The residents are so careful of the perfect appearance of all things that there is little work for a village improvement society to do. But, nevertheless, there is a Ladies' Village Improvement Society that has planted many hundreds of trees, kept the sidewalks in order, and looked after the neatness of the village. Most of the village houses are connected with Col. George E. Waring's sewage system. In four recent years the town spent $45,000 for various public improvements.

Notwithstanding the system of sewerage that was introduced a few years ago, the growth of the village since then compelled an enlargement of the system, and this was completed in 1889; so that Lenox boasts of the best sanitary arrangements in that regard of any village in Berkshire. The water supply is to be still further enlarged the present season at a cost of some $30,000. This will give a new and larger reservoir, supplied from mountain brooks, and a ten-inch main is to be put in during the summer of 1890. This will give the village ample accommodations in this direction for pure water for domestic use, as also furnishing an additional safeguard against serious damage by fire.

The necessity for a bank was apparent long ago, and it was sometimes difficult for a gentleman, however well fixed he might be financially, to obtain ready money, on account of getting a check or draft cashed. Besides, a place of deposit for moneys or valuables was also a growing necessity, and so that demand culminated in the organization of the Lenox National Bank, in the fall of 1889. The stock is largely held by city people, and it has demonstrated a paying investment as well as accommodation for the business men of the village as well as the people who come here for a summer or more transient residence. A savings bank is also to be established ere long.

Another season it is possible that electric lights will be introduced; in fact, a company for that purpose was organized some time ago, and it is now talked that a system by which Lee, Lenox and Stockbridge may be lighted from one central station will be adopted in the near future.

A substantial drinking fountain, made of Italian and Tennessee marbles, was placed in the "triangle" on Main street in 1885. It was a gift to the town in memory of Miss Emma Stebbins, the sculptor, from her friends, at a cost of $1,500.

The Late Season.

The season in Lenox ended the first week in September, many years ago. Now the height of the season is in October, and many people remain till November and December, while some tarry till far into January, or come for a visit at that time, and some even stay all winter. Main street is a lively scene in an October afternoon, with many people and carriages and vehicles of all sorts, drawn by the best bred horses. One of the more recently introduced forms of amusement is "hare and hounds" hunting, and the ladies as well as the gentlemen get much enjoyment and the most invigorating sport from these dashes across country. Hence the season is a very long one in Lenox, beginning moderately in the early summer, and making a round of summer, autumn, and part of winter. The charm of October in Lenox is incomparable outside of Berkshire. The brilliant foliage, the warm days with their invigorating climate, the beautiful drives, and all nature, visible, tangible and intangible, combine to make the region a paradise, in which living is a transcendant delight.

The October appearance of the country made the following impression upon the Lenox correspondent of a Chicago paper: "There are no autumnal pictures in any other part of our country more beautiful than those of Berkshire. The pictures the Great Master has painted upon the woody hill-sides are inimitable. The yellow leaves of the sugar maples, the combination of bright colors of the black maples, interwoven with the long, slender red leaves of the shumach, together with the purple and bronze of the oak, contrasted with the green of the hemlock and pine, all standing against a background of gray rocks, is a charming picture which the eye never tires of looking upon."

As winter comes on, the factors of the country aspect are changed, but not the charm of the result. A winter scene is not the dreary thing that people who have never seen it here think that it is. So beautiful are these scenes that the most artistic engravers nowadays reproduce them the best they can for magazine readers, and there is no place where they can find better originals than here in Berkshire. Miss Sedgwick's love of winter scenery manifests itself in a letter of December 1st, 1844. She writes "of the beauty of yesterday morning, when winter rose in her 'robes pontifical, ne'er seen, but wondered at.' Summer is but a drawing-room scene compared to it. The sun of these days rises behind the highest point in our eastern horizon, and consequently his beams shoot down the sides of the mountains, and even into the laps of the hills, before he is himself visible. A newly fallen snow covered the whole area between the hills from mountain top to mountain top, and every tree and shrub; not a breath of air had shaken the snow off the lightest twig. It was intensely cold, and the smoke from our village homes—the breath of their nostrils—rose in a solid column white and bright as molten silver. Here a rose-colored light flushed the hills, and then the light dropped down into their hollows like a cloth of gold. The whole vault of heaven was of the brightest blue; not a cloud, not a paling hue, over any portion of it; and far up in the clear atmosphere, and relieved against this blue, stood the magnificent trees, with their winter foliage of snowy wreaths. Then up came the sun, and the trees that crested the summit all along his horizon glittered as if they were shining in another world." Writing of the winter climate, Mrs. Hawthorne says: "This superb winter's morning, when to live seems joy enough. * * * There have been no winter horrors of great cold and storm here, as we were led to expect. The children have lived upon the blue nectared air all winter, and papa said the other day that he did not believe there were two other children in New England who had had such uninterrupted health and freedom from colds. Such clear, unclouded eyes, such superb cheeks, as come in and out of the icy atmosphere! Such relish for dry bread, such dewey sleep, such joyous uprisings!" Hawthorne himself went so far as to write in the winter: "On the whole, I think that the best time for living in the country is in the winter."

TRINITY CHURCH.

Lenox has an unpretentious, yet substantial and well-finished church in Trinity. It is built of dolomite, finished in 1886, at a cost of forty to fifty thousand dollars, and consecrated in 1888, Bishop Potter of New York preaching the consecration sermon. At the laying of the corner-stone, the sealed box was placed in position by ex-President Arthur. The tower and porch are the gift of F. A. Schermerhorn and Mrs. R. T. Auchmuty, in memory of their brother. The eight stained-glass windows in the chancel, representing scenes in the life of the Savior, are the gift of Mrs Charles Kneeland. The large circular stained glass window opposite the chancel is "The Children's Window," given by the children of the church. The chancel is the gift of the Misses Kneeland in memory of their brother, George Kneeland. The half-acre that is the site of the church, was bought for $8,000, and the whole cost, except special gifts, was paid by subscription.

The Congregational church, on the hill, will always be an object of interest. The Methodists also have a cozy little house of worship in the old Trinity church building, and the Catholics have also a pleasant and commodious house of worship on Main street.

THERE IS BUT ONE OPINION.

That Lenox really is what its admirers claim for it, is proved by the fact that the people who come here have most of them done extensive traveling where the finest scenery of the world is found, and that they are people of taste and culture whose opinion is law. This is referred to for the benefit of those who have not been here. Many landscape painters have been here, and many paintings of Lenox scenery have been made. Among the artists who came early were Inman and Gray, both of New York.

A correspondent of the Boston *Globe* from Lenox, in 1885, wrote: "It is not wonderful that visitors here are enthusiastic over the beauties of the Berkshire hills. The place has a charm peculiarly its own." A New York *Tribune* correspondent adds: "The region is becoming much like a large park." Prof. Thomas Egleston, of New York, has said: "Thirty years ago, every house in Lenox was the home of a refined and intelligent household." It is no less so to-day. President Chapin, of Beloit College, wrote: "Let me send a filial greeting to old Bald Head, and my thanks, that swell with precious memories, to the genii of the Ledge and its pine grove; of the Pinnacle and its rough, romantic paths; and to the naiads of the Mountain Mirror [Lake Averic], whose placid beauty must be forever enchanting."

Miss Sedgwick writes of a fine day in 1860: "It is a divine day—a day when hope and faith spring forth from the glorified earth in harmony with the soaring birds and the opening flowers. The air this morning is such as might come from Paradise, when the guardian angel opens its gates to happy mortals. There is a worship of beauty, a sweet breath of praise from all this wide landscape before my door. Nature is the heavenly messenger whose voice is melody and harmony."

But, perhaps, enough has been said to give the reader a good idea of Lenox and its people. Nothing remains now for the stranger to do but to visit the town and see for himself; and, if he has an appreciative and discriminating eye and taste, he will discover a thousand times more than this tells him of. Lenox is now in the fashionable age. Its literary age, so appropriate to this remarkable region, has passed, to give place to the luxuries of the wealthy and the fashions of the ceremonious. The people who come this way in the summer and autumn to live a long or short time, at home and hotel, number about 1,500 at any one time, and, as people are constantly coming and going, the total number of all is much larger. The town is now owned principally by those who have come here to establish country homes, and the almost complete acquisition of the town's territory by these people is in the near future. Already large portions of Lenox and Stockbridge constitute a huge garden, and it cannot be many years before their whole included region shall be one interrupted, magnificent park, tenanted by happy owners. The town is better for the influx of wealth and culture, and Berkshire as a whole is better in many ways for the growing demand for summer homes here in the leading resort of Berkshire.

STOCKBRIDGE.

NO ONE can undertake to describe Stockbridge without a deep felt realization of how inadequate both tongue and pen are to express the sense pleasures and the feelings they awaken, that fill the writer to overflowing. But regret gives place in time to a resignation to the incompetence of human communication to deal with such masterpieces of the Creator as are scattered lavishly over this town. Stockbridge is one of the two or three places on the continent where the distinguished men of the earth make pilgrimages to adore the acme of village and country beauty, and where travelers speak of the choicest scenes of the world in comparison; yet more of contrast than comparison, for it is here alone that the tone of scenery, peculiar to the town, is anywhere found. It is an indescribable cast of the beautiful and the picturesque, too fine for the common soul, too exquisite for a duplicate.

The youthful, intellectual fancy of the poet Bryant was touched to the quick upon his first entry into this town. While walking from Cummington to Great Barrington, to enter a law office, on October 3d, 1815, accustomed as he had been all his life to the charms of nature, he here beheld touches that he had never found before. Referring to the impression that the scene made upon him, he wrote, fifty-seven years after: " The woods were in all the glory of autumn, and I well remember, as I passed through Stockbridge, how much I was struck by the beauty of the smooth, green meadows on the border of that lovely river, which winds near the Sedgwick family mansion, the Housatonic, and whose gently flowing waters seemed tinged with the gold and crimson of the trees that overhung them. I admired no less the contrast between this soft scene and the steep, craggy hills that overlooked it, clothed with their many colored forests. I had never before seen the southern part of Berkshire, and congratulated myself on being a resident of so picturesque a region." But the poet could never do justice to Stockbridge, except in appreciation. He, like many others, must have felt that the mind was capable of entertaining emotions aroused by natural scenery, that no power of expression could truly represent.

THE SPIRIT OF THE SURROUNDINGS.

How thoroughly the spirit of the surroundings is absorbed by living among them is illustrated by an effort at their description by an old time resident, E. W. B. Canning, who begins with this striking incident: "An eminent son of Stockbridge—though for many years of his later life a resident elsewhere—escorted his newly married wife, who was an entire stranger to Berkshire, on her first visit to his native town. He planned that his arrival should occur at sunset of a bright evening in the time of the apple blossoming, and over the hill that rises north of the village. The wondrous beauty of the landscape, and the charms of its houses, nestled among the elms and maples of the quiet streets, left an impression which, thirty years thereafter, found joyous utterance among the last words of her death bed delirium. Had she confused that unforgotten scene of her early bridal with the prospect of the heaven on whose shadowy borders she was lingering?

"Beautiful for situation, and a joy of the whole Commonwealth, is Old Stockbridge on the Plain. The town singularly combines, in its scenery, grandeur and beauty. The wooded foot-hills of the Taconic range bound it on the west, sloping in places gently downward to its triple lakes and its winding river, and again boldly breaking off in abrupt precipices. The Housatonic comes placidly in from the eastward, and, after slowly executing numerous romantic curves through extensive meadows, makes a more rapid exit into Great Barrington. Rattlesnake Peak—the De-ow-hook of the Indians—dominates on the northeast border; Nau-ti-kook answers its defiance from the west; while Monument, famed in story and in song, bounds the immediate view on the south. Southeastwardly the hills ascend rather steeply to a high plateau called 'Beartown,' and, in a huge fissure of a spur ridge, lies Ice Glen, one of the 'lions' of the place, overlooked by the much frequented resort called 'Laura's Rest.' Such a variety of hill, plain and valley affords a corresponding variety of prospect; and it is a fact, often remarked by visitors, that rarely, if ever, elsewhere will a drive in any direction open so frequent a succession of views, so constant, so diverse, and all so beautiful."

THE SEDGWICK FAMILY.

As with other Berkshire towns, the character of the people who first resorted to Stockbridge was determined by the residents. The social status of the town was due, in the first place, principally to the Sedgwick family. In 1785, Theodore Sedgwick began to practice law in the village, and to him is due the credit of the first practical anti-slavery agitation. Col. Ashley, of Sheffield, who supposed that he owned a negro woman, who had run away from him, brought suit against the man who harbored her. Under Mr. Sedgwick's defence, it was decided that slavery was impossible under the State Constitution of 1780. The woman was so grateful that she became a member of his household for her life; she took care of his children, and was buried in the family lot, where a monument, inscribed by Catherine M. Sedgwick, commemorates her humble virtues. The first slave in America, whose chains were broken by the law as early as over a century ago, lies buried in Stockbridge. It was chiefly through the exertions of her benefactor that the Massachusetts law was made permanent. Among the earliest reported cases of the Supreme court, in Greenwood *vs.* Curtis, in volume VI of the Massachusetts Reports, Mr. Sedgwick, then a judge of the court, and an early member of the most distinguished line of judiciary of all the States, laid broad and deep the foundations of justice, in this State, by declaring that the law of nature should be the law of the land, and that no person could hold property in the person of another. Before he was judge, Mr. Sedgwick was a United States senator, and was a prominent man in launching the ship of State, under the Constitution, and such was his reputation that Aaron Burr studied law with him. Burr lived in the J. Z. Goodrich house.

Judge Sedgwick and his children, Charles and Catherine, were instrumental in attracting the first visitors to Stockbridge, who were at the same time their own visitors. The daughter has described how this began: "My father's public station and frequent residences in town gave him a very extensive acquaintance, and his affectionate temper warmed acquaintance into friendship. There were then no steamers, no railroads, and a stage route through our valley but once a week. Gentlemen made their journeys in their private carriages, and, as a matter of course, put up at their friends' houses. My father's home was a general depot, and when I remember how often the great gate swung open for the entrance of traveling vehicles, the old mansion seems to me to have resembled much more a hostelrie of the olden times than the quiet house it now is. My father's hospitality was unbounded."

Through the marriages, relationships, fame and friendships of the Sedgwick family, people of taste, refinement, intelligence and wealth were brought to Stockbridge from all parts of the East,—people, too, who could not behold the town and neighboring country, and breathe its enchanting air, without owning subjection to the matchless charms of the region.

EARLY VISITORS.

In time, the stage coach thoroughfare, between Boston and Albany, ran through Stockbridge, and travel increased so that eight stages passed each day—four each way. The late Daniel B. Fenn, who managed the Stockbridge House, from 1826 to 1831, for his father-in-law, remembered many of the distinguished men who tarried in the town a few days on their way through, during those years, and a few years before and after. They were Daniel Webster, William L. Marcy, Martin Van Buren, Daniel N. Dickinson, Robert C. Winthrop, Governor Strong, Governor Lincoln, Attorney General Davis, all the judges of the Supreme court,—in short, all the other executive and judicial officers for many years: Franklin Granger, of Canandaigua; Judge Buel, of Albany; Governor Van Ness, of Vermont; Silas Wright, John Van Buren, Harrison Gray Otis, the Danas and Appletons, and so many more of the distinguished men of the day that the names mentioned are but a few of the whole number. Thus it was that Stockbridge, through the Sedgwick family, became, in point of time, the first place of resort in Berkshire.

CATHERINE M. SEDGWICK.

Catherine M. Sedgwick attracted around her Bryant, from Great Barrington, and many other congenial spirits, and in the course of time her own literary works came to be published. Her "New England Tale" appeared in 1822, and was received with such interest and favor as to give its author an immediate position in the world of American literature. Then followed "Redwood," in 1824, which was published also in England, and was translated and published in France; afterwards "Hope Leslie;" "Clarence," in 1830; and, after 1834, "Linwoods," "Le Bossu," "The Poor Rich Man and the Rich Poor Man," and "The Love Token." Miss Sedgwick's precedence among American literary women was never questioned until "Uncle Tom's Cabin" was written.

Besides a wide acquaintance, Miss Sedgwick had an interesting correspondence with many of the distinguished people of her day, in this country and in Europe—with Sismondi, Harriet Martineau, Dr. Channing, Mrs. Jameson, and so on. Stockbridge became known to the literary people of the day, and to many others who were the patrons of literature and sought the society of its producers. Such people, among others, came to the town. The sympathy of the Sedgwicks was awakened for the Italians, who were exiled by the Austrian government about 1831, and Foresti, Albinola, Confalonieri and Castillia came here as their guests. About the same time, Miss Sedgwick went to live with her brother Charles, in Lenox, who was then clerk of the courts. The house in which Miss Sedgwick lived in Stockbridge is owned by H. D. Sedgwick, her nephew, on the south side of Main street, in the center of the village, and she was buried in the village cemetery.

A Perfect Inn.

It was but a natural result that, after the introduction of the outside world to Stockbridge by the Sedgwicks, the attractions of the town should bring a constantly increasing number of visitors from people of a kind with those who had been here. Public accommodations for those who had no private entertainment by friends were given by the Stockbridge House, which stands, to-day, under the proprietorship and management of C. H. Plumb, one of the choice hotels of the world. The oldest part of the building, the west end, was erected in 1764, or thereabouts, and was called for many years "The Red Lion Inn." People are now living in Stockbridge who can remember the old sign as it stood in front of the hotel with its picture of a lion, done "after the old masters," in red paint. This part of the hotel still preserves its olden architecture unaltered. There was not room enough between floors and in walls for the huge beams; so they project into the rooms and are encased. The ceiling in the rooms on the first floor is of varying height, a curious feature that a prominent architect, who has been Mr. Plumb's guest, has introduced in the plans of some old style houses. The rooms have quaint old cornices and other inside finish, with outside doors of Dutch fashion, and, extending nearly across them, are long hinges instead of the modern butts. The furniture of these rooms is in keeping with their antique appearance, being genuinely old, and not the product of a modern antique furniture factory. There are old tables, bureaus, chests of drawers, chairs, and so on. One article of furniture is an old sideboard with inlaid work, made by William Whitehead, one of New York's first cabinet makers. In the halls and rooms are placed spinning wheels, reels, warming pans, old sleigh bells, an Indian tomahawk found at Ticonderoga, deers' antlers, old clocks, and many other things that harmonize with the relics of the olden time. About forty years ago, an addition of thirty-six feet front was built on one side of the old house and the new addition of 1884 is of about the same size, the roof of the former addition being carried up to make three stories and an attic. Many of the rooms in the hotel have Franklin stoves, or fire-places, and they are cheerfully lighted and nicely finished and furnished. The hotel now accommodates about one hundred guests, besides giving table board to the occupants of about ten cottages outside. Mr. Plumb has a fine early garden for supplying fresh vegetables—those great luxuries to city people. A very large cold room, one of the largest and best in the county, is attached to the hotel, for keeping meats, fruits, and other perishable provisions.

This hotel is not so large that the guests must depend upon servants for the satisfaction of all their wants. In all matters where it is not out of place, they have the personal attendance and service of Landlord Plumb, a genial and model boniface. Many of the guests of this house have been here for many seasons, John H. Gourlie, ex-president of the New York Stock Exchange, for instance, for thirty-one years, including the season of 1880. The guests are upon the most friendly terms, and new guests, if they do not find friends among the old ones, as they generally do, at any rate soon find congenial company, or they need have none at all if they prefer. It is said by travelers that they never saw, outside of England, a hotel that reminded them of the best-kept English inns of the country towns so much as this one does. Be that as it may, this inn is not, while under its present management, the subject of improvement, while perhaps the English inn is.

Hotel Guests.

The Stockbridge House has always had a high quality of guests. As far back as 1856, such men as Charles Buckingham, the New York merchant; Frederick A. Burrall, the New York broker; William Clark, the Brooklyn merchant; Essex Watts, of New York, and Mr. Joslyn, one of the owners of the Buckingham Hotel, in New York, came here and stayed for the season. The hotel registers bear the names of many distinguished and prominent people, and every season the house is filled with well-known people from New York, Boston, Philadelphia, Brooklyn, Washington, Hartford, and other places.

One of the most sightly and picturesque views to be had in Stockbridge is from a point on the hillside where runs the western-most roadway from Stockbridge to Lenox, not far from the residence of David Dudley Field and Rev. Henry M. Field, and other places. This view overlooks the generally kept village cemetery, where many of the Sedgwicks, Douglass and others of noted family lineage "sleep their last sleep," is seen thickly set with pretentious shafts of marble and gleaming stones. Back of the old village and the Field family memorial tower, where its chime of bells is never more appropriately heard than when ringing out their melodious tones of "Home, Sweet Home."

Interesting Country Homes.

Visitors had not made Stockbridge a summer resort many years before some of them began to think of establishing country homes here. It is not certain who was the first one to do this, and the possibility is that two or three did this about the same time. About 1850. The first one seems to have been Daniel Stedman, of New York, a retired wealthy merchant, who bought what is now Mrs. E. D. Crane's "Orchard Grove," and built the dwelling house. About the same time, John Wayman, of Boston, who died years ago, bought village property and made a home. G. P. R. James lived on the road near Monument Mountain in 1850, and a few years thereabouts; but in his efforts to make a permanent home to his liking, he became so disgusted in his treatment by an Irish neighbor that he finally left. He was a world wide traveler, but remarked that though he had known many localities where individual features, constituting landscape properties, were more imposing, nowhere had he seen the more desirable of them all grouped in a combination so charming and so perfect. After 1860, at short intervals, others came and established some of the finest country homes in the commune. John Winthrop came from Boston and bought his "Ice Glen Farm." The Rev. Dr. D. D. Field, having gone to another parsonage, after preaching in town from 1819 to 1837, retired from active work, and returned to this town to pass the remainder of his days in one of the fairest spots on earth. Here he died, and was buried in the village cemetery. Some twenty-five years ago his son, David Dudley Field, repaired the old house, and bought the Rev. John Sergeants place, on Prospect Hill. The old house where that missionary lived is still standing, the second oldest building in town, and is supposed to have been built in 1737. It has been occupied, summers, by friends of Mr. Field, to whom it has been rented. Jefferson Davis's private secretary in the days of the Rebellion, Burton N. Harrison, lived there at one time. Near by, Mr. Field built "Eden Hall," which he has lately given to his daughter, Lady Musgrave. The grounds were laid out under the supervision of the landscape artist, Frederick Law Olmstead. Sir Anthony Musgrave, who has been Governor of British Columbia, New Brunswick, Natal, and Jamaica, and who is now

Governor of Queensland, in Australia, expects to retire to this place, it is said, upon leaving his present office. Mr. Field owns more real estate in Stockbridge than any other person; he has not lived here much of late years, but is often here for short periods.

Charles E. Butler, of New York, whose wife was a granddaughter of Judge Sedgwick, came from New York and bought the Morgan place, near Glendale, where he erected a fine stone house, and gave his home the name of "Linwood." His law partner, Charles F. Southmayd, bought the Nathan Appleton place, "Oak Grove," which had been given to the poet Longfellow, whose wife was a daughter of Mr. Appleton, but was never occupied by him. The Rev. Dr. Henry M. Field, editor of the New York *Evangelist*, bought the Rev. Dr. West place, on Prospect Hill, and put up a fine house, where he has entertained many distinguished people. He has occupied his "Windermere" for twenty seasons, during which time he has done everything in the way of making lawns and planting shade trees, to add to its natural beauty. Adjoining, a beautiful home was made by the late Henry Ivison, at "Bonnie Brae," on land that he bought from the founder of Williams College. He was a friend of Dr. Field's, whom he had long known in New York. Such was the intimacy and friendship between these neighbors, that they never had a fence between their grounds, the two lawns being like one, It is occupied summers by Mr. J. E. Parsons, of New York.

Lucius Tuckerman, of New York, bought the Missionary Kirkland place, "Ingleside," called generally the President Kirkland place, formerly, from his son, the president of Harvard College. Mrs. G. E. Beck, of Poughkeepsie, N. Y., bought from H. W. T. Mali, of New York, his "Edge Hill Farm," not far from the south end of Lake Mahkeenac. The late William Ashburner, a native of the town, but long a resident of San Francisco, has a place near Ice Glen, "Maple Hill;" and on the opposite side of the way is the place of the late Charles Boyden, of Boston. William E. Doane, of New York, who has a place on Main street, is very active in village improvement. Professor C. A. Joy, formerly of Columbia College, came here twenty years ago, and procured a home on the slope of Prospect Hill, and, a few years after, Professor Rood, of Columbia, made a country home as his near neighbor.

In 1885, Joseph H. Choate, of New York, who had spent many seasons in town, purchased land extending from Main street up to Prospect street, where he has recently built one of the loveliest homes in the country. The house on the lower side of Prospect street cost $100,000, it is said, and is a rare possession, with its many adornments, conveniences and comforts. It is finished in many handsome natural woods, and the windows are so arranged that the view from each one is like a framed picture of surpassing beauty. The greatest length of the house is 96 feet; breadth, 46 feet, and, on the lower side, three stories high. It is a wooden house, somewhat in the old English style of architecture. The outside is shingled down to the basement, and has no paint, except on trimmings. Five stacks of chimneys and two towers rise above the roofs, two spacious piazzas are on the rear, and the whole building is beautifully broken up with bays, angles, windows, and various architectural designs.

Just north of the Choate place is the new summer residence of Mr. Birdseye Blakeman, of the wellknown publishing firm of Ivison, Blakeman & Phinney, of New York. The house is large, constructed of marble, and is one of the finest homes in the county. The grounds are particularly fine, and in summer are turned into one vast garden. The views from these places are of surpassing loveliness. The handsome new home of Mrs. Iasigi, of Boston, is just opposite the Blakeman place.

Dr. Chapman, of Hartford, has lately bought land at the upper end of Prospect street, where he is to build a home. Mrs. Julia Van Rensselaer bought a house in the same quarter some time ago, and has replaced it with a handsome modern cottage, which she occupies with her sister, Mrs. Philip Livingston.

Bringing to a close the mention of the owners of country homes in Stockbridge, a delicate matter cannot be avoided. A petty jealousy toward each other possesses Stockbridge and Lenox, lest one shall claim some of the other's "glory." There was a time when the talk of a few Lenox people tried to belittle the other town, and the remembrance thereof still rankles. Indeed, Stockbridge claims that the grievance has not been suppressed. On the other hand, Stockbridge "claims" all that it can tax. The division line between the towns runs through the outskirts of Lenox village, on its southwest, and here, and in the north also, are places in Stockbridge territory owned by people who are four to five miles from Stockbridge village, and who are not identified with its society, but who are essentially Lenox people in spirit and association. What credit is due to Stockbridge for embracing the land on which these people live shall here be given, but the accuracy of this volume demands that they shall be classed where they belong. The homes that are the subject of this feeling are owned by W. D. Sloane, Charles Lanier, W. S. Bullard, W. A. Tappan, S. G. Ward, the Misses Tappan, and George Higginson, Jr.

Permanent and Temporary Residents.

There are a few people who may be called permanent residents among the people who have come here to find a home. These are W. E. Doane H. J. Canfield, John Winthrop, Harry D. Sedgwick, Miss M. A. Weyman, Miss Grace Stanley Parker, the Rev. Arthur Lawrence, rector of St. Paul's Church; Mrs. Samuel Lawrence, H. D. Cone, Mrs. Charles Adams, and Colonel James F. Dwight, from whose house, next to the Indian Burial Ground, the most delightful view in the village is to be had toward the southwest. His house is one of the old ones of the village, and is a fine survival of the old-time dwelling, as is Mrs. Ward's Edwards Hall, which is the oldest building in town.

First and last, Stockbridge has been visited by many distinguished people, some of them as the guests of residents, others at the hotel or as lessees of houses. Dr. Kane, of Arctic fame, came when the Grinnells lived here. In 1841 Lord Morpeth, later the Earl of Ripon, wanted to acquaint himself with the life and homes of American yeomanry while visiting here, and was taken to the house of Paul S. Palmer, in this town, where he ate dinner with a man who had been in the Revolution, and was introduced to a specimen of the best and most intelligent of Berkshire farmers, than whom there are no better representatives of American yeomanry. Harriet Beecher Stowe lived here several seasons, some of the time in the Timothy Woodbridge place, now owned by Lady Musgrave, one of the old houses of the village. The family of President Garfield was at the Stockbridge House in 1885. Frances Hodgson Burnett has been here; and General Armstrong, the Indian educator, often visits at D. R. Williams's. William M. Evarts and Judge David Davis have been here several times, and so has Longfellow. There has hardly been a governor of the State who has not visited the town—Andrew, Washburn, Bullock, and nearly the whole long line of executives. No one in town has entertained as many distinguished people here as the Rev. Henry M. Field. Among his earliest visitors was the Rev. Dr. McCosh, president of Princeton College, then on his first visit to America, who was so captivated by the prospect, as he stood on the piazza of Dr. Field's house and looked off upon the mountains, that he exclaimed: "There is not a finer view in all Scotland!"—which was a good deal for a Scotchman to say. In support of this he quoted Walter Scott, who was wont to say that the finest scenery in Scotland was not in the Highlands nor in the Lowlands, but midway, where the bald, bleak mountains lowered their rugged fronts, as if stooping to the vales between, so that the whole effect was one of grandeur, mingled with the exquisite beauty that it softened. This description, Dr. McCosh said, applied perfectly to the scene here before his eye. Dean Stanley, who was David Dudley Field's guest here in 1877, said that the view from this hill was the most beautiful that he had seen in America. Two years ago Sir William Thompson, among the first scientific men of Great Britain, spent several days with Dr. Field at "Windermere," and was equally enthusiastic over the view, combining the charms of hill and valley, mountains and rivers. As might be supposed, a home with such attractions and with inward charms, presided over by one of the best hosts in the land, has no lack of visitors from the city and from abroad. If we could trespass further on this private home, a long list of distinguished guests could be named. Dr. Field has been a great traveler, having been in all parts of the world, and he often has the pleasure of welcoming under his roof missionaries and others whose guest he has been in India, China, and Japan.

MEMORIES OF THE INDIANS.

Stockbridge has unusual memories of the aborigines. An early mission of the settlers was the Housatonic mission among the Stockbridge Indians. The matter was agitated as early as 1734, and the work was inaugurated by the Rev. John Sergeant, in October of that year, on the present location of Great Barrington village, where a school was opened. The Rev. Timothy Woodbridge, whose grandson wrote "The Autobiography of a Blind Minister," came to the mission soon after. For the purpose of giving the missionaries a better support, the town of Stockbridge was set apart, and some of it given to them. In May, 1736, the mission moved to Stockbridge, comprising some fifty souls, of whom forty were pupils in the school. Its fame went abroad, and such were the accessions from Connecticut and New York that, upon the general migration of the Indians westward, their number was about 400. Indeed, it seems to have been the most famous Indian mission of its day in the Colonies, and from it several missionary undertakings branched. Mr. Sergeant died in 1749, and was buried in the village cemetery. The epitaph on his tombstone is said to have been composed by an Indian. The conduct of affairs was taken in succession by Jonathan Edwards, 1751-8; the Rev. Dr. Stephen West, 1759-75; John Kirkland, and, lastly, John Sergeant, son of the missionary. But civilization crowded upon the Indians, and, in 1786-8, the Stockbridge Indians went to live near the Oneidas, in Central New York. Since that time, with four other removals, these Indians, about 250 in number, now live in Shawnee county, Wisconsin, where their existence is gradually fading.

OLD INDIAN BURIAL GROUND.

The services of the Stockbridge Indians to the Revolutionists were so valuable that Washington, on the declaration of peace, ordered that an ox for a barbecue, with whisky rations, be given to them to celebrate the event after their own customs. The ceremonies were performed on their council ground, at the slope of Laurel Hill, where, after an abundance of good cheer, they shot, scalped and burned an effigy of Arnold, and buried their war hatchet.

About $400 were raised in 1877, by the exertion of Mrs. J. Z. Goodrich, for a memorial for their Indians. Their burial place, before the establishment of the mission, was in the rear of the home of Col. James F. Dwight, on a bluff overlooking the meadow. A natural shaft, about fifteen feet long and two feet square, was got near Ice Glen and set west of Col. Dwight's home, on a base five feet high, concealed by a cairn of small boulders and covered with vines. A large flat slab was built into the front of the cairn, and inscribed: "The Burial Place of the Housatonic Indians, the Friends of our Fathers — 1734–1877." It has been greatly admired for its simplicity and appropriateness.

JONATHAN EDWARDS.

The name of the Rev. Jonathan Edwards is inseparable from Stockbridge. He was installed here August 8, 1751, and first occupied "Edwards Hall," now the oldest building in town and a place where summer guests find entertainment. It was built for the Rev. John Sergeant in 1737, and the front portion, minus the veranda and dormer windows, is the same now as then. Mr. Edwards erected an addition. In a closet in the house, six by fifteen feet, he wrote that great work, "The Freedom of the Will," which was followed by "God's End in Creation" and "The Nature of Virtue." Here he reviewed and prefaced his treatise on "Original Sin," "The Harmony of the Old and New Testaments," and prepared for the press his sermons on "The History of Redemption." Several characteristic stories of him are told, which may be got in the literature of the town. He left Stockbridge, January 4, 1758, to become president of Princeton College, where he died on the 22d of the next March of small-pox, at the age of 54.

The table on which President Edwards wrote is still here, in the hands of Prof. Hoffman. The outside of the house is still made of the original clapboards put on 149 years ago; they were not sawed, but were split from pine logs with axes, and were fastened with hand-made nails. The same ponderous doors that kept Indians out now let summer boarders in, three little glass windows at the top (it was in Queen Anne's time), a paneling outside, a heavy batten of plank inside, four wrought-iron hinges, each three feet long, an elaborate and ingenious latch, opened by a knob and closed by a spring, a brass knocker, and a great staple on each side within and a hickory bar six feet long standing in the corner and fitting the staples, with which the doors have always been fastened every night.

About 200 descendants of President Edwards gathered here, September 6 and 7, 1870, in commemoration of their great ancestor. They were hospitably entertained by the village people, and all united in public meetings, music, speeches, and festivity, which closed with a dinner, tendered by the citizens on the old Indian Square. The outcome of the gathering was the erection by the descendants of a monument to their great ancestor, of Scotch granite, costing $3,000. It stands within a few rods of the site of the old Indian meeting house toward the west end of Main street.

PUBLIC BENEFACTIONS.

Stockbridge is fortunate in being a place of monuments, drinking fountains and public benefactions of various sorts. The second soldiers' monument erected in Western Massachusetts was placed here and dedicated October 17, 1866, with orations by Governor Bullock and Harry D. Sedgwick.

J. H. Gourlie and G. Albinola have given fountains to the town, one of them being in the small park near the hotel.

By the efforts of George Lawrence, in 1881, $600 were contributed to the erection of a unique stone drinking fountain, with appropriate inscriptions, on the Library corner.

The literary taste, in which the town has never been lacking, found expression, in 1790, in the establishment of a public library, which continued until 1822, and in many other ways the inhabitants obtained much reading matter during that time and subsequently. In 1862 Nathan Jackson, of New York, born in Tyringham and educated here, gave $2,000 for a public library, provided that others would add $1,000 and erect a suitable building. The cash contributions nearly doubled the $1,000, a corner lot was given by Mrs. Frances F. Dwight, J. Z. Goodrich erected a fine stone building at a cost of $5,000, and 400 volumes were contributed. The Jackson Library Association has a permanent fund, and the town and many residents contribute generously every year. The Library has about 8,000 volumes, and over 9,000 volumes are drawn yearly.

A fund of $3,000 was bequeathed in 1842 by Cyrus Williams for the education of indigent lads at Williams Academy, in the village.

Cyrus W. Field, in 1879, added to the grounds on which formerly stood the Congregational church, ten or twelve acres adjoining, and laid out the whole for a public park, all at an expense of towards $15,000.

John Z. Goodrich gave Williams College towards $75,000, $50,000 being in cash. He gave the hall above the Library for the use of the Congregational Society. Miss A. D. Woodbridge left a legacy of $3,600 to the Laurel Hill Association. Mrs. H. D. Cone has made many public gifts and maintains in the village of Housatonic a free public library and reading room, for the special use of Mr. Cone's paper mill operatives.

On the site of the old Indian meeting house, David Dudley Field, in 1878, erected a Mission Tower of stone, in handsome design, and placed in it a clock and chime of nine bells, called the Children's Chimes, which are rung at his own expense during a portion of the year. The bells weigh 8,000 pounds, the largest one 2,000, and the nine cost $4,200. The Tower is seventy feet high. It commemorates the Indian mission, and the chimes are in memory of Mr. Field's grandchildren.

Mr. Field also built a road over Monument Mountain, by the way of the Smith farm, a few years ago, but it is now somewhat overgrown with bushes and trees.

The Laurel Hill Association and Village Perfection.

As lovely as Nature has been formed in Stockbridge, Art has contributed finishing touches to the village aspect, so that the artificial environment is absolutely matchless in unsullied beauty. This is due to the native taste of the inhabitants, who do what they can privately to enhance the charm of the village surroundings, and, for further work, have established a society for organized public improvement. The parent village improvement society of the nation was the Laurel Hill Association. In this village, in 1853, Mrs. J. Z. Goodrich, then Miss Hopkins, was instrumental, through agitation, in securing the organization of this society. The meetings have always been held on Laurel Hill, the ancient council ground of the Indians, which was made a play ground for school children by the Sedgwicks in 1834, and was deeded by them to the association in 1866. The scattered sons and daughters of the town, in all sections of the county, volunteered their aid, and, with $1,400 in cash and a large amount of promised labor, the association was launched on its æsthetic career. In its thirty-three years of existence, it has expended about $8,000, planted 2,000 trees, exclusive of hedges; and its watchful care for village appearance may be seen in the sidewalks, street crossings, foot bridges, village paths, drives and shades in the cemetery, in the shaven lawns, in the absence of street fences, in the constant cleaning and graveling, and, more plainly still, in the improved taste and culture of the people in all that tends to rational pleasure and refinement.

At the annual meeting there are an oration from a rustic rostrum, speeches, and music. In 1881, Prof. H. B. Adams, of Johns Hopkins University, traced the Germanic origin of New England towns; and, in the following year, he gave an account of the origin of Stockbridge and village improvements in Berkshire. The laws of village improvement, he says, beginning with restraining the wanderings of swine and cattle, have developed to this product of a refined community and of an educated common sense, and not only effectually prevent trespass upon open lawns and in attractive gardens, but even forbid the accumulation of rubbish about the village premises and along the highways and hedges; nay, these laws have even restrained the last vestige of swinish litter once caused by thoughtless persons scattering, as they came from the post office, torn envelopes and newspaper wrappers upon cleanly walks and drives.

The Unspotted Neatness of the Village.

The fame of this association has gone so far that the demand for its printed constitution comes from every part of the American Union. The village neatness is the wonder of every stranger. W. A. Croffut, writing to the Boston *Herald* in July, 1882, says: "Stockbridge is unique — the neatest, most orderly, and best kept town that I have ever seen in this country. The main street is 120 to 150 feet wide, and all the streets outside the wagon way are kept closely mown and swept clean of every twig and every dead leaf. Hedges, constantly trimmed, often supersede fences — hedges of privet, osage, orange, hawthorn, blackthorn, arbor vitæ, hemlock, cedar, and all sorts of thrifty evergreen. Everywhere one sees the hedge trimmer and the lawn mowers busy, and, as my eye strays out of the window, it rests on a man with a broom, with which he is carefully picking up every stray leaf. The first day I came here, I flung away a crumpled visiting card from the front porch. Then it looked so conspicuous on the lawn that I went and picked it up and flung it into the street. That, it was instantly apparent, was worse yet. It lay on the close cropped emerald stubble, and looked as if it could be seen for ten miles. I picked it up and carried it to the waste basket; there was no other way. Almost every house in town has a handsome lawn around it and flowers before it — flowers in beds of every shape, flowers over the doors in red boxes, flowers in pretty window ledges, flowers growing in crotches of the abundant trees, and the whole village has an ample shade. There is hardly a house or barn that needs a coat of paint; hardly a hedge with frowsy hair. Everything is in order, indicating not only wealth, but, what is much rarer, good taste and a love of beauty."

The æsthetic influence infects every visible village component. In 1884, the Town Offices were built at a cost of $10,000, a fine building with handsome rooms, surpassing anything that can be found elsewhere. The interior of the Housatonic Bank building is the most elegant one in New England outside of Boston; and one of the stores has no parallel in any other country place in the land in its appearance and appointments.

ST. PAUL'S CHURCH.

Stockbridge is fortunate in having a perfect gem of a church, St. Paul's, which was pictured and somewhat described in the *Century* soon after it was built, in 1884. It was given to the society by Charles E. Butler in memory of his wife, Susan Ridley Sedgwick Butler. The interior is open to visitors during the day time every week day, except Saturday, for prayer or inspection. The building and its belongings are choice works of art, the total cost being, it is said, about $100,000, exclusive of land. The stained glass pictorial window in the rear of the chancel is a memorial of the Rev. Dr. Samuel P. Parker, who was rector of the church for about fifteen years. The artist was La Farge. The window was given by friends of Dr. Parker. The massive chancel furniture of antique quartered oak, communion table and two chairs, was given by Mrs. Franklin H. Delano, of New York. The antique brass lectern was given by Charles S. Weyman. The pulpit, symbolically carved, was the gift of the Rev. Henry F. Allen, rector of the church, 1865-72, in memory of his mother. On the wall in front of the organ is a reproduction of the famous "Singing Boys and Girls" of Lucca Della Robbia, the Florentine sculptor of 1400-80. The original, ten panels sculptured in all degrees of relief, finished in 1445, was the marble frieze that was in front of the organ in the cathedral at Florence, but is now set up in the Uffizi Palace, in that city. A few copies have been made from a cast of the original taken by a Berlin art society. This work of art is given by Misses Emily and Laura Tuckerman. The baptistery is a precious work of art in fossiliferous marble from France and in brecciated marble. The memorial tablet was designed by St. Gaudiens, and the stained glass windows came from Tiffany's. The Roosevelt organ is a very effective

CHIME OF BELLS TOWER.

one for its size, with a carved case of quartered oak and with forty-seven front pipes peculiarly decorated. There are several memorial windows of stained glass, carved hammerbeams, and other choice belongings, all of which, with what has been mentioned, make this church one of the notable ones of the country. With singular propriety this work of art and beauty, and harmony and religion, is placed in Stockbridge and in Berkshire where nature is in harmony with art and beauty, and where religion should reach its purest and most exalted form. The church that this displaced was a wooden building, whose architect was the famous Richard Upjohn; the bell, now in the new church, was given by David Dudley Field; and the clock, also put into the new church, was largely the gift of G. P. R. James. In the old church had officiated many distinguished divines, and it had many noted attendants, among them Charles Sumner. Here Dean Stanley delivered a discourse, his only one in America.

THE HOME OF DISTINGUISHED PEOPLE.

Besides the large number of distinguished persons that have made Stockbridge their home, both native and adopted, already mentioned, there are many more, a few of whom ought to be mentioned, because of the pleasant association. "Cherry Cottage" was the birth place of the Rev. Dr. Mark Hopkins. The Rev. J. T. Headley preached in Curtisville from 1840 to 1842. The Rev. Dr. Kirkland, who was president of Harvard College, first became an educator in this town. The Rev. Dr. Stephen West, pastor of the Congregational church from 1759 to 1818, was a noted polemical preacher, who wrote "An Essay on Moral Agency," a treatise on "The Atonement," and many sermons and essays. The Rev. Samuel Whelpley, author of "The Triangle" and a "Compend of Ancient and Modern History," was born and reared here. Among citizens of the town have been Prof. Albert Hopkins, of Williams College; Prof. J. W. Hart, of Philadelphia; Miss Abby D. Woodbridge, of Albany and Brooklyn; the Rev. Henry Fowler, of New York and Chicago; Judge Ezekiel Bacon, of Utica, N. Y.; Judge Pierrepont Edwards; President Edwards, of Union College; Theodore Dwight, Henry W. Dwight, Henry and Robert Sedgwick, of New York; the poet William Pitt Palmer, who was born here. Timothy Woodbridge, Jahleel Woodbridge and John Bacon were judges of the Supreme Court, the former chief justice; Ephraim Williams was judge of the Court of Common Pleas; Horatio Byington was judge of the Superior Court. Nine judges, counting promotions, have been appointed from this town, and seven congressmen, among them Theodore Sedgwick, who was speaker. Judge Sedgwick was also United States Senator. John Z. Goodrich was congressman and lieutenant governor, and was one of the originators of the Republican party in 1856, being chairman of the National Committee which organized the party. Horace J. Canfield was president of the State Senate. Jonathan E. Field, whose distinguished brothers' names are so intimately associated with the history of the town, was president of the State Senate, and, when in that office, received the visit here of the whole Senate, and was a member of the commission to revise the Statutes. Stephen D. Field, his son, is an electrician and an inventor of a system of quadruplex telegraphy and an electric motor. Enoch, son of Timothy Woodbridge, was chief justice of the Vermont Supreme Court. Several devoted missionaries have gone from the town—the Rev. Cyrus Byington to the Choctaws, the Rev. Josiah Brewer to Turkey and Greece, Mrs. Catharine Watson to Burmah, Mrs. Catherine Sergeant De Forest to Beirut, Mrs. Sarah Perry Powers to Persia, Mrs. Mary Perry Ford to Aleppo, Miss Susan J. Johnson to the Choctaws. The subject of this paragraph could be continued much farther.

VILLAGE ATTRACTIONS.

The new Casino, on Main street near Edwards Hall, built in 1887, is one of the attractive features of the village. The lot was purchased with contributions from David Dudley Field, William F. Doane, John Winthrop, Lucius Tuckerman, C. E. Butler and Charles F. Southmayd. The building is two stories high, of the old colonial style of architecture, with a fine lawn in front, largely devoted to tennis courts. On the first floor is a very pretty little theater which is in constant demand during the season for theatricals, dances, etc., the upper floor contains billiard and smoking rooms.

The oldest shade trees in the village are the four elms standing before the premises of Mrs. Owen, on Main street, which were set by Col. W. M. Edwards, grandson of President Edwards, in 1786. The oldest maples are the remains of a row on the south side of Main street, which were planted by residents on Fast Day, 1814. Some trees were set in 1840, but a large part of the shades of the village and all those on the outleading roads were set by the Laurel Hill Association since 1853. The money has been promised, and will be some day forthcoming, for setting out a row of trees on each side of every highway within the town.

People who do not want to hire a house nor live at the hotel can obtain excellent keeping in and near the village in private families, eight or ten of which each offer accommodations to a few people.

There are about fifty miles of public roads in this town, all in a most perfect state of repair. Riding over them is as easy as over a railroad; they are well graveled, hard, smooth, and even, and the town takes a great deal of pride in them, as it ought. Over these roads the rides are enchanting, and on fair days most of the people are out with handsome turnouts and fine horses.

Ice Glen.

Walks about town are in numerous directions. A favorite one is to Ice Glen, a cleft across the spur of Bear Mountain, a short distance from the village. Here, in a deep, cool, shady, wild ravine of irregular formation, is a luxurious retreat in a hot day, where ice may be found all summer down among the fallen rocks. The ravine is forty rods long, and is thickly strewn with enormous boulders and the great trunks of fallen trees, all mossy and slippery and in wild confusion, so as to leave cavernous recesses and an often impeded passage for a lively brook. To clamber up this ravine in the dank air and gloomy shade is a most romantic undertaking, and a weird aspect is imparted to the scene by a torchlight visit in the night.

Laura's Rest.

Beyond Ice Glen, and about two miles from the village, a magnificent mountain outlook is had from Laura's Rest, where David Dudley Field had built an observatory fifty feet high, wrecked in a heavy wind last winter. Here the range of vision extends wide into Connecticut, New York, and to Vermont, on nearly every side of the observer, and the beauties that are spread before him are transcendent.

Where to Walk.

Fine sidewalks extend from the center of the village from one-half to three-quarters of a mile in every direction, and these, well shaded, make delightful strolls. Prospect Hill, just above the village, commands one of the choicest views of beauty in the world,—so say the Rev. T. T. Munger and every one else who has traveled enough to sustain so bold a comparison.

Of the view from Prospect Hill, Henry Ward Beecher, in one of his Star Papers, says Stockbridge is "famed for its meadow elms, for the picturesque scenery adjacent, for the quiet beauty of a village which sleeps along a level plain, just under the rim of hills. If you wish to be filled and satisfied with the serenest delight, ride to the summit of this encircling hill ridge, in a summer's afternoon, while the sun is but an

STOCKBRIDGE BOWL.

hour high. The Housatonic winds in great circuits all through the valley, carrying willows and alders with it wherever it goes. The horizon on every side is piled and terraced with mountains. Abrupt and isolated mountains bolt up here and there over the whole stretch of the plain, covered with evergreens."

The Rev. Henry M. Field has paid many a tribute to the beloved town. In a letter, he says: "The peculiar beauty of Stockbridge is that it is a valley set in an amphitheatre of mountains, which close round it like the walls of some mighty castle, as if to guard it from intrusion from the outer world. The point of view from which one takes in all its features best is the brow of the hill, on the northern side, where at the same moment we look down on the valley below, and round the whole horizon. There is one point, on the shoulder of the hill, which has an outlook up and down for miles, and, because of this, was chosen by the early settlers as the position for a watch-tower against the Indians. After those dangers were passed, this spot was always a favorite resort for the view. It is a tradition of the town that old Judge Sedgwick, the ancestor of the famous Sedgwick family, as he rode over the hill, always reined in his horse at this point to take in the enchanting prospect."

Laurel Hill, on the edge of the village, is the object of another walk, a delightful place that is a frequent resort. A walk to "Cherry Cottage," toward Monument Mountain, is often taken by those who want to go three miles. A four-mile walk is from Palmer's to East street, and a most wild, romantic walk of six miles may be had over the old Burgoyne road, which begins close by the artesian well, three-quarters of a mile beyond Ice Glen, and extends up the mountain. It is not a public road, but connects with the Beartown road, going down to South Lee, which is the way of return. But the stranger in Stockbridge needs no directions beyond these to find the beautiful. It is everywhere!

Where to Drive.

The town has three noted lakes—Mahkeenac (Stockbridge Bowl), at the north, covering 500 acres, gracing a scene of surpassing loveliness; Averic, half a mile southwest of it, covering fifty to sixty acres; and Mohawk, a mile northwest of Glendale, comprising about twenty-two acres. There are ample facilities for boating on these charming lakes.

Drives outside the town are made to Lenox, West Stockbridge, Richmond, Great Barrington, Bashbish Falls, The Dome of the Taconics, Lake Buel, "Highlawn Farm," and other places mentioned in the table of distances and drives.

Miss Sedgwick's Description of a View.

A view of Stockbridge is charmingly depicted in Catherine M. Sedgwick's "Hope Leslie:" "A scene of valley and hill, river and meadow, surrounded by mountain, whose encircling embrace expressed protection and love to the gentle spirit of the valley. A light summer shower had just fallen, and the clouds in a thousand liveries bright had risen from the western horizon and hung their rich draperies about the sun. The horizontal rays passed over the valley and flushed the upper branches of the trees, the summits of hills and the mountains with a flood of light, while the low grounds, reposing in deep shadow, presented one of those striking and accidental contrasts in nature that a painter would have selected to give effect to his art. The gentle Housatonic wound through the depths of the valley, in some parts contracted to a narrow channel and murmuring over the rocks that rippled its surface; and in others spreading wide its clear mirror and lingering like a lover amid the vines, trees and flowers that fringed the banks."

The Huge Old Willow.

About a mile south, on the road to Great Barrington, is the huge stump of a willow tree, whose branches, weakened by age, were blown down by wind a few years ago. It was said by all who saw it to be the largest willow they ever saw. The trunk measures 32 feet around, and the branches were 115 feet from tip to tip. This tree grew from a riding whip that a Mr. Goodrich stuck in the ground in 1794, when he passed that way on horseback on his way from Weathersfield, Ct. A finely written meditation, from the pen of the Rev. Dr. Henry M. Field, on the fall of this tree, was published in his New York *Evangelist*, in July, 1884, and we give it in picture, in connection with the initial letter of this chapter on Stockbridge, as it appeared a few years before its destruction.

Stockbridge Must Be Seen and Lived in.

The opinion of many visitors to Stockbridge might be quoted from their writings as to its attractions, for never a year passes without more or less of such publications; but the reader of this volume ought not to need the quotations. Yet, at best, words cannot do Stockbridge justice; they cannot describe its omnipresent charms, the exquisite quality of its beauty, the unspotted neatness of the village, nor the refined quiet of the place. The associations that group here are all matters that interest the exile from cities. The memories of Judge Sedgwick, who was one of the remarkable men of his time, and who should be remembered, as well as for other matters, as the first man who was instrumental in making slavery illegal ; of Catherine M. Sedgwick, who was the first American literary woman of her day ; of the great metaphysician, Jonathan Edwards ; of one of the first protestant missions among the Indians ;—all these and many more memories, and the absolute perfection attained in village life and aspect, together with the choice society of the town, make it of the highest interest to visitors. As with other parts of Berkshire, Stockbridge is still growing as a summer resort for the tourist and for those who stay a few days or weeks, and, at the same time, it is becoming the summer and autumn home of an increasing number of people. Most charming locations for new homes are still plentiful, and in the spreading tendency to come this way for a season's sojourn, it is probable that not many years will pass before the best of the remaining ones will be converted into many more precious Country Homes in Berkshire.

Great Barrington from the Northwest.

GREAT BARRINGTON.

ONE of the pioneer attractions in the Berkshire movement was Great Barrington. Here the singular beauty of the region first found appreciation, and a few devotees early made pilgrimages to the Creator's choicest shrine of Nature. As the late Rev. Dr. Samuel P. Parker remarked many years ago, nature has been most prolific with this town. While sharing in the marvelous beauty of the other towns, this one has appropriated the boldest and most daring touches, which, outside of Berkshire, instead of heightening the charm, would have ruined it. The factors of the landscape have been thrown into the most striking combinations, all in exquisite harmony, imposing in effect, multiplied into astonishing variety, and admirable to the last extreme of good critical taste.

The First Visitors.

Among the first in the county, this town was sought by refugees from the summer of the city and by country home seekers. Before a railroad came from Bridgeport on the windings of the Housatonic river, in 1842, these people were necessarily few; but after that their numbers soon and steadily increased. William Cullen Bryant frequently, after 1825, made summer visits; Elias W. Leavenworth, now of Syracuse, N. Y., who passed his youthful years here, often returned, and, in renewing fond remembrances, invariably first hurried to command the magnificent prospect from Berkshire Heights. William Sherwood came often from New York to visit his nieces, the Misses Kellogg, who kept a famous school for young ladies. This was attended by his daughter, Mary F. Sherwood, who here became acquainted with her future husband, Mark Hopkins, subsequently of Central Pacific Railroad fame. John F. Bacon, of Albany, came to visit relatives; and a guest of the Misses Kellogg was William Gilmore Simms, of South Carolina.

The coming of other visitors than former residents and friends and relatives of the town's people was conditioned upon good hotel accommodations, which were not provided till the Berkshire House was built by George R. Ives, in 1840. Then, with the railway communication with the outside world, which was established in 1842, came people who at once made Great Barrington an established summer resort. From 1842 to 1850, among the visitors who are remembered were Henry Bush, consul to China, who had a Chinese servant, a great curiosity in those days; Dr. Barstow and family, of Salem, Mass.; Dr. Prescott, who was a surgeon in the Revolution; Mr. and Mrs. Bamman, who remained during the winter, and were the first to make so long a residence; and Dr. Ticknor, who had been an army officer. W. B. Dinsmore, now president of the Adams Express Company, stayed at the Berkshire House in the summer of 1846, or thereabouts. Park Benjamin, who was a frequent visitor, read an original poem at a Fourth of July celebration in 1847, in the oak grove where E. D. Brainerd's house now stands, on the road to Berkshire Heights, and C. Edwards Lester, who was often here in those days, and whose "Glory and Shame of England" had given him notoriety at the time, delivered the address. Dr. Parker, when he preached at Lenox or Stockbridge, years ago, told a village inhabitant here that some years previously he stepped into the Pearl street store of a New York friend, who told him that he had sold his New Jersey property. "Why so?" asked Dr. Parker. "I'm going to the finest town on the American continent," was the enthusiastic reply; "and that town is Great Barrington, Berkshire County, Mass." The unfortunate merchant died before he could move to the earthly paradise.

The first country home seeker in this town was David Leavitt, the wealthy New York merchant, who, in 1852, bought the property that he called "Brookside," now owned by Mrs. Hotchkiss of New York, and located on the east side of the Housatonic River, below the Fair Grounds. There he meant to experiment in agriculture, and, at a cost of about $60,000, built a huge barn, then the largest and most costly one in the United States, and attracting so much attention that Horace Greeley came to examine it, and wrote an account of it for his *Tribune*. The barn was burned in 1885. Three sons of Mr. Leavitt subsequently established summer homes here, and also David S. Draper and M. Ludlow Whitlock, New York business men, and J. Milton Mackie, who came from the eastern part of this State, and whose "Pine Cliff," near Green River,

Hopkins-Searle Mansion—(South View.)

has a most beautiful outlook. Mr. Mackie is known for his literary work, as a leading Jersey cattle breeder, and as the president, a few years since, of the Jersey Cattle Club.

From Great Barrington, interesting journeys may be made in any direction—to Stockbridge and Lenox, to Sage's Ravine, Bear Rock, Bear Mountain, Lookout Point and the Dome of Mount Washington; to Alford and on up the Green River valley, of which Bryant said in his earlier writings:—

> I often come to this quiet place,
> And breathe the air that ruffles thy face.

Along the roadway of this river, whose incomparably clear waters pass leisurely upon and over beds of cleanest of slaty gravel, the way leads by and over the foot-hills of the Taconics into New York state, where Columbia county vies with Berkshire in the presentation of good farms, good homes and charming landscape layouts.

Mrs. Edward F. Searles.

Since the summer of 1883, Great Barrington has acquired increased fame from the doings of Mrs. Edward F. Searles, formerly Mrs. Mark Hopkins, and the visitor is now first concerned to know about them. The Kellogg Terrace property, just south of the central portion of the village, having been given to her by the will of her aunt, Miss Nancy Kellogg, in 1881, Mrs. Searles had the old house repaired and elegantly refitted, and has since made the place her home a part of the summer or autumn, her other home, for winter and spring residence, being her princely house in San Francisco. In the spring of 1883, a $45,000 barn was built for her, but it was burned in December, 1885, and afterwards rebuilt. Her large gifts to the Congregational society, consummated in the spring of 1884, had become widely known, when shortly after the news went to the remotest corner of the land that she would have a $1,000,000 house built here. This is now nearly completed.

The house has a frontage to the north of 180 feet, and is about 100 feet deep. Its massive walls are broken by seven beautiful towers and numerous gables. The material is native blue dolomite, taken from a quarry across the river and conveyed to the site by a tram railway constructed for the purpose. It is somewhat difficult to designate the style of architecture of the building, but it may be said to be a combination in which the old French style predominates. At the north the house has four stories, and at the south there are two more, made by the slope of the hill. On the south side is a high and massive terrace which is paved with marble, the rail being surmounted with the same stone. Under this terrace is a large winter conservatory in which are kept the palms and other tropical plants that beautify the grounds in summer. The appearance of this terrace gives the impression of a fortress, and it is one of the most striking features of the building. The main entrance to the mansion is through a grand porch on the north side. The doors for this entrance are to be historical solid bronze doors, and were cast in Munich. Their cost is $15,000, and they have not yet been placed in position.

From the hall-way immediately after entering, is the entrance to the grand atrium.

There are three of these atria and they are the central feature of the house. The grand atrium is of large size, and its angular lines are broken on either side by rows of massive marble pillars which support the roof. These pillars represent all the marbles of the world, no two being alike. As in the hall-way or passage leading to the atrium, the wood-work is all of the finest English oak and the ceilings and upper wall are of stucco-work, pure white and of exquisite design. Right here it may be stated that throughout this entire mansion there is not a particle of coloring, excepting that which may be in carpets, hangings or furniture. The walls and ceilings are all of oak and stucco, and not a drop of oil has been used in the finish of the wood. It is polished by hand alone and the finish is magnificent. To the right of this grand atrium, in one of the towers, is the library, and on the opposite side in another tower is a reception room. The library has the same finish of oak and stucco, and is lighted by an ingenious arrangement of windows over the shelves. The walls of the reception room are paneled in oak, these round rooms being extremely tasteful and handsome. Coming back into the grand atrium, one has his attention drawn to the brilliant light that comes through a massive arched door-way at the opposite end. Looking toward this, the main source of light for this royal chamber, the idea of light and distance obtained is marvelous, and a look between the massive marble columns, and a second double row of oak columns to the music room entrance, is like a glimpse of fairy-land. The floors of the atrium are of quartered oak, the walls are wainscoted high with oak, and above the beautiful marble columns rises the arched roof. The surrounding rooms are for domestic purposes, and are in perfect harmony with the rest of the house. The second row of columns, just mentioned, are all of a rare oak of tan-color, and are richly carved. The columns lead up to the grand entrance to the music room, and the oak, like that used in the grand archway, is of the same kind as that used in the music room. England and Scotland were hunted over to find enough of this rare wood, and its cost was $35,000.

Passing on under the arch, one enters the music room, which is 52 by 45 feet, and occupies an extension on the west side. Pages might be written about this music room alone, and it would not then be adequately described. The room is oblong, the organ being built at one end, while the other end is oval. The ceiling is arched and very high, the construction being with a view to getting the best possible musical effect. At one side, over the arched entrance from the atrium, are two balconies, which curve and sweep in irregular lines, giving a peculiarly pleasing effect. The side walls are wainscoted high up, and above the oak is again seen the marvelous stucco work, wrought in the beautiful musical designs. About the room in niches are magnificent carved oaken seats, so arranged as to be retired, and hung with beautiful tapestries. But the crowning glory of this room is the organ. The case is a beautiful musical temple, made of carefully selected oak, and is a work of art in itself that is probably not excelled in this country. The wood used in this case cost $12,000 and a large number of men worked two years in carving the elaborate designs. The organ case and the balconies are built into the room, and the effect is of an entire whole, not a room broken by protruding line of balcony or organ case. The lines are so softened that the harmony is perfect and the effect is marvelously delicate and beautiful. The organ, which cost $75,000, is of the best metal, and is one of the finest instruments ever made. The front of the organ is not marred by an organ-seat, but the organist is located on a conical shaped oak booth, depressed somewhat, and placed some distance from the organ. The room is lighted by several hundred incandescent lights, concealed in the ceiling. These are controlled by the organist, and the lights are raised and lowered in accordance with the character of the music. Above and apart from the music room is a beautifully finished chapel for the use of the family.

Leaving the music room and coming back through the grand atrium into the hall-way, the grand staircase is pointed out as an object of interest. It is made of oak, but the rail, which was made in France, is of hammered steel of unique design. There are also two elevators in the house, making access easy to the upper floors. The rest of the rooms in the house are of different designs and each is a study in itself. There is a Moorish room, Turkish room, Roman and Grecian rooms, and in each the stucco, the carving, the windows and everything are in keeping with the style of architecture represented.

All through the house are scattered the most magnificent bronzes, statues, and other works of art.

The kitchen has a tile floor and tile wainscoting, and is as nearly complete in its way as any room in the house. The plumbing is another feature, for it is made as nearly perfect as possible, and by no chance can any gases return to the living rooms.

The main idea of the building is a great musical palace, all else being subservient to this. The music room is the central feature, and the magnificent atrium is designed simply as a sort of preparatory chamber for the sublimity of the musical temple beyond. The living rooms are necessary adjuncts to the art rooms and are fitted up in harmony with them.

From the south windows of the house, the views are as fine as any in southern Berkshire. They take in the beautiful Berkshire meadows, the valley of the lower Housatonic and the range of East and June mountains. It is the intention of the owner to make of the 150 acres a grand park or garden, and a few years more will see this plan carried out.

Two beautiful and artistic bridges will be thrown across the river, the grounds will be traversed by carefully-constructed roads, and the whole will become a veritable garden of Eden. Along the front of the place a stone wall is now being built. It is of the same material as the house, and will be surmounted by a hammered iron rail of a peculiar design. Some $2,000,000 will have been expended on the place when it is finished.

On both sides of the river at this point Mrs. Searles owns about 200 acres of land, including the large meadow between the house and the river and southward, a quarry of 70 acres on the west slope of Mount Bryant, and nearly the whole north half of Prospect Mountain, which rises abruptly from the river.

THE HIGH FOUNTAIN.

In the large meadow below the terrace a fountain has been constructed that sends a large column of water aloft to the extraordinary height of eighty to ninety feet, with the mountain background to show it off. In the first frosts of autumn, the water has a remarkable appearance, for, at the rising of the sun, the spray that sheaths the column of descending water, is converted into aqueous vapor, so that it rises and floats upon the lazy air, following graceful lines a thousand feet or more till it becomes invisible, or joins the low clouds or early morning vapors. The projected water then has no appearance of returning to the basin below, but all seems to be taking flight.

ONE OF THE EARTH'S CHOICEST VIEWS.

The view from the street near Kellogg Terrace is one of the choicest ones on the earth. It is there had in greatest perfection, though charming phases of it are seen from other points, further south or up the westward hill. A gentleman who has spent several years in town, who has traveled extensively in Europe and America, and who has a keen and critical appreciation of the beautiful, is one of hundreds of similar people, who declare that there is no more lovely outlook than this, even in Switzerland or Italy.

THE SUNSETS OF MARVELOUS BEAUTY.

The sunsets that are thrown upon this East Mountain are often of marvelous beauty. Some years they are absent; others, they are frequent, depending partly upon meteorological conditions. The best effect is obtained from the lower portions of the valley, because the observer is then in the shade of the western hill. Though visible at all times of the year, the best sunsets are in June, October and November. The sunsets seen in the west by city, seacoast and prairie people, are incomparably inferior to the magnificent colorings of refracted sunlight, reflected upon the west side of this mountain on the east of the village, in mellow golden, in crimson, purple and many other tints. Several years ago a village resident was passing a man standing in the street below Kellogg Terrace when the latter, a stranger, waked from the spell that was upon him and ejaculated "There," with a gesture toward the mountain. No longer able to retain his admiration, he said that he had traveled far among the Alps and the Appenines, and beheld the richest sunshine of the old world, but had never found one that so deeply stirred his feelings as this one. The echoes of the locomotive whistle, from this mountain, continue for 50 seconds.

The transformation of this prospect into a winter's scene is often of wonderful effect. *The Berkshire Courier* describes one as follows: "These are the days when to live in the country and see the beauties of a frosty morning is joy enough. One morning last week the sun looked over East Mountain and saw a cloud of frost crystals suspended in the air and rising from the meadows to the top of the mountain; and as he threw the beams of his dazzling eye through the feathery prisms, a singular effect was visible to the observer from Main street. In the southeast stood a column of rainbow light, apparently a thousand feet high, and in the east was another of similar appearance. Berkshire in winter rivals Berkshire in summer."

THE CONGREGATIONAL CHURCH.

No religious society elsewhere in a country town, and few in cities, have such a possession as that of the Congregational society in Great Barrington. The cost of this was not far from $200,000, the cost of the land, which would be a principal item of expense in cities, being only an insignificant twentieth of the whole. The superiority of the blue dolomite, composing the buildings, over most other building stones, is here apparent. A description of the interior is unnecessary here, for visitors are admitted to the church, and as it is one of the notable churches of the country, all strangers coming to town ask permission to enter on week days, if they do not attend Sunday service. There is not a veneer about the whole building; all materials are the best and are "solid." The solid mahogany platform and pulpit are the gift of Mrs. J. M. Wasson of Pittsfield; and the mahogany furniture was given by Mr. and Mrs. Edward Leavitt of New York. The carved work, the decoration in colors, the stained glass and pictorial windows, and all the belongings are sure to attract admiring attention. The chapel is unexcelled and is connected with a ladies' parlor and kitchen thoroughly equipped with cooking utensils and chinaware. At the dedication, September 26, 1883, the Rev. Dr. Mark Hopkins preached the sermon.

ONE OF THE BEST ORGANS EVER MADE.

The Roosevelt organ in this church cost over $30,000, and in mechanical construction excels every other organ in Europe and America, with one exception, that in the Hopkins mansion, already described. The size equals that of the average large organs at home and abroad. The compass of the manuals is C C to A 3, 58 notes; of the pedals, C C C to F, 30 notes. The organ has 3,954 pipes, 60 speaking stops and 34 mechanical accessories of various kinds, among the latter being 13 combination pistons, which, in a fraction of a second, bring into use combinations that have been made among 309 adjusters on the face of the key box. By their recent invention, which has been applied to only a very few organs, all of the Roosevelt make, the player can make any combinations of stops that he pleases before playing (billions of them are possible), and bring them into instant use by pressing the pistons. The best organ in Europe operates by pistons only 24 combinations, all fixed.

An echo organ is behind the wall at the opposite end of the church and is operated over two and a half miles of electric wires. There are but few echo organs in the world.

It is only in the hands of a master that this organ ever begins to show its possibilities; indeed, only one of the expert organists who have played it, and he the most competent one in the New World, if not in the whole world, has been able to do justice to the instrument. Public recitals are given by Frederick Archer every summer. The ebony and antique mahogany case, ornamented by the best carvers in America, was the design of the London architect, G. A. Audsley. The 83 front pipes are decorated with $250 worth of gold leaf. The generosity of this gift has been ascribed to Timothy Hopkins, treasurer of the Central Pacific Railroad Company; and also to Mrs. Edward F. Searles.

The Parsonage.

The parsonage, its furniture, and the barn cost about $100,000. Here is a most luxurious home, that is all the gift of Mrs. Searles, in memory of her husband's great-grandfather, the Rev. Dr. Samuel Hopkins, the pastor of this church from 1743 to 1770, who was the author of the famous Hopkinsonian doctrines, and one of the vigorous thinkers of his time. Mrs. Searles and her brother-in-law, Moses Hopkins, of San Francisco, each contributed $5,000 toward the cost of building the church and chapel.

The First Armed Resistance in the Revolution.

Great Barrington has the honor of being the first place in the Thirteen Colonies where the first armed resistance was made to the dominion of George III, and his officers openly defied and bereft of authority. On the 16th of August, 1774, more than eight months before the battle of Lexington, the judges of the Crown came here, then the shire town, to hold court; but they were prevented from doing so by a large concourse of men, principally from the south end of Berkshire county and the north end of Litchfield county, Conn. The court house stood in the center of the street, directly in front of where the Berkshire house now stands. It faced to the east, and the street diverged here, passing on either side of the building. One of the three judges who was to hold court was David Ingersoll Jr., who resided in the house now used as a lodge at Mrs. Searles' Kellogg Terrace. He owned this property and was a pronounced Royalist. The crowd seized Ingersoll and placed him on an antiquated horse, with his face to the tail. His cocked hat was battered, his wig was knocked away, and in this undignified manner he was ridden out of town amid the jeers of the crowd. He was taken to the Litchfield jail, from which he afterward escaped and fled to Boston. While there he sold his Barrington property in order to raise money with which to return to England. The old house, of such historic interest, is well preserved, and can be readily seen from the street. In this old court house, in 1780, was made the first decision freeing a slave. The slave was Elizabeth Freeman, better known as "Mum Bet." She was the property of John Ashley, and her case was pleaded by Theodore Sedgwick, who secured her freedom under the Massachusetts bill of rights. The Shays rebellion of 1786-7, against burdensome taxes and imprisonment for debt, made Great Barrington a historical scene of action, and culminated in a pitched battle in the northwest part of Sheffield, a few rods south of the Goodale quarry. The men of Berkshire and other counties of Western Massachusetts constituted the two best and most famous regiments of the Army of the Potomac in the Civil War—the Tenth and the Thirty-seventh—adding new evidence of the patriotism and spirit of liberty pervading the region.

WILLIAM CULLEN BRYANT.

William Cullen Bryant's residence in this town, 1815-25, has left associations that will always endure. The strong impressions that the surroundings made upon his poetic nature found some voice in his poem on Green River, a stream a mile west of the village, that "glides along, through its beautiful banks, in a trance of song"; in his "Monument Mountain," an elevation in the town, half way towards Stockbridge; and about two scores of others, among them being "The Ages," "The Rivulet," "Autumn Woods," "After a Tempest," "Forest Hymn," "A Winter Piece," "The West Wind," and a "Walk at Sunset." These works of the poet were all the inspiration of the Nature in which he lived. Indeed, Berkshire is a vast volume of poems that no pen can fully transcribe, no words adequately express. Mr. Bryant was town clerk for several years, and the records, abounding in his autographs, are preserved. He made record of his marriage to Frances Fairchild, of this town, which took place in the Henderson house, June 11, 1821, and recorded the birth of his first child. The old house stands on Main street, opposite Kellogg Terrace—and was once used for storing Revolutionary supplies, and where General Burgoyne stayed for a time on his way to Boston after the Saratoga defeat, when Colonel Elijah Dwight lived there. General Burgoyne was riding by the house, when he was suddenly taken ill, and would have fallen from his horse but for the timely aid from one of his staff officers. Colonel Dwight witnessed the scene

BRYANT HOUSE—(WHERE WILLIAM CULLEN BRYANT WAS MARRIED AND WHERE HIS FIRST CHILD WAS BORN.)

from his piazza, and hastening out, he tendered the hospitality of his house to the sick general. The offer was gratefully accepted, and Burgoyne remained several days, his troops remaining in camp near by. The old house is now owned and occupied by Mrs. Culver, a niece of Bryant, and despite the fact that it was built in 1759, it is well preserved, and is one of the most interesting buildings in Berkshire. In connection with the Initial letter of this paper on Great Barrington, we give a picture of the house and a full page picture from an 1889 photograph.

Among the prose work that Mr. Bryant did while here was " A Border Tradition," that he wrote for the *United States Review and Literary Gazette*. The meadow south of Kellogg Terrace was once a swamp, and was supposed to be haunted. At any rate, strange lights had been seen there.

MONUMENT MOUNTAIN.

Long famous for the views of extraordinary beauty from its summit and from its dizzy precipice, Monument Mountain, four miles from the village, is a choice possession, even in Great Barrington. A fine tribute to this mountain comes from " Octavia Hensel " (Lady Alice Seymour), a native of this town, in a letter a few years ago from Austria, describing a concert given by Liszt, whose music brought back to her memory a visit to this mountain. The apparent fancy of the description has an objective reality; for Nature, in Berkshire, always goes hand in hand with Fancy:

"Liszt sat down to the piano. Many years ago a little child climbed to the top of Monument Mountain, among the Berkshire Hills. She wandered away from the merry party of parents and friends, and found a marble nook under a gray rock, fringed with ferns and lichens. Down on the moss bed, among the wintergreen berries, she knelt to look over the frightful precipice into the valley where pines and hemlocks waved. She heard only the sad sighing of wind in the pines, she saw only cloud shadows moving over the landsape, but they were replaced by a haze of golden glory; for, 'after the shadow, the golden sun' smiles on the field lily bells, and sets them ringing for joy. The child could not hear these flower bells ringing, but she thought she did; she saw the bright waters of the Housatonic ' winding through meadows in a path of light' and the sunbeams playing among the tree shadows over the stream, and the silly child thought she heard the fairies laugh at this game of hide and seek. The glorious mountains that wall in the Housatonic Valley stood solemn and dark away to the north; the awful precipice above which the

MONUMENT MOUNTAIN FROM UNDER THE CLIFFS.

child stood filled her with that unspeakable awe which we sometimes feel when organ notes announce in the *Te Deum* the majesty of earth's glory." Berkshire is not only a poem, but it is a poem set to entrancing music.

Of Monument Mountain, Prof. Hitchcock writes: "It does not rise more than 500 feet above the plain and 1,250 feet above tide water; but its eastern side is an almost perpendicular wall of white granular quartz; and, shooting out boldly, as it does, into the heart of a beautiful country, the prospect from its summit is delightful. * * * In several places frowning masses [of rock] are still left projecting from the cliff, more than 200 feet above the base, still holding on to the parent rock with apparent firmness. And it is an interesting trial of the nerves to creep to the edge of these jutting masses, and to look down upon the fragments some hundreds of feet below. * * * Near the highest part of this cliff, a pointed mass of rock, only a few feet in diameter, has been parted at the top of the mountain; but its base not giving way, it now stands insulated, and from 50 to 100 feet high" on different sides. It is called Pulpit Rock, and is very difficult of ascent, though a few people have been to its top.

The name of this mountain is derived from a monument of stones that had been made by Indians at the foot of the southern slope of the higher part of the mountain. The tradition on which Bryant's poem was founded was told by an aged Indian woman, who said that an Indian maiden, having formed a passionate attachment for a young brave, who was her cousin, and whom the customs of her tribe forbade her to marry, threw herself from the precipice, and that she was buried where the Indians, passing that way, have each placed a stone. Another tradition has it that the pile marks the spot where invading Indians were slaughtered by the resident Indians. Still another is that the heap was raised over the grave of the first sachem who died after the Indians came into the region; and, again, it is said to have been a territorial boundary between tribes. The accepted conclusion now is that the monument has a religious import, and was very likely connected with the burial of some Indian. Whites scattered the stones half a century ago, and dug to find treasure or human bones, but were unsuccessful. The cairn was replaced in 1884.

ELDON'S CAVE.

Eldon's Cave is a recently discovered point of interest, and is named in honor of Eldon French, its discoverer. This young man is a graduate of the Great Barrington high school and of Cornell University, and accidentally came across the entrance to the cave some three years ago. It is in the Tom Ball range of mountains near the village of Williamsville in the town of West Stockbridge, and is of limestone formation. The entrance is through a corridor some 500 feet long, and in places so low, that the explorer is compelled to wriggle along on his stomach, snake fashion. After passing through the many trials encountered in this dark passageway a large chamber 15 feet square is reached. The roof is some 30 feet high, is arched, and is covered with beautiful stalactites, each holding a globule of water. The sides are of marble, polished by carbonic acid gas dissolved in the water which trickles down from above. When lighted by a torch or candle, the cave has the appearance of being a cave of diamonds, and the sight is dazzlingly beautiful. Beyond the main cave are several smaller chambers, which are not without their attractions.

BELCHER'S CAVE.

In the north end of the village, where a spur of the mountains comes to an abrupt end, a cave is formed by the disruption and falling together of rocks. It is known as Belcher's Cave, because tradition says that a man named Belcher counterfeited silver coin there before the Revolution. The place is often made the object of easy, summer days' walks by those who want to see what the rough hand of Nature has done, and to get the refreshing coolness imparted to the air by rocks and shade.

MOUNT PETER.

A more pleasant walk, and an easy one, is to Mount Peter, in the south end of the village, from whose summit charming views may be had. On this mount, President Garfield sat, on August 25, 1854, on his way to college, and wrote some verses to an unknown maiden who had some stanzas on "Morning in Berkshire" published in the village paper, *The Berkshire Courier*, a few days before. The story and all the verses may be found in the files of the *Courier* in the issue of September 21, 1881.

BERKSHIRE HEIGHTS.

A walk or a ride of only a few minutes will take one to Berkshire Heights, the view of which is not excelled in all Berkshire. One hundred acres of the land here was bought in 1885 by the Berkshire Heights Land Company, for the purpose of opening it up for dwelling house building for city people. Beautiful streets have been made, lots laid out, and a few homes have been built.

Soon after the purchase of this property the gentlemen interested, organized the Berkshire Heights Land Company. The purest water from Green river has been carried up to the heights, the cost of this improvement being some $30,000. The property has been provided with ample sewerage facilities, new roads have been laid out, and a quarry has been opened near by, where plenty of good building stone is obtainable. A very beautiful spot was chosen as a site for the new hotel which Mr. Caleb Ticknor proposes to build in the near future. The grounds have been graded and the driveways laid out, and all is in readiness for building. The plan of the new hotel provides for a very handsome four-story building of modern design, with a frontage of 317 feet. The house will overlook Mansfield lake, only three minutes away, where fine fishing and boating can be found. The view down the valley from the hotel will be delightful. The prospects are that the hotel will be built within a year or two, and when completed, Great Barrington will have one of the finest summer hotels in New England.

A charming pine grove is reserved for a park and an observation tower, from which the view will be perfectly ravishing. The view is far superior to an adjacent one from a lower elevation, referred to by the Rev. T. T. Munger as one of the few most beautiful of the famous landscape views that are to be had in the world. The hill is one-half mile from the railroad station; its elevation is 264 feet above Main street, 980 feet above tide water, and from it scenery of great variety and a profusion of beauty spreads out on every side, extending into Connecticut, New York, and Vermont. One of the latest ideas is to change the location of the railroad station to a point nearer the Heights. This movement is the beginning of an enterprise that will make available for habitation a most delightful hill on the western edge of the village, and is one of the steps toward the end whither all Berkshire is tending—the creation of Country Homes.

East Rock and Prospect Rock.

A more difficult walk is the path to East Rock and the top of Mount Bryant, at an elevation of 1,448 feet above the sea, 725 feet above the railroad station, and about 775 feet above the river. This huge boulder, left by a glacier hanging on the brow of the mountain, affords a resting place commanding one of the broadest and finest of Berkshire's many mountain top outlooks. Its beauty is unspeakable, and no one should fail to catch its inspiration. The path leads across the top of the mountain to the eastern brow, where the scene from Forest View suggests the name. At a slight expense, a good road can be made to this summit. East Mountain, south of Mount Bryant, is 1,700 feet high.

A more easy walk, along a woodland path, is that to Prospect Rock ; and some visitors pause on the way to call on Crosby, the gunsmith.

JUNE MOUNTAIN.

A walk of perhaps seven miles, that is productive of much enjoyment, is to follow the road between East and Prospect Mountains as far down as "Brookside," and then leave the road and walk to the left, along the edge of the woods on the mountain side, up to the place where Roaring Brook comes off the mountain top. The view here is a choice one. Then cross over to June Mountain by Mark Laird's house, and get the southern view from that mountain, the beauty of which cannot be excelled. Return *via* the east road to Sheffield. The last view may be had easier by riding down this Sheffield road to a place just north of the first house ; then walk a few hundred feet up the mountain.

Another walk, but in the edge of the village, exposing some of the very best of Berkshire's scenes, leads a little past Major Gibbons's place on the Egremont road ; then off the road, up the hill through the small pines, where the views change every few feet; then up to Berkshire Heights, to Mansfield Lake and to Ames's Hill.

LAKE BUEL.

Lake Buel, six miles distant, is a beautiful sheet of water, lying a few rods beyond the eastern boundary of the town, to which thousands of people go every summer. Accommodations for the public are sufficient in the way of boats, picnic grounds, horse feeding, and so on, at both ends of the lake. The name of the Lake is from Samuel Buel, who, July 23, 1812, saved from drowning four of seven persons whose boat was capsized. This is one of the most frequented lake resorts in Berkshire, and of late years has come to be very popular. Several cottages have been built and many families spend a part of the summer there, enjoying a delightful "camping out" experience.

ICE GULF.

In the mountain west of the lake, half a mile back of the house of George L. Turner, is a singular chasm called Ice Gulf. The width is forty to fifty feet, the perpendicular walls are eighty feet high in some places, and the length is about eighty rods. Huge rocks have fallen from above and filled it twenty feet or more, and among them ice is found late, if not a'l summer. The mountain is actually cleft in twain. The place is exceedingly wild, an icy chill always pervades the air, and the light of day is hardly more than a gloom. Among the theories of this curious formation is that of an earthquake, while President Hitchcock's idea, in his "Geology of Massachusetts," is that it is a "purgatory" made by the sea during the partial submergence of the Atlantic coast.

MINERAL SPRINGS.

The Soda Spring, three miles from the village, in that part of Sheffield called Brush Hill, has long been sought for its curative effects on cutaneous diseases. The summer hotel that once existed there was burnt several years ago, but was never rebuilt. To this spring, and to a neighboring Sulphur Spring, many people go to fill jugs and kegs. It is suggested that the water from these springs be brought through glass lined pipes to a more accessible point, thus adding still another attraction to this region, and the idea may be carried out in a short time

LONG LAKE.

There is no lake in the county whose immediate surroundings are more picturesque than those of Long Lake, three miles to the west of north. Going over the Christain Hill road, one beholds the best scenery in panoramic array. The lake has an Adirondack appearance, with its forest margin, its clear water, and the overhanging mountain.

BEARTOWN.

The wildest inhabited part of the town is the northeast corner, called Beartown, and ascended from South Lee. Two miles from that village, at the end of a private road, beginning on the left at an old saw mill, lives Levi Beebe, a mountain farmer, who has attained reputation for great originality as a weather prophet. From his house the northern view is remarkably beautiful. The drive up the gorge, the ride through the woods and a talk with Mr. Beebe are a rare treat.

THE VILLAGE OF GREAT BARRINGTON.

The village of Great Barrington has unexcelled natural advantages in the picturesque and the beautiful. Variety is prolific, and suprises are unceasing. Village neatness is conspicuous, and is growing ; the street fences are nearly all removed; handsome lawns, nice houses and graceful trees are on every hand; and an air of thrift, comfort and substantial well-being pervades. Among the later improvements may be mentioned electric lights, an increased water supply, and a comprehensive system of sewerage which takes in the entire village. Many new sidewalks have also been laid, and improvement along this line is to be kept up.

A HUNDRED WALKS AND DRIVES.

While some walks and drives have been mentioned, they are but a few out of a hundred or more that are each different from the rest, and all which embrace myriad charms. Whatever way one turns, he cannot go amiss of seeing what will provoke his deepest admiration. Several views have been painted by artists of established reputation, among them being J. B. Bristol, N. A., who commonly spends the summer here. Within the town there are about ninety miles of roads. Beyond the town's limits, the objects of a day's or half-day's ride are many—in Mount Washington, Bashbish Falls, Bear Rock, the Dome, and other summits; in Sheffield, Sage's Ravine, White's Hill, near North Egremont; the Twin Lakes, in Salisbury, Ct.; on the north, many points in Stockbridge and Lenox; and many other attractions that will be found mentioned elsewhere in this volume. The roads over which these places are approached are most excellent. They are nearly all made of gravel; they are smooth, hard and free from loose stones. Great Barrington annually spends from $5,000 to $12,000 in the care and construction of roads and bridges.

THE SPORTSMEN'S CLUBS.

The South Berkshire Sportsmen's Club and the Berkshire Trout Hatchery Club are organizations made up of the best citizens, and the objects are indicated by the names. The first named has done much for the protection of game out of season and the maintenance of the game laws. The Trout Club is of more recent origin, but is an enterprising association. A fine hatchery, with a capacity of half a million, has been established on a tributary to Konkapot, about six miles from the village. Here has been erected a club house, a keeper's house, and ample barns for the care of horses, and this is really a most interesting place to visit. In the large exhibition ponds may be seen "speckled beauties" from the smallest size up to $3\frac{1}{2}$-pounders, a sight of which fairly makes one's mouth water. The purpose of the club is to restore and perpetuate the excellent trout fishing in this section, and it certainly seems as if the object would be attained. A visit to the hatchery makes a pleasant and entertaining trip.

A Remarkable Story

of a Hancock farmer is preserved. He was arrested for high treason in the Revolution, and was lodged in the Great Barrington log jail; but such was his character for honesty, that he was allowed to go out to work where he could pick up a shilling, upon promise to return at night. He did this for eight months, and when the sheriff was about to take him to Springfield for trial, he assured the officer that he would go alone, and was allowed to do so. After a journey of forty-two miles on foot, he arrived at court, was tried, and was sentenced to be hanged, but was pardoned. The story is found in the old-time school books.

Old Macedonia.

The old cannon in front of the Soldiers' Monument is the relic of a famous naval achievement, the capture of the British 38-gun frigate "Macedonia" by the "United States," commanded by Captain Decatur, October, 25, 1812, after a fight of two hours. For many years "Old Macedonia" celebrated Independence Day with as loud a voice as when it shot down Yankee tars, until a few years ago, when it became so honeycombed by rust that its firing was dangerous.

The Fair of the Housatonic Society.

City people who remain here till the last week of September will be much interested to see a country fair—the "honest farmers" showing their cattle, sheep and horses, and, above all, the queer mixture of humanity that assembles from farm, village, and remote hills. The fair of the Housatonic Agricultural Society, in this village, is next to the largest one in the State ; it has an attendance of 12,000 to 15,000 people, and a large show of domestic animals and manufactures of unquestionable excellence.

Some Natives and Residents.

The house on the summit of the hill on the old road to Seekonk was built by the Rev. Dr. Samuel Hopkins, and was tenanted by him. William C. Bryant had his office at one time in the wing of Bazy W. Pattison's house, and once lived in the house where Charles J. Taylor lives. In M. Ludlow Whitlock's house, General Timothy Wainwright once lived. In 1822, the Leavenworth house, the second on the right above the railroad on Castle street, was built—then the finest in town. Elias W. Leavenworth, who passed his youth in the village, late of Syracuse, N. Y., was a distinguished citizen of that State, and held numerous high offices, among them being that of Secretary of State. Theodore Sedgwick, a man of national distinction in his day, studied and practiced law here for a few years.

In later years other men, more or less known to fame, have found homes in this town. From 1840 to 1845, the Rev. Charles B. Boynton, previously engaged in business in West Stockbridge, preached in the Congregational church in Housatonic village; subsequently he became a well known preacher in Cincinnati, was chaplain of the XXXIXth and XLth Congresses, and wrote several books. His son, General H. V. Boynton, became the Washington correspondent of the Cincinnati *Commercial Gazette*, and another son, C. A. Boynton, Washington agent of the Western Associated Press. The Rev. Mr. Boynton's successor in Housatonic, was the Rev. J. T. Headley, famous for his biographies.

The Pope house on South Main street, the old brick house built in 1766, was the early home of Frank L. Pope, the eminent electrician, who explored Alaska and neighboring British America in the interest of the overland telegraph, who wrote "The Modern Practice of the Electric Telegraph," which has had a greater sale than all other works on electricity put together, was chiefly instrumental in establishing the stock reporting business, was originator of the private line service, was inventor of the first and best electric signals for railways, and has been constantly active in literary and scientific work. Mr Pope owns the ancestral homestead and the north end of June Mountain, where he has built a small house in a sightly location, and will build a much finer house for his country home. The old house on Main street has been remodeled, and while the ancient structure is maintained, its appearance has been vastly improved. Mr Pope's youthful associates here were Thomas Maguire, the late famous correspondent of the Boston *Herald*, and the late Merret Seeley, superintendent of the National Express Company. Mr. Pope's younger brothers are well known among electricians : Ralph W. Pope for his services to the Gold and Stock Telegraph Company, and, later, as editor of the *Electrician and Electrical Engineer;* and Henry W Pope as the chief organizer of the District Telegraph system of New York and eastern cities.

Of the children of Judge Increase Sumner, one of the leading lawyers of the State during his long practice in this town, Samuel B. Sumner, of Bridgeport, Ct., was colonel of the Forty-ninth Massachusetts Regiment and a judge in his adopted city; Charles A. Sumner, of San Francisco, is one of the orators of the Pacific coast, where he has made a wide reputation as a talented journalist and politician; and Albert I. Sumner, the musician and composer, was lost in shipwreck. Some of the best business blood in Chicago, the most energetic city in the world, has gone from Berkshire, and among the representatives from Great Barrington are Charles H. Fargo, one of the first men of the city; Rufus P. Pattison, James L. Pattison, and the late Henry K. Buell—all well-known business men.

The Berkshire House and Other Accommodations.

Summer and autumn guests find ample accommodations in public and private houses in Great Barrington. For many years the Berkshire House, in the village center, has been famous among people who come this way for its choice entertainment, and it never stood so high as under its present landlord, Caleb Ticknor. It is not so large nor so small that a guest feels lonesome; on the contrary, he becomes the member of a large family, as it were, where his comforts are looked after attentively, but not with obtrusion. Mr. Ticknor is one of the few men born to manage the affairs of an inn. His natural politeness, affability and accommodating disposition are such as to win for him the liking of all his guests Under such administration, the Berkshire House has attained an enviable reputation, and has become a choice resort for those who want to spend the season or a vacation at a hotel.

The Collins House, in the south part of the village, under the proprietorship of Alfred Peck, makes a specialty of summer and autumn guests. It has entertained many noted people, and is particularly agreeable in having a village situation and yet in being quiet and having country surroundings that are delightful.

There are many boarding-houses in the village and among the farm houses outside, and several furnished houses may be hired for the season.

The Miller House makes a specialty of accommodating travelers, and has never stood so well with the public as under the proprietorship of W. B. Loveland, for the last few years.

The People Who Come Here.

A stranger coming to Berkshire can find congenial, social surroundings, no matter what his wants are; but he must use discretion in selecting the place. Some idea of what Great Barrington offers has already been given, but the mention of at least a few of the people who come here is in order. Of the people previously named, nearly all who are living are visitors for long or short time.

Referring to people who have other homes in cities or elsewhere, country homes are owned in Great Barrington by Mrs. Searles, of "Kellogg Terrace;" Howard Ackerman, of New York: H. M. Johnson, of Buffalo; Frank L. Pope, Elizabeth, N. J., " Wildwood."

William E. Tefft, of the large dry goods house of Tefft, Weller & Co., of New York, has just completed "Elmwood," a large and tasteful dwelling, built on the former site of " Jumbo Cottage." Col. W. L. Brown, proprietor of the New York News, bought the Major Gibbons place a few years ago and occupied it during the summer. In 1888 the house was burned down, and its place has been taken by a more pretentious house, just finished (summer of 1890). Among others having fine places here are William Stanley, a prominent New York lawyer, and his son William Stanley, Jr. The latter is the electrician of the Westinghouse Company, and is an inventor with a well-established reputation. D. W. Morrison, a wealthy saddlery dealer of Newark, N. J., has nearly completed a comfortable home on the west slope, overlooking the town.

Among those who have come here to retire to a country home are J. Milton Mackie, of New York; E. D. Brainard, from Albany.

Within a few years houses were rented to these people : Mrs. Emma J. Peck, Brooklyn, N. Y.: Samuel L. Harris, Brooklyn; Miss Sarah E. Wickham, Brooklyn ; Mrs. J. H. Heroy, New York ; E. A. Doup, Brooklyn; G. W. Peters, Newark, N. J.; G. T. Harris, Philadelphia. Judge Dewey of the Superior Court is a regular summer visitor to Great Barrington, his former home.

Among the Berkshire House guests within a year or so have been J. W. Emerson, A. P. Burbank, W. D. Howells, Edward G. Dickson, B. G. Talbert, W. E. Cooper, T. J. Pell, W. D. Ryder, Woodruff Sutton, all of New York; Capt. Henry Erben, of the Portsmouth Navy Yard; J. M. Brookfield, William H. Wright, Abram Lowerre, all of Brooklyn; W. D. Bishop, Bridgeport, Ct.; Frank A. Day, Boston; Prof. H. F. Walling, Cambridge, Mass.; Thomas G. Ritch, C. H. Lounsbury, both of Stamford. Ct.; N. H. Sanford, Prof. James D. Dana, both of New Haven.

At the Collins House, L. M. Bates, of New York, stayed several seasons. Among other guests have been the following: Mrs. B. H. Van Auken, William H. Bradford, S. Inslee. Jr. (of Calhoun, Robbins & Co.), John LeBoutillier (of LeBoutillier Bros.). J. T. Sparkman, William O. Sumner, Leonard J. Carpenter, Samuel Keefer (proprietor Grand Central Hotel), all of New York; Mrs. E. Reid, New Rochelle, N. Y.; William J. Sayres, John Vanderbilt, both of Brooklyn.

Most of the boarding-houses of Berkshire accommodate from five to fifteen guests each. In the houses in and around Great Barrington village. any one desiring entertainment will find everything to his comfort. and such varied social surroundings that he will find anything to his liking. For young people, all sorts of outdoor sports are feasible, on land and water. with no lack of companions and contestants—in tennis. base ball. foot ball. wheeling, swimming, boating. and so on.

The mail facilities of Great Barrington are excellent. There are three mails each way between the town and New York. A letter mailed in New York in the evening is received here at 9.30 A. M., and a letter mailed here at 8 P. M. is received in New York at the first delivery. An Albany evening paper is received at 5 P. M., New York evening papers at 8 P. M. New York morning papers are received at 1 P. M. There is a Sunday mail, arriving from New York with morning papers at noon and letters mailed Saturday evening.

A PAINTERS' PARADISE.

For the last half century, Great Barrington has been known to many of our great masters of landscape painting. Here came Durand and Kensett, besides many of their associates, and here Bristol often has his summer home. Artist Church of New York, a famous landscape painter has spent several summers here. These lovers of the beautiful in scenery have sketched many of the picturesque views of the vicinity, and have done their share with Bryant to make the whole region classic.

VARIED SCENES.

Henry Parker Fellows, who has made several canoe voyages, in a description of a canoe trip down the Housatonic in 1881 says of the journey through Great Barrington : "The Housatonic is a confirmed coquette, constantly flirting with one mountain range or another, and frequently several at the same time. * * * The sun after a while disappeared in a cloud of fire behind the Taconic Dome, which towers 2,000 feet above the valley, a solemn mass of darkest green, while Monument Mountain, at the other end of the valley, stood out in purplish glow, clear and distinct in the still air. I remember no river scene. indeed, of greater beauty. The stream itself, too, was very beautiful. The banks on either side sloped down to the water's very edge of smooth turf, broken, however, by a clump of trees, or masses of clustering vines, and we occasionally passed a little inlet, usually guarded by a martial array of cat-tails. * * * There is a stateliness and dignity about Great Barrington as great in reality as its high-sounding name would imply. It is a rare combination of New England thrift and New York opulence. Beecher it is, I believe, who once declared that he never entered the village without wishing that he was never to leave it."

"Octavia Hensel," referring to the scenes about town, tells how they will hold sway after they have become impressed upon the beholder: "Mount Peter will still rise high above the Housatonic meadow, its gray marble rocks half hidden by nodding hairbells and tufts of red columbine, and the village will peep out from the groves of elm and maple, while far to the north the Mountain of the Monument will fling its boldly curved outline against a turquoise sky. Over the winding oziers that border the Housatonic on the east, the great rock of East Mountain will rise in solitary grandeur above the dark green masses of the woodland hills, and reflect in splendor of topaz and amethyst the sunsets burning behind the distant Dome of purple Taconic's mighty range. Away to the south, the low mound of the Indian burial ground will lie an embankment across the shadowy Mahaiwe vale—an outpost to guard the village homes from the ghostly array which imagination pictures in the white birch forests stretching away to the Sheffield plain. To the west, reaching almost to the woodlands at the base of the great mountain dome, where the purple light deepens to Tyrian hues in the coming on of night, the Egremont plains will appear like an emerald clasped on the hills' imperial mantle."

HOUSATONIC.

One of the busy, thriving and growing villages of the country is Housatonic, situated at the northern extremity of the town of Great Barrington. Here the wild and rugged precipitous western slope of Monument Mountain descends abruptly to the Housatonic River, which dashes down rocky rapids and mill dams, in full sight of the traveler on the railway cars. Since 1850 the Monument Mills have been making cotton warps and, since 1866, the Wawbeek Mills, owned by the same company, have made Marseilles counterpanes of the highest quality. The Owen Paper Company has been in existence since 1856, and now makes some of the fine writing paper for which Berkshire is famous. The mercantile interests of the village have grown with its manufacturing industries and a large trade now centers here that formerly went elsewhere. A large and handsome business block recently erected by the Monument Mills Company near the railroad station contains stores and a large hall for public meetings.

In the village of Van Deusenville, midway between Housatonic and the village of Great Barrington, a blast furnace for the manufacture of pig iron was built in 1834 ; since 1844, this has been owned and operated by the Richmond Iron Company. The product is some of the toughest and best iron made in the United States, and is unsurpassed for car wheels. The ore comes from West Stockbridge.

Housatonic, and Van Deusenville as well, is finely situated with reference to the natural attractions of the region. Stockbridge begins at once on the north of Housatonic, and Lenox is just beyond. The lower end of the romantic West Stockbridge valley begins at Housatonic, reaching northward a few miles to the beautiful country of Lebanon Springs and Queechy Lake. One of Berkshire's best surprises may be had by a short drive to Long Lake by the way of Williamsville; the battlements of Monument Mountain face the eastern storm three miles away; while all the glorious scenery of Southern Berkshire is southward and on every hand.

Under the new life that has been given to Great Barrington within a few years, the town is coming into greater prominence than ever as a summer and autumn resort; and, while it is sought more than ever by appreciative tourists, and by the visitors of a week, a month, or a season, it is also becoming highly valued, by people who retire from work or leave the city, as a most perfect location for Country Homes.

SOLDIERS' MONUMENT.

PITTSFIELD.

AROUND the city of Pittsfield, the valley in which it lies, is practically a large amphitheater, nearly hemmed in on all sides by mountain ranges or high hills. Washington Mountain walls in the city from the east; the valley narrows to the north, with occasional spurs of the mountains and hills in Lanesboro and Cheshire; to the south are seen the South Mountain, and the range further west towards the Richmond line; and on the west are the Taconics, with Perry's Peak in Richmond, and Potter Mountain to the northwest. This first city in the county, with its wide streets, stately elms, the thrift and intelligence of its inhabitants, at once apparent, and the general appearances on all hands, denoting substantial well being,—possessing all these, Pittsfield has a dignity, a maturity, a stability, that are impressed upon every visitor.

GENERAL ASPECT.

In Berkshire, where every one of its thirty-two towns has its own peculiar natural advantages and attractions, it is difficult to say what is the most pleasing or abounding most richly in that which is grandest and best. Pittsfield has six lakes, either wholly or in part within her borders, some of them of considerable size; and at each side of the town, east and west, flow the two sources of the Housatonic River, uniting nearly at its south border line. There is no end of "views," some of them bewitchingly grand, and many quiet nooks, suggestive of romance and legend; while, from almost any point, Greylock looms up in all its grandeur and pride, as though keeping sentinel over the northern portal to the valleys lying at its feet—the Hoosac and the Housatonic. Pittsfield, as seen from such an elevation as that on the hillsides of Washington up to Lake Ashley, or from Potter Mountain, with the great village in the distance, and the two lakes, Onota and Pontoosuc, apparently at your feet—from South Mountain, or, in fact, from any point—is a lovely picture.

Town Affairs.

Pittsfield has a history peculiar to itself, from the earliest times taking pride in its traditions and its records, so that, whatever the angry debate of the town-meeting or the internal dissensions there may have been over policy and measures for the government of its affairs, in the end the best has generally prevailed, the good judgment of the wisest and those having its affairs most deeply at heart has been finally adopted.

Pittsfield has laid aside the old town form of government, which became her so well for more than a century, and has become the first city in Berkshire county. The charter was accepted by the voters in February, 1890, and the new city government will be inaugurated in January, 1891. The government will consist of the mayor, a board of seven aldermen, and 14 common councilmen, and the change is expected to be of great benefit to the town. In all but name, Pittsfield has been a city for some time. The population is now about 18,000, there are regularly organized police and fire departments, fire-alarm telegraph, fine water supply, carried letter delivery service, telephone facilities, electric lights, first-class sidewalks, a well-equipped street railway, and many other modern conveniences ordinarily found only in cities. The demand for a new form of government was imperative, and though many were loth to give up the old town-meeting, which in its plain democracy has been such a feature of Pittsfield, the majority voted for the change, and Pittsfield modestly takes her place in the lengthening list of the cities of the Commonwealth. But the change from a town to a city will not in any way make Pittsfield less desirable as a summer resort or as a permanent home. It will still be the same beautiful place it has always been, with its broad, well-kept, shady streets, its air of refinement and prosperity, and its many other attractions which have won it the well-deserved title of "lovely Pittsfield."

Railroad communication has done a great deal for Pittsfield, even before most of the other parts of the county were so highly favored; New York and Boston are only about five hours away, with many trains daily each way. In 1868 the town became the county seat, and with that change has come the addition of the fine marble court house, opened in 1871, as well as the jail, which is one of the places of interest in the town to visit.

The manufacturing of Pittsfield, while extensive and increasing, is to a great extent hidden away, as it were, in the extremities of the town, and there is little or none of it along the principal streets. There are several thriving and well kept manufacturing villages; so that, while adding wealth and prosperity, they are not as detrimental to its attractiveness as a resort as they would be were the industries sandwiched in with handsome residences and its public buildings, or occupying its most attractive sites.

A HEALTHY ARISTOCRACY.

The earliest settlers were among the best. Men with a reputation, men of influence, patriotic in time of war, and earnest in everything which, according to their judgment, augmented the interests of the town in an educational, social and religious sense. The famous "Fighting Parson Allen," when he left his sermon to participate in the Battle of Bennington, was a fair type of his parishioners then, and that same spirit prevails yet. It was early made a residence by a healthy aristocracy, not purse-proud or arrogant; but the history of the town shows that its wealth and its culture, its bravery and its social element, have all been the instrumentalities in keeping Pittsfield in the ranks of "the best," and her people all along its history have caught the spirit of the grandeur about them, vieing with each other—speaking in general terms—in making the town a pleasant and safe dwelling place for its people, and offering them all the advantages possible under the circumstances. The "old families," like the Pomeroys, the Williamses, the Allens, the Francises, the Parkers, the Goodriches, the Churchills, the Colts, Dunhams, Stearnses, Plunketts, Clapps, Campbells, Barkers, Brewsters, Merrills, Russells, Childses, Col. John Brown, and scores of other names, who have been instrumental in moulding the town in its early days, have in their descendants men and women who love Pittsfield because they think the good old town is worthy of it, which has a healthy stimulating influence on the rest of the community. Thus much for the social atmosphere of Pittsfield; and, year by year, the improvements in better things—better schools, better sidewalks, better homes, and, in fact, better government every way—goes on, to the end that the visitor seeking rest may be attracted to its gates and within its walls, while at the same time its own children may also be educated to know more of the better ways of living.

The character of its visitors has, in a great degree, been moulded by its citizens, and during the past few years the attractions of Pittsfield, as well as other portions of Berkshire, have been very effectively set forth by the advertising literature of the Berkshire Life Insurance Company, which, while advancing its own interests in a very praiseworthy manner, has also given the great world outside to know more and more of the attractions of Pittsfield and Berkshire than had been known before.

A LITERARY TONE.

Pittsfield has, from its earliest time almost, been known as a literary town, and as one looks back over the pages of its history, so pleasantly and accurately told by J. E. A. Smith, he finds that there have been scholars and writers, poets and novelists, and others of that class, who have given the town a healthier atmosphere for their having lived within its borders. Its appropriations for schools are always large and generous; its churches are, as a whole, prosperous and well supported, while the church edifices are in keeping with the spirit of the town—commodious, comfortable and attractive, without show or gaudiness. Its pulpits have always been filled by prominent clergymen of the type of Parson Thomas Allen, who for many years served at the First church, taking an active part in moulding its affairs and those of the town, so that the present generation is reaping the benefits of his teaching. There were the Rev. Dr. Heman Humphrey; the Rev. Dr. John Todd, whose memory is still green in Pittsfield, whose books have gladdened many hearts and been translated into many tongues; the Rev. Dr. William C. Richards, who for some time officiated at the Baptist church, a poet and scholar; while, later, came the Rev. J. L. Jenkins of the First church, Rev. William Wilberforce Newton of St. Stephen's, an author of note and the originator of the plan for the Church Congress, whereby all denominations may work in unity—a creation worthy of the grand old town in which it first saw the light of day and the liberal, progressive men who originated it.

Dr. Oliver Wendell Holmes, a lineal descendant of Jacob Wendell, one of the early proprietors of the territory now comprising the town, was for a long time a summer resident, and still keeps up his attachment for Pittsfield. Henry W. Longfellow was a frequent visitor at the summer home of his father-in-law, and Herman Melville resided for many years at "Arrowhead."

For many years Pittsfield was the seat of the Berkshire Medical College, whose graduates are still among the foremost in the profession in different parts of the country. The late Dr. Josiah G. Holland was a student at this institution at one time. "Maplewood," originally a cantonment for troops during the war of 1812, had for a long time been known as a young ladies' school, with beautiful grounds. The property in 1887, passed into the hands of H. L. Plumb, formerly of Stockbridge, who, with Arthur W. Plumb, previously a popular assistant at the Stockbridge house, keeps here a choice summer hotel. Arthur W. Plumb now owns the property, and is making Maplewood one of the most popular summer hotels in New England. "Springside" once a flourishing boys' school is now used as a summer hotel, and is conducted very successfully by Mrs. Tetley, and Miss Saulsbury's young ladies' school is still in successful operation. As early as 1796 several libraries were founded, and in 1850 a young men's association was formed. Its library building, the Athenæum, is the gift of the late Thomas Allen, of St. Louis, who went out from Pittsfield a poor boy, carving his way to fame and fortune. Its shelves contain several thousand volumes of the best books, while the reference library is a fine one. Its benefits are absolutely free to all the people of the town, which appropriates liberally to its support until the bequest of about $60,000 by the late Phineas Allen becomes available, which will then make it self-supporting. Its museum, reading room and art gallery are well worth a visit, and the privilege of taking books is allowed to the summer visitors on the payment of a small guaranty fee. There are held the debating societies that wish to occupy its rooms; the ladies have their meetings there for their Wednesday Morning Club, of which Miss Anna L. Dawes, daughter of Senator Dawes, was the chief promoter, and before which association there have been lectures of a high order from time to time. These meetings are held during the summer. The Berkshire Historical and Scientific Society also holds its quarterly meetings there, and, in a word, it is the center of the educational interests of the town.

LOCAL ASSOCIATIONS.

Pittsfield from an early date has always been social, and many new associations abound. It is the boast of Pittsfield that it has more societies, secret, and for literary and other purposes, than almost any other place of its size in the State. Nearly all the secret orders are represented in Pittsfield, and one of its Masonic lodges dates back its origin to about 1795. The Monday Evening Club, an institution of the town, of which Thomas F. Plunkett was chief organizer, is composed of a limited membership of twenty-five prominent gentlemen in the town, who meet fortnightly during the winter months at the houses of the members, the host usually reading a paper, and a discussion following, afterwards coming the spread. Few towns of its size in the State have a similar organization as flourishing as this. The Business Men's Association, organized in 1881, has a membership of about 125 of the leading men of the town and vicinity, having an elegant suite of rooms in the Central Block fitted up for social purposes, which are resorted to by its members for the discussion of business or other matters, and pleasant games, without gambling. Its rooms are always open to gentlemen visiting or sojourning in the town. The Academy of Music has a large stage, and, such is the local appreciation of the best drama and music, that frequent entertainments are here given by the best theatrical companies. Its coliseum is also utilized for fairs and large gatherings.

WITHIN THE "CITY LIMITS."

The roads of Pittsfield embrace some of the finest drives in the county. The city's principal streets, North, South, East, and West, diverging from the Park, are wide, straight, and lined with huge trees, mainly elms and maples, on each side. On North and South streets is a clear view from the High School building (the former location of the Medical College) to Maplewood, of nearly a mile; and in summer especially, so hidden are the buildings, that the eye seems to look through a long avenue of trees. Down East street is another broad view, for half a mile, with great trees each side, and back from the highway are beautiful and cozy residences, with well-kept lawns and yards. A street railway is in operation, extending from the railroad station to North street, up to Wahconah street, Bel Air, Pontoosuc, and to the lake of that name.

WHERE VISITORS LIVE.

Among the many noted inns that the town has had, an old one, built in the last century, after being closed for years, was reopened in 1885—the Homestead Inn, on East street. This building has now been demolished to make room for the new residence of H. W. Bishop, of Chicago. The Berkshire Life Insurance Company's building stands on the "Berkshire Corner," which was the site of the famous old Berkshire Hotel, whose Federalist landlord, in 1808, refused to furnish a dinner for Democrats, who were compelled to make their repast in a neighboring orchard. Pittsfield now has the American House, owned by Major Quackenbush, formerly of the Stanwix Hall, Albany, and managed by Plumb & Clark; the Burbank House, opposite the railway station, and in summer Maplewood and Springside. A popular house for permanent or transient boarders is Wendell Hall on Wendell avenue; there is the attractive house of Mrs. Backus, on South street, which was the resting place of Lieutenant Greeley in the summer of 1885. Maplewood is a delightful stopping place, and is excellently managed by Mr. Plumb. Its large buildings at the upper end of North street are set back from the road, and the grounds are unusually pleasant and attractive. It entertains hundreds of guests each year, from New York, Boston, Washington, Philadelphia, Chicago, Brooklyn and other places, and the scores of coaching parties which "do" Berkshire every summer never fail to stop at Maplewood. "Springside," further up the street is finely located, and from its windows are obtained the most charming views of the city and its surroundings. Its grounds are large and nicely laid out.

In the center of the city is Park Square, which, up to 1812, was an open space where the noted "Pittsfield Elm" lived for untold years and fell in 1864, from old age, leaving many to sorrow for its loss as that of an old friend. In 1825 the appearance of the plat was improved for the purpose of making a suitable place for an ovation given to General Lafayette, who visited Pittsfield that year. Here, in 1809, the first "cattle show" in the country—a simple display of a few animals—was held, giving to Pittsfield the honor of holding the first agricultural fair in this country. The Park occupies a sightly location and is held in high estimation locally, more particularly, perhaps, by old-time residents. Here is located the unique Pittsfield Soldier's Monument—"The Color Sergeant," by Launt Thompson—which stands on the western approach of the Park. On the occasion of the dedication of this monument, in September, 1872, there was present the largest assemblage ever witnessed in Pittsfield. On the north and south shields are inscribed the names of the Pittsfield soldiers who fell in the war; on the west are the arms of the United States and on the east the arms of the Commonwealth of Massachusetts, in bronze relief. The monument consists of a pedestal, base, shaft and capital, the capital being enriched by a wide abacus, on which the statue stands and by wreaths of laurel in high relief. It is built of light-colored granite from Millstone Point quarries, near New London, Ct., and cost $10,000. On the west face is this inscription:— "For the Dead a Tribute: for the Living a Memory: for Posterity an Emblem of Loyalty to the Flag of their Country." On the east face:— "With Grateful Recognition of the Services of All Her Sons who Upheld the Honor and Integrity of our Beloved Country in the Hour of Peril, the Town of Pittsfield Erects this Monument in Loving Memory of Those Who Died that the Nation Might Live."

1.—Wonderful Birch Tree Near Lanesboro Line. 2.—Wahconah Falls, Windsor.
3.—Pontoosuc Lake. 4.—Onota Lake.

BEAUTIFUL ONOTA LAKE.

The lakes of Pittsfield are an important feature of its attractiveness, and every year the two principal ones have become resorts either for a day's pleasure or for camping parties. Onota Lake, formerly called West Pond, is one of the largest, at the same time one of the most beautiful, sheets of water in the whole county. From various points along its shores some of the most beautiful views in the region are obtainable, especially from the southwestern, where in the days of the French and Indian wars, there were fortifications. In front of the beholder are the Washington Mountains; to the northeast, as one stands facing the east, are the hills of Windsor, many miles away; to the north, Greylock and the other peaks in the neighborhood are clearly seen, and still further to the east, the Green Mountain range above Adams; to the south is the mountain defining the southern boundary of the basin in which Pittsfield is situated. A charming view is obtained from the field of Mr. Chapman, whose farm extends along the western border of the lake. The lake lies in a pretty upland basin, and contains, since its enlargement in 1864, 683 acres. Prior to this enlargement it was practically two independent lakes, the smaller one being formed by a dam or causeway, thrown across by the beavers. Its west shore was a wall of pebbles and boulders thrown up by the action of the ice. The lake is easy of access and can be driven to from nearly every point. Under the compromise of the will of the late Abraham Burbank, Pittsfield becomes the possesor of some fifty acres of land lying along the east shore of the lake. The compromise has yet to be passed upon by the Supreme Court, and if approved will give the city a charming resort. It will be improved, and will be known as "The Burbank Memorial Park."

PONTOOSUC LAKE.

Pontoosuc Lake, two miles north of the center, is the next largest in size and lies partly in Lanesboro. It was enlarged as a reservoir, in 1867, so that its present area is 575 acres. The highway skirts its eastern shore, and is one of the popular drives out of Pittsfield. At the lower end, in Pittsfield, are two lovely pine groves, where camping and picnicing parties find a day's outing most enjoyable. From this place the view to the north is delightful, taking in the hills farther on in Lanesboro, with Greylock beyond, Constitution Hill and others, while to the west are the Taconics, two miles away, the reflection of whose peaks in a bright day is plainly seen on the bosom of the placid lake. Gunn's Grove, a point on the northwest shore, is also a delightful camping ground. The south end of the lake is the northern terminus of the horse railroad and it has come to be one of the most popular spots in the county. Several fine pavilions have been built upon its shores, several small steamers and scores of smaller craft have been launched upon its surface, and other necessary accessories have been provided. During the summer months, hundreds of private picnic parties spend the day here.

OTHER LAKES.

Richmond Lake is practically a reservoir, in both Richmond and Pittsfield, and has been enlarged within a few years for the accommodation of the factories on Shaker Brook, which flows from it. It contains about 250 acres, but it has not the attractions of the other lakes, and is therefore not a place of resort. Silver Lake, in the east part of the village, contains about sixty acres, and with a little improvement might be converted into a pleasant resort for boating; a drive around its shores has been talked of. Sylvan Lake is about half the size of Silver Lake, but is not important. Morewood Lake, known to some as Melville Lake, and by others Lily Bowl, is in the south part of the town, near South Mountain, and covers about thirty-five acres. It is almost hidden from view in the trees along its banks, and its waters are fed largely from clear springs. It being to a great extent private property, it is not resorted to by the general public. It can be seen from the Housatonic Railroad trains.

Streams are numerous and many of them picturesque, in different parts of the town. Some of them still afford passably good fishing, though of late years the supply has diminished. The town maintains a sportsmen's club, composed of prominent gentlemen of the village, and there is also a well sustained association of marksmen, who make visitors, having a taste in that direction, welcome to the use of their range just outside the limits of the village.

THE CEMETERY.

The principal cemetery of Pittsfield is the finest in Berkshire, and is a little more than a mile from the Park. It is a portion of a farm of 150 acres, and is in the control of a corporation. It is picturesque in the extreme. Trees and wooded slopes dot the landscape, while from the higher grounds a beautiful view of the village is obtained. There are several pretty drives through the undulating grounds, which are often resorted to by those who wish to spend a quiet hour. Thomas Allen of St. Louis, who dearly loved the home of his birth, bequeathed $5,000 for the erection of a suitable gateway, and his monument, a monolith of polished Scotch granite is probably as large a shaft, quarried from a single stone, as can be found in any other cemetery. The cemetery dedication, in 1850, was in keeping with the spirit of the city. Everybody attended the ceremonies; there was a procession formed at the park which marched to the grounds in solemn order; an address was made; Oliver Wendell Holmes read a poem, for he was no stranger to Pittsfield; and there were original odes sung, composed by former residents of the city. There is a healthy pride, in the case of the cemetery. This grows every year, in making it attractive to the visitor.

OUTDOOR SPORTS.

The Pleasure Park is about a mile east of the center of the city. This was organized by a number of the leading gentlemen of the town years ago as a private course for driving, with a commodious house within the enclosure. Here are annually held several interesting races, and it has also been the scene of some spirited bicycle races. The grounds of the Berkshire Agricultural Society, two miles north of the village, have also a good track, and the annual "cattle show" is a feature of Pittsfield in September which attracts large crowds during the four days' exhibition. Of late years the showing of standard bred trotting stock has come to be one of the leading features of the occasion. The finely bred horses from the W. R. Allen and the W. F. Gale stock farms at Pittsfield, the Elizur Smith farm at Lee, and the Payne farm at Hinsdale, are shown, and a finer lot of horses is not shown anywhere in this country. From this elevated position, still another view of the town is obtained, different from all others.

Pittsfield is also the headquarters of the Berkshire County Wheelmen's organization, nearly all of whose members are connected with the League, and they have an elegant suite of rooms fitted up in the England block, in the center of the city. Excursions during the season are of almost weekly occurrence, and there are some of the finest tours to be taken, with Pittsfield as the center of the radius, in all the county. The young men connected with the organization are from among the best, and their rooms are open to their brethren whenever they are in the town.

THE LEADING RESIDENTS.

As before stated, Pittsfield early became the dwelling place of a most excellent class of citizens, who made the town the place of their abode for years, became identified with its good name and its interests, and many of the old homes still remain. As a rule they were large and roomy, and some of them, even in their dilapidation, give evidence of the hearty good cheer and hospitality that must have reigned within.

From the Park east, as one strolls leisurely down the way, there is the country seat that belonged to Thomas Allen, a substantial stone structure, with delightful grounds, and the family yet cherish its cozy surroundings. Just beyond, and opposite, on the site of the old Pomeroy homestead, stands the new residence of Henry W. Bishop. It is of pure old colonial style and is a notable addition to the Fifth avenue of Pittsfield.

On Bartlett avenue, named in honor of the brave General William F. Bartlett, whose life was peacefully breathed out in Pittsfield, are several beautiful specimens of cottage architecture. The Episcopal rectory is situated on Bartlett avenue. On the north side of East street, fronting Bartlett avenue, is the house of ex-Senator Jones, formerly the home of Colonel George S. Willis, a public spirited citizen and once the high sheriff of the county.

Farther along on East street are the homes of Cashier Warriner, the new cottage of Dr. W. F. Paddock, the place where W. B. Cooley (now dead) used to live, the home of Dr. J. M. Brewster, and the Mrs. Clapp homestead, in an inviting location. The old homestead of Dr. Brewster, the elder, is now the site of the handsome new house of W. R. Allen, of St. Louis, which is one of the most expensive as well as one of the model houses of the county. Beyond lives Jabez L. Peck, active in the upbuilding of the town, and near by was the home of N. G. Brown, when living. On the south side of the street, and somewhat back, is the Ensign H. Kellogg homestead, standing back from the street, with its shady lawn, its vine covered columns, a substantial brick house, one of the old landmarks of the town.

Further east is the Thomas F. Plunkett house, now the home of Mrs. H. M. Plunkett. This was the home of Thomas Gold, who, tradition says, though the story has been exploded, sat in an upper chamber and witnessed his own funeral as the procession passed away to the cemetery. It was necessary, it was said, that, owing to some financial transactions, he should be dead, and, after the funeral was over, he made his escape to other lands. In this house the famous poem, "The Old Clock on the Stairs," by Longfellow, was written, and the clock remains to this day in the same hall-way.

This house commands a fine view from the summit of a knoll. Mrs. Plunkett may claim the honor of being one of the pioneers in the organization of the present sanitary system and the boards of health, urging the subject to her husband during his legislative terms until it finally became a law, and from Massachusetts the system has extended to other States. She is the author of a widely circulated book, among other works, on "Sanitary Plumbing." The dwellings of James W. Hull, Dr. W. E. Vermilye and Congressman F. W. Rockwell are on Appleton avenue, just south of East street.

At the foot of East street are the homes of Mrs. W. M. Root and of the late W. G. Backus, while near by, on Elm street, is a plain, nearly square house, the residence of Senator Henry L. Dawes. He came to Pittsfield many years ago, and has been in hearty accord with all its improvements and watched its prosperity with great interest. His daughter, Miss Anna L. Dawes, president of the Wednesday Morning Club, is a lady of literary talent and accomplishments. Elm street, across the east branch of the Housatonic River, is a lovely walk or drive, and further on is the residence of Mrs William Pollock, at "Greytower," which is one of the most magnificent country seats in all Massachusetts. On William street, near the Pollock property, is the new summer home of E. T. Sampson, of New York, which in many ways is one of the most complete in its grounds, outbuildings, and the residence of the gentleman itself, in all Pittsfield. His location commands a sweep of vision for many miles around; and the view to the south is especially bewitching. Farther east, Mrs. Ogden, of New York, and her son-in-law, F. T. West, of New York, will finish this season two cottages for summer occupancy which are also eligibly situated. There are several shady roads and pleasant drives in this part of the city toward Lenox and Washington. On the middle road to Lenox, we come to the farm of Col. Walter Cutting, which, as "Canoe Meadow," was occupied for some time by Oliver Wendell Holmes, whose grandfather in the maternal line settled in this town in 1735. For the cattle show of 1849, he composed and read his poem "The Ploughman." Col. Cutting has a fine herd of Guernsey cattle at this farm. The country seat of John Kernochan is also on this delightful drive. A short distance south is the famous "Abbey Lodge," owned for several years by Col. Richard Lathers, of New York, and which from time to time was the place of entertainment of noted visitors to Berkshire.

THE WESTERN PART OF THE CITY.

On Jubilee Hill, west of the railway station, still remains the Dr. Childs homestead, from which some fine views of the city may be obtained. On this hill the famous Berkshire jubilee was held. The houses of Cashier E. S. Francis, and "Prospect Villa," erected by S. V. R. Daniels, are prominent here. From this point the eye takes in new beauties not seen in any other part of the center, there being an unobstructed view for many miles in all directions. The Governor George N. Briggs place lies to the westward. Turning north from here for a moment, through Onota street, there is a lovely drive ; the village lying to the east, and Greylock full in one's face. This road can be followed for two miles nearly to the west entrance of the cemetery. In some respects West street is the handsomest drive in town. The Crook farm, owned at one time by Mr. Crook, the famous New York restaurateur, with its mammoth barn, occupies a fine and commanding site. Methodism had its first meeting house in this part of the town, although the first preaching was in the east part, where the eccentric Lorenzo Dow at one time preached. For nearly three miles West street is almost straight; in many places finely shaded, and a beautiful landscape greets the eye during its entire length to the eastern base of the Taconic Mountain in Hancock, and thence to Lebanon Springs, to which it is the direct highway.

A little more than a mile out is Onota lake, on whose southeastern shore is the country seat of H. C. Valentine, of New York. It has been extensively improved since its ownership by Mr. Valentine, whose grounds of meadow and lawn and wood are among the finest in Pittsfield. It was occupied for one season by Minister Thornton, of Great Britain. Mr. Valentine's extensive farm is a little southwest, overlooking a valley which presents many attractions to the eye. Attorney General A. J. Waterman has also a farm as a country residence near by, and the neighboring F. A. Hand estate is attractive. Directly opposite is Mrs. Buckingham's summer home. A little farther on is the Chapman farm, which was bought a few years ago by Wirt D. Walker, a Chicago lawyer, who has made a charming place out of the old farm house, and he is to build a villa on his own land on the west shore of Onota lake, which commands a charming view. Turning to the north through Churchill street, the road is along a romantic drive for some miles, through a farming section of the town, to the famous "North Woods" district. From the elevations along the route, many fine views of Lake Onota, and the hills east and the range in which Greylock is always in the center, are obtained A drive on through the "North Woods" district brings one in view of the Shaker Promised Land, or Holy Ground, in Hancock.

South of West street there is a fine drive to Stearnsville, with the South Mountain and Osceola Mountain beyond, and to the right the valley stretching on towards Richmond and West Stockbridge. On West street is the city's farm, where the poor and mild insane are well cared for—

an interesting place to visit for an hour. One of the attractions of the street is to drive a short distance farther, rising the hill into Hancock, when the eye to the east, back over the way, to the north and the south takes in a kaleidoscope of natural beauty, that once looked upon can never be forgotten.

ATTRACTIONS ON THE NORTH.

Up North street is Maplewood, with its attractive grounds, opposite which is the home of T. A. Oman, which was occupied one year by the late ex-Senator David L. Yulee, of Florida, who had as his guest the late Dr. J. Marion Sims, the famous surgeon. Senator Eustis, of Mississippi, has lived on the corner of Bradford and North streets. Near Maplewood is the fine Catholic church and grounds and the parochial residence of Father Purcell, the veteran priest of the county. Opposite this is the new Unity church, a neat frame edifice which shelters a young but prosperous Unitarian society. Going further north, we come to the House of Mercy, created and sustained by the ladies of Pittsfield—the model cottage hospital of Massachusetts. This charity was supplemented in 1889 by the erection of the Henry W. Bishop, 3d, memorial training school for nurses. This was built and furnished by Henry W. Bishop, of Chicago, as a memorial to a beloved son, who died while a student at Williams College. The building is a commodious three-story brick building, complete in every detail, and a most valuable accessory to the House of Mercy. A short way further is "Springside," before referred to, and on the summit of the hill is the property of the Davols, who maintain this as the summer retreat for their families; a bewitching landscape is here presented. The Learned farm, a short way beyond, is now owned by W. F. Gale and used as a stock farm, where much fine stock is bred.

On North street, near the House of Mercy, is Wahconah street, leading to the main entrance of the cemetery. This road can be continued on to the village of Bel Air, past the grounds of the Agricultural Society, to Taconic, and again to Pontoosuc. At Bel Air a fine drive can be taken to the west, past Russell's and Peck's mills, bearing a little north on the Hancock road, over Potter Mountain, in that town. It is a popular drive, through a quiet portion of Pittsfield, and the scenery, while not so grand, is still very attractive. The road to Potter Mountain is taken by bearing again to the west; directly ahead is the road to the famous Balanced Rock, in Lanesboro; or the drive may be continued, after pausing a while to view this wonderful freak of Nature, past the Hurlbut farm, and crossing the north end of Pontoosuc Lake, taking the road again from Lanesboro to Pittsfield, on the east shore of the lake, and making a very pleasant half-day's excursion.

In the northeast part of the city, on Burbank street, is the Judge B. R. Curtis place, which half a century or so ago, was one of the finest country seats in the town. Judge Curtis, who was a judge of the United States Supreme Court, made Pittsfield his summer residence for some time. From this house is obtained a lovely view to the south, east and west, which in some respects has but few, if any, equals in Pittsfield. From the higher ground back of this property the valley below and on to the north is a perfect panorama of loveliness and the locality is easily reached as a drive. The place is now leased to and has been occupied for two or three seasons past, by Count DeCerkez, of Paris. Further east is the "Maplehurst" farm of Mrs. Thomas Allen, where there is probably one of the finest as well as the most expensive herd of Jerseys in all Berkshire. On the north end of this farm, on the new Dalton road, are also some very fine views, especially looking to the north, with Greylock in the foreground.

Near the Coltsville Junction is the farm of W. Russell Allen, where he formerly kept a fine herd of Percheron horses. In 1889 Mr. Allen laid out more than $100,000 in fitting up this farm for the breeding and training of high bred trotting stock, and purchased some $200,000 worth of the finest bred horses in the country. Three very large barns were built, forming three sides of a square, the other side being partly filled by the residence of the manager. In the center of the square was built a water tower, and around the whole was laid out a half-mile race track. Near by were erected three cottages for the occupancy of the men employed on the place. Water is brought to the barns in pipes from the old Benedict farm, farther north, which Mr. Allen purchased, and every stall is supplied with running water. A road has been cut from the barns to the new Dalton road which passes the place, and the entrance is to be graced with a handsome granite gateway. This is the finest stock farm in New England, and the buildings form a prominent spot on the landscape. At Coltsville is the Crane government mill, where the distinctive paper used by the government for the printing of bank bills, the postal note paper, and bond paper for numerous governments, are manufactured. The Unkamet Brook, flowing near the Pittsfield & North Adams railroad and into the Housatonic, has its source up in the meadows and the swamp in the northeast portion of the town, within a few feet of the source of the little brook feeding the stream flowing north towards

Cheshire and into the Hoosac River. Thus the common fountains of two rivers are so close that it often depends upon chance which of the drops bubbling up side by side in the springs at the common source shall flow into Unkamet Brook and thence to the Housatonic and reach the sea down in Long Island Sound, or to the other, thus swelling the source of the Hoosac River, flowing north, thence to the Hudson River and the sea in that manner. So slight is the slope of the valley bottom, according to the surveys, that a dam raised four feet above the level of the highway at Coltsville would turn Unkamet Brook and the waters of the branch of the Housatonic coming in from Dalton northward into the Hoosac and thence to the Hudson.

To the west from Coltsville station is the handsome villa and farm of W. F. Milton, a New York merchant, in trade with China for some years, who came to Berkshire and Pittsfield, first as a summer visitor. His house is a model of architecture and each of its rooms is fitted up with different woods. He has probably the finest collection of *bric-à-brac* in Chinese curios, and also in fine bronzes, in Berkshire. Mr. Milton's view of the valley is peculiar and indescribable. North of his place, on the hills east of Lanesboro, the drive has many attractive features and fine views. Next west of Mr. Milton's is the farm of Zenas Crane, Jr., with its fine herd of Guernsey cattle and notable barn. Another panorama is here opened out, and away to the east and the north, on beyond Greylock, even, the eye wanders seeing new beauties at every turn. The admirer of fine cattle with choice pedigrees, and of a well-kept and well-tilled farm will find pleasure in viewing Mr. Crane's possessions in this line. If desired, turning from this place, a fine drive is had, past the house formerly owned by Oren Benedict and now owned by Russell Allen on the highway which has its junction with the Dalton road. Going farther west from Mr. Crane's farm, rising a little higher, are some other good views, especially to the west, and of the Taconics, with Greylock still at the north, and this highway has its junction with that running north from the center to Pontoosuc. The drive from the center, east past the Curtis place to the junction, then to Coltsville, thence west and past the dwellings of Messrs Milton and Crane, to Taconic and then south past the Davol country seat, is one of the finest in the city.

IN THE SOUTHWEST.

In the direction of Barkerville and Stearnsville, beyond the west branch of the Housatonic, is the house of Mrs. Pomeroy, built a few years ago.

Keeping directly south from the Shaker Brook, the road runs on the high ground and is a fine drive, with the Taconics to the west, and on the left the Lenox range, South Mountain and Mount Osceola to the left and south. If this highway is followed, not turning west when above Barkerville, a pleasant trip is made on towards West Stockbridge or Richmond. Another drive from this highway a little south of the point of divergence with the other Barkerville road, is to turn east, following the highway known as South Mountain street, which joins the Lenox road near the Morewood property.

Barkerville is the birthplace of Judge James M. Barker, of the Superior Court. A mile west are the Hancock Shakers, quite as often known as the Pittsfield Shakers. This community is partly in both towns of Hancock and Pittsfield, and is among the oldest of the sect of the country. They have four families, with all the auxiliaries of a typical Shaker community, though their church is not opened to the public as at Lebanon, a few miles farther beyond, over the mountain, and to which this is the principal highway. The Hancock or Pittsfield Shakers own several square miles in the two towns in Massachusetts and in Lebanon over the line in New York, and have been here for more than a century. Their community is a pleasant place to visit, and they entertain callers simply, but agreeably.

Down South Street.

Down South street, elegant in shade and quietude, is the Martin property, one of the oldest houses in the town. Just beyond is the new Berkshire Home for Aged Women, a charity originated by Rector Newton of St. Stephen's church. The handsome new building was the gift of the Crane family, of Dalton, who in building it, carried out the expressed design of the late Zenas Marshall Crane. The building also shelters the Union for Home Work—a most practical charity. Further south is the house of Thomas F. Pingree, the homestead owned by Ezekiel R. Colt, when living, the Dr. Strong villa. The houses of the late S. W. Bowerman, the brothers West—John C. and Gilbert—the homestead of Daniel Stearns, a manufacturer in the past, and of F. W. Hinsdale, are situated on this street. The home of Mrs. Redfield, opposite the high school, has been occupied for several seasons by a New York publisher. Down the hill is the residence of J. N. Dunham, president of the Springfield Fire and Marine Insurance Company. The road crosses the Housatonic at this point, and in the deep pool by the bridge occurred the romantic suicide of a young lady student at Maplewood, whose rashness was the result of disappointed love, and at the time made a sensation in all the region. It is often referred to yet, and was the foundation of a romantic novel.

Half a mile farther on, we come to "Broadhall," the Morewood property, and known by many as the Melville place. It has a history full of interest, and it is but little changed since it was erected, in 1781, by Henry Van Schaack. At sundry times it has been used as a boarding house, and among its guests have been Longfellow, Hawthorne, Herman Melville, President Tyler, and many others of note. A few years ago it was the summer home of Count and Countess Llewenhaupt, the Danish minister, and many foreign notables were their occasional guests. To the southeast is the Melville estate, named "Arrowhead," from the Indian relics found near by. Some of the best writings of Herman Melville were written here, among them being "Moby Dick," the "Piazza Tales," "My Chimney and I," and "October Mountain," the name being taken from a neighboring mountain of that name. Beyond the Morewood estate the road passes under the shadow of South Mountain, known as Snake Hill from its tortuous windings, and from the summit one looks down into the city of Pittsfield with delight. A good road was built to the top of this mountain recently by Charles Wakefield, and accommodations for picnic parties are provided on the mountain. It is now a popular resort, and a most delightful spot. A striking view of Greylock to the north, the hills to the east and west as far as the eye can reach, makes a pleasing picture.

On East Housatonic street are the homes of Judge Barker, ex-Lieutenant Governor and Judge Joseph Tucker and his brother, George H. Tucker (the treasurer of the county), Henry W. Taft (the clerk of the courts), and the homestead of Henry W. Dwight, superintendent of the American Express Company. In the Dwight homestead, when occupied by the Rev. William Wilberforce Newton as an Episcopal rectory, was the birthplace of the "Congress of Churches," an idea which has crystallized into a grand, progressive plan of church unity. Mr. Newton's charming sketch, "The Priest and the Man," was finished here. On the corner of East Housatonic and Gold avenue is where Judge James D. Colt lived, and opposite is the new residence of Frank W. Dutton. Across the avenue is the John L. Colby place, now owned by a Chicago gentleman. Farther on is the dwelling of Treasurer Adam, of the savings bank. On Wendell avenue, at "Wendell Hall," was the home of the late General W. F. Bartlett; here are the homes of Col. Walter Cutting, James H. Hinsdale, and also the Joslyn estate, whose owner was interested in hotels in Boston and New York—the Buckingham and others—for many years; the homes of Thaddeus Clapp, O. W. Robbins, Frank Russell, D. M. Collins, Frank D. Taylor, and architect H. Neill Wilson, Dr. J. F. A. Adams are on the same street. Mr. Wilson is a comparatively new comer in Berkshire, but has already raised the standard of architecture here, and has designed many of the handsomest buildings in the city, besides some of the most tasteful in Lenox. The new Dalton church was designed by him. We now come to "Elmwood," the country seat of Edward Learned when living, and one of the finest in the State. Its great elms make the name appropriate. It occupies a prominent situation in the village, and its handsome grounds are highly attractive. It was occupied during the summer of 1888 by President Bliss of the Boston and Albany railroad and his family. It is stated that the original owner was a baker, who had accumulated a fortune and removed to Pittsfield to establish a home. His vocation followed him, and he was so continually annoyed by the exclamation of "Crackers" and other epithets pertaining to his trade that he sold his property to Mr. Learned and quit the town forever.

Delightful Homes.

In cottage architecture especially, in taste so far as regards homes of moderate price, Pittsfield has taken a long stride within the past decade. The locality in the vicinity east of Maplewood avenue is building up rapidly with houses of this character, the names of whose owners would fill a long list. It shows an improved taste in the citizenship of the town, and the old-fashioned, unattractive homes of the past are fast disappearing, or, at least, are not duplicated in the present generation. The most costly house is that of W. R. Allen, of St. Louis. The Milton house, near Coltsville, has also many special attractions, and the cottages of H. H. Ballard, on South street, are also models in their way. The Valentine places, on West street, have been remodeled, and, together with their surroundings, especially the Allen place on the south shore of Onota, are decidedly attractive and pleasing. Congressman Rockwell's cottage on Appleton avenue, the dwelling of the late Dr. W. E. Vermilye, a representative of the New York family of that name, and the home of James W. Hull, are all on the same avenue, each attractive and cozy. The homes of Pittsfield are peculiar in their coziness and their air of comfort, rather than brilliant in many colors or adorned with angles and an attempt at overdrawn architecture. The attractions of the city are in its natural beauty rather than its grand houses; and so, while its homes and its cottages have few striking features, ample and well-kept lawns are

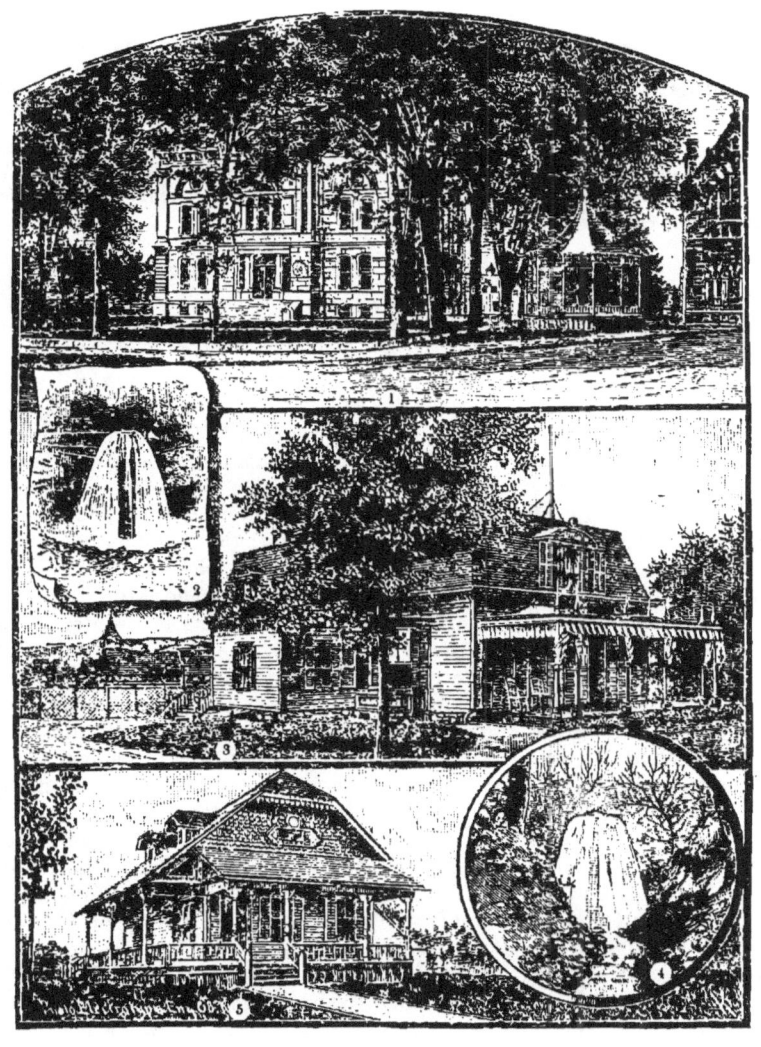

1.—Berkshire County Court House, Park Square, Pittsfield. 2 and 4.—Dalton Flowing Artesian Wells. 3.—Lenox Club House. 5.—Crane Library, Dalton.

everywhere; shade, inviting rest and comfort, is on every hand; the wide streets have an air of quiet and attractive peacefulness, and the walks are broad and well-kept. There is a great deal of wealth in the town, which is liberally drawn upon for the beautifying of Pittsfield or the furtherance of its industries and substantial prosperity, and the city has a most thriving appearance in consequence.

Names That Are Widely Known.

Gordon McKay, the inventor of the sewing machine bearing his name, was for many years a resident of the town. Elias Merwin, the Boston merchant and banker, was a citizen of Pittsfield, and always loved its attractions; the Rev. John E. Todd, the well-known New Haven divine, was a Pittsfield boy; Jacob L. Greene and John M. Taylor, both successful insurance men in Hartford, received much of their early business training in Pittsfield; Prof. C. E. West, of Brooklyn, one of the most successful educators of the day, was a farmer's boy here. The late General H. S. Briggs, one of the most efficient men in the customs service, was for many years a resident of Pittsfield; the Rev. O. P. Gifford, the eloquent pastor of the Warren Avenue Baptist church, Boston, and the Rev. Wayland Hoyt, of Brooklyn, had in the Pittsfield Baptist church their first pastorates; the Rev. Dr. John Todd, famous as a writer and a preacher, left a lasting impression for good on the town, which he did so much to make an ideal New England village; Rev. Dr. Harris, afterward president of a Maine theological school, and a vigorous writer, was once pastor of the First church; William Miller, the father of Millerism, or the Second Advent, was a native of Pittsfield. Vice-President Hendricks was a guest in Pittsfield in the summer of 1885 for a short time; Dr. J. Marion Sims spent the last months of his busy life in this town, and would have made it his summer home, especially on account of its mountain water. His autobiography was written in the Oman house on North street. The English, French, Danish, Spanish and Portuguese ministers have all been temporary residents. Baron Struve, of Russia, spent a season here in a house that he hired, in 1883. Gen. Greeley, the Arctic explorer, spends a part of the summer each year in Pittsfield. Each year more and more houses in town are rented to city families, whose desire is to escape the exactions of "society," and yet who do not want to abandon the solid comforts of civilization. For such people, and for all others who would enjoy a combination of city and country life, difficult to obtain elsewhere, and certainly not obtainable in the pleasurable degree found in Pittsfield, this city offers the choicest inducements.

PARK SQUARE, PITTSFIELD.

Henry L Dawes, long a resident of Pittsfield, was for eighteen years a member of the National House of Representatives, for years a leading member and the chairman of the Ways and Means Committee, and since 1876, a representative of the Commonwealth in the U. S. Senate. Thomas Allen, a most distinguished native of Pittsfield, who died in 1882, came into prominence in 1836, in Van Buren's election; in 1837 he started the " Madisonian " in Washington, a paper that had much influence, and was shortly after made public printer. Moving to St. Louis, in 1842, he took a leading place in affairs, was chief promoter of the Pacific railroad, and was president of the first company that began its construction. He bought the unfinished Iron Mountain railroad and finished it, and was one of the prominent men of the country. James M. Beebe, a noted Boston merchant, a member of the firm that was the predecessor of Jordan, Marsh & Co., was a Pittsfield boy. The Rev. William Allen, another native, was a professor in Dartmouth College and president of Bowdoin College, and the author of several literary works, among them being the first biographical dictionary published in America. Congressman Francis W. Rockwell is a loyal as well as a distinguished resident of Pittsfield, and numerous natives of this town have held high places in political, business and professional life.

ENCIRCLED BY INTERESTING PLACES.

Pittsfield, with all its attractions, is surrounded by numerous others of a varied nature in adjoining towns. The delightful drives are omnipresent, and a few of them are mentioned elsewhere in this volume. South are the beauties of Lenox and Stockbridge, six to twelve miles distant. Southwest, Perry's Peak in Richmond, eight miles. West, Lebanon and the Shakers, seven miles. Northwest, Potter Mountain, between Lanesboro and Hancock, nine miles; Lulu Cascade, four miles; Berry Pond, in Hancock, five miles. North, Balanced Rock, six miles, and several sightly hills in Lanesboro; the glass works in Berkshire Village, six miles. To the east and northeast, in Dalton, are the Wild Wizard's Glen, four miles; Mount Weston, eight miles, and the fine paper mills; in Windsor are Wahconah Falls, eight miles. On the southeast are Lake Ashley, and the magnificent outlooks from Washington Mountain, about seven miles, one of them being from October Mountain, and Tory Glen, on the west slope of the mountain, five miles. With all these neighboring objects of interest added to its own, Pittsfield is a most delightful place for summer and autumn sojourn.

WILLIAMSTOWN.

WILLIAMSTOWN is named in honor of Col. Ephraim Williams, who fell in the battle of French Mountain, near Lake George, September 8, 1755. The college which bears his name and whose record is one that Berkshire is proud of, was founded by him. In area, this is a large town; its boundaries are mainly the "grand old hills of Berkshire" on all sides, and its scenery is fascinating. Standing in the village, which is on an elevated plateau, as it were, one looks in all directions and sees the peaks rising on every hand. In the village there is a sentiment characteristic of many of the Berkshire towns and yet peculiarly strong in Williamstown, of great admiration and love for the old college town. The students when they return to reunions and "commencements," somehow seem to come no more to shake hands and recount the pranks of their college days than to see the old campus, and gaze again upon the hills, on every hand, changing with every month of the year, and get another breath of the pure air of the beloved town.

Green River, aptly named, and a stream of some proportions, formed by the junction of the Hancock River, the New Ashford Brook, the stream from the "Hopper," and some smaller ones, forms a north and south valley, which stands at right angles to the Hoosac, at the north end. The central parts are valleys made by the Green River running north to the Hoosac, of which it is the principal tributary, and the town is again cut by the Hoosac, which runs west. In this compound valley is situated Williamstown village, where the valley is quite extensive. It is surrounded on every side by mountains. On the west are the Taconics, a grand range at this point, with many prominent peaks. On the east is Saddle Mountain, a part of the Green Mountain range. At a

Main Street, Williamstown.

point where the Hoosac River falls out of Massachusetts into Vermont the ground is about 100 feet lower than any other land in Berkshire, the next lowest being where the Housatonic leaves the State below Ashley Falls. Every stream in Williamstown finds its way into the Hoosac, and there is but one water way to the ocean; in many of the other towns there being two. The old Mohawk trail between the Hudson and the Deerfield Rivers, the latter east of Florida Mountain, passed along on the north bank of the Hoosac from the place where Braytonville, (a manufacturing village on the North Adams road to Williamstown) stands, to the New York line. What is a fact and only recently discovered, is that the present highway from Braytonville along the north bank is almost exactly, if not quite, on this same Indian trail. It is not close to the river, for the Indians did not like wet ground, but only a few rods distant. Along this trail the Mohawks passed in 1662 to their great battle with the Deerfield Indians in the Connecticut Valley. The highway varies but a few rods from this trail. When Fort Massachusetts, only a little beyond the Williamstown line, and now in North Adams and referred to elsewhere in this book, was captured, the captives, who were marched to Canada, were taken over this route, which Chaplain Norton calls the "Hoosac road," through Williamstown, down by the "Dugway" in Pownal, and thence through the State of New York. This region of Berkshire is historic ground as well as classical, but we can barely mention the fact in passing.

THE MOUNTAINS.

In the mountain chains or ranges on nearly every side, with the high ground near the college buildings as a center, are peaks or prominent points, and these have names, most of them of local interest. To the east, the furthest to the left, as one stands near the chapel of the college or the Mansion House, is Mount Hazen, for the first surveyor who ran the lines in 1741; the next south is Hudson's Height, so named for Captain Seth Hudson, the last commander of Fort Massachusetts and the last survivor of the original settlers. The next is Mount Emmons, 2,276 feet high, where a copper bolt was placed in the early survey; the next is Smedley Height, so named from one of the old settlers in the valley and still owned by one of the descendants. Still looking east and farther south as the range swings around southerly, is the Saddle Range. Saddle Mountain, as it appears from the distance, is practically in three lobes, there being Raven Rock with the road to Greylock in the valley between that and the Greylock lobe, which is the highest, and Mount Prospect which is the western lobe, cut off to near the middle by the streams issuing from Greylock, making "The Hopper," so-called. The north end of the central lobe, and in plain view from every part of the village, is Mount Williams, so named in honor of the founder of the college. The next peak to the south on this central lobe, is Mount Fitch, commemorative of the first President of Williams College. The next is Greylock itself, seen from every part of Berkshire and 3,535 feet above sea level. Greylock, whose summit is in Adams, is more particularly referred to in the article on that town. The next on the south is Mount Moore, commemorative of the second President of the college, and the southernmost of the central group is Mount Griffin, for the third President of Williams College. Then on the western lobe is its highest peak, which is Mount Simonds, commemorative of Colonel Simonds, which overlooks the "Hopper." The next in order south of the "Hopper" is Bald Mountain, sometimes called the "Bluffs," 2,597 feet high, and the southern end of that lobe is Mount Chadbourne, so named in memory of Paul A. Chadbourne, one of the deceased Presidents of the college.

On the west are the Taconics, which give the name to the new age of geology, known as the "Taconic system," of Professor Emmons. The northern end so far as it relates to Williamstown, at the point where Hazen's line crosses the Taconics, was named by him Mount Belcher, commemorative of the then Governor of Massachusetts and New Hampshire, who had commissioned him to make the survey. The fine swell to the south of Mount Belcher (we are now on the west range or the Taconics) is called Leet Hill, from an interesting old character of 100 years ago in town. The pointed peak to the south of Leet Hill is Dodd's Cone, so named for Professor Dodd, of Williams College, professor of mathematics for many years. The highest point in the Taconics in Williamstown—twin peaks—were long ago named Mount Hopkins, 2,790 feet high, taking the family name of President Mark Hopkins and his brother Albert, who was for many years a professor in the college. Both are names that are prominent in Williamstown and are revered in the history of the college. The next swell is McMaster Mountain, so named from an old family of that part of the town. The next point, hardly visible from the village, but nearly west of the cozy village of South Williamstown, is Mount Mills, so named for Captain Samuel Mills. The last is Sabin Heights, so named in memory of Lieut. Zebediah Sabin, one of the minute men in the Revolution, who lost his life in the Expedition with Arnold up the Kennebec to Quebec in the winter of 1775-76. It is unnecessary to state that most of these points are accessible, some of them can be driven to and their summits are placed where grand views can be obtained. From the village in all directions are many fine views of the valley and there is a panorama of rare loveliness laid out before the beholder.

There are four passes over the Taconics into the State of New York. The northern is called Petersburg Pass, 2,075 feet high; next to that is Berlin Pass, 2,192 feet high, which was a turnpike in the early part of the century; both are passable and afford fine drives and magnificent views. The third is Kidder Pass, which is fine for horseback riding, and the southernmost is the Johnson Pass, so named from David Johnson who lived at its foot, and who also went up the Kennebec with Arnold.

Village Perfection.

The village itself is a gem, a college town with many buildings, college and society houses, some of them of unique architecture. The college buildings are well worth a visit, and the chapel, with its ivy for each of the classes for many years back, is suggestive of a great many recollections dear to the alumni. The main street of Williamstown is sixteen rods wide and beautifully laid out, running over the hill and through the depression of the valley. The dwellings on each side suggest quiet and comfort. Besides the main street, on which most of the college buildings are located, there are several lateral streets, all of them finely shaded and with handsome dwellings. The Fields, David Dudley, Cyrus W., and the Rev. Dr. Henry M., all, or nearly all, of whom are alumni of the college, have been actively interested in the village as well as in the college itself. There is a thriving village improvement society, and the citizens take great pride in their village. It has been greatly improved and beautified, through the liberality of Cyrus W. Field, who gave $10,000 for this purpose, with the condition that the street fences be removed. This was done, and consequently the village seems like a large park, characterized by perfect neatness and rare beauty. The direction of the work was in the hands of Frederick Law Olmstead, the noted landscape gardener. Well kept lawns extend the whole distance of Main street, planted here and there with shrubs and shaded with gracefully spreading trees. The street passes over three small hills, on which the college buildings stand, offering Mr. Olmstead unusual opportunities, which he has not failed to use, in producing charming effects. The upper end of Main street has been greatly improved of late years by Col. Anthony Bullock, a Cincinnati millionaire, and his son, James W. Bullock. The street and walks were graded and turfed, where necessary, and a large amount of money was laid out here.

Mission Park.

Here is the birth place of the American Board of Foreign Missions. In 1806, and even before, the students of the college had been wont to seek some quiet retreat where they might pray, and there are still the remains of a large willow, near the dwelling of Prof. A. L. Perry, where they gathered under its secluded branches; down by the river is another place, but on one occasion they met in a small grove, and, a thunder shower coming up, they fled to a haystack, under the shelving sides of which they gathered and held their meeting; and there the first missionary work began. We give a view, in the initial letter of this article, of the monument erected on Missionary Park, to commemorate the event, by Harvey Rice, of Cleveland, Ohio. Directly behind Mission Park lies the old college cemetery, a very beautiful spot, where rest the dust of many of Williams' honored sons. The remains of the beloved Dr. Hopkins lie buried here, and not far away is the resting place of Dr. Chadbourne. There are monuments here to two other of the college presidents, Dr. Fitch and Dr. Griffith, although their remains are not buried here. This cemetery is also the burial place of many professors and students, and is probably the most hallowed spot on the college property.

Many Choice Drives.

There are many fine drives about Williamstown. Like nearly all the other valley towns of Berkshire, there are three drives through it, one each side under the mountain and another through the center. The drive to North Adams is a pleasant six miles trip, one route being south from the village through the pretty village of Blackinton, and the other past the Greylock Mills. To Pownal, five miles, is a pretty drive along the river. To Hancock, through South Williamstown, is delightful. Over the mountain, through the passes mentioned, there are fine views. There is not a more romantic road in all Berkshire than from Williamstown to Pittsfield *via* New Ashford, Lanesboro and back *via* Cheshire, Adams and North Adams. Two popular drives in the village are known as either the "Long Oblong," or the "Short Oblong." A drive takes the west road from the Greylock House, following the Taconics up Hemlock Brook, then turning near the school house to the main road from Hancock north through South Williamstown, and back by the river road to the village again at its east end. The road to Greylock is also a fine drive, striking the new road to Greylock Park by an easy grade, making a distance of about fifteen miles. The drive to Bennington, Vt., sixteen miles, is also a delightful one over the hills, and has many nice bits of scenery on the way. The attractions in the neighboring towns are numerous, and extended reference to them will be found in the articles on those towns.

Near the railway station, on a very commanding height, John M. Cole has fitted up Cole's Grove for picnicing and excursion grounds at great expense, and has made a very attractive spot. There are roads and walks, paths and arbors, and a large dining hall capable of accommodating a large party, a dancing pavillion, facilities for cooking and all the accessories of a resort of this kind. It is only a few rods from the station and in summer is visited by many excursionists.

A Valley Outlook.

In the east part of the town, two miles from the village, are the Sand Springs with a temperature which is uniformly 72 degrees, and the water being a cure for many skin diseases. Here was located Greylock Hall, which was burned May 14th, 1886. A most delightful view is obtained from the piazzas of this excellent hotel. The building stands on an elevated place near the northern rim of Williamstown basin and with a southern frontage of 165 feet, and its windows and broad verandas command a prospect seldom equaled. The Rev. Washington Gladden, referring to it in a private letter, says: "In the sublimity which belongs to magnitudes and distances,—which arises at the sight of mere bulk, or the signs of mere force,—the White Hills or the Yosemite Valley are, of course, far richer than this region; but the beauty that attracts and charms the eye, the calmness that gives rest to the distracted sense, the peace that at once restores and satisfies the soul, have taken up their abode among your Berkshire Hills. Such a sight as that upon which you look from your windows, is good medicine for any tired citizen. The Hoosac Mountains, far off to the left; the Greylock group, with Williams and Prospect in the foreground; and Bald Mountain, sitting like a lion couchant, looking down into the Hopper; the ribbed and buttressed Taconics, ranging themselves along the western horizon; and the Dome, looming up in the north; while Williamstown, with its colleges, sits on its three hills in the center of the scene. The picture is as vivid as if I had seen it but yesterday."

Williams College.

The college has its graduates by the hundreds, and they fill all the stations in life. It was to attend the commencement of his alma mater that President Garfield had started when struck down by the assassin. Williams College was proud of her son, and he loved her as fervently as she was his pride. The list of her graduates would fill a volume, and the history of the town and the college forms an interesting chapter in this part of the State and the county.

The college began as a free school, endowed by Col. Ephraim Williams; and with $3,500, raised by lottery, and $2,000 by subscription, a building was erected, now West College, and in 1791 the school was opened, to be incorporated, less than two years later as a college. The proceeds of two townships in Maine, $10,000, granted by the Legislature, and $2,000 more, were applied in 1798 to build the old East College, which was burned in 1841. The present East and South Colleges, built in 1842, occupy in part the same ground. Griffin Hall, standing on the eastern eminence, nearly opposite East College, was built in 1828 for $10,000, raised by President Griffin. College Chapel and Alumni Hall, on the west brow of East College grounds was built in 1859. Among other fine windows, the chapel contains a beautiful memorial window to the late President Garfield. It represents an angel pointing out the beauties of the promised land to Moses. It was the gift of Cyrus W. Field, and was done by Lafarge at a cost of $3,500. A very fine organ, costing a like sum, has recently been placed in the chapel by the class of '76. Clark Hall was the gift of Edward Clark, of New York, in 1881, and is situated on the eminence east of East College; it is a fine building and was to furnish a safe place for the Wilder mineralogical cabinet and the college archives. Near the South College is the Astronomical Observatory, the first erected in this country for this exclusive use, in 1836, by Prof. Albert Hopkins. To the east of this is the Magnetic Observatory; Lawrence Hall was built in 1846, through the liberality of Amos Lawrence, of Boston. It is near East College, and contains the college library of 30,000 volumes, with room for 5,000 more. During the year 1889 two additions were built on Lawrence Hall, one east and one west. The additions are of brick, two stories high, and contain several fine study and reference rooms. In addition to the library in Lawrence Hall, there is another in South College of 9,000 volumes, belonging to the literary societies of the college. In Lawrence Hall is kept the Lange collection of pamphlets, some 3,000 in number, on classible subjects. It is a very valuable collection. In the additions is to be kept the valuable collection of pictures, potteries and bronzes, and the art library, to be known as the Field collection, and given in honor of the late John W. Field of Philadelphia. The library is constantly increasing under the $18,000 endowment of the Lawrence and other funds. Kellogg Hall, south of West College, built

Mark Hopkins Memorial, Williams College, Mass.
Allen & Kenway, Architects — Boston

in 1847, takes its name from Prof. Ebenezer Kellogg, who was long the Professor of Ancient Languages. Jackson Hall was built for the Natural History Society by Nathan Jackson, of New York.

John Z. Goodrich, of Stockbridge, gave Goodrich Hall, in 1870. It is on the North side of Main street, west of Griffin Hall. The Field Memorial Observatory, situated on high ground, southwest of the principal college buildings, and intended to supplement the old Astronomical Observatory, was the gift of David Dudley Field, in 1881. Mr. Field has been a liberal benefactor of the college, and was the principal donor of the Soldier's Monument, erected in 1867. Morgan Hall, the most valuable of the college buildings, situated east of West College, was erected out of a principal part of a gift of $100,000, from Governor E. D. Morgan. On the south side of Main street, east of Morgan Hall, stands the Laselle gymnasium, which was finished in 1886. It stands as a monument to Prof. Edward Laselle, for many years professor of chemistry in the college, and to Hon. Josiah Laselle, of Whitinsville, Mass., both graduates of the college. Its cost, with equipment, was $50,000, of which $35,000 was given by the widow of Josiah Laselle and his son Josiah W., who graduated in 1886. The latest addition to the college buildings is the Mark Hopkins memorial building, situated a little east of opposite the chapel. It is a beautifully proportioned structure, three stories high, and was completed in 1890. The material is limestone and brick and the cost was $80,000, of which $25,000 was given by Frederick F. Thompson, of the class of 1856. The remainder was raised by subscriptions from the alumni and President Hopkins' friends.

Among the fine society buildings erected in recent years are those of the Sigma Phi, the Delta Psi, the Kappa Alpha and the Chi Psi fraternities. Massachusetts has given to the college, besides the townships mentioned, two others in 1819: $4,000 at incorporation in 1793; $3,000 annually for ten years, beginning with 1814, and $25,000 annually for three years, beginning with 1868, provided that a like sum should be raised by subscription, which was done, mainly by the efforts of President Hopkins.

The house occupied by President Carter standing on the north side of Main street opposite West College, is a notable structure. The front portion was built about 1800, and is one of the finest specimens of the old colonial style of houses in this section. It was given to the college in 1858, together with twenty acres of land, by Nathan Jackson. The property cost him $6,000, and to-day is worth $50,000, at the least.

Weston field, is the ball and athletic grounds, and lies south of the southern line of the old college property. It is the gift of Hon. Byron Weston, of Dalton, who has spent much money on it, and has been the scene of many athletic victories.

The presidents of the college have been : The Rev. Dr. Ebenezer Fitch, 1793–1815; the Rev. Dr. Zephaniah Swift Moore, 1815–1821; the Rev. Edward Dorr Griffin, 1821–1836; the Rev. Dr. Mark Hopkins, 1836–1872; the Rev. Dr. Paul A. Chadbourne, 1872–1881; Dr. Franklin Carter, since 1881. Among the distinguished professors of Williams were Prof. Emmons, who was a pioneer geologist; Prof. Albert Hopkins, who built the first permanent astronomical observatory ever connected with an American college, and whose influence as a religious leader of students has never been surpassed; Dr. John Bascom, late president of Wisconsin University, and Prof. Perry, a well-known free trade advocate and now president of the Berkshire Historical and Scientific society.

For many years Williamstown has been a favorite summer resort, and its development in this direction during the past few years has been remarkable. No town in the county has more charming sites for summer homes, and several have been built upon recently. John B. Gale, a prominent Troy lawyer, has built a handsome residence on South street, where he lives the greater part of the time. Mr. Gale has done a great deal in the way of improving the town. The house of Mrs. Luther Clark, of New York, is occupied during the summer by her son-in-law, Samuel P. Blagden, of New York. Mr. Blagden is a nephew of Wendell Phillips, and the house is full of furniture which belonged to the latter. The residences of N. H. Sabin and Eugene M. Jerome, of New York, and of Prof. Hewitt, are among the recently erected homes which are worthy of mention. Mr. Doughty, of Troy, has built a fine country seat; the Rev. Harry Hopkins, of Kansas City, son of Rev. Dr. Mark Hopkins, has built a nice summer cottage there; Col. Archie Hopkins, of the Court of Claims at Washington, has a summer cottage in the neighborhood ; President Leake, of the bank, has a delightful home near by; Mr. Harrison, of Milwaukee, has established a summer home, and Mr. Markham, of New York, has a country seat and farm here. There are also several houses, where the faculty and other residents of the town reside, which are tasteful. Williamstown has its share of prominent guests. Hardly a commencement passes that does not bring back for a time many of its alumni, who are glad to return to her shades, and there are also many permanent summer guests. As a place of residence, as well as resort, this town has an educational attraction to those having young children, as well as numerous natural attractions. Pupils can prepare for Williams College, at Greylock Institute, in South Williamstown, about four miles distant. For all purposes of country life Williamstown stands high in the estimation of all who have lived here. The social and educational features, and the natural beauty, wildness and picturesqueness of the town and its neighbors, make it a choice place of resort, whether for a short vacation, or for the season; for a country home in addition to a city home, or for permanent residence. The changes in the hotels during the past three years have been very great. Col. Bullock, whose name has already been mentioned, purchased the old Kellogg House and transformed it into the cozy Taconic Inn. The house was entirely remodeled, a large addition being built on the south side. It now has accommodations for about 150 guests, and is one of the model hotels of Berkshire. The Mansion House standing directly opposite the Taconic Inn was purchased in 1888 by Col. Bullock, and is now known as The Greylock House. It has been thoroughly remodeled and renovated, and makes a fit companion for its handsome neighbor across the way. This house accommodates about 150 guests, and is only open during the summer and autumn. The town also contains several private boarding-houses where excellent accommodations can be obtained.

SHEFFIELD.

"IN following the course of the Housatonic through Berkshire, the southernmost of the villages strung like beads upon its shining thread, is Sheffield, lying in a peaceful breadth of valley, where every thing speaks of calm and repose. The soft curves of the hills and mountains surrounding it are repeated with constant variety of outline, but all impressed with the same gentle character. On the west, Taconic swelling to the rounded height of the Dome, nearly 3,000 feet above the sea, broods like a vast bird over the valley. On the south, the Canaan Hills, from their direction east and west, take all changing effects of sunshine, and offer an endless study of variety in color, and light and shade, while to the north and east the river meadows, dotted with graceful trees, and watered by

'Streams that with their bordering thickets strive
To hide their windings,'

lead the eye to the upland farms beyond, and to the wooded hills which crown and protect them. Among the heights are wild and romantic ravines, shaggy precipices, and leaping brooks, easily to be reached by the adventurous explorer, but the prevailing expression of the open valley is slumbrous tranquility, and its most fitting atmosphere the tender, Indian summer-like haze which frequently enfolds it. Yet often it is no less beautiful in those resplendent days with which our New England climate makes us all familiar, when the sky is sapphire, and the air is crystal, and there is a keen invigoration in the breeze, and a quick sparkle from the water, and a crisp splendor over the entire landscape. If seems then as if you could count the leaves in the deep forests on Taconic, and it must have been under this aspect that it was seen, according to a village tradition, by the celebrated John C. Calhoun. Passing a night at the inn, and finding in the morning that he had half an hour before breakfast, he said, much to the amusement of the landlord, that he would employ the time in taking a walk to the foot of the mountain. It is four miles as the crow flies, but on a clear morning, an unaccustomed eye still finds it hard to believe it more than one-fourth of that distance." So writes Miss Mary E. Dewey, with a keen appreciation of the charms of her native town, and yet unable to exaggerate them.

THE SHEFFIELD ELM.

An Attractive Resort.

When coming to Berkshire, people have been too neglectful of this town and village. Every glance around the village brings repose to the visitor and admiration for its neatness. The broad Main street has perfect lawns, smooth and well cared for, and few streets are so finely shaded. Four rows of maples and elms extend along this street, a rare sight in any village. The elms were set out in 1843. In a hot summer day, to sit under these trees or stroll among them is a refreshment of no common order.

There are ample accommodations for visitors in Sheffield at the hotel, in village families or among farmers around town. The Conway House offers good entertainment to guests, under the proprietorship of James E. Conway. In and near the village of Ashley Falls, four miles south of Sheffield village, boarders are taken at a few houses.

Walks and Drives.

The roads of Sheffield are improving under a more intelligent working than they had not many years ago, and afford a great number of delightful drives, the principal of which are included in the table of drives. No town in the county has more miles of roads than this one, there being over a hundred, and the rides that may be had over them are all truly Berkshire in their characteristics.

A delightful walk is down Main street to the Big Elm, a mile south of the center. This tree is one of the giants of its kind, long famed for its wide spreading branches. Dr. Holmes refers to it in his "Autocrat of the Breakfast Table." A walk of a mile out to the east side of the river, near William M. Chapin's place, will secure a most delightful view of the Housatonic Valley, which, in Sheffield, is at its widest place, with the magnificent background of the Taconics, with the Dome in the center, to the westward. The drive along this east road from Alum Hill, where the view is very fine, to Great Barrington, is one of Berkshire's best. Pine Knoll, on the eastern outskirts of the village, overlooking the meadows, is a place to which a very noteworthy walk of a few hundred yards is often taken. Through the liberality of several people then present, and former residents, three acres, composing the Pine Knoll were bought, fenced and fitted up in 1884 at an expense of $1,000, and placed in perpetual trust as a public resort, for strolling, picnics and meetings under the tall pine trees that constitute a shady grove. A walk of one mile out to the west is to Bear's Den, a wooded mount that rises to a height of 200 feet from the plain. From the summit of precipitous rocks on the east side, there is a fine outlook, where picnic parties often go, and on the west slope there is a deep ravine, darkly shaded and cool, where fissures and disrupted rocks constitute cave-like places, one of which used to be the home of a bear.

SAGE'S RAVINE.

Sage's Ravine, in the southwest corner of Sheffield, and partly in Salisbury, Ct., and Mount Washington, is nowhere surpassed in wildness and general effect. To reach it, visitors leave the under mountain road a little south of the place where the brook crosses it. Here the scene is enough to give the visitor a sharp appetite for what he expects to see further up the mountain. An old mill was once situated by the roadside, whose wheel was turned by the water of the stream, and the view from below, which was very striking and still is, though the mill is gone, was engraved for "Picturesque America." The ravine is situated between Race and Bear mountains, and the water that comes down descends in many cascades and falls, a distance of several hundred feet in about as many yards. Here the very extreme of wildness is reached, among the boulders and walls of rock, the ragged cliffs and crags, the dark, tangled forest, the roar and splash of the mad waters. The ascent may be rather difficult for timid ladies, but no one who is not a weak invalid should or need be deterred from the undertaking. The darkest time is in the afternoon; in the morning, when the sun shines directly on the main fall, a rainbow is seen in the spray, a most charming effect. It was Henry Ward Beecher who declared that a visit to this ravine was worth a trip from New York every month in the year.

THE UNDER MOUNTAIN VIEWS.

The views from the under mountain road going north of the ravine, awakened the profoundest admiration in Mr. Beecher. Of it he writes: "Meanwhile the sun is wheeling behind the mountains. Already its broad shade begins to fall down upon the plain. The side of the mountain is solemn and sad. Its ridge stands sharp against a fire bright horizon. Through the heavens are slowly sailing continents of magnificent fleece mountains—Alps and Andes of vapor. They, too, have their broad shadows. Upon yonder hill, far to the east of us, you see a cloud shadow making gray the top, while the base is radiant with the sun. Another cloud shadow is moving with stately grandeur along the valley of the Housatonic; and, if you rise to a little eminence, you may see the bright landscape growing dull in the sudden obscuration on its forward line, and growing as suddenly bright upon its rear trace. How majestically that shadow travels up those steep and precipitous mountain sides! How it swoops down the gorge and valley and moves along the plain!"

In a clothier's shop on the roadside at the south side of the ravine, strange occurrences began November 8, 1802. Stones and other articles were thrown through the windows night and day for several days, and, though many people came to discover the authors of the disturbance, the origin of the doings has always remained a mystery. The operation was soon transferred to a house 100 rods north, and though the stones came with great velocity, they often stopped at the window sill. Witchcraft was supposed to be at the bottom of the mystery, which has been made historical.

WORKS OF NATURE.

The Ice Gulf, mentioned in the account of Great Barrington, is approached over Brush Hill, and entrance is made at the west opening.

Mossy Glen, back of the home of Isaac Spur, under the mountain at the base of the Dome, is a wild, cool, shady place, where people often go and have picnics.

A mile above Frank Curtis's place, under the mountain, and half a mile back of Langdon Hulett's house, is a small natural cave called the Bat's Den, which is a curiosity to those who have never seen natural caves.

People often ascend the Dome from the east side on foot, if they are good at mountain climbing, after riding to the base.

The greatest attraction for Sheffield people is the beautiful Twin Lakes, and on the road thither, the outlook from Cooper Hill is too exquisite ever to be forgotten.

Ashley Mountain, southeast of Cooper Hill, east of the Twin Lakes, and bringing to an end on the south the broad part of the Housatonic valley is a broad, easily ascended mountain partly in Sheffield and partly in Salisbury seven to eight hundred feet above the valley, that offers one of the most varied and wide panorama of views that can be had elsewhere in the whole Berkshire region from a hill of no greater eminence. The summit is wooded and the views must be had lower down. A two or three-mile circuit of the mountain exposes every point of the compass. The view to the north is probably the best northern view in the whole region; the west takes in the Salisbury landscape with the lovely Twin Lakes and the Taconic background; on the east are the Canaan Valley and the bold Canaan Mountain, and on the south appear an extensive list of components. It is a pity that there is no public road up the mountain; one can ride over a poor private road part way up the mountain, but most of the sightseeing must be done on foot, and where the forest does not obscure the outlook.

Among the out of town excursions, besides those mentioned, are those to Lake Buel, Bashbish, Great Barrington, Stockbridge and Lenox.

SOCIAL FEATURES.

"Without water-power, or any manufacturing interest," writes Miss Dewey, "Sheffield is exclusively a farming and grazing township. Rye, corn, oats, and potatoes, delicious butter, rich milk, and ruddy apples are her contributions to the comforts of the world, nor does she lack for fruits, but can show large vineyards, and cherry, pear, and peach orchards. There is a general diffusion of comfort, though little wealth, among her scattered farm-houses, and much shrewdness, and what might be called latent intelligence among her people, who feel to the full the advantages and disadvantages of a purely agricultural district." With other agricultural products may be mentioned tobacco, of which the Sheffield farmers raise much that is declared by the United States census of 1880, in a special report, to be, with the tobacco of the other Housatonic valley towns, the best that is raised in the nation.

One of the principal winter pleasures of the quiet village is a society called the Friendly Union, which meets on Friday evenings for social, and literary purposes. The sessions usually begin with a lecture, or reading, or concert, or dramatic entertainment, or debate, after which games may be played. This was organized in 1871, principally through the efforts of Miss Dewey. These social meetings have attained some celebrity in their way and have been the means of suggesting organization of similar "friendly unions" in other parts of the country.

DISTINGUISHED NATIVES.

Sheffield has been the native place or the home of many remarkable persons, principally in branches of the Dewey and Barnard families. The Rev. Dr. Orville Dewey who was born here and who passed the latter part of his life at his home on the south part of Main street, "St. David's," "ranks as one of the ablest and best beloved of the early exponents of American Unitarianism." His "Problem of Human Destiny," written in Sheffield in 1850-1, is one of the ablest works of the American intellect. Several volumes of published sermons show that Dr. Dewey was master of a most perfect style. He preached in Boston, New Bedford, New York, Washington and several other places. For many years Dr. Dewey entertained noted friends at his home here.

among them the Rev. Dr. Henry W. Bellows; and Catherine M. Sedgwick, in 1854, wrote, after a visit here, "I never saw a less ostentatious, or a more cordial and effective hospitality." Dr. Dewey's daughter, Miss Mary E. Dewey, of Sheffield and Boston, has long been known for her literary and philanthropic efforts, and his sister, Miss Jerusha Dewey of Bridgeport, Conn., has written much on religious topics. Major-General John G. Barnard, who was born here and who always had a country home in the village, "Netherby Hall," now owned by his widow, served in the Mexican war with distinction, was superintendent of the Military Academy, as an engineer he superintended the construction of fortifications at San Francisco, New York and elsewhere, he directed the siege operations of the armies of the Potomac in the Peninsular campaign, had charge of the defences at Washington, he was General Grant's chief engineer of the armies in the field, and was the author of more than half a dozen scientific works. Dr. Frederick A. P. Barnard, his brother, President of Columbia College since 1864, was previously prominently connected with many institutions of learning, and during his life has been active and leading in literary, scientific and educational matters. He has written many works, principally of a scientific nature. Daniel Dewey, a native of Sheffield, was Judge of the Supreme Court; the Rev. Dr. Chester Dewey, also a native, was professor in Williams College and the University of Rochester, and was long principal of the Collegiate Institute at Rochester. Daniel Dewey Barnard, long distinguished in political life, was minister to Prussia, 1849-53. Sheffield also was the native town of Bishop Edmund S. Janes, who had reason to say, as he did, "I have always been proud of my native town." Robert G. Fitch, once editor of the Boston *Post*, went from the eastern part of Sheffield, now in New Marlboro. Paul Dewey, uncle of the Rev. Dr. Orville Dewey, was a man of strong parts, though not known beyond this limited region. It is traditional that the celebrated French author, Châteaubriand, staying at a Sheffield tavern one night while on his way to or from Albany, casually entered into conversation with Mr. Dewey in the evening, and that the Frenchman found the conversation so interesting, in which Mr. Dewey paid him the same compliment, that neither knew that the whole night had passed, till dawn had brought the fact to their notice. Theodore Sedgwick practiced law in this town for several years. In the lower cemetery are the graves of General John Ashley and General John Fellows, the former born in town and both nearly life-long residents, and revolutionary officers.

Sheffield has been famous for building marble. A part of the Girard

College building is made of marble from an old quarry in the northern part of the town, and marble was supplied from this or some other quarry for the inside finish of the Boston Custom House, for the New York City Hall and Court House, and for the Berkshire County Court House in Pittsfield.

Two years and four months before the Mecklenburg "Declaration of Independence," January 12, 1773, Sheffield, in town meeting assembled, passed a remarkable series of resolutions that were a Declaration of Rights and Grievances. They have been hidden away from the historian, but they undoubtedly place the town first of all in the Thirteen Colonies in point of time in announcing the right of self-government, independent of British rule. In 1774 the town had up for consideration the question of the "inhuman practice of enslaving our fellow creatures, the natives of Africa."

This was the stuff that the ancestry of most of the present town's-people was made of. Nowhere can now be found better specimens of the "independent farmer" than in this town. Among them and the village people, and at the village hotel, the people of cities who would escape from unhappy living, will find quiet, agreeable and well kept resorts.

EGREMONT.

THE PARISH OF SOUTH EGREMONT.

EGREMONT is divided into two villages, South Egremont and North Egremont. Situated midway between the excellent facilities, busy life and social brightness of Great Barrington on the one hand, and the airy, prospect-commanding summits of Mount Washington on the other, the pleasant little village of South Egremont always receives a generous share of Berkshire's summer patronage. Nestled in a quiet nook of the broad but broken Egremont Plain, under the very shadow of the grand old Dome, with its pretty white church spire and cool, shady streets, it is one of the most perfect specimens we have of the unspoiled New England village. In every direction are most delightful drives over smooth, level roads, some of the very best in the county. They will take you north to Prospect Lake, three miles and a half distant, and to White's Hill; west through Guilder Hollow to the foot hills of Mount Washington, with Bashbish Falls and the Dome, and Bear Rock a few miles beyond; south by a pleasant winding way to Sheffield, Sage's Ravine and Twin Lakes, or east four miles by the gentle waters of Green River, and past beautiful homes with park-like grounds to the elm lined streets of Great Barrington, and beyond to Lake Buel, Monument Mountain, Stockbridge and Lenox. The list of these drives is about the same as that for Great Barrington and the distance in most instances may be quite accurately estimated by taking into account, when necessary, the distance between these villages, which are four miles apart. However, there are some special drives and distances that ought to be mentioned and these may be found elsewhere in this volume. The shriek of the locomotive has never disturbed its Sabbath-like repose, yet the village is easily reached from the Hillsdale station of the Harlem railroad, six miles distant, and from Great Barrington on the Housatanic road, four miles off. Stage leaves Great Barrington at 10 A. M., South Egremont at 5 P. M. Stage leaves Hillsdale 3 P. M., South Egremont at 11 A. M.

MOUNT EVERETT HOUSE.

People of quiet tastes, whose means may or may not be limited, love to come here in an unostentatious way, enjoy a brief respite from care, turmoil and excitement, and when they have drunk their fill of country invigoration depart as quietly as they came. For more than twenty years they have come and gone in this way, and of late their number has steadily increased.

The Mount Everett House, where most visitors expect, as a matter of course, to stay, stands on a pleasant corner facing north, where a hotel of some kind has flourished since 1780. Under its inviting sign the stage coaches of the famous old Hartford and Albany turnpike used to stop in former days for "refreshments." W. B. Peck, the present proprietor, has been in charge since 1871. To his judicious management very much of South Egremont's popularity as a summer resort is due. He has thoroughly mastered the most difficult of all arts, that of making his guests feel not only well treated but quite at home. On his register are the names of such men as Charlton T. Lewis, J. F. Mead, Robert Carter, John T. Baker, J. E. Browning, E. C. Dillingham, J. H. Goodsell, R. W. Ross, Walter Hanford, Rev. T. A. Eaton and John L. Kennedy, all of New York; Dr. L. J. Sanford, Judge E. J. Sanford, Lewis Hotchkiss, all of New Haven, Conn.; Walter Callender, Providence, R. I., and John J. Lambert, Troy, N. Y.

There are several houses in the village where boarders are taken, or where people who take meals at the hotel may find lodging, and sometimes there is a house or so to rent.

There is an old brick house in the village, built in 1761, with the date on the front wall, and A. for Anna, and J. T. for John Tuller, with a heart represented between them, signifying the happy union between Mr. Tuller, the builder, and his wife.

Some Men who have Lived Here.

Associated with Egremont are the names of several men who have attained more or less reputation. Grosvenor P. Lowery, who was born in North Egremont, is one of the leading members of the bar in New York city, where he is counsel for great telegraph, railroad and express companies. He comes this way now and then. Andrew Reasoner, born in South Egremont, achieved success in railway construction and management for the Harlem, the Hudson River, the Long Island, the Milwaukee & St. Paul, the Great Eastern, the Morris & Essex and the Delaware, Lackawanna & Western railroads, and of the last two consolidated, he is now superintendent, living at Morristown, N. J. Governor H. B. Bigelow of Connecticut, received his school education at the South Egremont Academy, and was a railway station agent in Housatonic.

Chester Goodale, who died here at the age of 93 in 1884, was a leading man in town during nearly his whole life. He put the Mount Everett House in its present shape in 1853. The buttonball trees near the brook opposite the hotel, he set out in 1813. He was the grandfather of the "Sky Farm Poets," the Goodale sisters. In 1836 he bought quarries two miles on the road to Sheffield and during the 40 years that he worked them he furnished the marble of which the columns, bases and architraves of Girard College were made.

THE PARISH OF NORTH EGREMONT.

This village is very favorably situated for making country life agreeable to city people. The quietude that reigns is supreme, the roads are unexcelled and the mountain resorts are near at hand. Prospect Lake is only a half mile away, where there is every convenience for aquatic sport, picnic parties and camping out, with a building for shelter, if needed. The lake has thousands of visitors every season.

REMARKABLE ECHOES.

At the top of the mountain on the road to Hillsdale, two miles distant, is a place, at the Summit House, where several Echoes are returned to every noise in rapid succession. There is one place where a single Echo is returned, one where two Echoes are heard, another where three, and still another where four are heard, and, when the air is tranquil, the Whispering Echo is audible. The reflected noise comes back with the greatest distinctness, and the places where the sound is returned with so many variations are all within twenty rods of each other.

There are several boarding houses in the village and outside, mostly owned by farmers, where the fare is good, but not high priced. Stage leaves Great Barrington at 10 A. M., and North Egremont at 3 P. M. Stage leaves Hillsdale 3 P. M., and North Egremont 11.30 A. M.

Green River, that charming little stream, with its clear water, shady banks, overhanging trees and vines, and pebbly bottom, runs close by the village.

WHITE'S HILL.

Now and then Berkshire people wake up to the fact that some hill or some road that has been slightingly familiar to them for years, is a place of fine outlook, and at once the spot is raised to local fame; or, so numerous are such places, that the people are indifferent explorers, and occasionally discover one by accident. Of this kind was White's Hill, three miles northwest of North Egremont village, and a little over the State line in New York. The view from this hill is far reaching, and so grandly beautiful as to be beyond description. One can drive to the very summit, where a rustic observatory protects the visitor from sun and storm. Few people are masters of the language enough to do a tithe of justice to the views; perhaps no one has succeeded so well as "Octavia Hensel," whom we quote from the *Home Journal:* "A more perfect evening could not be imagined; the sky was that peculiar gentian blue, seen nowhere but in Italy and Berkshire, while great banks of fleecy clouds, like frosted silver in sunlight, floated away to the north. The air was full of the perfume of wild raspberries, in tangles of fern and briar roses. The chestnuts shook their tasseled blooms of emerald, and the mountain pines murmured in the soft scented breeze.

"Words cannot describe the wonder of the scene. We have ascended the Swiss mountains, wandered over Tyrolean heights, ridden through the mountain fastnesses of the Karpathians, and penetrated the depths of the Bohemian forest hills; but never before has such perfect grandeur of mountain scene, splendid expanse of valley, plain and woodland, filled the circumference of the earth! High up on this pinnacle, turn which way you will, the sight stretches away a hundred miles to mountain ranges, meeting the cloudland of the horizon. * * * To the north the Austerlitz Valley seemed balanced in a moss-cushioned swing, so strangely semi-circular is the curve of its hills upon the east and west. Along the northern mountain ranges, until Greylock's saddle-shaped mountain towers up blue and dim into fleecy cloudland. Then along to the east, where the Monument Mountain seems but a tiny hill against a triple range of earth waves, rolling their broad billows away into the boundless blue of infinite distance. Mahaiwe's Valley, defined by morning mists floating up into the rose light of the upper air, sparkled with the silver threads of its streams,—Green River twining through meadows 'in a path of light,' and Housatonic's deeper waters gleaming gold in the sunshine. But, grandest of all, rise the superb domes of the Taconic range. Below them, over the southern plains, dimpled with valleys, dotted with hills, extend gardens of beauty, pines and elms, and fields of golden grain, among which the little villages of Copake and the Hillsdale hamlet lie in loveliest grouping. But the eye turns again to the far off cloudlands of the southwest, where the dim outlines, blue and misty as the heaven above them, of the Hudson highlands extend along the horizon. Then the Catskills take up the sublime story of eternal repose, and along the western sky they lead on to the Helderberg range and the Adirondacks of the north."

MOUNT WASHINGTON.

THIS town is one of the highest in the county and, of course, in the State, and its dry, salubrious, cool summer climate is extremely refreshing to the city resident. The habitable portion of the mountain is a broad valley, on the slopes of which a few people live, above them rising many summits, down which come the cooler breezes of the upper air. To this mountain city people have come for years, and found entertainment at farmers' houses; and, with the increase of their profits, the farmers have enlarged their houses and prepared them comfortably for the reception of boarders. The first people who came to the mountain found keeping at " Farmer " Smith's about 1850, and it is believed that his first guests were Dr. Torrey and family, of Boston. Since that time the house has contained many people, some of them famous, as the old registers of visitors prove. All that the autograph fiends have left of them are now in possession of Isaac Spurr.

The next one to keep boarders was Isaac Spurr, in 1861. He recalls in pleasant memory that the first dollar he earned after he was 21 was from Mrs. Charles Sedgwick, who came with a party of girls from her school in Lenox, and hired him to leave the coal bush and pilot them to the summit of the Dome. It was to this place that Catherine E. Beecher and her sister, Mrs. Perkins, of Hartford, came years ago. At that time *Harper's Magazine* published a fancy sketch, entitled " The Little Black Dogs of Berkshire," written by Miss Beecher at Mr. Spurr's. Among his guests have been Prof. Joseph Henry, of the Smithsonian Institution; Prof. Short, of Columbia College, and members of the Livingston, Ogden, De Puyster and Hoguet families. A few years ago a party of sixty-four of the members of the American Institute of Mining Engineers stayed here for dinner, and the register of that date bears the names of T. Sterry Hunt, Joseph D. Weeks, and many other familiar names.

Such people as the following now come to Mount Washington: Isaac Spurr's—Mrs. Thomas D. Pearce, Mrs. M. A. Chapman, Miss M. Cresson, all of Philadelphia; Frank Goodrich, Oswald Jackson, New York; Mrs. C. B. Williams, Whitestone, L. I.; Miss Gummere, Burlington, N. J.; Miss S. F. Corlis, Miss Olivia Rodham, Swarthmore, Pa. At William H. Weaver's—Miss B. D. Sharpless, Mrs. Elizabeth Williams, Miss B. Farnall, Philadelphia; the Rev. Thomas Fisher, Hartford; A. A. Patton, Yonkers, N. Y. At Ira L. Patterson's—Mrs. H. C. Meinell, Montclair, N. J.; Mr. and Mrs. Janes, New York. Mrs. Janes has been here every year since she was a girl. At O. C. Whitbeck's—Dr. Charles Milne, A. Frissel, New York; Miss Lever, West New Brighton, Staten Island; Lieutenant Schroeder, of the United States navy; Prof. Jean Roemer, C. H. Flagg, Thomas S. Strong, New York; Isaac H. Allen, Brooklyn. Mr. Whitbeck's is the most elevated boarding house on the Taconics. At Frank B. Schutt's there is always a houseful.

At the Alandar House, which is the largest house on the mountain at the south end, and an exceedingly well kept house, too, the following have been guests: Mrs. Charles Dudley Warner, Hartford; W. H. Hamilton, Mrs. W. B. Wooster, both of Albany; John Ritchie, Jr., Boston; the Rev. J. M. Taylor, Providence, R. I.; Captain A. L. King, Clifton, Staten Island; Prof. E. D. Cope, Newbold H. Trotter, Dr. Spencer Trotter, all of Philadelphia; William Evans, Dr. Joseph Stokes, both of Moorestown, N. J.; Dr. Norman Smith, Dr. John T. Metcalf, the Rev. N. E. Cornwall, A. Slaight Jones, all of New York; Mrs. C. P. Newbold, Alexander H. Stuart, both of Brooklyn; H. J. Gelien, Whitestone, L. I.; the Rev. James M. Bruce, Hudson, N. Y.

Several years ago, the late Mrs. T. L. Walsh came here and bought a place, to which she came every summer during her life.

In 1884, Philip C. Garrett, of Philadelphia, who had been a guest of the Alandar House, bought 150 acres of land and built a large, fine cottage on a high hill, having the vast side of Mount Alandar, with its many gorges, in sight on the west, and mountain tops and wild forests on all sides. At this "Wyldmere," Mr. Garrett lives every summer. The beginning thus made in establishing mountainous homes here must, in time, lead to the acquisition of the principal portions of the mountain for this purpose.

PECULIARITIES OF THE TOWN.

The eight or ten boarding houses of the mountain are only three to five miles from the Copake Iron Works Station of the Harlem Railroad.

New England people commonly go to Great Barrington, where they are met by their future host, who carries them in a wagon ten to fifteen miles to his mountain home, a most delightful ride. A stage runs over the mountain from Great Barrington to Copake Iron Works, leaving the former place at 10 A. M. and the latter at 2 P. M., both daily, except Sundays. Less of the friction of life one could hardly hope to find than in this mountain town. Here is no railroad station or express office, no telegraph office, no "store" or manufactory of any description, no grist mill, no blacksmith shop, no brass band, no resident lawyer, doctor, or clergyman.

The roads of Mount Washington, though level in few places, are easily traveled over and are kept in a good state of repair.

The Goodale Family.

At "Sky Farm" at the north end of Mount Washington, at the top of the long ascent from Guilder Hollow, for many years lived Henry S. and Mrs. D. H. R. Goodale, and their children, Elaine and Dora R., all more or less known for their writings in verse and prose. Mrs. Goodale has long been a contributor to the best periodical publications, and her daughters, at first known as the "Sky Farm poets," achieved fame in early girlhood as promising poets of nature. Readers often come across the productions of Mrs. Goodale and her daughters in *Harper's*, in *Good Housekeeping*, in *St. Nicholas*, and in other publications. The Misses Goodale have issued several volumes of poems, but the first one, "Apple Blossoms," perhaps, met with the best reception, "In Berkshire with the Wild Flowers" coming next. The Goodale family left the mountain several years ago.

The Dome of the Taconics.

There are many places of interest on this mountain, remarkable for extensive, wild, picturesque and beautiful scenery. There is no mountain outlook in Berkshire, indeed there is said to be none in all New England not even excepting the White Mountains, that equals, in the last two respects, the outlook from the top of the Dome. In a clear day, land is visible in Vermont, New Hampshire, Connecticut, and New York, and it is said that mountains in New Jersey and Pennsylvania have been sighted. The intervening country affords a vast domain for the eye to feast upon, as one stands upon this Dome of the Taconics, 2,624 feet above the ocean and about 2,000 feet above the Housatonic valley below. Greylock stands out boldly 40 miles toward the north; the chains of the Catskills, with sharp outlines and peaks, wall in the west

Sky Farm Cottage.

at a distance of 35 miles. The Shawangunk Mountains can be seen far in the southwest; the low hills of Long Island, 100 miles to the south have been seen, and blue water beyond, though rarely. The Housatonic Valley lies in beauty on the east and the broader Hudson River Valley spreads out on the west. Near by, the mountain valleys and summits catch the eye, on the remainder of Mount Washington. These appear at their best in the early autumn, as may be inferred from a description by the Rev. S. W. Powell in the New York *Evangelist:* "I could see looking westward, that the dark green of the hemlock was everywhere 'picked out' by the scarlet of the sumac and soft maple; while the oak, the beech, and the chestnut gave less vivid browns, reds, and yellows. Here and there the bright gold of the sugar maple lit up the space around it. Everywhere birches and hard maples just beginning to turn, afforded lovely olive tints. Several side-hills were solid masses of gold, while in some places naked cliffs that were almost waste gave, so to speak, a deep bass to the great symphony of color."

The first published reference to an ascent of the Dome was that of President Dwight of Yale, in 1781. The following is an extract from Prof. Hitchcock's Geology of Massachusetts, relating to the Dome: "The central part is somewhat conical, almost naked eminence; except that, numerous yellow pines, two or three feet high, and huckleberry bushes have fixed themselves wherever the crevices of the rock afford sufficient soil. Hence the view from the summit is entirely unobstructed. And what a view!

'In depth, in height, in circuit, how serene!
The spectacle, how pure!—of nature's works
In earth and air,
A revelation infinite it seems.'

You feel yourself to be standing above everything around you, and feel the proud consciousness of literally looking down upon all terrestrial scenes. Before you on the east, the valley through which the Housatonic wanders, stretches far northward in Massachusetts, and southward into Connecticut, sprinkled over with copse and glebe, with small sheets of water and beautiful villages. To the southeast, especially, a large sheet of water appears (Twin Lakes), of surpassing beauty. In the southwest the gigantic Alandar, Riga and other mountains more remote, seem to bear the blue heavens on their heads in calm majesty; while stretching across the far distant west, the Catskills hang like the curtains of the sky. Oh! what a glorious display of mountains all around you! And how does one in such a spot turn round and round, and drink in new glories, and feel his heart swelling more and more with emotions of sublimity, until the tired optic nerve shrinks from its office. This certainly is the grandest prospect in Massachusetts [Prof. Hitchcock had explored the whole State] and the first hour that one spends in such a spot is among the richest treasures that memory lays up in her storehouse."

The Rev. J. T. Headley, the biographer, is among the many men who have gone into ecstasies over the scene from the Dome. He writes: "You are the center of a circle of at least 350 miles in circumference; and such a circle! I cannot tell of the prodigality of beauty that meets the eye at every turn. You seem to look on the outer wall of creation, and this old Dome seems to be the spot on which nature set her great compasses when she drew the circle of the heavens. A more beautiful horizon I have never seen than sweeps around you from this spot. The charm of the view is perfect on every side—a panorama, which becomes a moving one if you will but take the trouble to turn it round."

There has long been a protest against adopting the name that Prof. Hitchcock gave to this summit—Mount Everett—and as the way to abandon the name is to first make beginning, we voice the united public sentiment of the region and use "The Dome of the Taconics" (often abbreviated to "The Dome,") to designate this mountain. As long ago as 1850, Miss Sedgwick, during one of her visits from Lenox, wrote in the register at "Farmer" Smith's:

> "Oh call it not Mt. Everett!
> Forever 'tis the Dome
> Of the great Temple God has reared
> In this, our Berkshire home."

The best authorities now say that Taconic is the corruption of an Indian word meaning the smaller of two sources of a river, and applied to the Bashbish stream. Through the misunderstanding of the settlers the name was given to the mountain down which the stream comes, and later the whole range got the name. The town of Mount Washington ought to have been named Taconic, for the present name is not so appropriate and is misleading. The main road leading to the Dome begins on the opposite side of the road from the Walsh place, but a road from the Smith place joins it.

BASHBISH.

Along the eastern side of Alandar runs toward the north a stream that, lower down, is called the Bashbish. It has been said to be an Indian onomatopoetic name, suggested by the sound of the falling water, and

BASHBISH LOWER FALLS.

Miss Sedgwick thought it to be of Swiss origin; but these are errors, for the name is undoubtedly of vulgar origin, coming to its present form from the Dutch corruption of English. Just opposite the perpendicular north end of Alandar, after plunging 200 feet, in all, down through a narrow rocky gorge, whose sides tower 200 and 300 feet above, over several precipitous slopes that, taken together, are the noted Bashbish Falls; and just after the last leap of sixty feet, where the water is divided by a huge boulder on the brink, the stream turns sharp to the west, and goes dancing away to join the Hudson through a gorge made by the north end of Alandar and the south end of Cedar Mountain. Below the falls it descends 300 feet in a short distance. Into the valley of this romantic stream, from either side above the falls, come several tributary narrow valleys, which in their lower portions are narrow gorges, and to clamber through them is so difficult, and often so dangerous, as to be very enticing to those of an adventurous turn of mind. A trip to the Falls is always a day's excursion, and should include a walk from the lower falls to the Eagle's Nest, to the Look-off, and to the upper falls, and returning by the highway. When going down the road in the gorge above the falls, the Old Man of the Mountain, or Profile Rock, will be seen high up on the right. This towering head is approachable from above, and commands a magnificent view of the gorge, the Catskills and the intervening country.

Beecher wrote of this place in his Star Papers: "I would willingly make the journey once a month from New York to see it." A sample ride to Bashbish from any of the towns of the Housatonic Valley is thus described by a Lenox correspondent of the *Home Journal* in early autumn: "Last week twelve ladies and gentlemen, on pleasure bent, filled a mountain wagon, and, with six good horses, took the drive from this dear old Lenox through the lovely village of Great Barrington to Bashbish. Soft autumn winds, laden with balm, and the mingled odor of late fruits, pine, wintergreen and flowers, came to us from the beautiful Berkshire Hills; winds which felt as if they might drive away all care and trouble, fine old elms arched overhead, fields spread out far and hazy, unseen brooks babbled by, all seemed full of so much peace that I longed for the language of a poet to express my uplifted joyous feelings." On the way home in the evening, "the tender glow of the sunset lingered over the darkening mountains; stars peeped out here and there; the Housatonic River softly rushed along the base of the hills, while 'in Nature's eyes we looked and rejoiced,' and wished our New York friends could have longer enjoyed this peace, this absolute repose, this regular life, which secures bodily health and gives tone to the mind; away from the great centers of culture, yet so much mental and social refinement within our reach, so much that is beautiful in nature to make the current of existence flow placidly on."

A pupil in Mount Holyoke Seminary visited this place many years ago, and was moved to compose a fanciful legendary poem, in the preface of which she wrote: The Bashbish Falls "are the anthem of Nature's hymn in New England, sent up to heaven from her wildest work. As I gazed upon those falls and the gray old mountains between which they dashed, I could exclaim: 'Oh! there is in Nature's charms a poetry so wild and deep that even a savage soul must bow and own its magic power.'" A traveler writes: Though the visitor "may have gazed upon the wonders of Alpine scenery and the sublime revelations of the Valley of the Yosemite, and have listened to the awful thunder of Niagara, it is not without a silencing thrill of delight that the cataract of Bashbish greets the vision." After lying on the rock at the "Look-off," and looking over and down, "steady, indeed, must be the nerves that can arise from the prostrate position entirely unshaken." "It may be safely averred that there is scarcely on all the earth's surface so sublime a freak of nature as little known beyond its surrounding neighborhood."

Prof. Hitchcock wrote a long account of Bashbish. Here, he says, is "the most remarkable and interesting gorge and cascade in Massachusetts." Referring to the Look-off, he writes: "I have scarcely ever felt such a creeping and shrinking of the nerves and such a disposition to draw back as here. Even though I took hold of the bushes with both hands, I could not comfortably keep my eye turned long into the frightful and yawning gulf. * * * Many persons who visit the falls do not ascend this precipice, but they lose more than half the interest of the scene. I feel the paucity of description for delineating such scenery." From the Look-off to the water directly below it is 194 feet, and to the foot of the lower falls about 350 feet, in a line somewhat inclined from perpendicular, but seemingly almost directly below.

ALANDAR RAVINE.

Along the eastern base of Mount Alandar is Alandar Ravine, one of remarkable wildness, where the old forest, the ragged rocks and the stream make some uncommon effects. A little below the old mill dam are noteworthy cascades. From this old mill site, which is a mile from the Alandar House, a path leads to the top of Alandar, a rare walk of three miles.

Mount Alander.

From the Bashbish Look-off a path runs to the north end of Alander and along its ridge for about four miles south, where, after a sharp rise of about 100 feet, it goes on rising gradually to its highest point, which is marked by one of the signal poles of the United States Geological Survey at an elevation of 2,200 feet. "All along the ridge of Alander," writes a correspondent of the New York *Evening Post*, "one gets a succession of beautiful views; and, especially, when the autumn colors are in their glory, one seems to be walking upon a great cloud shot through with the richest hues of sunset. Crimsons, scarlets, bright and old gold, bronzes, mauves, olives, etc., mingled with the various shades of green afforded by oaks and birches not yet touched, by the laurel, by pine of two or three varieties, and by the sombre hemlocks—all these, and many intermediate tints of brown, red, and gray are exquisitely mingled and proportioned."

At the foot of Alander on the west side, half a mile south of the Douglass place, is a great rock with a cavity underneath. From this issues a large stream of the purest and coldest water, and a very perceptible current of cold air. Tracks of animals have been seen leading into the cavern at one side. It is said that a boy has crawled into this crevice a considerable distance, and it is thought that there is a lake and a cave under the mountain. The water does not change with season in temperature or volume.

Bear Rock and Taconic Falls.

A most sightly and easily accessible place on the brow of the south end of Mount Race, a quarter of a mile in a direct line from Sage's Ravine and about a mile above the under mountain road, is Bear Rock, over which the outlet of Plantain Pond descends and makes the Taconic Falls. The water makes short work of a fall of several hundred feet, and the plunge over the rock in an early perpendicular cascade is visible from many points in the Housatonic valley in the south end of the county. The water descends 405 feet in falls and almost perpendicular cascades. The view from this rock is as indescribable as any in the county, it is so extensive, grand, beautiful, everything in one. Looking north one sees a mile away a precipice of more than a thousand feet on the east side of Race Mountain. The rock is generally approached over the east road on Mount Washington when the wagon is well loaded. A shorter way is up the steep road from below, a little north of Sage's Ravine; this road is so nearly on end that some people are frightened in riding over it; horses cannot draw much of a load up the ascent, nor hold back much going down. A few feet north of the place where the stream crosses the road, turn to the east and a few steps will take one to the rock. A walk of 2½ miles from the Alandar House follows an old road through the woods west of Plantain Pond to Bear Rock.

OTHER PLACES OF INTEREST.

Plantain Pond, a short distance back of Bear Rock, and Guilder Pond, at the north base of the Dome, are sheets of clear water, surrounded by mountain summits and with a forest margin, so that they look precisely like many an Adirondack lake. Guilder Lake is seen on the trip to the Dome, and Plantain Lake on the Bear Rock trip.

There are paths to nearly all the mountain tops, to Ethel, Cedar, 1,775 feet high; Fray, 1,915 feet; Race, 2,300 feet; West, 2,300 feet; and Bear Mountain. The last is in the territory of Salisbury, Conn., and is the highest land in Connecticut, with an elevation of 2,250 feet. It is but two miles from the Alandar House on Mount Washington, by a new path of half a mile leading from the highway. Fifty rods back of Mr. Garrett's house is a small lake of eight by ten acres, called Wyldmere, and immediately back of this is Lee Mountain, to the summit of which walks are made from the Alandar House.

Drives are often made from Mount Washington to Lakeville, Conn., a distance of 12 to 17 miles, and to the Twin Lakes, 15 to 20 miles distant. Mount Riga lies south of Mount Washington, and for its attractions see the article on Salisbury. Monument Mountain, south of Alandar, has on its summit a monument that was erected in 1725 at the northwest corner of Connecticut.

SUNSET MOUNTAIN.

One can drive to the top of Sunset Mountain, 1790 feet high, half a mile southwest of O. C. Whitbeck's, and hence it is more frequently visited than any other summit. Here, writes Mrs. D. H. R. Goodale, "The grandly outlined hills seem to stand about with a friendly nearness, even when the purple duskiness of twilight is in all their folds, while, to the west, far off the slow-dropping sun floods the blue Catskills with his golden glory, and illumines their shadowy cloves, as he paints upon the sky above them all the evanishing splendor of his cloud-castles! The beautiful valley between, with its breadth of forest and field, with its nestling homes, its waving grain and clustering orchards, takes on, moment by moment, those wonderful gradations of light and color that are the despair of painters. Through the air comes the soft tinkle of a distant cow-bell; peace is descending with the gathering darkness; the twilight is creeping on, but through its hush, the warmth, the glow, the promise of the sunset glory lingers in our hearts."

What was formerly a part of the town of Mount Washington, Boston Corners, was set off to New York, because a prisoner arrested there could not be brought to a Massachusetts court without taking him through New York territory. At that place the celebrated fight between Tom Hyers and Yankee Sullivan took place, with an accompanying assemblage of ruffians.

About half a mile north of the Boston Corners station of the Harlem railway is a steep gorge on the west side of the mountain called the Blow Hole, where the wind concentrates and rushes down with tremendous force when it comes from the east. It sweeps across the Harlem railroad at this place and is sometimes dangerous to passing trains. Several years ago a passenger train was blown from the track by the wind coming down this Blow Hole.

A Few of Many Tributes.

Prof. Hitchcock, in his report on the geology of Massachusetts, says that the scenery in and from this town would almost repay a lover of nature for a voyage across the Atlantic. "To one who has a taste for the wild, the romantic and the grand in nature, those two days [spent on the Dome and at Bashbish] will be a season of delightful emotions."

A part of Mrs. Goodale's tribute to this town is as follows: "High amid the hills of extreme Southern Berkshire, uplifted skyward where light and air. color, perfumery. song and silence of the summer days all come and go. pure, free, spontaneous, each with its own delicious, subtle charm, lies Mount Washington. Girt about with the everlasting hills in their serene steadfastness, with the wild Bashbish gorge on the southwest, and the western outlook bounded by the beautiful range of the Catskills, in no part of Berkshire is to be found more of the native majesty and loveliness of Nature. Green fields, cattle upon the hills, and scattered farm-houses speak of the hand of man, and yet there are broad stretches of woodland, occasionally, indeed, laid low by the woodchopper's axe, and plumed with the soft, wavering smoke column of the charcoal pit, but oftener answering only to the rhythmic fingers of the wind, and echoing no harsher sounds than the cooing of the wood-dove, or the persistent plaint of the whip-poor-will."

An autumn correspondent of the New York *Evening Post* writes: "I had a large parlor, with a stove in it and a bed-room connecting. From all my windows the grandest and loveliest scenery was always inviting the eye. Within a few minutes' walk over a notch in Ashley Hill, I could be in the great lonely wilderness, stretching away west and north to Alandar, and which at all times of day, but especially in the afternoon, was fairly palpitating with vivid color. On returning from long, bewitching tramps in that fairy-land to my good supper, my cozy lamp and long, restful evening over easy vacation reading, I was not obliged to take off my comfortable, easy flannels, or to listen to the chatter of a lot of fashionable fellow boarders; and, withal, the price at which I was gladly accommodated was less than that which in the summer months I must have paid for far more contracted and less comfortable accommodations. By all means, let the lover of color, of tramping, and real comfort come just as the leaves begin to turn," about the 20th of September.

1.—Campbell's Falls, New Marlboro. 2.—Hotel, Bashbish Falls. 3.—Eastern Portal, Hoosac Tunnel. 4.—Natural Bridge, North Adams. 5.—Upper Bashbish Falls.

NORTH ADAMS.

NORTH ADAMS is the largest town in Berkshire county.* The peculiarity of this part of the county is that the valleys are narrow; there are no sweeps or basins like those at Pittsfield and at Stockbridge, nor yet at Great Barrington. The mountain peaks, thrown up in great profusion, among which Greylock sits as king wherever you go, are nearer together and the valleys are in some places little more than defiles or gorges. Coming from the south, the Hoosac Valley is the path over which you go, beginning below Cheshire, nearly to Pittsfield, where the head waters of the Hoosac and a branch of the Housatonic rise almost in the same spring. At Adams, the valley is quite narrow, widening a little at the north line of that town and the boundary of North Adams until nearly to North Adams village, where it narrows again to a width of about a half mile. Looking straight ahead north, as one enters North Adams up this south branch of the Hoosac, the mountains rise up before one as though a dead stop had come; but the river finds its way to the west through a narrow pass for some distance, on towards Williamstown. In that direction, called at North Adams, the Williamstown Valley, it is wider again, and yet the grand old hills are on both sides with delightfully panoramic views, as the distance opens, one after another. From the village of North Adams, as a base of observation, the other valley is to the east, following close the east branch of the Hoosac, a goodly stream tumbling turbulently down the incline, all the way through Clarksburg. This east valley is narrow, in places almost a gorge, along which the highway winds, while on the right, following that stream northeast from the village, the everlasting hills rise continuously. This valley runs on through Clarksburg into Vermont and widens out into a magnificent valley at Stamford; in that state to be sure, but so near North Adams and having its business so closely identified with it that it hardly seems that Stamford is out of Berkshire.

The Busy Village.

So, the peculiarity of North Adams lies in the fact that it has three valleys, each with many natural beauties, peculiar to itself, and these are, the Hoosac, coming from the south, its continuation to the west, called

* Pittsfield having foregone that distinction by becoming a city.

the Williamstown Valley ; and, to the east, down which the east branch of the Hoosac runs, that known as the Stamford Valley. Along these valleys lies the village of North Adams, sometimes called "The Tunnel City," and it is so hidden in the valleys, in quiet dells and nooks, that a good view of the village is not obtained unless from some lofty height. Its population is estimated at about 15,000, and is a busy and enterprising hive of manufacturing and commercial life ; every man is a laborer, as it were, and there is probably no other village of its size in the state which has so many self-made men. The Hoosac is lined with mills and factories and the different industries have given names to the villages grown up about them, as, "The Union," "Braytonville," "Greylock," "The Beaver," "The Glen," and many others. The main village is compactly built, and its mills are in the very center.

The town's history runs back to the French and Indian war, and the site of the old Fort Massachusetts on the Hoosac River, near Braytonville, between North Adams and Williamstown, is marked by an elm tree which was planted many years ago by the Williams College students. It is on the Harrison farm, and it is a wonder to many why the fort should have been placed there, for on each side are sharp ledges, from which the Indians could command almost with ease the interior of the stockade and fort.

NATURAL SCENERY.

The natural scenery of North Adams is unexcelled in the county. It is all the more grand because the narrow valleys bring it so near. There are no distant outlines to cut the horizon but, rising almost abruptly from the valleys, the mountains lift their majestic heads. Coming up the south valley, the Hoosac, on the right, to the east, are the Green Mountains, or the Hoosacs, as they are called, and, by some, the Florida range, under which, two miles from the village, the vast Hoosac Tunnel was bored. To the left of this valley are the Taconics, with Greylock in plain view. There are first the foot hills, then a valley beyond and, farther on, the peaks of the more abrupt mountains, such as Mount Williams and Bald Mountain. The eye rests on many prominent clear-cut views of mountain scenery in this valley, which are almost indescribable. To the west, in the Williamstown valleys, are the same ranges, this spur of the Taconics, thrown off, as it were, from the main range, the Saddle and Pine Cobble on the left, and the other peaks farther in Williamstown, making a beautiful valley and superb mountain views. North of the village, and almost making an impenetrable barrier, is the Pine Cobble, which, in the earlier years, was a great resort for rattlesnakes, and it was the holiday of the town at the proper season to make a "bee," and go thence to dispatch the reptiles; there are yet many snake stories to be heard in the village of the wonderful exploits on these occasions. In the east valley, or the Stamford, the Green Mountain range is unbroken, excepting by this valley, which affords many beautiful views.

In the Hoosac Valley, a mile or so below the village towards Adams, are several hills like haystacks, say fifty feet high, and a perfect cone in some instances, resembling an Indian mound. Prof. Hitchcock says of them that, in the glacial period, these were brought down from the Hoosacs. In many places in the valley there are clear evidences of the work of the glacial period, and in the village, at Furnace Hill, the glacial scratches are plainly visible. One case near the little tunnel is peculiarly marked.

To the north is Clarksburg, and the hills on the north boundary of the village, in the locality known as Houghtonville, are in that town. From this portion of the village a magnificent view is had down the valley to Adams. On the hills west of the village and on the top of which the reservoir of the village water-works is located, another excellent view of North Adams is obtained. Witt's Ledge, a stone quarry in the edge of the village, one of the prominent hills of the Taconic range, is a fine walk of ten minutes and opens an enchanting panorama below, while its geological formation is also a most interesting subject for the student.

The Natural Bridge.

Emptying into the east branch of the Hoosac a mile from the center, is Hudson's Brook, rising in Clarksburg, and upon which stream is the great curiosity of Northern Berkshire, the Natural Bridge. This was the spot which entranced Hawthorne, who spent a long time in North Adams and whose "American Notes" brings into prominence many characters of the town in past years. This enlarged fissure, down through which the water rushes, is in white marble, discolored by time and the action of the water so that the stones are gray. A view of the bridge is given in this book. The depth of the fissure is at least sixty feet and at several points the stone almost closes over. The upper end of the chasm is very narrow, but it widens after the plunge of the stream and is accessible, forming a spacious chamber. The echoes are grand in the subterranean passage. There are numerous pools, and protruding spurs or rocks divide the stream, so that each fissure is almost a cave by itself. The stream once fell over a high precipice on the south, but, through chemical action, has disintegrated the limestone beneath it, leaving two masses of rock connecting the sides and forming natural bridges, though the upper one is much broken. The lower one is arched and the stream runs 50 feet below it, the average width of the brook being about 15 feet. In times of low water, people walk beneath the bridge. A cave exists a little west of the top of the chasm, large enough to be entered with some trouble, and permitting one to stand erect in some places. The history of this discovery is that a man named Hudson, living in Clarksburg, carrying home a deer and passing this spot, let it slip from his shoulder and lost it down a hole into the cave. It is without doubt one of the most romantic spots and one of the rarest bits of the work of nature, in all Berkshire. It is within easy walking distance from the village.

POINTS OF INTEREST.

Up on the Florida mountain east of the village some of the finest of views are obtainable. From this point the Rev. Washington Gladden received an inspiration which kindled his soul as he gazed on the enchanted scene far below him. In a word, while the village below is unattractive in broad avenues and shaded walks, and while there are no lawns and grounds and surroundings of the ideal "country seat," yet, from any eminence where the village is snuggling at your feet, you are struck with its unique situation, hidden away in the glens and dells.

The Notch is an interesting part of the town, west of the village. The foot hills, Witt's Ledge and the other hill continuing south, are its eastern boundary and the mountains in the Taconic spur, its western. The Notch brook supplies the town with water, and the stream has upon it "The Cascade," where the mountain stream comes tumbling saucily along until it makes an abrupt plunge of about 40 feet into the abyss below. There is a deep gorge between the hills, with overhanging rocks covered with moss and ferns, and here in the deep shade of the pines the situation is somber and romantic. In this range of foot hills tradition has it that there exists a cave, but of late years its exact location is not known.

BUSINESS CHARACTER.

There have been no old families to give the town a social reputation, and it has never been a resort for the summer visitors. It is too busy, and there is a hum in the air of the industry and push of the place. But the visitor will find the friendliness and the hospitality of the town wonderfully refreshing and cordial. The building of the Hoosac Tunnel, the greatest engineering feat of the kind in the country, gave the town a great start in a business way. The work, while altogether under the Hoosac Mountain in Florida, and in part the other side, was, nevertheless, a North Adams affair, and the village reaped a substantial benefit from it. The tunnel, of which we give views and a sketch elsewhere, is 25,081 feet—or four and three-quarter miles—long, through solid rock the entire distance. It has cost millions of money, and is the property of the Fitchburg Railroad Company which purchased it from the State in 1887, together with the forty-four miles of road-bed between the Vermont line and the Connecticut River at Greenfield.

North Adams is the greatest railroad center in Berkshire. From the south is the Pittsfield and North Adams branch of the Boston and Albany Railroad; from the east the Fitchburg Railroad, now connecting with the New Haven and Northampton Railroad. The Fitchburg has absorbed the Troy and Boston, and the Boston, Hoosac Tunnel and Western Railways, and now furnishes connections west. A street railroad was built in 1886-7 between North Adams and Adams, six miles south. The road was purchased in 1888 by the Thompson-Houston Electric Company, and the year following was equipped with the electric system.

The Fitchburg Railroad, Hoosac Tunnel route, is the only line which runs to Williamstown. Passengers from the south should see that their tickets read, Troy to Williamstown. During the summer the train service from Troy and from Boston to Williamstown is all that can be desired.

Some Village Institutions.

A few years ago S. A. Kemp gave to the town twenty acres of land, on which is a grove, on the hillside just east of the village, for a park, and every year the town is making a good appropriation for its improvement. A free library was established in 1884, now having about 12,000 volumes, and a free reading room. A mile west of the village are the grounds of the Hoosac Valley Agricultural Society, with a fine half-mile track, where racing is often indulged in. The schools of North Adams are probably the best in Berkshire. As the result of a serious accident in the railroad yard, in 1883, the citizens of the town subscribed liberally for the erection of a hospital, which occupies a place on the hill north of the village, and from its veranda a charming view of the landscape below is enjoyed. There are three social clubs—the North Adams Club, with a membership embracing some of the prominent business men of the town, who have tastefully arranged rooms on Main street, the Club Brunswick, composed of younger men, who occupy cozy quarters on

Main street, and the Washington, which is pleasantly located in the new Blackinton block on Main street. In addition to these clubs there are numerous secret orders, all of which seem to flourish. The receptions given by the social organizations of the town are noted, and at more than one of them the governors of the State have graced the occasions with their presence.

The pulpit of the Congregational church has been filled by men of wide reputation, among them being the Rev. Washington Gladden, who as a writer has made a national reputation; Prof. Llewellyn Pratt, of the Hartford Theological Seminary, and the Rev. Theodore T. Munger, now of New Haven, whose books have attracted much attention.

THE DRIVES.

The narrow valleys in which North Adams is located makes it impossible to have such numerous drives in the immediate vicinity as there are in many other towns. What there are are romantic, and make up in beauty and variety of scenery what they lack in number. No town in Berkshire offers more rare views and glimpses of the valley and mountain, with far-reaching lookouts and look-offs, than North Adams; for a new view, or a new panorama, as in the turning of a kaleidoscope, is offered at almost every turn.

The drive up the Notch road is romantic. This was the old route to Adams, and is one of the wildest in the county. The road in many places is exceedingly steep, and, running along the mountain side, above the valley, the villages are in plain sight away down below. This road is continued for six miles after leaving the Notch road proper, and comes out in Adams by the old Quaker church. In many places the trees overhang the highway, making a delightful shade, and some abrupt turn in the road will open to view a most magnificent surprise of scenery below. The trip this way and back from Adams up the valley is about twelve miles. North Adams, seen below in the night from this road on the mountain, is beyond description. The drive east, from Main street at the Wilson House or Richmond House as starting points, through Union street, past the Freeman Print Works, through the Beaver, to Briggsville, following the east branch of the Hoosac, to Clarksburg, is a pleasant one, over a highway finely shaded. Continuing to Stamford and the Paradise Hotel, famous for its trout suppers, is an easy grade and a drive of about five miles. It is the most frequently taken of all the drives out of North Adams. Another drive, longer, but highly romantic, is to take the east road out of the village to the "Five Roads," 1½ miles, then turning directly to the left, and thence to Stamford, having the summit of the mountain for the highway and the valley below as the picture, returning from Stamford by the other route named,—a very good twelve-mile drive. In the east part of the village are many views of the town.

There are many walks of a few minutes that open wonderfully interesting views. To Witt's Ledge; to Thayer Pond, now the reservoir of the Freeman Manufacturing Company, on the hill east of the village; to the Hospital and the road leading east from there to the Natural Bridge; up in Houghtonville on the high ground in Clarksburg, and many others, as fancy leads. All of them present different pictures, and it is peculiar of North Adams that its short walks brings out as many pretty views as a drive of two or three miles would afford in other places where the valveys are wider.

The west shaft of the Tunnel, two miles southeast of the village is a romantic spot. The buildings are decayed, but the pile of debris is simply remarkable. Here are the works of Prof. Mowbray, who, during the building of the Tunnel, manufactured nitro-glycerine; the place has been the scene of two or three serious and damaging explosions. It is easily reached with a carriage, and there is a good view of the village in the south valley and down towards Adams, that is worth a trip there. The place is frequently resorted to. Near this place is the reservoir of the Arnold Print Works, collecting the 600 gallons of water which flows every minute from the west portal of the Tunnel and conveying it in pipes to the railroad station and the mills farther down in the village. The west portal of the Tunnel is near and is worth a visit. Huge doors close the entrance to the Tunnel, when necessary, and there is a block signal station at this point. Another short drive and one frequently made is to go down Church street into a by-road leading to the west shaft, then turning north, following a valley with a view of the village to the left and the high range of mountains abruptly rising opposite, to Main street back to the village—a drive of four miles. Still another drive is to the central shaft of the Hoosac Tunnel in Florida. The view of the valley below when the summit of the mountain is reached beggars description. It makes a pretty ten-mile drive there and return.

What is called the grandest drive of all, and occupying a day, is to go east over through Florida with its many romantic views, to Hoosac Tunnel Station in the Deerfield Valley; then going north, following the Deerfield Valley to Readsboro City, where are the extensive operations of the Messrs. Newton, who have built a narrow gauge road thereto; then to Hartwellville, in Vermont, and to Stamford, returning direct to North

Adams, the trip being about 35 miles. This gives a good view of both the Hoosac and the Deerfield Valleys. A complete list of drives will be found elsewhere, and mention of the numerous attractions in neighboring towns appears in the articles on those towns.

THE BRAIN AND BRAWN.

The town has an excellent set of business men, and has sent out some good representatives. Hiram Sibley, the head of the great seed houses at Rochester and Chicago, was a North Adams boy. The handsome Episcopal church in the village was the gift of Mrs. Sibley, also a native of North Adams. The Tinker family has been identified with the growth and prosperity of the town. The Blackintons have also added their energies to advance its temporal interests; the Braytons and the Richmond families have been identified with the town in many ways from its earliest days. George Millard was the pioneer of the shoe industry. James Marshall was pioneer in the business life of the town; Sylvander Johnson's efforts succeeded in aiding the Tunnel work in its darkest hours. A. B. Wilson, the inventor of the Wheeler and Wilson sewing machine, went out of the town with his model under his arm and achieved fortune; the Wilson house is his local monument.

The Hodges were among the pioneers; there were Samuel Gaylord, A. W. Richardson, the Cadys, the Arnolds, for many years the print works' owners and men of character and stability; W. W. Freeman, the early manufacturer of calicoes; and Judge James T. Robinson, editor and orator. Senator Dawes began his practice and made his first political reputation in North Adams. In the life's busy day there are the Gallups, A. C. Houghton, Col. John Bracewell; Prof. Mowbray, of nitroglycerine fame; O. A. Archer, of Blackinton; Cashier Wilkinson, Judge George P. Lawrence, Frank S. Richardson, president of the gas and electric light companies; F. E. Swift, the Messrs. Cady, W. H. Gaylord, C. H. Cutting, Dr. George L. Rice, Postmaster Tyler, S. Proctor Thayer, a local writer and author. C. T. Sampson, the shoe manufacturer, was among the first to utilize Chinese labor in the time of unjust strikes, and it may be thrown in here, as a matter of history, that the first Chinese to become a naturalized citizen of this country was a resident of North Adams. G. H. B. Fisher, W. L. Brown, E. B. Penniman, Austin Bond, Manager A. W. Locke, and others might be mentioned, who have taken a lively interest in the welfare of the town.

FINE PLACES FOR SUMMER RESIDENCE.

A portion of the Richmond House was built in 1816. The principal hotels are the Wilson House, of which Foster E. Swift, who was also the landlord of the recently burned Greylock Hall at Williamstown, is proprietor; the Richmond House, of which Mr. L. L. Scott is the proprietor; and the Mansion House.

There are no summer homes in the town as yet; but within a few years several handsome dwellings have been built. The hillsides are dotted with cottages, and the slopes make sightly places of residence. The elegant house of the late Sanford Blackinton, on Main street, was for many years considered one of the most complete in Berkshire. Then there are the houses of A. W. Hodge, W. L. Brown, F. A. Walker, E. B. Penniman, F. S. Richardson, and some others, which are tasteful designs of architecture.

As a whole, North Adams possesses many attractions, and the tourist will have much to repay him for the time he may spend in drives, and rambles, during the stay that he may make within the town and its neighborhood.

ADAMS.

THE valley in which lies nestled the busy town of Adams is about four miles long, through which the south branch of the Hoosac runs quite swiftly. The south end of the valley is practically walled in, the Hoosac finding its way through a narrow defile, while high hills and ragged peaks almost entirely make a barrier of rock and wooded slope, which is nearly impassable. By its peculiar formation, the town abounds in hundreds of slopes and views.

GREYLOCK.

To Adams belongs the honor of owning Greylock, the highest peak in the State and a monarch of all its fellows,—a point seen from every town in Berkshire, almost, and a grand, wild piece of mountain scenery. As in North Adams, the valley here is too narrow to admit of many drives in the town, excepting as one drives up and down the valley, or to the eastward to Savoy, climbing the hills all the way up to the summit. There are, however, no finer views of valley scenery in all Berkshire than Adams presents. In the village of Adams one looks Greylock full in the eastern face, and, standing in the valley, the ascent looks to be not very tedious or difficult; but the reverse is the fact, and, while there are those who have made their way to the summit, 3,535 feet high, it is not an undertaking to be repeated. The description of this sightly place, and the views to be obtained there, are in another chapter, under the heading of "Greylock Park."

The early settlers of Adams were largely from Rhode Island,—Baptists and Quakers,—from whom excellent citizens have descended. The old Quaker meeting house, the only one of the denomination in the county, yet stands, although its congregations have long since ceased to worship within its walls; but it is not allowed to go to decay, and will always be maintained as one of the landmarks of the town. It stands on an eminence west of the village.

THE VILLAGE.

Adams, as a whole, has about 10,000 people; but the village proper has only perhaps half that. In fact, it is a continuation of villages, known as Maple Grove, Adams, Renfrew, and Zylonite, which is the station at the Zylonite Works. The town has gas and electric lights, and has of late begun to pay attention to its sidewalks. The growth and prosperity of Adams has been added to largely within the last decade; new streets have been opened, new manufacturing industries added; and so the villagers have been too busy to pay much attention to beautifying the village until recently. There are seven churches in the village, viz., Congregational, Baptist, Methodist, two Catholic, Universalist, and Episcopal. The latter has a beautiful stone edifice, dedicated some three years ago, the gift of L. L. Brown, the wealthy paper manufacturer, near his own dwelling. To this was added in 1889 a handsome parish house. In the upper story of this building is the fine gymnasium of the Adams Athletic Club, an organization made up largely of the business and professional men of the town. A new town hall, costing some $50,000, was built a few years ago, and the upper story is one of the finest play-houses in the county. The village has its bank, Masonic lodges of the various degrees, and other secret organizations. The best citizens of the town maintain a Rifle Club, which has a reputation of more than local renown. A military organization was formed in 1887. It is called Company M, and is part of the regular state militia. The population, because of its manufacturing establishments, is mixed; but, as a rule, the town is orderly, and it is in a great degree a village of homes. It is not, therefore, a resort as yet, for everbody is too busy to make it one.

Sample Drives.

The drives are many and fine. From the Quaker church, north, is one of the wildest and most romantic drives in all Berkshire, following up the mountain side west of the village, and thence along the "Notch" road to North Adams. The road is probably 1,000 feet above the valley, and the view in all directions is one of the rarest grandeur. Hills upon hills, and peaks on peaks, are spread out to view. This is a favorite drive from Adams, on through the Notch above North Adams, and so on to Williamstown, leaving North Adams to the east. Another drive is to go east through Hoosac street, in the village, which is a little north of the center of the village, and go directly east, climbing the east range by an easy ascent to North Savoy. From that place, turning north through Florida to the village of that name, a fine view of the Deerfield Valley is obtained. Then returning westward to North Adams, and from there down the valley to Adams again, completes a popular drive of say twenty-five miles. It is spoken of as an afternoon drive, especially in the autumn, when the frost has touched the foliage, as most remarkably enchanting, and, if it can be taken as the sunset is about approaching, when the summit above North Adams is reached, it is said to add a fascination which nowhere else in Northern Berkshire can be obtained. A drive to Savoy Hollow, the location of Bowker's Hotel, is another popular seven-mile drive up the hills overlooking the village, and this is taken by the villagers and others a good deal, both in winter and in summer, for clam bakes, trout suppers, and social parties. On the road east of the Zylonite Works, towards the north line of the town, is also another fine drive and view. It is near the Richmond farm, now the town poor farm. The writer remembers a genuine surprise he received at seeing such a beautiful view laid at his feet; for, as far south as the eye could reach, there was a succession of rare bits of scenery, and northward the view is equally magnificent. It was all the more surprising from the fact that the altitude, apparently, above the valley is not very considerable.

One may take the highway a little east of the station at Cheshire Harbor and drive along the east slope of the town, under the base of the range of hills and mountains there, with the village of Adams below, to North Adams, seven miles, with a magnificent view of the valley all the way and the stream and the clustering villages many feet below, and enjoy a panorama all the way. Or he may start at Cheshire Harbor, turning west a little and then north, in the little valley made by the foot hills at his then right as he drives north, with the base of the Saddle Mountain range to the left, through a farming region, until he emerges in the village near the old Quaker church. Then if fancy dictates he may go on north over the romantic Notch road to North Adams, and have at his feet the busy valley again and an entirely different view. There are several fine views right in the village, for the high range of hills each side of the valley, make a thousand points of varied interest. A pretty drive is what is known as the "Pumpkin Hook" road, south on the east side, towards the Dry Brook and then to Cheshire, five miles.

A THRIFTY TOWN.

The extensive "Greylock" paper mills of the L. L. Brown Paper Company are situated in this town, with an auxiliary mill at West Cummington, 12 miles away. The mills have long been some of the government paper contract mills and the company has the only mill for producing hand made papers in the United States. L. L. Brown was the first manufacturer in the country to successfully make a specialty of ledger and record papers. Beginning in 1850, he soon gained for his paper a reputation second to none in the world. Mr. Brown has had valuable aid from his treasurer, T. A. Mole, one of the most genial paper manufacturers in the country. The extensive gingham mills of the Renfrew Manufacturing Company are situated in the north part of the village proper; the Plunkett Manufacturing Company and W. B. C. Plunkett's Sons are large manufacturers of warps besides gingham fabrics at Greylock. Near the north line of the town has grown up within a few years one of the greatest industries of Berkshire, the manufacture of zylonite, and a village has grown up about it of unique and tasteful cottages, a model in every way. Besides Mr. Brown and his son-in-law, Emil Kipper, several New York gentlemen are interested in the enterprise, and artesian wells of great depth have been sunk, bringing up water of extreme purity. The pay rolls of Adams amount to millions of dollars annually, and the manufacturers are proverbially helpful to their employes in assisting them to homes and caring for their interests.

THE TOWN'S ANCESTRY AND DESCENDANTS.

The town has had a good ancestry. The Uptons were an old Quaker family, of which Daniel Upton, now a prominent resident, is a good representative. The Anthonys also were an old family, and Susan B. Anthony, the well known advocate of the rights of women, was a native of Adams. The Fisk family, of which James Fisk, Jr., was a member also lived early in the town. The Bowermans, of which were the late S. W. Bowerman of Pittsfield and other wealthy members in New York city, were an old family; the Almys of Salem came from Adams. The Howlands settled in that portion of the town now near the northern border and have assisted in giving a name and character to the town. The Wilmarths were a good family and have descendants in Adams yet; there was a large prominent family of the Jenks name, and the Richmonds and Deans were of the early families. So, as the years have come and gone Adams has had families and men who have sought to give it a business name and a good record for the future to look back upon. William C. Plunkett, a member of the family prominent in other parts of Berkshire, came to Adams a young man of limited means, but of great executive ability and amassed a fortune, gave the town a great deal of its thrift and died only a few years ago at a ripe old age, and his sons, now here in business are maintaining the honor of the family. Governor George N. Briggs, whom all Berkshire speaks of reverently for his goodness of heart and purity of life, was born in Adams. The Wheelers were a family who have left an impression for good on the town. William Pollock of Pittsfield, whose country seat was the finest in the county, made much of his fortune in Adams and was the founder of the Renfrew Manufacturing Company. The Moles, several brothers, are active and substantial citizens of the town. James Renfrew, a nephew of Mr. Pollock, of Scotch birth, is also a prominent citizen and one of the Renfrew Company's busiest and most energetic stockholders and managers. The Adamses, the Phillipses, H. T. Bliss, Cashier Wellington and others, are now among the active men of Adams.

There are no special summer homes in Adams; the town is too much of a manufacturing center and its industries are too much in the village to admit of it here, but, outside the village the situations for country seats are endless and summer visitors would live in a constant round of delights. Within a few years there has been an advance in permanent homes of architectural beauty and the hillsides scattered all through the town afford rare sites for them. The home of L. L. Brown, while unpretentious, is nevertheless a model, and his greenhouses are unexcelled, with possibly one exception, in the county. The Plunkett family home is also cozily situated in the village and has a home-like air. James Renfrew has built within a few years a large cottage of unique architecture on one of the slopes in the east part of the village which has one of the most commanding lookouts of the valley to be found in the village. The cottage of Mrs. Bliss, daughter of Daniel Upton, is a tasteful bit of architecture and well situated. A. B. Mole's new dwelling on the Savoy road and overlooking the village, is a fine addition to the town, and there are several other dwellings especially on the hill to the south, which are really artistic and model homes. The village has taken a new start in its homes recently and the move is creditable. The old Howland homestead, which is plainly seen from the railway at Zylonite station to the west, has been entirely remodeled within a few years and is the home of Emil Kipper, of the Zylonite Company. The exterior, while attractive, is not to be compared to the interior decorations, which are after the Egyptian style, largely, with choice furnishings, many of them from Cairo and Turkey.

We cannot leave Adams without a parting glance at Greylock. The ascent is now from the north towards Williamstown or North Adams. The road in North Adams, known as the Notch road, is utilized as a part of the new highway which was built to the summit in 1885. From the terminus of this Notch road, a new highway has been made, bridges have been constructed across the little mountain streams, so that it is a comparatively easy grade all the way to the summit, 8 or 10 miles.

GREYLOCK PARK.

To Berkshire and the town of Adams is accorded the king of the New England mountains, outside of the White Mountains—Greylock, the highest point in Massachusetts, 3,535 feet above sea level, and 2,800 feet above the valley of the Hoosac, at its base. Poets and writers have vied with each other, in song and sketch in praise of Greylock, a name applied to the peak from its resemblance to the grey locks of an old man, when the stern old summit is crowned with the frosts of winter or late autumn. The range or cluster, of which Greylock peak is the center and crowning feature, has six or seven distinct points of prominence, all within the space of about seven miles in the towns of Adams, Williamstown and North Adams, with a spur thrown off from the south through Cheshire, New Ashford and Lanesboro and ending in a slight hill in Pittsfield. The former name of the peak, taken in connection with the point next south, was Saddle Back, so named from its resemblance to a saddle, but the name Greylock, a fit appellation, as one sees it when the frosts of winter are crowning its summit, with its dome-like top often far above the clouds, is the poetic title and one that gives it significance and prominence the country over. Greylock Park is its new christening, now that improvements have been begun upon its summit and the approach thereto.

If Greylock stood alone in the center of a great plain, or even if the other and somewhat lesser mountains were carried away, its gigantic height would be more impressive; but the fellows of Greylock detract a good deal from its real glory, and one who stands in the village of Adams and looks fully into the breast of the monster pile, and then to the summit hardly realizes that he is gazing upward 2,800 feet. Its beauties and its attractions, its views and its morning panorama of peaks on peaks, and sleeping valleys and peaceful lakelets—Greylock by the early sunrise or the deepening sunset—all these have been woven into pleasant sketch, or poetic strain by pens like Fanny Kemble's, Catherine Sedgwick's, President Hitchcock's, Washington Gladden's, "Godfrey Greylock's," and many others. There is hardly a point in Berkshire from which Greylock cannot be seen, and its form is always discernable and recognizable from its graceful slope to the east. The nearer views of it are grander yet, and from those points where one looks directly into his stern old face, as from above Adams, Windsor, or Peru, there steals over the beholder a sense of awe and of majesty.

It always seems as if Greylock stood as a silent, yet ever watchful sentinel of the north portal of Berkshire and the valley below, conscious of his grandeur, and not a little proud of his few hundred feet of elevation more than his fellows on either side. One who rides by Greylock on the cars through Adams, and takes a good look upon its forest-covered side, with the gray frost lingering on the spruces which run up the eastern slope almost to the summit, can well agree with the application of the name, which many have asked the reason for, as on a clear winter morning it fairly glistens in the sunlight. It is cold, forbidding and stern except in summer, when its shaded sides invite rest and repose; and its summit, even from a distance, inspires one with the belief that Greylock must, from the very nature of things, be a most charming and sightly retreat. It is strange, however, that so few of the dwellers in Berkshire have been to the summit of Greylock and enjoyed for themselves the magnificent view here spread out on every hand. The narrow valley at its base seems cramped by the Saddle Back range on the west and the Green Mountains on the east; but when the summit is reached, there seems such a sense of relief; there is more "elbow room," as it were, while the eye feasts until weary on new scenes and new beauties; yet a day's sight leaves many, many interesting views yet untouched. It would take a week to analyze and digest all of them satisfactorily.

GREYLOCK PARK ASSOCIATION.

There are three ways of reaching Greylock; one west from the village of Adams, bearing a little north, and climbing directly up the sides, another through a portion of Cheshire, and the south part of Adams, following a wood road for some distance and then leaving teams and climbing for about two miles to the summit; the third was until recently by the way of the Notch, in North Adams, then walking the rest of the distance, through an easier grade, and yet a longer tramp, to the summit, from the northward. All these were hard jaunts, and that probably accounts for the fact that so few have ever seen the wonders of the realm round about from this lofty height. In 1885, the long-cherished hope of a road to the summit of the mountain crystallized into action, and a number of gentlemen in Northern Berkshire associated themselves together under the title of "The Greylock Park Association," and set about the improvement of the mountain summit. A highway was built from

North Adams in September and October, 1885. When the contemplated improvements are finished, Greylock will be a strong rival to other mountain-top resorts, and one of the most popular places in Berkshire.

The Greylock Park Association is composed of several enterprising gentlemen, and these officers: President, L. L. Brown; vice-president, W. B. Plunkett; clerk, S. Proctor Thayer; treasurer, W. W. Butler; directors, W. L. Brown, A. C. Houghton, James H. Flagg, George B. Perry, Austin Bond, A. W. Locke, W. B. Plunkett, J. C. Chalmers, of the Renfrew Manufacturing Company, H. H. Wellington, cashier of the National Bank of Adams, Franklin Carter, President of Williams College, and J. M. Waterman, and they remain practically the same. An act of the legislature was granted, authorizing the association to have a capital stock of $50,000, and it is authorized to hold 600 acres of land on the mountain. Governor Ames contributed $250 to the work. The first work of the association was in building the road, which has been completed at a cost of about $4,000. Later the association built an iron tower upon the summit. The tower is simply a frame with a well-protected platform at the top, and as the wind cannot secure a "hold" upon it, it seems safe to predict that it will stand for many years. The tower is some fifty feet high, and the view to be obtained from its top surpasses description. Other improvements made were the building of a double house, and a commodious log barn. The house affords welcome accommodations for visitors and is open during the summer. These improvements have made Greylock even more attractive, and the number of visitors increases every year.

Ascending the Mountain.

Parties desiring to ascend the mountain find the best facilities at North Adams. A message to the livery establishments will engage large or small wagons, made for mountain climbing, with safe horses and careful drivers. The turnout will meet the party at the depot and start at once for the summit. The rates are very reasonable.

With North Adams as a starting point, we begin the ascent. We follow the highway towards Braytonville, on the Williamstown road, a little way, and turn to the left and west, on the Notch road, as far as Mr. Walden's, where the new road of the association begins, three miles from North Adams. This notch road is also intersected by the road from Williamstown, as part of the old road to Adams, or the "Shelf road" overlooking North Adams. From Mr. Walden's house, the Greylock road passes through the hitherto unbroken forests, five miles farther, to the summit. The grade is easy all the way; there are no steep ascents, for the building of the road has been of the most thorough character. The association has taken a strip five rods wide all the way through the forest, in order that the shade may be maintained, and also that adjoining land owners, who may wish to cut their timber, cannot encroach upon the drive. Two miles up the mountain from Walden's, we cross Money Brook over a strong bridge.

THE HOPPER.

Near here is the famous Hopper, down into which from the top one may look a thousand feet, its sides, steep and rugged, overhung with shrubs and trees and vines. The woods at this point in the highway are to be cleared away, so that tourists may obtain a view of this great abyss to greater advantage. Several slides have occurred on the slopes of the Hopper, one of them 1,600 feet in length. The most remarkable one of all was in 1784, when a dwelling house was swept away, though the inmates escaped.

PAUSING FOR A FORETASTE.

Near Money Brook is "Wilbur's Clearing," as it is called, and we stop for a short time to breathe and to take a look at the view which is beginning to be a slight foretaste of the summits. It is such a superb scene to the north and west! Williamstown and the college are sleeping down in the valley, and, away beyond, are the Taconics on the one hand, the Green Mountains to the northeast, and we follow the Hoosac as it winds through the meadows and the pass towards Pownal, and so on its way until it is lost like a thread in the distance. North Adams is seen occasionally below, and a background for miles is the Hoosac range, to the east of the village, and away on to Clarksburg and Stamford. Even this view, only part way up the mountain side, is almost sufficient to take the breath away, and creates a desire to linger on the scene before us. Three miles more of easy riding,—eight miles from North Adams, for a good horse easily carries two in a buggy all the way with little effort,—and, emerging from the woods into an open space, we are at the very summit of Greylock. The view bursts upon the vision in all its grandeur on a clear day, and we are glad now that we did not linger to merely *lunch* on the more limited view from the "Clearing," three miles below, but came at once to partake of the genuine *feast* offered on the summit of this lofty, stern old peak.

The "Near View."

The pen cannot describe the scene; for over 100 miles in all directions, the view is laid out before the beholder. Five states can be looked into with ease,—Massachusetts, Vermont, New Hampshire, Connecticut, and New York. It is claimed that with a strong glass the shipping in New York harbor can be seen with ease. The "near view" down below us enchanted us more at first; there was an irresistible desire to see from whence, and to where, we had come since we left the busy village two hours before, and we looked down from a perch, as it were; for the valley seemed only a little way off, and yet so small and insignificant. The Hoosac River was flowing like a silver thread in the bright sunlight through the valley, with graceful, serpentine curves. We could follow it from its very source now; in fact, both sources of the two branches,—one creeping lazily through the meadows from Cheshire through Adams, and so along to North Adams; the north branch, from its mountain pond in Stamford, rushing and tumbling down the hillside and joining its sister stream in North Adams, and both tripping along merrily through Williamstown and on to the west in its course to the Hudson.

Like a bird in mid-heaven, we looked down at Adams, now a little, diminutive village, as it were, and yet apparently only a little way off. To the north of us, in this near view, was Williamstown,—a picture of quiet contentment as it sat with the great hills all about it and the college buildings the center of the amphitheatre. To the west, we looked down into the little hamlet of New Ashford, and then on beyond that to the other valley in New York State, apparently only a stone's throw away. Southward lay Cheshire village, so near as almost to leave the impression for a moment that we could speak to the pigmy of a man we saw somewhere near it. Pittsfield, with its lakes and encircling hills and mountain tops farther on, was in easy sight, its spires shimmering in the sun, and the village lying in the center of a plain, which looked even larger than we had imagined.

This was the "near view" that we instinctively longed to take first. Then, as we ascended we looked out in each direction in successive order, gradually extending it, as we took in peak after peak and point after point, with the "near view" as the beginning, in each point of the compass. The mountain tops rolled out before us as the waves of the ocean come, one by one, as we allowed the eye to take them in. To the north were numberless points, with villages occasionally, valleys whose depths we could not see, and a clear range of the Green Mountains for at least thirty miles, or until the eye could see no longer.

A Far Sweep of Vision.

But we get tired of looking. That is the trouble of Greylock; and still you cannot rest, for the temptation is too strong for "just one more look." Northwestward, the Adirondacks are plainly seen in their prominent points, and from Greylock and one of their summits the surveyors in the United States coast survey, a few years ago, signaled each other by flashlights in the process of their work. To the east are Monadnock, in New Hampshire, and Wachusett, in plain view, and scores of smaller points, while Mounts Tom and Holyoke, in the Connecticut Valley, are apparently but a little more than neighbors from where we stand. Southward the eye takes in the Dome of the Taconics, the southern sentinel of Berkshire, and a fellow guard with Greylock of the two portals of the county. The whole space between is literally sprinkled with mountains and hilltops, and with lakelet gems on every hand reflecting them in the sunlight. The prettiest view to many minds is that southward covering the entire length of the county, and taking in most of the "grand old hills of Berkshire." The eye does not stop with the Dome, but wanders farther on into Connecticut; and, westward of the southern views, takes in the Catskills. The beholder realizes what human weakness is when he longs for the words that shall express the volumes of thought and emotions that swell his brain and heart. He is filled with delight, with awe, with reverence, at the outlook, which inspires him with a grander idea of Creation and of God. Here is true sublimity, and its emotion, mingled with numerous others, ill defined but powerful, moves the observer to the very depths and impresses him with the majesty of Nature.

Vastness, Beauty and Sublimity.

Of the view from this mountain, Prof. Hitchcock says: "I know of no place where the mind is so forcibly impressed by the idea of vastness, and even of immensity, as when the eye ranges abroad from this eminence. I have rarely, if ever, experienced such a pleasing change from the emotion of beauty to that of sublimity, as at this spot. The moment one fixes his eye upon the valley of Williamstown, he cannot but exclaim, 'how beautiful!' But ere he is aware of it, his eye is following up and onward the vast mountain slopes; and, in the far off horizon, he beholds intervening ridge after ridge, peering above one another, until they are lost in the distance; and unconsciously he finds his heart swelling with the emotions of sublimity; nor can the soul of piety cease its musings here, until the tribute of reverence has been paid to that Eternal Power who has driven asunder these everlasting mountains."

THOREAU ABOVE THE CLOUDS.

A sunrise view is particularly transporting. The lighting up of this great panorama, as on the sunbeams come, to open all this grandeur gradually to view, is not only inspiring, but sublime. Of this scene, Thoreau breaks forth into the most ravishing descriptions as the sum of all his sight-seeing and the fruition of more than his fancy had pictured. "I was up early," he writes, "and perched upon the top of the tower to see the day break. As the light increased, I discovered around me an ocean of mist, which reached up by chance exactly to the base of the tower, and shut out every vestige of the earth, while I was left floating on this fragment of the wreck of a world,—on my carved plank in cloud-land, a situation which it required no aid from the imagination to render impressive. There was not a crevice left through which the trivial places we name—Massachusetts, Vermont and New York—could be seen. All around me was spread for a hundred miles, on every side, an undulating country of clouds. It was such a country as we might see in dreams, with all the delights of Paradise. When the sun began to rise on this pure world, I found myself a dweller in the dazzling halls of Aurora,—into which poets have had but a partial glance over the Eastern hills,—drifting among the saffron-colored clouds, and playing with the rosy fingers of the Dawn, in the very path of the Sun's chariot, and sprinkled with its dewy dust, enjoying the benignant smile, and, near at hand, the far darting glances of the god. The inhabitants of Earth behold commonly but the dark and shadowy underside of heaven's pavement; it is only when at a favorable angle of the horizon, morning and evening, that some faint streaks of the rich lining of the clouds are revealed. But my muse would fail to convey an impression of the gorgeous tapestry by which I was surrounded, such as men see faintly reflected afar off in the chambers of the east. Here, as on Earth, I saw the gracious god

> 'Flatter the mountain tops with sovereign eye. * * *
> Gilding pale streams with heavenly alchemy.'"

When Mr. Thoreau descended the mountain he found himself in the region of clouds and drizzling rain, though he had previously had no suspicion of rain.

GREYLOCK'S FUTURE.

To make this mountain more of a resort, the Park Association made the improvements already described. A year or two since an iron tower forty feet high was erected and this affords a beautiful view over the treetops; so that one may look almost directly into the village of North

Adams. Mr. L. L. Brown is the new president of the Association and at this writing a good many improvements are projected. It is said the Fichburg railroad are also contemplating taking an interest in the scheme, in order to make it a place of resort for people who naturally come over their line.

The sunrise view is grand beyond description. The valley below is ordinarily shrouded in a misty fog, as the sun comes over the eastern hills after leaving Monadnock. Gradually as the mist clears away, the hill-tops come out and resemble great islands in what before had been a vast sea. The spires of the churches begin to prick through the mist; then the stacks of the factories below. It is a beautiful sight, and one never to be forgotten. It is worth rising from one's couch in the cabins on the summit to drink in a beauty that words or pen cannot describe. The writer, who has spent several nights on the summit to obtain the early view, has distinctly heard sounds in the village of Adams, five miles below in the valley, the whistling to dogs, or the loud shout re-echoed against the mountain-side. The sight of the lights, coming out, one by one, in the village below in the early evening, is also a novel sensation; reminding one of the coming out of the stars. The memory of a night on the summit, in the silence of the great vastness that settles over one, leaving the visitor to his own reflections, or possibly a communion with the great Creator, is one never to be effaced.

The project of another road, leading from Pittsfield to Lanesboro, thence up an easy grade, direct to the summit of Greylock, received quite an impetus last year, and if this is done, southern and central Berkshire will find it more convenient to visit the summit than now. A favorite plan is to go to Adams by the afternoon train, and make the trip on foot by the circuitous foot-path to the summit. This taking the pedestrians from Adams, past the Old Quaker Church and the locality of the Quaker settlement and the home of Susan B. Anthony. Greylock is worth a visit by the tourist, either for a day's entire restfulness, the sunrise view, or the impression that strikes him of the immensity of the scene. Water will be brought to the summit, and many other improvements made. Already about $13,000 have been raised and will be expended. In time, cottages will be erected, and there is talk that some day in the near future, a road from Adams will also be built, so that tourists may make the ascent by one drive, and the descent by the other.

The mountain-side is full of interesting views and charming, rugged bits of scenery. The Hopper is of itself a study, and the Cascade is also on this route. The return trip from the mountain summit to the Wilson

House in North Adams, can easily be made in an hour and fifteen minutes, though three may well be occupied in the leisurely ascent. Such wonderful, sublime and soul-satisfying views are the glory of Berkshire, for, as a means of bringing one in contact with the grandeur as well as the repose of nature, Greylock has no equal; while its attractions, enhanced by the art of man, for the accommodation of those who seek its retreat, will make it in time the great object of visitation in all the "Berkshire Hills."

TYRINGHAM.

THE sightly location at "Fernside," the pure mountain air and water, the good table and the various accommodations of the place attract many summer and autumn guests every year. The elevation of the eight houses, barns and many outbuildings at "Fernside" is 1,160 feet above the ocean; that of the highest point on the property, 1,900 feet; the mountain some distance back is 2,200 feet high. These mountains are easily accessible. "Fernside" lies on the southern, steep slope of the narrow Hop Brook Valley in Tyringham, three miles from the railway at South Lee, and but a short distance from the Tyringham post-office. The scenery from the premises is some of Berkshire's best. Prof. Gildersleeve of Johns Hopkins University, says that this is the only place he was ever in where he could walk all day and find a new and charming view every five minutes. This may, indeed, be true. After enjoying the sights near the buildings, one is ambitious to climb the mountain to the southward and westward. A good path has been prepared through bushes and woodland and over pastures, and a delightful walk it is to follow its easy ascent.

THE SHAKERS.

As early as 1792 a society of Shakers was organized in Tyringham, consisting of nine members at first. They purchased a large tract of land and made two settlements—one at "Fernside," and the other half a mile west. The community soon numbered 100 and once it contained 185, and until after the middle of the present century it was very flourishing; but, in 1858, 23 of their number ran away at one time, and in 1874 their number was so reduced that they sold their property in Tyringham and joined the communities at Hancock, Enfield and New Lebanon.

MOUNT HOREB.

The summit of the first mountain is bald and is covered with grass; there, the prospect is beautiful, magnificent, imposing, charming—everything. The place was selected for their "Horeb" by the Shakers in 1844. They received the suggestion from Isaiah II-2: "And it shall come to pass in the last days, that the mountain of the Lord's house shall be established in the top of the mountains and shall be exalted

"FERNSIDE," TYRINGHAM.

above the hills, and all nations shall flow unto it." These places were selected under the supposed influence of divine messengers from Heaven. Every Shaker society in the land has its Mount. When the Shakers, then living at "Fernside," desired to locate their Mount, a dozen or more set out one day and stopped where the controlling spirit commanded them to stop, and that place was the mountain we have mentioned. There they cleared a small piece of ground and built a fence around it and an inner fence around the spiritual fount, and erected a marble monument, with an engraven message on both sides purporting to come from God, himself, warning all to keep sacred the grounds and never desecrate them. The Shakers held services there for several years and finally discontinued them, after which the warning on the monument was violated and it was carried away piecemeal for relics. The base stone is now left, somewhat mutilated in breaking off mementoes. The Shaker burying ground is also on the premises. The stones lie flat on the graves after the Moravian fashion. The oldest is dated 1793.

Dr. Jones's "Fernside."

The Shakers' original building was erected in 1776, but was torn down in 1881. An old building, still standing and now used as a shop, is over 100 years old. The house built next was a brick one, put up in 1823, as indicated by a tablet of marble with the date chiseled in it. The Shakers were running out, and they left in 1875, selling the buildings and about 1,200 acres of land to Dr. Joseph Jones, of Honesdale, Pa., who is the present proprietor, looking after the comforts of his guests with unremitting attention.

Among his guests have been the following: The Rev. Dr. James Mason Knox, Bristol, Pa.; Mrs. N. P. Willis, widow of the poet: Prof. H. D. Noyes, John J. Wood, Charles D. Neufville, J. Evarts Tracy, E. Vermilye, all of New York; W. H. Matthews, New Orleans; Prof. Edward S. Doubleday, Brooklyn; E. Smith Kelly, Philadelphia; H. J. Haynsworth, Albany; Prof. H. Rowland, of Johns Hopkins University.

The outlook from the buildings, or from almost any portion of the farm, is exceedingly fine. The spires of Lee and Lenox rise far to the north, with dreamy blue hills in the distance. Towards the east at your feet, (for you are high up on a breezy summit, from which you can look complacently down on the morning fogs) lies a broad, fertile plain stretching away towards the north as far as Lee. Towards the southeast three-quarters of a mile away, and hidden by a round, bald-headed hill called the Cobble, the village of Tyringham is snugly nestled in the valley. The air is delightfully cool and refreshing; in the warmest seasons and at all times of the day, a breeze is constantly perceptible.

Fine drives abound on every hand, through Lenox, Stockbridge, Lee, and Great Barrington. The road from Monterey shows a magnificent view from the top of the mountain. The walks are unlimited all over the mountain and valley, exposing ever changing views of the highest charms. Mr. L. B. Moore a few years ago converted his cozy farm house into a summer home naming it "Riverside," and the past season he has had to enlarge and beautify and improve it. He has a delightful location on the main road through the village. Several New York families come to Riverside for a whole summer's rest and recreation. Here are other houses in the village, where boarders are taken in the summer, amid surroundings of no common order. Stage leaves Tyringham 3:45 P. M.; Lee, 2:30 P. M.

NEW MARLBORO.

SECLUDED, quiet and healthful, New Marlboro village is situated at an elevation of 1,470 feet above the sea. The whole North Parish, as this village and its neighborhood are sometimes called, is an elevated plateau of more than a thousand acres, with rims of higher hills around portions of the northern and eastern horizon, while off to the south and southwest and northwest are miles of hill and valley, woodland and meadow, with mountains rising one above another in the distance, all together forming one of the grandest panoramas that even Southern Berkshire can boast. To the southeast, as one looks from near the South Berkshire House, is the pretty little village of Southfield, perched on a mountain terrace and half shut in by wooded hill.

The village people have begun to give portions of their houses to summer guests, but the principal accommodations are given at the South Berkshire House with accommodations for about 150 people. This village was first made a summer resort by I. N. Tuttle in 1878 and he since obtained possession of the South Berkshire Institute buildings, after the school was abandoned. The boarders at this house find a phase of the best country life, and they value it particularly for their children, who have a large area of clean ground to play upon, where their noise is not annoying. The boarders pass time in many agreeable ways suitable to their surroundings, in outdoor life, in games, dancing, theatricals, etc. The music rooms of the Institute open into each other *en suite*, afford ample room for indoor entertainment, and the school-room has been provided with a permanent stage, curtain, etc., for amateur theatricals. Picnics and drives around the wild and picturesque country are had frequently, and fishing and hunting receive the attention of their devotees. Four sets of lawn tennis are provided for the guests and there is room for all of them at once in the village park, as well as room for two sets on the Institute grounds. Wells & Jenks are the proprietors.

In 1881 Marvin Chapin, proprietor of the Massasoit House in Springfield, was driving over the hills in Southern Berkshire and stopped at Mr. Tuttle's with the intention of staying only one night and then resuming his journey. He was so pleased with the place that he remained eight days and came again next year with his family and stayed several weeks. Seth H. Moseley, proprietor of the New Haven House in New Haven, Ct., came along in a precisely similar way,—discovered the house by accident, as it were, tarried a few days and came again the next year. The proprietors of these famous hotels have stayed at Mr. Tuttle's many summers. A large number of its guests have come year after year; among them are the following: John L. Drummond, C. E. Mallor, R. Major, Mrs. M. A. White, H. Carter, all of New York; H. B. Vandervere, Aug. Colson, Chris. Joost, all of Brooklyn; Frank A. Monson, New Haven, Conn.; F. W. Keith, D. H. Clark, both of Stamford, Conn.; Judge Turner, New London, Conn.

NATURAL OBJECTS OF INTEREST.

The exceedingly interesting drives around New Marlboro are numerous. Lake Buel, situated partly in the northwestern corner of the town 3¼ to 5 miles distant, according to whether one goes to Gibson's or Turner's, is a delightful lake, a mile and a half long, where the accommodations are ample for every purpose.

Lake Garfield in Monterey, a little larger than Lake Buel, is 5 miles distant, and there visitors are well provided for.

The Otis Reservoir, the largest natural lake in the county, is 11 miles away, and a lovely lake it is, too.

The Cat Hole in the southwestern part of the town, about three miles northeast of Clayton, is a natural cave of several chambers. The descent is rather difficult, and few persons but boys would care to go into it in the present condition of its entrance.

CAMPBELL'S FALLS.

In the south part of the town on the state line, about three miles east of Clayton, are Campbell's Falls, where the Whiting River pours about 80 feet down rocks, in an almost perpendicular fall. Above the falls are numerous cascades where the stream flows through a dark, wild ravine, and below is a gorge walled in by steep, wooded and rocky mountain sides, seven or eight hundred feet high. The falls are the resort of many picnic parties. A saw mill used to be on the rocks above the falls and from its carriage, which was made to slide out over the abyss, a little girl once fell to the bottom, a distance of about 95 feet, but she survived and lived to be over 90 years old.

In the Umpachene Falls, where the Umpachene stream joins the Konkapot, a little below Mill River on the road to Clayton, the water de-

"Gibson's Landing," Lake Buel.

scends over quartz rock by two leaps, to a depth of about 30 feet, the upper cataract being about 10 feet. Though there is nothing striking about these falls, they are an interesting natural object.

Eastward of New Marlboro in Sandisfield and Otis is a sparsely settled country where the Green Mountains are divided by deep gorges and wild streams, and covered with forests.

TIPPING ROCK.

Tipping Rock, two miles off, a little below Southfield village, is a great curiosity. A huge boulder, weighing 40 tons was left here by the retreating glacier of the ice age, on the bed rock on the summit of a low hill, where the stranger has ever since abided, so well balanced that the strength of one finger can rock the huge mass, yet many oxen could not overturn it. There are but few of these boulders in the world.

Favorite excursions outside of the town are to Stockbridge, Lenox, Great Barrington, Monument Mountain, Bashbish and the Dome.

The autumn foliage in New Marlboro is gorgeous, as may be understood from the following description by a resident: "The grand panorama is now spread before us in all its magic beauty; north, south, east and west it is the same wonderful, flaming, shading, rioting of color; every maple blazing at top with tint of scarlet or orange, every ash tree turned from green to straw color, every birch tree shimmering and quivering in the sun, as if golden beads were strung upon its branches; sumachs turned into ladders of fire; poplars marked and spotted with vermilion; not a single tree left of solid green, except the pines, firs and hemlocks, which look darker and greener than ever by contrast with the masses of flashing color."

In an old brass foundry blacksmith shop, that was situated on the eastern edge of the village on the stream, Elihu Burritt worked over an anvil two or three years about 1833.

New Marlboro is reached from Great Barrington, 9 miles distant, every day except Sunday by a stage that leaves at 1:30 P. M. Stage leaves New Marlboro at 7:30 A. M.

MILL RIVER.

Mill River is a village lying three miles to the southwest in a narrow valley through which the Konkapot flows, 8 miles from Great Barrington, from which place a daily stage leaves at 1:30, except on Sundays. A few summer boarders are kept in this village at the hotel and at private houses.

CLAYTON.

Clayton, in the southwest corner of the town, is 2¼ miles from the Ashley Falls station of the Housatonic railroad, and is a place that city people would find delightful for summer residence. Here are the China Clay Works, where a high quality of clay was for many years mined and prepared for the use of paper makers in giving paper a finish, for making fine crockery, vulcanizing rubber, making "pure lead" paints, soap, face powder, fire bricks, lead pencils, crayons, and for kalsomining. Mr. Taft's "Elm Brook Farm," is a fine one of 600 acres, 400 of which are cultivated and produce a great quantity of crops. It is one of the model Berkshire farms, with beautiful home buildings, which are charmingly situated on the banks of the Konkapot River.

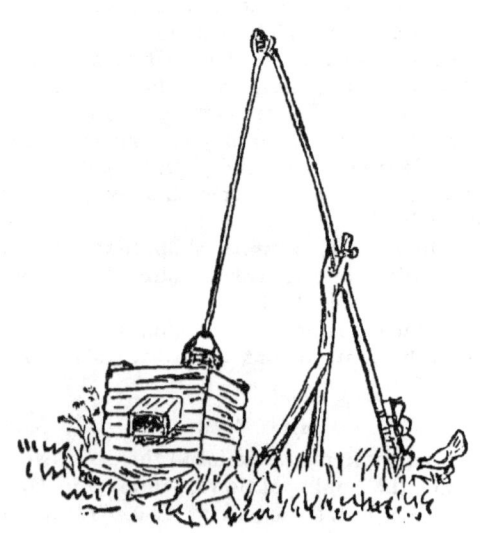

LEE.

LEE is a very small name for a beautiful, and what Yankees call a smart town. Franklin Chamberlin, the Centennial orator of Lee, who has had abundant opportunities for studying the scenery and institutions of both the old and new world, thus compliments this town: "Nestling among the foot hills of these mountain ranges, midway between old Greylock on the north and Mount Washington on the south, and divided by the swiftly flowing Housatonic (a river beautiful in name and in all its bed and border, from its source in lake and mountain spring, down among its wooded hills and pleasant valleys to its outlet in the sound), Lee has enough of beauty to satisfy the desires of its children, while they remain at home, and to be a pleasant memory when they are away."

Many portions of Lee are exceedingly beautiful; indeed, the whole western part is the same as the Stockbridge and Lenox region in character. Into this territory the country home purchasers will come in time when they are crowded from making purchases in the neighboring towns. The people of Lee have never encouraged the coming of city people to stay here for the season and the boarding houses in town are few though they are placed where very good entertainment is given. The Morgan House, in the center of the town, is under good management, and the accommodations are good for transient guests. A few natives or old-time residents of the town come back annually for a summer's sojourn, or casually to mingle again with old-time pleasant associations, and to keep unbroken old-time friendship or to renew old acquaintanceship. Aside from these and a few summer boarders, the comers to Lee are from neighboring towns, bent on enjoying the many attractions the town has.

FERN CLIFF.

On the east of the village of Lee and in close proximity to it rises the rocky eminence called Fern Cliff, the summit of which is crowned with a beautiful grove of hemlocks. This is the trysting place of the villagers, and no spot could be more charming for picnics, and walks and talks by daylight, or moonlight. This cliff extends about a third of a mile parallel with the village, and pleasant, shady walks, commanding delightful and ever varying views, traverse the whole distance. At the north end stands a large boulder of gneiss, called Union Rock, probably from the union of so many hearts consummated on this favorite resort of young lovers. On its broad back a dozen couples can stand at once and trace the windings of the Housatonic at its base and through the distant meadows, and satisfy their eyes with the cultivated farms to be seen at the north and west, while the grand hills of Beartown stand out prominently in the south. The Rev. Dr. Barnas Sears, for many years president of Brown University and accustomed to Berkshire scenery, having been born in Sandisfield, once visited Fern Cliff, and was so charmed with its walks, trees, and views, that he said, "If I am ever able to retire from public life, I should like to build a cottage and spend the evening of my days on this delightful eminence." This cliff is 200 feet above the village and on one side is a small cave.

A half hour's walk to the top of East Mountain (one can drive very near) shows a fine view of the Catskills and a good deal of Berkshire territory. The drive over Washington Mountain shows a magnificent view of Pittsfield and the surrounding country, far and near, with the illusion of bringing Greylock to within half its real distance; drive via Lenox Furnace, Ashley Lake, and return via New Lenox. Another delightful drive is to come from Monterey over the road to "Fernside," to get views of wonderful effect from the summit of the mountain. The drives to Lenox, to "Fernside," to South Lee over the Merrill Hill, to Beartown, to Lake May, to Lake Mahkeenac, and Bald Head Mountain, are so full of changing beauty that they never tire though repeated a hundred times.

LAUREL LAKE.

One of the most charming features in the scenery of Lee is Laurel Lake, a beautiful sheet of water, covering some six hundred acres, and situated in the northwest part of the town. The outline of this lakelet is marked by bays and capes, and one bold, rocky promontory; and its shores, here and there beautified with groves of pine, hemlock and maple, are remarkably free from swamps. The land rises in gentle slopes from the water, furnishing beautiful sites for country seats, which have been generally appreciated and purchased. At the east of Laurel Lake rises a graceful eminence on which Arthur Gilman, of Cambridge, built an attractive cottage and laid out pleasant grounds, all since sold by him.

In South Lee, just below the dam of the Hurlbut Paper Company, one may see hundreds of "pot holes" in the bed rock of the river, so plenty here that no one notices them, though such holes are great curiosities in other regions. A rock in the meadow on the east side of the river, a very short distance north of the South Lee railway station, observed from the railway, looks like an elephant lying down.

The quarries in Lee have furnished marble for a large part of St. Patrick's cathedral in New York, the Philadelphia Trust and Safe Deposit building, the new City Hall in Philadelphia, and in that city the Farmers' and Mechanics' bank, the enlargement of Girard college; the two wings of the Capitol at Washington, part of Washington Monument, and for the soldiers' head-stones in the national cemeteries. The marble for the extension of the State house at Boston, is quarried here.

Lee is famous all over the country for its paper manufacture. Here paper was first made in 1806 in South Lee village. In less than 50 years the town made more paper in quantity and value than any other town in the United States, and only three cities are now ahead of it in the value of their paper. The Smith Paper Company is one of the principle ones of the country, and makes 160 tons a week of news, book and manilla, besides many tons of wood pulp. This was the first company in the United States to make paper partly of wood pulp and get an established sale for it. Wellington Smith, the manager of the business, has been Executive Councilor, member of the national republican convention of 1880, and president of the American Paper Manufacturers' Association. The famous "French Linen" paper is made by the Hurlbut Paper Company in South Lee, a paper that carried the highest honors at the international competition at Paris in 1873 and at Philadelphia in 1876.

A sadly memorable day in East Lee was April 20, 1886, when the dam of Mud Pond, in the mountain, near Becket, gave way.

The water descended four miles to the Housatonic River, two miles of the distance being through the village, confined in the narrow valley. Every building bordering the stream was wrecked, several dams and bulkheads demolished, seven lives were lost and damage was done amounting to a quarter of a million. The scene of devastation was fearful.

HORSES.

The horse breeding farm of the late Elizur Smith at "Highlawn Farm" on the south side of Laurel Lake, is one of the notable ones of the United States, whose fame has gone far and wide. The farm itself consists of 700 acres of highly cultivated land situated in a very sightly location, and of several hundred acres of leased land. It is drained by 37 miles of tile, has all kinds of machines and steam engine for operating them, has eight separate sets of large barns, and six wind mills that pump water through five miles of pipe. The stud was established in 1882 and soon grew to large proportions; it now consists of the stallions "Alcantara" and "Alcyone," each a $20,000 horse, "Montezuma," a beautiful $4,000 stallion, about 50 mares and more or less colts, making about 100 animals in all, worth $150,000 or more, besides the 700 acres of land, which may be worth $200 to $500 an acre, according to the notion of the purchaser. Farm and all, there is probably no other so costly a horse breeding establishment in the United States. Those who visit the farm on business are entertained at a private hotel on the premises, where the surroundings are decidedly agreeable. Visitors and purchasers come from all over the eastern part of the United States, as far south as Washington and as far west as Kentucky.

One of the notable collections of orchids in the United States, was for many years, that of De Witt Smith, in Lee, whose greenhouses were visited by many in winter, when orchids are at their best. These orchids came from New Grenada, Brazil, the Andes, Gautemala, Oaxaca, Mexico, Assam, Burmah, Rangoon, Java, Manilla and other of the Phillipine islands, Japan, Madagascar, United States of Colombia, Costa Rica, the Rio Negro Choco, Bogota, La Guayra, Nepaul, Mount Ophir, Chiriqui, Borneo, Syllhet, Moulmein, Australia, the Himalayas, Guaina, Peru, Guayaquil, Organ mountains, Arracan mountains, Trinidad, Panama, Khoosea hills, Island of Pulo-Copang in the Chinese sea, the Malay islands, and parts of India, Africa, the East Iudies, South America, Mexico, Central America, the West Indies, and the far East, not mentioned The collection has recently been sold to a New York party, much to the regret of Berkshire people.

SANDISFIELD.

FEW towns in Berkshire abound more in the wild scenery, romantic drives, and delightful look-offs from its elevations than Sandisfield. At New Boston there is a good hotel, kept by Mr. C. H. Hunt, where summer guests occasionally pass a few weeks. Of late there has been some inquiry for "abandoned farms" for summer homes, and it is probable that within a few years many of these quiet places will be occupied in that manner. The drive from New Boston to Otis, some ten miles, along the west bank of the Farmington river, is pronounced by a gentleman who has made the whole tour of Berkshire, either in driving, bicycling, or on foot, as the most romantic and entertaining of any in the county.

This location in the summer is a desirable one for any one seeking retirement and quiet, and one of the most healthful localities in the country. The elevated situation commands an expansive view of the surrounding country, at once romantic and attractive. A lover of fine scenery, embracing a wide stretch of country, would at once be attracted to this location, and the bracing atmosphere and salubrious water are conducive to health and enjoyment. Distance from Great Barrington or Winsted, Conn., 15 miles. Stage leaves Winsted 1.00 P. M. and Westfield at 1.30 P. M., and leaves Sandisfield for those towns early in the morning. Not so richly endowed with lake scenery as Monterey and Otis, Sandisfield possesses a full share of the hill and valley prospects, which are the common heritage of the county. There are no summer hotels, strictly speaking, but many of the farmers' families receive guests for the season, and those who find them out get their money's worth in health as well as pleasure.

OTIS.

THE region included in the towns of Monterey, Otis, and Sandisfield is a broad upland tract, agreeably broken with hill and mountain summits, 1,500 to 1,800 feet above tide. The people, so far as the "old stock" at least goes, are plain, warm-hearted country folk, hospitable and intelligent, always ready to enjoy the society of strangers who come for a season of rest and wholesome rural pleasure, and to help in making their stay pleasant. But city people have not yet actually appropriated the region, as they have some other places, so that those who do resort there are sure of country life in the true, old-fashioned sense of the word.

Otis, sloping down to the valley of the Farmington, has always been noted for the number and beauty of its so-called "ponds." Those who never care how far removed they may be from railway facilities, find them a never failing delight. The largest, lying off in the lonely wooded basin near East Otis, Rand Pond or the Reservoir, as it is called, is known through all Berkshire and northwestern Connecticut, as an unrivaled fishing place. It looks much like an Adirondack lake, so wild are the surroundings. The water, after issuing from this lake, has a rapid descent over precipitous ledges of rocks, forming what are known as Otis Falls. When viewed from an advantageous point, in this romantic and weird ravine, the scene is grand and sublime. In the southerly part of Rand Pond is a floating island of considerable extent. It is composed of débris and the tangled and matted roots of shrubbery, and when one walks over it a quaking motion is imparted to it, extending some distance on either side. Thirteen lakes, great and small, are situated in this town. Rand Pond is the largest body of water in the county, and Great Lake, a mile from it, is next in size. The drive from Lee to Otis is a delightful one, and abounds in many pretty views, while the stage road is well kept and of easy grade. Within the past year or two, a number of gentlemen from Lee have leased a pretty sheet of water called "Shaw Pond," about eight miles from Lee and on the direct road between there and Otis, have built a pavilion, cleared up the shrubbery and thus made it a delightful camping ground, and also, by the cottages put up, a fine place for an extended stay for themselves and families.

There are many pretty drives between Otis village and Sandisfield or down the river, through New Boston to Colebrook and Winsted. Otis has for years been the resort of sportsmen and people fond of camp life. Its reputation stands high among such people in Springfield, and it is their habit to visit the town every season. Several residents of the town take summer boarders, who may be sure of good entertainment.

ALFORD.

THE quiet village of Alford is beginning to attract summer visitors who become attached to the place, for its rustic peculiarities, its native beauties and wild belongings. The drives are fine to Egremont, Great Barrington, Green River, White's Hill, State Line, and West Stockbridge, and there is no end of walks in all directions, and of all varieties. Tom Ball Mountain on the east is of high elevation and commands a varied and extensive outlook. A few rods back of Mr. Fitch's quarry is the Frying Pan Spring, a place where water, falling in a cavity in the ground, makes the peculiar sound of a large frying-pan over a hot fire. One must not fail to visit Crowned Head, so named by Mrs A. D. T. Whitney, so truthfully described by her in her book, "Odd or Even," written in this town: "We climbed the steep sides and reached the summit, to view one of the grandest landscapes ever spread out for human eyes to feast upon. The mountains stand around like huge sentinels to guard the little hamlets scattered up and down the valley. We see the Hudson River, like a golden thread, while above and beyond the grand old Catskills pile up like mighty snow drifts, lost in the blue of heaven." Stage leaves Great Barrington at 3 P. M., leaves Alford at 11 A. M.

WEST STOCKBRIDGE.

WEST STOCKBRIDGE has many attractive features, and the town is romantically situated for the summer residences of city people. From this town there is a wild drive over the mountain to Stockbridge. West Stockbridge Center is the "old parish" of the town, and while of easy access, is probably the most perfectly secluded village in south Berkshire. Its views are very fine, with the Dome to crown all, off on the southwestern horizon. Here has been for over a generation the home of the Rev. Lewis Pennell, whose life-long devotion to Hebrew studies has earned for him among his brethren of the cloth, the title of Rabbi. The quarries of the town have furnished marble for many buildings in cities, among them being the old City Hall in New York, part of Girard College, and of the State House at Boston. There is a small natural cavern in the southern part of the town.

The mountain called Tom Ball, situated in this town, though it is equally accessible from Alford, affords one of the most charming outlooks to be found in Berkshire from mountain summits. The ascent is not very easy, because of tangled forest, clifts and general steepness, but, when once accomplished, the views on every side are intensely effective. The range of vision is wide, both in points of compass and in distance. This mountain is one of those picturesque elevations so common in Berkshire, rising abruptly from the adjacent valleys, without foot hills to dwarf them. Tom Ball, like many other summits in the county, is neither of the Taconics nor the Green Mountains, but stands in proud independence, apart from the main mountain ranges.

BECKET.

THE general elevation of this town is about 1,200 feet, its breezes are delightfully cool and invigorating and there is no malaria. The scenery is wild and romantic in places. Boulders of almost every kind abound, and in this town we are truly among the "Granite Hills," for this stone is prevalent and there are some fine quarries of it in this part of the range. It is indeed one of the summit towns of the county. North Becket, the principal place of business, is a thrifty and clean little village of 500 people, lying along the branch of the river; Becket Center is farther to the south, delightfully situated; and West Becket is near the town line of Lee and Tyringham, on the south end. The mountain scenery is varied and grand in different parts of the town. Becket Mountain, in the northwest part is only two and one-half miles from the Claflin House at North Becket, and is 2,194 feet high; it is easy of access, and almost at its feet is the Bulkley, Dunton & Co.'s reservoir. Wadsworth Mountain is three miles south of North Becket, about 2,000 feet high, and from its summit the steeples of seven churches can be counted.

In the vicinity of the village (North Becket) are Yokun Lake, so named from the Indian chief who lived near there, and Center Lake, both of which are attractive sheets of water. There are many others, in different parts of the town, but the two first named, and Greenwater Pond, are easy of access.

The Claflin House, owned and kept by W. A. Schlesinger, is an excellent and popular resort, accommodating 50 guests. His guests are mainly families who come from New York, Brooklyn, New Jersey, St. Louis, Hartford, St. Paul, New Orleans, Washington, and even Louisiana. Some of the towns-people take boarders at their farm houses.

The former residents of the town, who have gone away and become wealthy, remember it with pleasure and within a few years a fine library building, called the "Athenæum," has been built by the donations of the town's loyal sons who have been blessed with means in other places. Many of the farmers of the town accommodate summer guests. The drives in all directions, either to Lee, Lenox, Pittsfield, or across the country to the higher lands of Peru and Chesterfield, are fine.

CLAFLIN HOUSE.

MONTEREY.

MONTEREY has drawn to its boarding houses of late years a goodly number of summer guests—houses environed by the majesty of beauty afforded by extensive vistas of glorious scenery of vale and mount. It is charmingly attractive as a peaceful spot wherein to while away a summer vacation.

Monterey boasts one of the most beautiful of Berkshire's lakes, Lake Garfield, a mile from the village, which from its absolute seclusion and the wildness of the surroundings is a favorite "camping out" place of South Berkshire. It is a mile and a half in length by three-quarters of a mile broad, of irregular outline and shut in around much of the shore line by picturesque groves, admirable for camping purposes. At the northern end is a natural curiosity that has attracted much attention; a floating island, two hundred or more feet long, that rises and falls regularly with the water. Formerly it "hung around" the south end, now and then floating from one side to the other; but a few years ago, when the banks were very full and a smart gale blowing, if drifted up the lake to its present moorings on a sand bank where it seems likely to stay for some time. Near the lower end of the lake is the home of Mr. M. S. Bidwell, where a number of summer guests are entertained. Mr. Bidwell is one of the Trustees of the Hampton Institute, and through his instrumentality a number of the Indian students, boys and girls, find summer homes among the farmers of Southern Berkshire.

Two miles south of the village is the romantic glen known as Hyde's Falls, through which a brook descends in a series of beautiful cascades for a mile. This is the favorite picnic ground of the entire vicinage.

The drives around Monterey and the neighboring towns are numerous. Lake Buel, 4 miles distant, situated partly in the town in the southwest corner, is a favorite object of a day's or half a day's excursion. Ice Gulf is near by. The drive to "Fernside" exposes a memorable view from the top of the mountain. Stockbridge, Lenox and Great Barrington make drives that are frequently taken.

RICHMOND.

RICHMOND is a quiet farming region, excepting in the southwest corner, where are the extensive iron mines and furnace of the Richmond Iron Company. In this town was reared Henry W. Dwight, the manager of the American Express Company, and Judge Dwight of Auburn. Among eminent natives were Judge Henry W. Bishop, a leading member of the Berkshire bar after his removal to Lenox; President Rowley of Du Pauw College; the late George Perry, once one of the editors of the New York *Home Journal*; Susan Teall Perry, of much literary fame, and several Congressmen. The house of the late Miss Catherine Pierson, near the Congregational church, was built by her father in 1790, and she has preserved it since, making it one of the most comfortable country homes in the county.

PERRY'S PEAK.

In the northwest corner is Perry's Peak, 2,089 feet high, from which one of the finest views in all Berkshire can be obtained. The valleys below open a scene of rare panoramic beauty. The Catskills on a clear day can be distinctly seen, and the craft sailing on the Hudson river; while on the west at one's feet is Queechy Lake in Canaan, the Shakers in that town, and the lovely valley of Lebanon for many miles north on the western slope. The Lebanon Shakers' settlement and the Columbia Hall farther north are nestled below, apparently only a short distance away, To the east is the Lenox range; north is Pittsfield and the entire valley in which it lies, Greylock farther beyond, and south the hills in West Stockbridge and Alford, a continuation of the Taconics. The summit of Perry's Peak is bare of trees and almost of soil, and the ascent is easily made in a wagon either from Richmond or the western valley from Lebanon. In summer it is a favorite resort, and in the autumn, when the foliage is turning, the view is bewitching. Some who have seen the view from this peak pronounce it to be much finer than from the famous Richmond Hill in England.

In Richmond is a queer geological curiosity in the celebrated "Boulder Trains," which continue through the town of Lenox and into Lee, though not so marked as in Richmond. The famous Balanced Rock is of this family. Many eminent geologists have examined them—Sir Charles Lyell among others—and they have always excited wonder and interest. They were first discovered as such, and their presence given to the world by Dr. Stephen Reed, a native of the town. They are simply huge boulders, either wholly or in part on the surface, strung along the ground, but with an interesting geological history.

There are numerous fine drives in the town, especially in the eastern part, along the base of Osceola and the Lenox Mountains, to Pittsfield. Near the church is "The Kenmore," which is now occupied in summer by a New York scientific school, whose members find ample range for study in nature all about them. Several of the town's people entertain visitors in the summer.

Queechy Lake, over the state line, in Canaan, is a lovely sheet of water and only a short drive from Richmond. The Canaan Shakers, a branch of the New Lebanon family, are also near the lake. It is a fascinating drive to leave Pittsfield, go through Richmond, swing around the base of the spur in the gap at this point to Queechy Lake, thence up the valley by the Canaan Shakers to New Lebanon and the Mount Lebanon Shakers, back over the Taconics, in sight of Perry's Peak and the other hills in that part of Hancock, through the settlement of the Pittsfield and Hancock Shakers to the village of Pittsfield again. The iron mines and furnace in the south part of the town are interesting places to visit.

HANCOCK.

THE town of Hancock is a strip of land one-third the width of the State on its western border and two miles wide. There is no village in Berkshire so peculiarly situated as Hancock, with the Taconics to the east, towering above it, and beyond them to the west the valley and the farms over the line into New York. The first settlers called the place Jericho, but it finally took its name from John Hancock. Asa Douglas, from whom Stephen A. Douglas descended, was among the first settlers and Charles Shumway occupies the site of the old homestead. The Hands were another of the old families. The elder Samuel, after a great many reverses, at last became wealthy and died in New Lebanon, so the historian tells us, and left his wealth in Spanish milled dollars in iron pots in his cellar, and his heirs, in distributing it, some of them drew their shares to Hancock in wagon loads. Martin I. Townsend of Troy, N. Y., one of the most noted lawyers and politicians, is a native of Hancock. The house of Kirk E. Gardiner was the first hotel in the town, and the old clock, the first one in Hancock, built into the wall of the house, is still doing duty as a time-piece and is a great curiosity. Richard Jackson, who was taken as a tory on his way to the battle of

Bennington, sent to Great Barrington jail, and who afterwards went to Springfield, where he was convicted of treason, was of Hancock. He was the soul of honor, and walked the entire distance unattended and delivered himself up. His singular conduct finally procured his pardon.

POTTER MOUNTAIN.

The drives in the town are charmingly magnificent. The road over Potter Mountain from Pittsfield, passing up through the west part of the town of Lanesboro commands one of the most entrancing landscapes in Berkshire. The road winds up the mountain from a few miles northwest of Pittsfield, making an easy ascent, and when the summit is reached, to the east is a rare panorama. Pontoosuc and Onota Lakes are at your feet. Pittsfield is just beyond, and presents a lovely picture, while farther to the south the eye wanders down the Housatonic Valley, or to the east further to the range east of Pittsfield and on to the Washington Hills. To the east is Lanesboro, and the prominent points in that town. Northward is the old familiar outline of Greylock and its fellows. Turning to the west, the village of Hancock is seen sequestered and snug in the valley, while the fertile farms and the lovely valley beyond, over in the other State, are taken in at a glance. From no other drive in Berkshire can so much be taken in at a glance as on the summit of the Potter Mountain road. A favorite drive from Pittsfield is over Potter Mountain to Hancock, then north to South Williamstown, and then back through New Ashford and Lanesboro to Pittsfield. The Berlin Mountain Range is on the west of the valley between Hancock and Williamstown, and is a charming region.

In Hancock, on the summit of the Taconics, off the highway, is Berry Pond, on whose outlet is the Lulu Cascade, a pretty waterfall much visited. On this summit, seen from Pittsfield, is the Shaker Promised Land, the Tower Mountain, and many other interesting points, from whose summits excellent views of the surrounding landscape are seen. South of the Lebanon highway, is the Shakers' Holy Ground, where their spiritual feasts were once held.

The town is quiet, peaceful and healthful. Its principal attractions are such as God has given it in its natural beauty. It is not a resort to any extent, and the homes are of the architecture of other times. The farms are well kept and the farm houses cozy and tasteful. Its drives are among the most romantic and singular in the county, and Pittsfield and New Lebanon utilize the mountain summits and the valleys for this purpose. Stages leave Hancock 5 P. M.; Pittsfield, 3 P. M.

LANESBORO.

ADJOINING Pittsfield on the north, Lanesboro is the northern town of the Housatonic Valley. Its scenery and attractions, as in every other Berkshire town, are peculiarly its own. With wooded heights, fruitful hillsides, blossoming valleys and picturesque scenery at every turn, it is an interesting place. It is quiet, sequestered and peaceful, and has no large villages. Pontoosuc Lake is partly in this town and partly in Pittsfield, and with its pretty groves, pavilions, sail and steamboats, has become a very popular resort for pleasure parties. The horse railroad from the railroad station at Pittsfield to the lake, adds much interest to its natural attractions. Standing near it one looks northward toward a most beautiful prospect. It is a lovely road and drive from Pittsfield to Lanesboro. The town commemorated Centennial year by planting on each side of the main highway a row of maples the entire length of its Main street.

THE LOOK-OFF SUMMITS.

There are several summits and prominent points in the town, among them Fairview, Savage Mountain, Farnam Hill, Constitution Hill, and The Knobbitt, all in the vicinity of the Main street; while in the eastern part, near Berkshire village, the location of the famous Berkshire Glass Works, are Crystal Hill, so named for the fine quality of glass sand found there, and a rugged point called Briggs' Cobble.

Constitution Hill, west of the village affords a fine outlook, of which J. E. A. Smith, in his "Taconic," thus writes: "Lying under its druidical oaks, or seated farther up, upon a pearl white quartz rock, in the shade of a whispering birch, you will see below you, groves and farms, and broad fresh meadows, with laughing lake and winding rivulet." The autumn "leaves here seem to have a perfection of beauty not attained elsewhere; you shall not desire to see a more gorgeous sight than Constitution Hill in October." On the western declivity there is a small cavern. From the piazza of the Royce homestead a view south is obtained, sweeping away down beyond Pittsfield and taking in the Housatonic Valley for many miles.

The iron furnace of the Lanesboro Iron Company, in the village, is an object of curiosity when in blast. The ore, taken from the beds in the west part of the town, also worth a visit, is among the finest for the manufacture of car wheels. In the stone school-house, at the north end of the main street, Arthur Gilman and Horace E. Scudder had a literary workshop, a few years ago, and here the Bodley Books, the works on Chaucer, and some other books were penned. The hills on both sides of the valley are easy of access, and some lovely views are obtained from them.

BALANCED ROCK.

A great curiosity is the famous Balanced Rock in the southwest part of the town. It is located on the farm of Grove E. Hurlburt, and is a few rods distant from the highway, an easy drive through the field being the route thereto. It is a huge, irregular mass of massive marble, grown gray by age and exposure, 30 feet long and 15 wide, poised on another rock three feet from the ground, and so evenly balanced that at first glance it seems as though it could easily be pushed from the smaller stone—a feat often attempted. There is many a legend connected with it. In the same pasture is another curiosity—a huge tree growing out of the solid rock. This locality has also the iron mines, and still farther north is a cave which has something of a legend to make it interesting. It is several rods long, and is almost at the base of Potter Mountain.

THE DRIVES.

There are many fine drives in the town. The road through the village and northward is one of them, either straight ahead, north to Pratt's Hill, or bearing to the west a little, the road to New Ashford and thence to Williamstown. East of the village are also some fine views. Taking the road at the Babtist church east, the drive of two or three miles to Berkshire Village is a pleasant one. "The farm house of the Messrs Owen, recently purchased by Edward T. Whiting, a New York gentleman, is a cozy country seat; and Prof. E. M. Fisher, formerly of Adelphi Academy, Brooklyn, also has a pretty place near by. Both gentlemen, with their families, now spend the entire year in this town. Several other city families own places here, and spend a portion of the season in this beautiful retreat among the hills, which will be more appreciated when it is better known. Turning a little south from there the trip to Dalton can be made, through the "Gulf," which on each side is a wild and pleasing piece of scenery. Or from the Owen place directly east to Berkshire Village is also a good drive. A fine grove for picnicing parties is on this road, near Berkshire Village. Back to the village again over another road, near the Congregational church, is a drive for a mile east, then to the north over the highway leading to Cheshire, on the west of the reservoir— a most lovely drive. A great many excellent and prominent men have at various times been residents of Lanesboro; in fact at one time it was quite famous for its lawyers, among them being Governor George N. Briggs in the early part of his practice. Henry Shaw, father of Henry W. Shaw, ("Josh Billings") was in his time one of the most prominent lawyers and politicians of the country. The homestead, which was the home of "Josh Billings," still remains in the village, commanding a beautiful sight, and is now occupied by William B. McLaughlin, formerly of Baltimore. The remains of the famous humorist lie in the little cemetery in the south part of the village, as he requested, and it was also his desire that his monument be a rough boulder from one of the marble quarries in the town, without adornment or polish, with a simple inscription on it, giving his real name and nom de plume. The Rev Dr. Samuel Brenton Shaw, who at the time of his death in Rhode Island in 1885, was the oldest living rector in the United States, was pastor of St. Luke's in the town for more than 30 years. His remains are buried here.

Within a few years Lanesboro has become a place of resort for city guests for boarding. The town has many beautiful locations for summer villas, and it possesses a great many attractions for those who desire the quietude of rural life, away from the railway. The "Brookside Farm" of Josiah A. Royce, $6\frac{1}{4}$ miles north of Pittsfield, entertains guests, and is in a delightful situation for the enjoyment of country life. Stages leave Pittsfield, 3 P. M., Williamstown, 6 A. M.; leave Lanesboro, 4.10 P. M. and 9.45 A. M.

WASHINGTON.

WASHINGTON (to be distinguished from Mount Washington) touches the southeast corner of Pittsfield, and is about 700 feet higher, or, say, 1,700 feet above tide water. There are some most charming views from different portions of the town, especially on the west slope, overlooking Pittsfield, and from near the old Congregational church.

Ashley Lake, which supplies Pittsfield with water, lies in a basin of white granular quartz, and is fed with numberless living springs of the finest quality of water. It is about a mile long, and just beyond is a bed of white sand, which for many years was used for glass-making. Undine Glen is near this point. There are two delightful drives out of Pittsfield to Washington. Just beyond the east line of Pittsfield, one can turn to the right, and, bearing south, follow up the hill, a new view opening at every turn, until the summit is reached. The center of the town near the old church, was the birthplace of Governor Edwin D. Morgan of New York. The Rev. Elijah Kellogg, one of the old-time circuit rider preachers of the New York conference, a chaplain in the Connecticut State prisons, was also a native of the town.

October Mountain, the range on the east of the Housatonic, near the Lenox station and north, is in this town; the outlook from it is charming, and in the autumn, with its variegated foliage, it is a lovely sight. Roaring Brook, which having its source in West Pond near the eastern base of October Mountain, is a wild stream running through Tory Glen, a place visited from Pittsfield and Lenox. The "City" is a small settlement near the Boston & Albany railway station, about a mile south, where a view of the eastern valley is obtained. A few city guests have made this a summer home, and there are several cozy farm houses where people are entertained.

Another drive from Pittsfield is to follow the course of the old Pontoosuc turnpike up the hill, along a most romantic drive, near which flows the Sackett Brook. When the summit of the hill is gained, two miles further a table land is reached, and the view is quite pleasing, especially to the east. It is sometimes a favorite drive to take this route from Pittsfield to the Washington railway station, go from there to the "City," and from thence by the first-named highway, back by way of the old Congregational church down the mountain to Pittsfield again. In the night, from the brow of the hill, Pittsfield in the distance and in the valley 700 feet below, with its lights gleaming, makes a novel picture.

DALTON.

DALTON village lies sequestered in the busy valley, through which runs the Housatonic River's east branch, furnishing the motive power, largely, to the great paper mills which have made the town famous. There is a great deal of natural scenery in Dalton. To the south is Day mountain, 700 feet above the village, and from its summit, which is a little difficult of access, but nevertheless approachable, a fine view is obtained almost to the northern extremity of the county. Warner Hill is in the southern part of the town, toward the junction with Washington. West of here, in the valley where the lines of Pittsfield and Dalton meet, are several fine drives. The traveler on the Boston and Albany road, gets a fine view of Dalton as the train passes along on the side hill. This hill was formerly covered with a thick growth of timber, making it impossible to get anything but occasional glimpses of this charming village. But in 1888 the timber was cut off, so that the entire town can now be seen from the cars. No town on the line shows to such good advantage from the railroad as does Dalton, and one cannot but be impressed with the extent and beauty of the town as seen in this way. The Dalton of to-day is hardly recognizable as the Dalton of four years ago, for the changes there have been so great as to make almost a new place of it. But while its appearance has undergone such a decided change, it still remains the same busy, thrifty town, and in fact its thrift is what has wrought the transformation. The improvements began about 1886, and since then the handsome new Congregational church, the cozy and attractive Irving House, the large shops of the Dalton Shoe Company, and more than a hundred new houses have been erected. Most of these buildings are located in the center of the town, on what was known as "Carson Flat." These are all new, cozy cottages, many of them of unique design and of many attractive features in cottage architecture. The land here is high, the soil gravel, and it is really the natural center of Dalton. Foremost in the matter of these changes, were the Messrs Crane, and Dalton's obligation to this well-known family has been immeasurably increased.

At the upper end of the town, Hon. Byron Weston, from the promptings of his proverbial energy and public spirit, has built three handsome business blocks, which add much to the importance and appearance of this section. The drive from Pittsfield to Dalton is a most interesting one. In 1886-7 the new Dalton road was built between here and Pittsfield, and by taking this, all grade crossings, and the danger of driving in such close proximity to the Junction where the Boston and Albany trains are constantly passing and switching, is avoided. The new road leaves Pittsfield in the northeast part of the city proper, and runs to the northeast, joining the old road a little east of the Coltsville station. The drive leads one through a pleasant section of farm country, where the views are exquisite. Soon after leaving Pittsfield the visitor comes to the new stock farm of William Russell Allen. The large buildings, with the tasteful cottages for the use of the employes, are located a few rods to the north of the road, on rising ground. These buildings, with the new half-mile track, represent an outlay of more than $100,000, and are more fully described in the chapter on Pittsfield. To the north is a fine view of the valley, and one of the prettiest views of Greylock from a distance in all Berkshire.

From the high ground on the Allen Farm, just east of Pittsfield, is an amphitheatre, with a kaleidoscope of views on every side. After reaching the old road one passes the "Government Mill," where the Cranes manufacture the distinctive paper for the United States currency and bonds. The building stands at the right side of the road, and, when in operation, a large national flag floats from the tall staff in front of the building. A little beyond this mill, is the Dalton line, and very soon "Cranesville" is reached. Here are the large mills of Z. & W. M. Crane, where the finest ladies' stationery is made. Thirty-three neat tenements near by are used by the employes, and on the Main street stands a neat frame building, where the Cranes have established a free library and reading room. This institution is very generally used by the employes of the mills, and the residents of this section. Opposite the library stands the new brown stone mansion of Hon. Zenas Crane, one of the handsomest and most tasteful homes in Berkshire. The residence of Mrs. Z. M. Crane is just beyond the library, and is a magnificent country home, with ample grounds, in the rear of which is a beautiful lakelet, fine conservatory, grapery, and the other accessories of the ideal Berkshire home. Further east is the house of J. B. Crane, who, with his brother, the late Zenas Marshall Crane, has made bank note paper for more than an ordinary lifetime. The house is fronted by a small park, and the grounds are well kept. The handsome house of John D. Carson stands nearly opposite. Passing there, the tourist drives on by the "Old Berkshire Mills" at the foot of the hill. On the right are the new hotel, the Irving House, the new Congregational Church, the new street leading from the main avenue, and so on to the "Center," where are located the extensive mills and handsome residence of Hon. Byron Weston. The Weston mills are very extensive, and here is manufactured the highest grades of ledger and record papers. This trip is full of interest to a visitor and gives him a good idea of what is Berkshire's thriftiest town.

Fine Papers.

The hillsides of the town abound with the purest water, and it is to this source that the town is indepted largely for its reputation in paper-making. Who has not heard of the "Old Berkshire Mills" of Carson & Brown, or "Weston's Ledgers," or the famous bond papers of Crane & Co., nor yet of the ladies' stationary of Z. Crane, Jr., & Brother? The second paper mill in the state west of Worcester was built here in 1801 by Zenas Crane, the pioneer paper manufacturer of western Massachusetts. The hillsides are full of springs of water so pure that for months the water may be run through the whitest flannel without discoloring it. Added to these are the four artesian wells of ex-Lieutenant-Governor Byron Weston, from 100 to 500 feet deep, all discharging over 1,000 gallons a minute; the Carson & Brown Company, have one of the most abundantly flowing artesian wells in the country—700 gallons a minute.

Dalton's Industries.

The principal industry of the town is, as is generally known, paper-making. Crane & Co. manufacture bank-note and bond paper. This concern was founded by Zenas Crane, and the original mill was erected in 1801. The present owners are James B., Zenas and W. Murray Crane, and the products of these mills has a world-wide reputation.

Z. & W. M. Crane, already mentioned, manufacture ladies' fine writing-papers and envelopes, and a few years since built a large addition to their mill, in which they manufacture all the paper boxes used in packing their product.

The Old Berkshire Mills Company was established in 1801, and until 1889 had been, for twelve years, carried on by Carson & Brown. In 1889, Mr. Brown sold out his interest to Z. & W. M. Crane, who with John D. Carson carry on the business under the name of the "Old Berkshire Mills Company." The mills turn out a superior quality of linen writing-papers, and the "Old Berkshire Mills" paper has an established reputation all over the country.

The Weston Mills, at the upper end of the town, constitute a large and valuable plant. The ledger and record papers made here are of the highest quality, and have taken numberless medals. The business was established in 1863 and has grown to large proportions. Mr. Weston has served in the state senate, and as Lieutenant-Governor, and is a highly-esteemed and most successful business man.

The latest addition to the industries of Dalton, is the Dalton Shoe Company, which was organized in 1889, with H. A. Barton, Jr., as president and treasurer, and M. V. Waring, manager. A fine new factory building was erected, and the finest grades of ladies', misses' and children's shoes are made.

The Glennon and the Kittredge woolen mills and the Renfrew cotton mills complete the list of Dalton's principal industries. Both are well-established concerns, doing a good business and giving employment to a large number of persons.

The employes of the Dalton mills are intelligent and well-informed people, who take a deep interest in the town. Between them and their employers kindliest feeling exists, and the result is a model manufacturing town. Its water supply is ample—from a mountain brook—and at the village the pressure is about 150 pounds to the square inch. The last spring a generous appropriation was made for sidewalks.

A new road from Main street to the pretty depot on the hillside, was laid out from Main street. The ravine in the river is crossed at this point by a substantial iron bridge, and from this, a wild gorge makes a weird picture.

As a Summer Resort.

The fact that Dalton is the home of so many large manufacturing establishments, might naturally create an impression that it is not a desirable summer home. But a person who forms such an idea has only to visit the place to be convinced of his mistake. The mills are all located in the valleys and almost hidden from sight; so that Dalton has none of the appearance of the ordinary New England manufacturing town. It is delightfully located, and affords opportunity for some of the loveliest and most romantic drives in Berkshire county. The first attempt to cater to summer visitors was successfully made a few years ago by W. B. Clark, who built the "Elmwood Cottages." For several years Mr. Clark entertained large numbers of people from New York, Brooklyn,

Hartford and other places. The building of the Irving House in 1889, gave more opportunity for accommodating summer visitors, and Mr. Clark has recently sold one of his cottages and is to rent the other. The new hotel is very pleasantly located on the main street. It is a very tasteful frame building, and is peculiarly cozy and attractive. It is elegantly fitted up throughout, is supplied with all modern improvements, and is under the management of Frank L. Bourne, an affable and experienced young hotel man. A fine livery is attached to the house, and the fame of this most excellent summer stopping place has already spread far and wide. The view from this house is exceptionally fine, especially to the west.

WAHCONAH FALLS.

Dalton's most romantic and delightful attraction is Wahconah Falls, a wild little cascade situated on Wahconah brook, just at the line dividing Windsor and Dalton. The falls are reached by a very pleasant two-mile drive from Dalton, and of late years have become one of the favorite spots in this section of Berkshire. The brook runs through property owned by the Messrs. Crane, and in 1889 the surroundings of the falls were greatly improved. The place was given the name of "Wahconah Falls Park," and signs were put up along the roads, directing people to the place. Just below the falls a good-sized pavilion was erected, and from a piazza on the back of this building is obtained a fine view of the falls, so near at hand that the spray is blown into the faces of the delighted onlooker. A path has been made over the rocks and through the woods along the brook above the falls, and seats have been put in at pleasant spots along the way. A rocky eminence at one side of the falls, has been crowned with a small arbor, and the view down the ravine from this spot is not surpassed by anything in all Berkshire. The water goes tumbling in a foamy mass over the rocks, and then sweeps on over its rocky bed until it hides itself from view among the trees far below. On either side, the high banks are covered with fine old trees, which bend gently over the stream, as if rejoicing in its beauty. Near the foot of the falls may be seen the remains of the foundation of the old grist mill which formerly stood here, and near at hand lie the old millstones, now green with moss. Farther up the stream are the remains of two other mills, and a word regarding the history of these mills may not be amiss. Considerably more than a century ago a saw mill was built on the stream, near the present reservoir, by Messrs. Bassett & Cleveland. This was carried away by a flood in 1779, and the following year the owners built

Wahconah Falls.

the grist mill near the foot of the falls. This was the first grist mill built in this section, and for many years did a good business. It had a corn and wheat mill, and two days in each year were set aside for grinding salt. The farmers would buy the coarse salt and dry it, and on the allotted days take it to the mill to be ground. Bassett & Cleveland sold the mill to Samuel and Joseph Talcott, who sold it to the state of Connecticut in exchange for a grant of land. The property was then purchased by Jacob Booth, who turned it over to his son, Philander F. Booth (now living at Dalton). It went through several other hands, and a few years ago was purchased by the late Zenas M. Crane, who willed it to the present owners, his sons. The latter have laid out considerable money in making the place attractive, and contemplate still further additions. The pavilion spoken of is supplied with an oil stove, and parties desiring to spend the day at the falls can secure keys to the pavilion at the Z. & W. M. Crane mill, the hotel, and other places. There is no charge made, and the grounds and buildings are absolutely free. The third mill was a saw mill, built some 50 years ago by Jacob Booth. A writer says of Wahconah : "The stream has been constantly gaining an impetus in its descent, now flowing through the meadow or pasture, leisurely, and, again, maddened and hurried, running quite rapidly. It is a succession of cascades, until at this point, hemmed in by rocks and stones of quite large size, the stream makes a leap of some eighty feet, and lies for a time, partially calm, in quite a deep pool in a basin below. A pupil of Maplewood, a few years ago, visited the spot, and, becoming giddy, fell from the rocks into this pool, and was drowned before her school-mates could rescue her. Wahconah Falls have a history, pleasantly told in the legends given in "Taconic." The stream is named for the Indian maiden Wahconah, the daughter of Miahcomo, the chief of the tribe residing in the valley where now is Dalton. The tale is interesting, and was a romance indeed, but too long for these pages. The falls decided eventually the fate of this fair Indian maiden, giving her to the brave of her choice rather than to the rival, who was ugly and painted."

WIZARD'S GLEN.

The principal natural curiosity is the "Wizard's Glen," in the west part of the town, known as "The Gulf," on the road leading west from near the Methodist church to Lanesboro. Here the road passes through jagged rocks, and in some places the merest ripple of water, or laugh, or word is echoed and re-echoed. The shade in some places is delightful and overhangs the highway. Tradition says that long before the paleface came to the valleys, this glen was the place where the priests of the Indian tribe made their incantations and slew their victims as a sacrifice to their god; one large rock is known as Devil's Altar. This spot has its legends and wild stories, in keeping with the grandeur and loneliness of the place. In Mr. Smith's "Taconic" is an interesting legend of the adventure that one Chamberlain had, after slaying a deer and lying down to sleep in the glen, on a night of thunder and lightning. A view of the devil and his imps holding high carnival was opened to him, and finally, in mortal fear, taking out his Bible, he pronounced the Name, which dispelled the vision and gave him rest and quiet.

Dalton has its old families; families who came with the beginning of the town, worked for its interest and grown deservedly wealthy and well-known. The Crane's, among the first settlers of the town, have been honored as well as widely known. Three generations have been in the Governor's Council. The development of the paper trade in the country has been aided largely by this family. Gov. Weston, the Chamberlains, Merriams, Greens, Carsons, Browns, Marshes, the Williamses of the family whose name is linked closely with other portions of Berkshire, and many others, all left their impress on the town for its greatest good.

It is a remarkable fact that in the town of Dalton, artesian boring should have developed a series of wells furnishing the most desirable water for paper-making use, superior in quality, perfect in temperature, unvarying in flow and abundant in quantity. Such marvelous results have been had from the Dalton artesian wells, that we present illustrations of two of them, showing the flow of water before the piping and covering. The first shows a well connected with the famous "Old Berkshire" mills, of which Messrs. Carson & Brown were proprietors in 1884, when the well was sunk. The boring on this well had been in progress for 22 days, when the drill, at the depth of 147 feet, apparently broke through a rock crust, and a flow of 700 gallons per minute of the purest, sweetest water burst forth.

The "Bonanza" artesian well was sunk the same year by Hon. Byron Weston, and was an equally remarkable success. It is 240 feet in depth, and flows a 12-inch stream of the purest water, which never varies from a temperature of 48 degrees Fahrenheit, summer or winter. Mr. Weston has three other wells for the supply of his mills, all of which are like the "Bonanza" in quality of water and in temperature, but none of the others gave an equal volume. The first was sunk in 1854 by Captain Chamberlain, a predecessor of Gov. Weston, was 150 feet in depth, and has since given out a continuous stream of 125 gallons per minute,

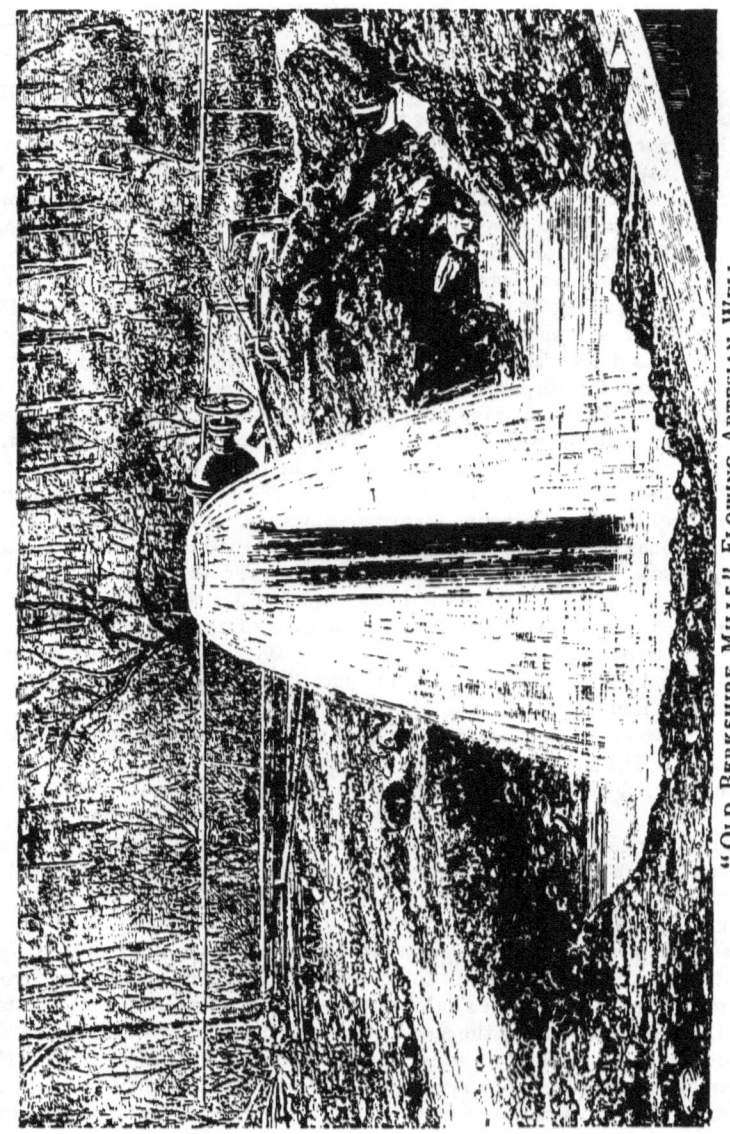

"Old Berkshire Mills" Flowing Artesian Well.

Weston's "Bonanza" Artesian Well.

through a five-inch pipe. In 1876 Gov. Weston sunk the second well, obtaining at a depth of 76 feet a three-inch flow, and in 1883 another boring was made, which was carried down 511 feet, producing a six-inch stream. Although these wells are at different localities, and vary so much in depth, the volume of each is constant, the quality of the water never varies, and is remarkably pure.

MOUNT WESTON.

The view from Mount Weston, to which one may drive, two miles from the village center, is exceedingly fine. Here Governor Weston has his chalet, a log house, where, with the coziest sort of comfort, parties of

SWISS CHALET ON MOUNT WESTON.

friends are entertained, from time to time, with rare good feeling. The view from the chalet on Mount Weston is one of the finest and far-reaching of the many similar ones to be found in Berkshire, and Mr. Weston generally gives the use of his "log cabin" and surrounding grounds to his wide circle of friends for picnic purposes, and to tourists and mountain climbers for temporary shelter, rest and refreshment serving. On the mountain above the depot is also a fine view, and here a local club have built a cabin, so that parties camping here may be accommodated.

HINSDALE.

HINSDALE is located on the high lands of the county, on the main line of the Boston & Albany railroad, which at the station is 1,431 feet above tide water. The Ashmere Reservoir, in the east part of the town, covers several hundred acres on the road to Peru Center. In the north part are some fine drives, the roads gradually descending and opening a constantly-changing landscape and giving new views to the west. The Plunkett Reservoir, covering many acres, is in the southwest part of the town and is much resorted to. In fact, the town has several fine brooks and lakes, the latter reservoirs, which are famous for angling, while game abounds plentifully in the woods and the mountain peaks.

West of the village is a pleasant hill from which a fine view is obtained, especially at the house of Milo Stowell, nearly on the summit. Following this road farther west, on the side of the hill, a beautiful view of Pittsfield and its surroundings is taken in at a glance. There is a mineral spring near the village, the waters of which have had some local reputation.

The town has had a high reputation for good citizenship from its earliest days. It was named from the Rev. Theodore Hinsdale, who removed here in 1785, and his descendants are still honored both in his name and the branches of the parent vine throughout Berkshire. His eldest daughter, Nancy, was the first teacher of a female school in Pittsfield and assisted largely in making the Willard College at Troy what it has become; the sons and grandsons of the first Theodore, have been active men in the town, being at present the Hinsdale Manufacturing Company. The Whites were another old family in Hinsdale, and from the town has gone out the head of the great firm of R. H. White & Co., of Boston, whose summer vacations are spent in his native town. A. D. Matthews, the well-known Brooklyn merchant, is a native of Hinsdale. E. A. Hubbard, for many years the superintendent of schools in Springfield and well known throughout the State, is a native; Henry C. Haskell, a missionary in Turkey, and Chauncey Goodrich, of a family connected intimately with the history of the town, and a missionary to Pekin, China, were both natives of this good old town; William E. Merriman, president of Ripon College, Wis., Francis E. Warren, governor of

Wyoming are also natives, and many others could be named, who, catching the inspiration from the town of their birth, have gone out to useful and prominent places in life in other parts of the country. Lyman Payne, who came some years ago to Hinsdale, and whose elegant country home is near the locality known as "The Flat," has one of the finest stud of blooded horses, as well as cattle of rare excellence in the county. The Congregational church on a slope overlooking the village is among the oldest in the county.

The town has as yet few or no country homes for city families, although recently a New York gentleman has purchased the old Hinsdale homestead for that purpose. There is but one hotel in the village, and there have been but little efforts made to attract summer tourists and guests to the town. There are several drives of from four to six miles about the town, which are very pleasant, and the roads are so laid out that in many instances the drives are practically around "squares."

PERU.

PERU, four miles from the railroad at Hinsdale, has the honor of being the highest inhabited land in the State. The Congregational church stands on the very summit, and its old-fashioned box pews still remain. The winds blow fiercely on this summit and to prevent the demolition of the steeple, there are heavy cables running down each side and fastened securely in the rock; for verily the church at this place is "founded on a rock." Another prominent feature of this old edifice is that the rain falling on the east side of the roof runs eastward and thence to the headwaters of the Connecticut and that on the west side finds its way through the headwaters of the Housatonic. No other place in Massachusetts can boast of such a novelty.

From this point the view to the north is very fine, and the stern old sentinel of the Hoosac Valley is plainly visible and even mountains farther beyond in Vermont. French Mountain, 2,239 feet high, a short distance south of the church, is the highest of the summits in the Green Mountain range in this part of the county. Its summit is quite easy of access and the look-off, especially to the north and south, is magnificently grand. The surface of the town is so broken and hilly, that there are fine drives in all directions. In the southern part of the town there are many charming slopes and hill-top views, which are so numerous and varied as to beggar description. Going northward through the towns of Peru, Windsor, Savoy and Florida to North Adams, a charming view is afforded, as the tourist keeps all the way along the top of the Green Mountain range,—a ride that has become quite popular for a day or two of outing. The town has abundant natural attractions, but its isolation has prevented any great influx of summer guests. It is purely agricultural, quiet, peaceful and very healthy. Stage leaves Hinsdale, 12, noon; Peru, 2 P. M.

A number of summer visitors find Peru a stopping place for a few weeks in the heat of summer, and, like Mount Washington, it is said to be a sure cure for hay fever. Many city parents, notably from Pittsfield, send their children among the Peru farmers for a few weeks, for genuine rest, recreation and the opportunity to romp and recreate. Some fine trout brooks abound.

WINDSOR.

ON the east slope of the town there are numberless interesting drives, through a fine farming region. On the Westfield river is a settlement of good families where a few summer people have tarried for a season. Of late the town is having a good many tourists who are attracted to it by its quietude and the home life of its people. Stage leaves Hinsdale, 12, noon; Windsor, 2 P. M.

Windsor Hill, rightly named, is reached by an easy though somewhat hilly road from Dalton, up the Waheonah Brook. From this hill, one stands nearly in front of Greylock, looking almost into its very summit, apparently only a short distance away. It is one of the finest views from the range. It is a treat to climb to the belfry of the old Congregational church and look upon the glorious landscape. The road north to Savoy, or northwest to Cheshire is an attractive drive. There are several old burial grounds in different parts of the town which have some queer epitaphs.

The family of which Senator Dawes is a worthy descendant, was among the first settlers, and he tells now with a good deal of relish how he walked six miles to the old church, one winter day through the snow, to be examined by the school committee as a pedagogue in one of the schools of the town. Men of prominence in professional life have gone out from Windsor, and one of the originators of the prayer meeting under the haystack at Williams College, from which sprang the missionary effort of the new world, was a Windsor young man.

CHESHIRE.

THIS town presents twenty-five angles in its outline. The range of hills to the east are of the Green Mountains. The best way to reach Stafford's Hill, the first place in town inhabited by white people, is to follow the Savoy road, east, for a short distance to the Jacques district, so-called, and then turning north to Stafford's Hill. From the top of this hill the view is most charming. On the same range, near the extreme southern border of the town and above the residence of George Fisher, east of the middle of the reservoir, is another magnificent view, to the south especially. In fact there is no end of views at nearly all points in this part of the town. The scenery around Cheshire Harbor, in the north part of the town, where the river lies landlocked in a snug harbor, is also strikingly beautiful.

On the west side of the village is a range of hills which are also rich in variety of scenery. Going west of the village a little way, then turning northward through the road known as "Pork Lane," there is a fine drive, and, from the R. C. Brown farm is a wood road which leads nearly to the summit of Greylock; it has for years been the favorite route to the top of that interesting place. Further on the west line, among the hills plainly seen from the railway and the village, whose slopes are dotted with farm houses, is Little Mountain, which is next to Greylock in point of view in the northern part of the county; its summit is bald, and from it in a clear day, five different states, Massachusetts, Vermont, New York, Connecticut and the peaks in New Hampshire, can be easily seen with the naked eye. The Catskills, forty miles away, are clearly seen.

The sand beds, from which the purest of silex is obtained, in the east part of the village, are a curiosity; the furnace where iron is made is worth a visit at night. The Berkshire Glass Works, only four miles south are often visited in summer, at evening especially, when the blowing is in process.

The Northrup Brook, emptying into the reservoir near Farnum's, is a curiosity. After leaving its source for some distance, it suddenly enters the ground and is lost to view for a considerable way and finally emerges from a cave materially increased in size. A little way further is Barker's

Falls, with a single leap of about 75 feet. Nearly all the places of interest on the west slope are easily accessible and can easily be driven to with a team.

The Fisks, of whom the famous "Jim" Fisk was a descendant, were for many years residents of Cheshire; the elder James, was born in town and lived here for years. The eccentric Elder Leland, a divine of the Baptist denomination, widely known in his time, was for many years the village pastor, and his old house still stands a little west of the village toward the cemetery. The old cemeteries of the town are numerous and they are worth a visit by the curious. The famous Cheshire Cheese will go down in history as the idea of this eccentric parson. He was a great admirer of President Jefferson, and, accordingly he invited a contribution of the cheese curd of the town to be made into a cheese for him. It was gathered at the cider mill of Captain Brown and into the hoop on the cheese press the curd was turned. The result was that nearly every family and nearly every cow in the town had contributed to it, and when finished the mammoth cheese weighed 1,235 pounds. The cheese was taken to Hudson, in a wagon and shipped to Washington by water. The anecdotes of this celebrated, eccentric parson are still told with great zest in the town.

The village wears an air of cozy thrift and comfort, and from it the drives are legion. The valley is so situated that one drives up on the east side for example and back by the west road and the traveler finds not only many new things to attract the eye, but an entirely different picture as the scene is reversed. A fine drive to Pittsfield, is down the west bank of the reservoir, rising the hills to Lanesboro and thence to Pittsfield, ten miles, and back by the Junction, through the Berkshire Glass Works and on the east side of the reservoir to Cheshire again. Going north toward Adams through "The Harbor" to Adams village, then turning by the paper mills there, striking the east slope of that village and back by the "Pumpkin Hook" neighborhood, striking the east road in Cheshire and back to the village again, is a lovely drive of ten miles with new scenery at each turn. The road east of Cheshire Harbor is romantic, among rocks and hills, a good highway all the distance. Pittsfield is ten miles, Lenox 16, Williamstown 15; North Adams at the other and northern extremity of the valley is ten miles; Adams, five miles; and Savoy, with a number of pleasant mountain drives, seven miles.

The town has an abundant and never failing supply of fine water, brought in iron pipes from springs and brooks in the hills west of the village. The supply has never been affected by a dry season, and there has never been a case of typhoid fever in the town since the water has been in use. The sanitary conditions of Cheshire are excellent, and the place has never known an epidemic.

Cheshire is situated on the Pittsfield and North Adams branch of the Boston and Albany railroad and has superior accommodations in the New York and Boston connections at Pittsfield.

The town has become a summer resort for people from New York and Brooklyn largely, though Philadelphia, Buffalo, and other cities have been represented. The development in this direction is only limited by the accommodations. Ten years ago, the country seat of the late R. C. Brown was opened for a summer rest as "The Cedars," by his son, Fred C. Brown, and it has been a resort for many people, among them Judge Hall, of the New York Marine Court, Warren Brown, a New York lawyer, Mr. Studley, manager of the Goodyear Rubber Company, Mr. Rintoul, manager of the Morgan estate of New York, the Thompson, an old family from Buffalo, and many others. The Cedars is still the principal resort of the town, and its capacity is taxed every summer. Mrs. N. W. Mason's "Brookside Cottage" and Mrs. Daniel Wood's "Maple Hill Farm" entertain a number of city people every summer, and the roomy farm house of W. A. Pomeroy in the east part of the town, is filled with guests each season. As a rule the families going to Cheshire are among the more cultivated and educated people of the cities. A few years ago Mrs. Dumont, of New York, purchased the Richardson estate north of the village and christened it very properly "Greylock Villa." This house is now occupied every summer by Asa Hull, the well-known composer of sacred music. The Hoosac Valley House, in the south part of the village, has also had several summer guests, and is a well-kept hotel. At the foot of the hill, north of "The Cedars," still remains the old tavern built by the King family in the Revolutionary days, and at this tavern the signal guns were fired, calling the militia together to march for the battle of Bennington. The old house is well preserved. Cheshire is rich in many ways, both in its natural beauty, its peculiar early history, and its traditions. A number of prominent men in other parts of the country have been reared in this town, among them Gordon Cole, a prominent lawyer of St. Paul, Minn., Captain Turtle of the United States Engineer Corps, and others.

SAVOY.

THIS is one of the hill-top towns of Berkshire, grand in a good many bits of scenery, and cold in winter. Spruce Hill, in the north part of the town, Lewis Hill, and some others, are prominent, and from their summits a good many fine views are obtained. A trout supper at Bowker's, the only hotel in the town, is a treat which many from Adams and North Adams often enjoy. He has been for more than sixty years the village postmaster, and the house contains many rare relics, especially in old books, etc. The little Baptist church in this hamlet was established over one hundred years ago. The longevity of the town is proverbial, and a lady (a native of Savoy) died only the past year, who had reached her 100th birth-day. Of late the town is resorted to a good deal in the course of a drive by tourists, and the main road through the town east and west is the thoroughfare to Cummington and other Hampshire towns. From some of the points in the town, a clear sketch from Monadnock to Greylock is obtained, and the course of the tunnel, under Florida Mountain, is clearly defined. There are "Savoy Hollow," the center, South and North Savoy, villages—all mere hamlets—in this town. Savoy is quite a resort for driving parties from northern Berkshire and even as far south as Pittsfield.

The eastern range of the hills overlooks some grand pieces of scenery in the Deerfield Valley, and to the rugged hills beyond in Franklin County. There are five hamlets in the town; Savoy Center and Savoy Hollow are the principle ones, in the latter, in the south part of the town, being the only hotel. It is an old-fashioned hostelry well-kept, with country fare; but a Stockbridge tourist, on a recent summer, said of it, that he found it his ideal of an inn, in a town of that rank.

Artist R. G. Shurtleff, of Springfield, whose easel frequently holds some of the finest landscape views in Western Massachusetts, is not unmindful of the beauties which Berkshire keeps in store for him, has made this hotel his headquarters for a season's sketching, and speaks of the scenery of the region as being very fine, the village life quietly fascinating and the hotel an attractive place for temporary sojourn. The latter is also a favorite place for a night's tarrying for those who go up to the hill-tops of Northern Berkshire in carriages for a brief outing of rest, relaxation and sensible enjoyment.

Many of the religions of the day have flourished in this little town; there have been Mormons, Adventists, Baptists, Methodists, Congregationalists, Shakers, who remained only a few years however, and some others. William Miller, the father of Millerism, labored here for some time. Excellent families have had their origin in Savoy. Abel Carpenter went to Chicago when it was but a village of logs, delivered the first temperance lecture in that city, and started the first Sunday school there. Jarvis N. Dunham, President of the Springfield Fire and Marine Insurance Company, is a native of the town. There are many fine drives, and the town is easily accessible by stage from Adams, only six miles away. The town is also in the line of the drives on the mountain top from Hinsdale to Florida and North Adams.

NEW ASHFORD.

THIS town is a picturesque gorge, lying between the giant foot hills of Saddle Ball on the east and a spur of the Taconics on the west. The scenery is grand, and there are few drives in the county so romantic as this part of the old country road between Pittsfield and Williamstown, which passes through what is locally and appreciatively termed the "Switzerland of Berkshire."

Sugar Loaf is a shapely mountain, with several small caves, and its dens have been the resort of coons and mountain cats for a long time. An autumn hunt at night for these animals is among the attractions of the place. Saddle Ball is eastward from Sugar Loaf, a continuation of Greylock and a prominent peak in Northern Berkshire. It cuts the horizon with a bold and symmetrical outline, and the view from its summit, which is accessible with but little effort, is one of the grandest in the country. The view from Beach's Hill is especially fine, and from its summit, which is easy of access, one looks down over the town as into a basin; the deceptive arrangement of the hills give the appearance of sloping walls, with no possible outlet for road or river.

In the north part of the town is the old Brown sawmill, spanning a chasm of great depth, which a mere railing separates from the highway. This view is of more than common interest, and is the subject of a fine painting. The stunted hemlocks over the rocky edge of the narrow abyss, the ruins of the old mill, the crumbling and mossy pillars of the old dam and the general wildness of the locality, as a background, make a most charming picture.

Near the village is the old cemetery where the "rude forefathers of the hamlet sleep," and far outnumber the living. The inscriptions are some of them quaint. In the southwest part of the town is Baker's Cave, the entrance to which is through a circular opening in the meadow. From this, a cavernous passage extends 100 feet or more with a sharp descent, to a cold spring at the bottom.

The stage from Pittsfield and Williamstown makes daily trips through the village. The air and scenery and mountain drives are all that can be desired, but as yet there is no hotel, and but few people have been attracted to the town as a resort. Its attractions, however, will amply repay the tourist for a close intimacy with them.

FLORIDA.

FLORIDA possesses some of the most attractive views in all northern Berkshire, and is almost entirely in its length and breadth on the summit of the Green Mountain or Hoosac range, as it is called at this point. It is a barrier of rock and mountain between Berkshire and the Deerfield Valley, and through its entire width the Hoosac Tunnel pierces its heart; in fact all but a few feet of the tunnel is in the town of Florida, although the great work is intimately associated with North Adams, which is only a mile or so away from its western portal. The town has an elevation of from 1,000 to 1,400 feet above the valley.

Its drives are a panorama at every hand. On the west side, after the summit is reached, and especially on the road over the mountain to North Adams, it is a grand picture. In fact the village of North Adams is hardly left before the hill-top opens its grand views. The town is a succession of hills and valleys when the top is fairly reached, until the slope towards the east side is approached. On the east slope is another magnificent view, although not so far reaching. There is a narrow valley of the Deerfield, near the east portal of the tunnel, and here, rising at least 1,000 feet to the west, is the range of mountains, down the side of which the stage road has come, and the passenger, when he alights, is almost dizzy as he thinks of the rugged passage he has made. Florida is really on the top of the mountain, its east side presenting an unbroken succession of hills and mountain peaks, while its west side towards North Adams is also steep and not easy of access, excepting over the established roads.

Hoosac Tunnel.

During the building of the tunnel, in a depression of the valley, a shaft was sunk, known as the Central Shaft, to the depth of over 1,000 feet, so that the tunnel had four headings, one each from the east and west ends, and two from the central shaft. Here was a busy settlement of miners and workmen, and during the work a fearful accident occurred whereby nearly forty men lost their lives and were buried, more than a year, 600 feet in the bowels of the mountain, while that space was filled with water. An accident to the pump house, which was destroyed by fire, prevented them from being rescued and the pumping of the water cost the State an immense sum. The place is an interesting one to visit, and it is a wonder how the great hills of stone piled up on every hand were ever raised out of the interior of the mountain. The shaft is protected by a wall 16 feet high, so that there is no danger of falling down its cavernous mouth. The spot is easily reached by a highway turning south just as the town line is reached out of North Adams, above that village. The length of the Tunnel is 25,081 feet, or about $4\frac{3}{4}$ miles.

Florida village is a little hamlet on the top of the mountain, with no special attractions excepting its isolation and quietude. The other village is Hoosac Tunnel Station. From Florida village north and east is a well kept and romantic road to Monroe in Franklin County and thence to Readsboro in Vermont, which latter town is also a summer resting place of considerable note. Near Mr. Whitcomb's the road bears to the south and east, and all the distance presents many views which attract the beholder. The road through the town, north and south, is a delightful one for an easy carriage drive through Savoy, Windsor and Peru to Hinsdale.

Whitcomb Brook flows east and joins the Deerfield River near the east portal of the Tunnel. One of the famous waterfalls in Berkshire is at this point, known as the Twin Cascades. Two tiny brooks join each other after their chase down the steep mountain sides and make a leap of nearly forty feet.

On the east side near the Tunnel portal is a beautiful bit of scenery. The mountain rises abruptly, and away on the hillsides farm houses are seen as though they were fastened to the side of the mountain. At this portal there is a ravine which is quite charming. A few feet south of the entrance is seen distinctly what appears to be an immense auger hole, where the first attempt was made to bore through the mountain, by a huge machine. A fine dam was built a short distance up the river, and altogether the scenery, the narrow valley, the rushing river and other surroundings are well worth a visit. A path, several rods wide, leading directly over the mountain through the woods, is exactly over the Tunnel and was made to assist in the engineering operations.

On the east side of the town, down by the Deerfield River, is a lovely narrow valley, with the river as the east boundary; beyond, high on the bank, is the railway, and then the towering hills of the range in Franklin County. Here is the Hoosac Tunnel Station, and it is a pleasant drive down this valley through Zoar, to Charlemont, Shelburne Falls and thence to Greenfield. A good many summer people have sought rest and quiet at the Station. Jenks & Rice have a house for summer guests and can accommodate 50 or more very comfortably. The Hoosac Tunnel House also accommodates a number of people. The village is easily reached by trains on the Fitchburg, and also the New Haven & Northampton railroad. The place is also a resort for excursionists who spend the day very profitably about the tunnel and the works there. The Messrs. Newton have built a narrow gauge railroad running up the river to Readsboro, to which there is a delightful trip of a few hours, or a carriage drive up the valley is a pleasant recreation.

CLARKSBURG.

THE eastern boundary of the town is the Green Mountain range, or the Hoosacs, as they are termed here, and commanding peaks arise in all directions in that part of the town. The great mountain in the western part plainly seen from North Adams, with a dome-like summit and almost bald, affords one of the finest points of observation in Berkshire, 2,272 feet high. The western part of the town has few or no roads, but the eastern part has drives and attractive scenery on every side. From any of the points, and especially the road from North Adams directly north through Houghtonville, the picture is grand, particularly toward the south when the summit is reached.

The road from North Adams through Clarksburg is a romantic drive. Up Union street past the great printing works of the Freeman Manufacturing Company, are other mills, like the Union, the Beaver, and so on following the stream, the Hoosac, to Briggsville, which is the real village of Clarksburg, where the postoffice is located. High mountains are on the east in Florida, and on the west the more fertile hills of the farms, while all along is a most delightful shade. This highway is the main road to Stamford and Bennington, Vt., a most charming day's outing. There is no hotel in the town suitable for resort. Here is neither church, doctor nor lawyer; North Adams being so near at all points that none are necessary, and, the inhabitants find their church affiliations either in that village or in Stamford, a few miles away.

From North Adams, again, another pretty drive is up Eagle street, and on the high ground just above the village another view of the valley below is obtained. This drive of about four miles to its junction with the other road up the Hoosac branch, is a fine one.

As yet few summer residents have come to Clarksburg; and while there are many fine farms in the town, the surface of which is broken and uneven, and though there are many good farm houses, architecture of modern style has obtained no foothold, and the town's best attraction is that which Nature has so profusely lavished on every hand and which is better appreciated by the sight than by a description. Its citizens are excellent people, and some of them would entertain guests in the quietude of their homes.

WILD FLOWERS AND PLANTS.

In these days of æstheticism, flower worship is a prominent characteristic of the times. Wild flowers that our forefathers passed by without regard, or knew not the existence of, are now eagerly sought. Berkshire has choice attractions in this line, for it is famous for having in plenty great varieties and many species and families of rare and beautiful wild flowers.

There are only two plants poisonous to the touch—the poison ivy and the poison sumach, otherwise called dogwood. After the earliest spring flower, the Hepatica (two varieties) comes Trailing Arbutus, which thrives hardly anywhere so well as in Berkshire. The Azalea is hardly out of bloom in the woodland, when some of the handsomest Ladyslippers to be found in the world are in blossom. Four kinds of these orchids are found—the Stemless Ladyslipper, the Small and the Large Yellow, and the magnificent Showy Ladyslipper. Among other orchids are the Showy Orchis and the Purple Fringed Orchis. There are in all 23 kinds of orchids. Of the two Anemones, the Woody blossoms in May and the Virginia in June. Three kinds of Meadow Rue appear from May to July, the last being the most beautiful; during the same time four or more kinds of Buttercups appear. The Marsh Marigolds, or Cowslips, are plenty in wet places in May, when the Gold Thread, with its pretty white flower and golden roots is also seen. The spring brings the Wild Columbine, commonly called Wild Honey Suckle, and the Red and White Baneberries. The Tulip tree, with its faint orange yellow large bell-shaped flower, blossoms in June, and the May Apple or Mandrake, is an edible July fruit. There are the White and Yellow Water Lilies, the Purple Pitcher Plant or Huntsman's Cup, of the bog, the Bloodroot of April and May in rich woods, the Dutchman's Breeches of May, two kinds of St. John's-wort in June, the early Spring Beauty and eight or nine Violets. The Herb Robert is a little geranium, and the Cranesbill is a variety of the same. There are two kinds of Jewel Weed, the Flowering Wintergreen, and five kinds of Clover. The Vicia Cracca is a climbing plant with purple flowers. Wild roses are numerous, the Purple Avens is found in three kinds, and the Shrubby Cinquefoil grows in neglected meadows.

All berries are numerous—Strawberries, Blackberries, Dewberries, Red and Black Raspberries, Black and Blue Huckleberries, so that there is plenty of berries to eat all summer. The Hawthorne is the genuine Mayflower, the Shadbush blossoms early, the Saxifrages may early be seen climbing on rocks. The Bishop's Cup comes out in May, the pink-purple Witton Herb is seen in August; there are two Orpines, yellow and purple, and three or four brilliant yellow Evening Primroses. The Star Cucumber with its pretty flower in July and August, climbs over bushes, the Aralia has a June flower, the Carnel bushes have bright red berries, and there are yellow and red Wild Honeysuckles, the real, not the Columbine. Many of the fields are so thickly covered with Bluets all summer that they seem to have a reflection of the sky.

Over 100 members of the Aster family are found here and over 20 kinds of Golden Rod. Several varieties of the Lobelia are found, among them two or three of the blue, and the Cardinal flower, which may be found in Berkshire in greater quantities than elsewhere in all New England; this flower, with its bright cardinal tint, grows so plentiful that acres are colored with it, and an armful may be picked by one standing in one place. There are Bell Flowers and Indian Pipes, the latter in woods. The Heath family is very plenty; the Mountain Laurel, Sheep Laurel, Swamp Laurel and Azalea grow in all woodland. In woods there are three pretty varieties of the Pyrola. The red False Beech Drops are found in September in oak and pine woods, the Star flower is plenty, the Broom Rape has one flower and no leaves, and grows as a parasite from the roots of trees. There is the Snakehead, the Monkey flower that makes the road sides blue a quarter of a mile in a place, the Gerardia with its large yellow bells, and two wild Verbenas, blue and white, blossoming in July.

The mints are numbered by over 20. The Viper's Bugloss has a brilliant blue, the Hedge Bind Weed flowers in July, the Climbing Bittersweet shows its orange and scarlet berries in autumn, and three kinds of Gentian, one of them Fringed, are plenty in September. Buckwheat is found in ten varieties, the Iris is represented by two kinds of Blue Flag, Blue Eyed Grass is common, the Carrion flower comes out in June, the Trillium grows in three varieties—the Yellow, Purple and Painted. Indian Cucumber Root, three varieties of Bellwort, the Clintonia, a wild lily, Solomon's Seal in several kinds, several varieties of Wild Lilies, Wild Lupine, Pickerel Weed, and Dog Tooth Violets are all found more or less plenty.

Here are the Staghorn Sumach with its crimson spikes, the Crocus, the numerous Cat-tails, Exquisite Ferns, including Maidenhair, four kinds of Club Moss, commonly called Ground Pine, Tree Pine, Club Pine and Running Pine, Jacob's ladder, several kinds of Rushes, 83 kinds of Sedge Grasses and numerous Grasses and Rush Grasses; the Sassafras abounds, the Aromatic Wintergreen or Checkerberry, the crimson-purple Poke Berries, the Mountain Ash, Daisies in many varieties, the early Coltsfoot, Wild Sunflower, the Sidesaddle flower, Water cress, omnipresent Frost Grape vines. Among the numerous nuts are the chestnut, butternut, walnut and hazelnut. Mosses grow in 60 varieties, and Lichens in many kinds. The Clematis, climbing over dark alders, becomes beautiful in the autumn, and in Williamstown a purple variety has been found. The Witch Hazel blossoms close the flower season as late as December. There are nearly 200 kinds of trees in the county and about 1,100 varieties of wild plants.

"If it be summer," writes Prof. Hitchcock, "these vast slopes are covered from base to summit with a vegetable dress, embracing every hue of green, from the dark hemlock and pine to the almost silvery whiteness of the white oak and poplar. If it be autumn, that same foliage, now assuming almost every color of the spectrum, and of hues almost as bright, presents one of the most splendid objects in nature."

CLIMATE.

THE air of Berkshire is dry, extremely pure and bracing. Its humidity is considerably less than that of sea coast air. The county is but little affected by the disagreeable east winds so much complained of along the Atlantic coast and interior of New England, east of the Connecticut River. The wind is from the northwest through the day about half the year.

The autumn is later and the spring earlier in the county, south of Lenox, by one to two weeks, than in the region north. The following table which compares the temperature taken at Williams College at an altitude of 708 feet with the temperatures of several cities, shows a higher summer temperature than is found in many places in the county at places more exposed to cool winds and at greater elevations:

PLACE.	MEAN TEMPERATURE IN DEGREES.					YEARS OF OBSERVATION.
	SPRING.	SUMMER.	AUTUMN.	WINTER.	WHOLE YEAR.	
Williams College,	43.44	67.25	47.36	23.28	45.33	37
Boston,	45.61	68.68	51.04	28.08	48.35	38
Albany,	46.54	70.43	49.56	25.26	47.95	46
New York,	48.26	72.62	54.54	31.93	51.83	22
Philadelphia,	50.07	73.	54.	30.05	52.01	57
Hartford,	47.89	69.75	51.70	29.89	49.81	17

The summer temperature is from 1.43 to 5.75 degrees cooler at Williams College than at the cities named—cities that send many of their residents hither at this time of the year; and, on account of the dryness of the air here and the humidity of the air near the sea coast, the difference in summer and in all other seasons of the year is vastly greater, measured by sensation, the feeling being much more comfortable in Berkshire whether in hot or cold temperature.

POPULATION OF PRINCIPAL TOWNS, 1885.

Adams,	10,000
Alford,	341
Becket,	938
Cheshire,	1,448
Dalton,	2,113
Egremont,	826
Gt. Barrington (error in census), about	4,900
Lanesboro,	1,212
Lee,	4,274
Lenox,	2,154
Monterey,	571
Mount Washington,	160
New Marlboro',	1,661
North Adams,	14,500
Otis,	703
Pittsfield,	16,000
Richmond,	854
Sheffield,	2,033
Stockbridge,	2,114
Tyringham,	457
West Stockbridge,	1,648
Williamstown,	3,729
Berkshire County, 32 towns, about	74,000

1880 CENSUS.

Salisbury, Ct.,	3,715
North Canaan, Ct.,	1,537
Norfolk, Ct.,	1,418
Hillsdale, N. Y.,	1,939
New Lebanon, N. Y.,	2,245

BERKSHIRE'S TOPOGRAPHY.

The Berkshire region is not quite confined to the county limits. Beyond these the choicest extension is on the south three or four miles into Litchfield county Connecticut; on the west the country peculiar to Berkshire goes a mile or so into New York; on the north Vermont is an inferior continuation of it; while on the east it is lost in a few miles in the western margin of the Connecticut river valley. Comprehending these narrow strips of country around the county of Berkshire, the region is about 55 miles long, and averages about 25 miles in width, and contains about 1,400 square miles. The natural features of the southern half of the county have been the most known to fame, but the northern half has many attractions, and recent local enterprise is bringing some of them to notice.

The western boundary of the region is the Taconic Mountains, a narrow range, which begins on the north at the Hoosac River valley and runs into hills in Connecticut on the south. The New York state line runs along these mountains. East of them is a composite valley, five to ten miles wide, unlike other large valleys and constituting the greatest source of Berkshire's beauty. Eastward of this is an extension of the Green Mountain range, about thirty miles wide, broken into many ranges and spurs by gorges and narrow valleys. The wild and picturesque are found in these ranges of mountains, but the beautiful belongs to the valley alone.

Here, whatever way one looks, there is a mountain background, dark and harmonizing in tint with the intermediate landscape. The broad valley is called composite, because it is made up of hundreds of smaller valleys between spurs of the main mountain chains and isolated hills and mountains. The most conspicuous of these is Greylock Mountain, the highest in the state, which extends a few miles north and south and east and west and divides the north end of the great valley into two parts. The finest background is made by the Taconics in the southwest corner of the county, where the Dome rises, the second highest mountain in the state. Every view is a symphony of many natural effects—of mountain range, of lake, of hill, of forest, of separate hills in all sorts of restful shapes, of ravine and precipice, of river and brook, of farm house, of meadow with graceful elms, of country home of some city inhabitants—all combined to make a perfect whole, without imitation and without duplicate. Every observant visitor to Berkshire has noticed how suddenly the views change and how radical the change often is. Governor John A. Andrew spoke of "the delicious surprises" of Berkshire rides; but he is only one of thousands who have remarked them. There are no two views in the broad valley or on the adjacent mountain slopes, 200 yards apart, that do not possess decidedly distinct differences; and places are very common where 50 steps will quickly change the scene as by the wand of magic.

Just above the middle of this long valley rise the Housatonic and the Hoosac rivers, the one flowing north and northwest, and the other one flowing south, and both possessing many tributary streams to grace their valleys. Within the county are 55 natural lakes, principally in the southern half, and half as many artificial reservoirs, while in the narrow margin outside of the county there are twenty or thirty more lakes, making, in all, about 100 bodies of water that lend charm to the landscape and sport to the fisherman and boatman. The altitude of the great valley at the south end is about 700 feet above the ocean; in the middle it is about 1,000 feet; at the foot of Greylock it is about 1,100, from which it descends considerably, northward. The mountain elevations range from 2,000 to 3,500 feet, and are inhabited on nearly every square mile.

In the following table of elevations, the village elevation is that of the railway station, where there is one.

The elevations on the following pages must be taken as more or less correct approximations. Those obtained by leveling, are from railroad surveys, which have started, some at tide, and others a few feet above, the number not being known, and such elevations apply to the track at the railway station of the village mentioned. The figures here given are not in all respects harmonious, though apparent errors are not great. Elevations taken by barometer vary considerably, and it is only by repeated trials that accuracy is reached, which has not always been the case in this list. In the following table L means engineer's level; B means barometric measurement; (?) expresses some uncertainty.

ELEVATIONS IN BERKSHIRE.*

ADAMS.

	Feet above tide.		Feet above tide.
Greylock,	3,585B	Spruce Mountain,	2,588B

BECKET.

Becket,	1,200L	Ward Pond,	1,600L
Becket Hill,	2,194B	Greenwater Pond,	1,873L
West Becket,	1,380L	Viet's Summit,	1,728L
Shaw Pond,	1,380L		

CANAAN, CT.

Canaan, Ct.,	670L	Canaan Mountain,	1,500B
East Canaan,	790L		

CLARKSBURG.

Clarksburg Mountain,	2,272B

COPAKE IRON WORKS, N. Y.

Copake Iron Works, N. Y.,	670L

DALTON.

Dalton,	1,197L	Mount Weston,	2,200(?)
Day Mountain,	1,900(?)		

FLORIDA.

Hoosac Mountain, east summit over tunnel,	2,209L	Hoosac Tunnel, central shaft,	829L
		Hoosac Tunnel, west portal,	766L
Hoosac Tunnel, east portal,	706L		

GOSHEN, CT.

Ivy Mountain,	1,640B

GREAT BARRINGTON.

Great Barrington,	723L	Water Company's Reservoir, east of river,	793B
Mount Bryant,	1,448B		
Highest part of East Mountain,	1,740B	Street at J. A. Brewer's house,	704B
Berkshire Heights,	980B	Street at Berkshire House,	716B
Van Deusenville,	726L	Housatonic River Bridge near "Brookside,"	672B
Housatonic,	740L		
Three Mile Hill,	930L	Green River Bridge, (Egremont Road),	673B
Monument Mountain,	1,260(?)		
June Mountain, (Wildwood Cottage),	865B	Summit in Highway south of Mark Laird's,	1,092B
June Mountain, (June's Spring),	958B		

HANCOCK.

Potter Mountain,	2,410B

HILLSDALE, N. Y.

Hillsdale, N. Y.,	670L	White's Hill,	1,510B

* The town elevation given is at railroad station, when there is one.

HINSDALE.

	Feet above tide.		Feet above tide.
Hinsdale,			1,430L

LEE.

Lee,	865L	South Lee,	843L

LENOX.

Lenox Village,	1,268	Lenox Furnace Mill Pond,	934L
Lenox Station,	957L	New Lenox, or Dewey's,	977L
Lenox Furnace,	937L	Yokun's Seat,	2,080B

LITCHFIELD, CT.

Litchfield Hills,			1,200

MONTEREY.

Monterey,	1,230L	Lake Garfield,	1,250L

MOUNT WASHINGTON.

The Dome,	2,624B	West Mountain,	2,300B
Fray Mountain,	1,915B	Bear Rock,	1,575B(?)
Mount Alandar,	2,200B	Isaac Spurr's,	1,653B(?)
Race Mountain,	2,300B	O. C. Whitbeck's,	1,698B(?)
Cedar Mountain,	1,775B	Mount Ethel,	1,833B(?)
Sunset Mountain,	1,790B		

NEW MARLBORO.

New Marlboro,	1,470L	Lake Buel,	900(?)

NORFOLK, CT.

Norfolk,	1,250L	Bald Mountain,	1,770B
Haystack Mountain,	1,670B	West Norfolk,	1,080L
Dutton Hill,	1,632B	Norfolk Summit,	1,335L

NORTH ADAMS.

North Adams,			701L

NORTHEAST, N. Y.

Rudd Pond,			796L

OTIS.

Otis,	1,200L	Great Pond,	1,540L
West Otis,	1,350L	Parish Pond,	1,515L
East Otis,	1,440L	Thomas Pond,	1,620L
Otis Reservoir, (Rand Pond,)	1,480L	Cold Spring,	1,200L

PERU.

French Hill,			2,239B

PITTSFIELD.

Pittsfield,	1,013L	South Mountain,	1,870B

RICHMOND.

Richmond,	1,046L	Perry's Peak,	2,089B

SALISBURY, CT.

	Feet above tide.		Feet above tide.
Salisbury,	690L	Monument Mountain,	2,300B(?)
North Pond, (Mt. Riga),	1,732B	Lion's Head,	1,675B
Round Pond, (Mt. Riga),	1,722B	Bald Peak,	2,000B
Water Shed, west of Round Pond,	1,760B	Bear Mountain,	2,250B
Lake Wononscopomuc,	723	Ore Hill,	830L
Barac Matiff,	1,250B	Lakeville,	720L
Prospect Mountain,	1,450B	Twin Lakes,	740L
Indian Mountain,	1,360B	Foley's Summit, H. & C.W. R. R.	772L

SANDISFIELD.

Seymour Mountain,	1,698B	Montville,	1,300L
South Sandisfield,	1,350L	West New Boston,	1,010L
Upper Spectacle Pond,	1,575L	New Boston,	980L
Lower Spectacle Pond,	1,540L		

SHEFFIELD.

Sheffield,	675L	Red Bridge at Kelloggtown,	648B
Bridge, Sage's House at Ravine,	783B(?)	Summit Pitcher's Notch,	719B
Ashley Falls,	683L	State Line, Housatonic R. R.,	690L

SOUTH EGREMONT.

South Egremont,			700L

STOCKBRIDGE.

Main Street,	833L	Glendale,	826L

TYRINGHAM.

"Fernside,"	1,160(?)	Mountain near "Fernside,"	2,200(?)

WASHINGTON.

Washington,	1,436L	Highest Railroad Point,	1,451L

WEST STOCKBRIDGE.

West Stockbridge,	901L	State Line,	913L
Williamsville,	798L	Rockdale Mills,	840L

WILLIAMSTOWN.

Williamstown,	594L	Sunset Rock,	1,992B
Berlin Mountain,	2,814B	Berlin Pass,	2,192B
State Line, Mass. & Vt., (Troy & Greenfield R. R.)	577L	Petersburg Mountain,	2,534B
		Petersburg Pass,	2,075B
Williams College, (Old Observatory,)	708L	East Mountain, (copper bolt,)	2,276B
		Stone Hill,	1,086B
Mount Hopkins,	2,790(?)	Summit between Williamstown, and Hancock on highway,	1,215L
Greylock, center peak,	2,591B		
Bald Mountain,	2,597B		

SOME OF THE DRIVES AND DISTANCES

IN AND AROUND BERKSHIRE.

SUCH are the extraordinary profusion and variety of Berkshire charms that the drives are limited only by the roads. Hardly a drive can be found that is not worthy of note. However, there are some drives that are particularly desirable and these are embraced in the following tables. It is a happy fact, most strikingly found in Berkshire, that, no matter what way one drives, he may return by some other route that does not vary much in distance from that of the outgoing route, so that the scene is constantly changing to the very end. For the benefit of tourists, on foot, with horse, or wheel, distances between towns on the main lines of travel are given. All routes mentioned are the most direct, unless otherwise specified. There are numerous fine short drives of two to five miles near each village, which it is unnecessary to mention.

FROM PITTSFIELD.

	Miles.
Potter Mountain,	9
Hancock, via Potter Mountain,	11
Balanced Rock,	4
Lanesboro, via Pontoosuc Lake,	5
Constitution Hill, in Lanesboro,	7
New Ashford, via Lanesboro,	12
South Williamstown, via Lanesboro and New Ashford,	16
Williamstown, via Lanesboro, New Ashford and South Williamstown,	20
Williamstown, return via North Adams, Adams, Cheshire, Berkshire and Coltsville,	45
Adams, via Cheshire,	15
North Adams, through the Hoosac Valley,	20
Cheshire, via Lanesboro, and over the hill keeping west of the reservoir, return via east side of the reservoir, Berkshire, Coltsville,	20
Lanesboro, thence to the road to Cheshire, crossing the reservoir to the east about midway its length, return via Berkshire Glass Works,	16
Berkshire Glass Works,	6
Boulder Trains, Richmond,	8
Perry's Peak, Richmond,	9
Queechy Lake, Canaan, N. Y., via Richmond,	12
Queechy Lake, north through Lebanon Valley to Mt. Lebanon Shakers, return,	25
Onota Lake,	2
Pontoosuc Lake north end, to Balanced Rock, return,	9
Craneville,	5
Dalton, via Coltsville,	5
Dalton, via Junction and Bartonville,	7
Wahconah Falls, via Dalton,	9
Windsor Hill, via Dalton,	13
Peru meeting house via Hinsdale,	17
Worthington, via Peru,	22
West Cummington, via Windsor Hill,	22
Goshen and Plainfield,	25
Cummington,	23
Hinsdale, via new Pittsfield and Dalton road,	8
Hinsdale, via Dalton village street,	11
Hinsdale, via back road,	12
Ashley Lake,	5

FROM PITTSFIELD.—(Continued.)

	Miles.
The Gulf and Wizard's Glen,	4
Dalton meeting house, west through the Gulf and Wizard's Glen, return,	10
Lanesboro, Berkshire, and return,	12
Pontoosuc, Z. Crane, Jr's., farm, Oren Benedict's,	4
Pontoosuc, farms of Z. Crane, Jr., and W. F. Milton, Coltsville and return,	6
Pontoosuc, W. F. Milton's, north past Thomas Barber's to the road running from Berkshire to Lanesboro, Lanesboro and return,	7
Shaker Promised Land, via West street, north through a delightfully romantic part of the town, return,	8
Lebanon Springs, directly over the mountain,	7
Lebanon Springs, return via Lebanon Shakers, through Hancock Shaker community, Barkerville, and Stearnsville,	17
Lebanon Shakers, via Hancock Shakers,	8
Hancock Shakers,	4
Lulu Cascade,	4
Berry Pond,	5
West street to Francis place, Stearnsville and return,	5
West Stockbridge, via Barkerville and Richmond,	11
Richmond Congregational church,	7

	Miles.
Washington church,	7
Washington, at the "City,"	10
Washington, via direct road east, to Washington Station, return via the "City," Ashley Lake,	22
Becket, via Washington,	18
Barkerville,	3
Barkerville, via Stearnsville, turn east, return via upper or hill road,	6
South Mountain, and "Broadhall," on Lenox road,	2
Lenox,	6
Stockbridge, via Lenox,	12
Stockbridge, via Curtisville,	13
Lake Mahkeenac,	8½
Lee, via Lenox,	11
Lee, via Lenox, return via Lenox Furnace,	20
Tyringham, via Lee.	16
"Fernside" (Tyringham), via South Lee,	17
Otis, via Lee,	23
Lenox, return via old Lebanon turnpike, West Stockbridge road,	16
Around Onota Lake, out via North Woods, return via Peck's,	6
Greylock Mountain, via Cheshire,	16
Barkerville, Branch's Corners, Hancock Shakers, return,	9
Cemetery,	2
Tory Glen,	5
Mount Weston, Dalton,	8

FROM LENOX.

	Miles.
Pittsfield,	6
Pittsfield, return via east road,	14
Pittsfield, return via mountain road, New Lenox,	16
Lanesboro,	12
Williamstown,	26
North Adams,	26
Adams,	20
Cheshire,	16
Dalton, (railway station),	12
Lebanon Shakers,	9
Lebanon Shakers, return via Pittsfield,	21

	Miles.
West Stockbridge,	6
State Line, via West Stockbridge,	9
Chatham, via West Stockbridge,	20
West Stockbridge, Richmond, return,	15
Richmond Hill,	9
Richmond, Barkerville, Pittsfield, return,	16
West Mountain Drive,	10
Under West Mountain Drive,	5
Over Bald Head Mountain, return,	7
Higginson's Corner, "Highwood," return,	4½

FROM LENOX.—(Continued.)

	Miles.		Miles.
Lebanon Springs,	12	Lake Mahkeenac,	2½
Lebanon Springs, return via Pittsfield,	25	Lily Pond,	1¼
New Lenox,	4½	Laurel Lake,	3
New Lenox, return via Lenox Station,	11	"Highlawn Farm,"	4
Lenox Station,	2½	Bradley's Corner, Palmer's, return via Lake Mahkeenac,	11
Lenox Furnace,	2¾	Rathbone's, Dorr's, return,	5
Lenox Furnace, return via Lenox Station,	6	Rathbone's, Dorr's, return via Lenox Station road,	6
Lee,	4	Lebanon Road, via Happy Valley, to Bradford's, return,	5½
Lee, return via Lenox Furnace,	10	Through "Cliffwood" Park,	4 to 6
Washington Mountain, via Lenox Furnace, return via New Lenox,	18	Curtis's Farm, to the Lenox Furnace road, return,	5½
Lee, return via "Highlawn Farm," Stockbridge road,	10	Sand's place, Lake Mahkeenac, return,	6½
Tyringham, via Lee, return via South Lee,	20	Lanier's farm, private road to Stockbridge road, Thomson's private road to Lee road, return,	3½
East Lee, return via Lenox Furnace,	14	Bashbish,	27
Fernside,	9	Bashbish, return via river road,	55
Fernside, return via Lee,	19	The Dome of the Taconics,	27
Stockbridge, via Lee, return,	15	Twin Lakes, East Side,	27
Stockbridge, return via lake road,	13	Sheffield,	20
Stockbridge, return via Curtisville,	14	Salisbury,	30
Stockbridge, return via West Stockbridge,	16	Otis,	16
Curtisville,	4½	Hartford, via Lee, Otis, New Boston, Colebrook,	60
Around Lake Mahkeenac,	10	Hudson, via West Stockbridge, State Line, Canaan, Chatham, Ghent,	32
Curtisville, West Stockbridge, return,	14	Albany, via Lebanon, Brainard's Bridge, Nassau,	40
Glendale, via Stockbridge, return,	16	
Housatonic,	10	
Great Barrington, via river road,	15	
Great Barrington, via Stockbridge,	14	Springfield, via Lee, Becket, Blandford, Westfield,	42
West Stockbridge, Williamsville, Housatonic, return,	22	

FROM STOCKBRIDGE.

	Miles.		Miles.
Lee, over hill,	4	Curtisville, through [Lake Averic, base of West Stockbridge mountain, return by turnpike,	7
Lee, via river,	5	
Pittsfield,	12	
Great Barrington,	7½	W. Stockbridge, via Williams River, Fuary's Quarries, Glendale, return,	12
Great Barrington, via Glendale,	9	
Glendale,	1½	Lake Buel,	10
Housatonic,	4	Lake Mahkeenac, (Sayles's),	3
West Stockbridge,	5	Lake Averic,	3
"Fernside,"	6	Monterey, via Monument Valley, Blue Hill, return via Beartown,	18
Tyringham, Hop Brook road,	8	

FROM STOCKBRIDGE.—(Continued.)

	Miles.
Curtisville,	3
Lebanon Shakers,	18
Bashbish,	21
The Dome of the Taconics,	21
North end of Lake Mahkeenac,	4
Around Lake Mahkeenac,	8
Glendale, return through Mr. Butler's,	8
Around Monument Mountain,	10
Lenox,	6
Lenox, via Lake Mahkeenac,	7
Lenox, via Curtisville,	8
Monument Valley to Blue Hill,	5
W Stockbridge, ret. via L Mahkeenac	13
Perry's Peak, via West Stockbridge, Richmond, ret. via W. Stockbridge,	24
Richmond Church, via West Stockbridge, return,	18
Monument Mountain, return via Smith Farm, (horseback ride),	8
Monument Mountain, summit,	5
Long Lake, via Glendale, Housatonic, Williamsville, return via Van Deusenville, Monument Mountain,	16
Lenox, via Lee, return direct,	14
"Highlawn Farm,"	5

FROM GREAT BARRINGTON.

	Miles.
Stockbridge,	7½
South Lee,	9
Lee,	11½
Lee, via South Lee,	12½
Lenox,	14
Pittsfield,	20
Housatonic,	5
Glendale,	7
Curtisville,	9
West Stockbridge,	10
North Egremont,	5
South Egremont,	4
Mount Washington, P. O.,	10
New Marlboro,	9
Otis Center,	16
Monterey,	8
Mill River,	8
Sheffield,	6
Clayton,	11
Ashley Falls,	10
Canaan, Ct.,	12
Canaan Camp Meeting Grounds,	14
Norfolk, Ct.,	18
Winsted, Ct.,	26
Salisbury, Ct.,	15
Lakeville, Ct.,	17
Millerton, N. Y.,	22
Hillsdale, N. Y.,	10
Hudson, N. Y.,	27
Springfield, via Sandisfield, New Boston, Tolland, Granville, Southwick,	42
Otis Reservoir,	19
Lake Buel,	5 to 6
Lake Buel, return via Brush Hill,	14
New Marlboro, return via Brush Hill,	22
Lake Garfield,	10
Stockbridge, Lenox, return via Lake Mahkeenac, Stockbridge, Glendale,	29½
Stockbridge, Lenox, return via Curtisville,	28
"Highlawn Farm,"	12½
Monument Mountain, Summit,	4½
Williamsville, return via Long Lake,	11
Alford, via new road, return via old road,	11
Alford, return around Tom Ball mountain, via marble quarries, Williamsville,	17
Green River, N. Y., via Seekonk, return via North Egremont,	17
Prospect Lake,	5
White's Hill, via North Egremont,	8
White's Hill, via Seekonk, Dr. Beebe's, return via North Egremont,	16
North Egremont, via Seekonk, return via Egremont Plain,	10
Mount Washington, Whitbeck's, Sunset Mountain,	11
The Dome Summit, via Walsh place,	13
Bashbish,	13
Bashbish, return via Copake Iron Works, Hillsdale,	28

FROM GREAT BARRINGTON.—Continued.

	Miles
Springfield, via Monterey, Otis, Blandford Center, Westfield,	42
Westfield,	32
Stockbridge, return via Glendale,	16
Stockbridge, Curtisville, and return,	18
Between Sheffield and Great Barrington there are seven roads—the meadow (6 miles), east (7), Brush Hill (8), west (7), So. Egremont (9), So. Egremont and "Bowwow" (10), So. Egremont and under mountain (15), 21 round trips by different roads,	13 to 23
Six roads to cross roads, between Great Barrington and Sheffield, 15 round trips,	7 to 14
Clayton, return via Ashley Falls, Sheffield,	23
Tipping Rock, via Mill River, return via Southfield, New Marlboro, Lake Buel,	26
Bear Rock, via Mount Washington,	15
Bear Rock, via Sheffield roads,	13
Bear Rock, via Mount Washington, return via Sheffield roads,	28
Sage's Ravine,	12
Sage's Ravine, return via Chapinville, Cooper Hill,	27
Twin Lakes, east side,	13
Twin Lakes, between the lakes, Gardner's,	14
North Egremont, via Seekonk, return via Baldwin Hill, Egremont Plain,	12
Around Mount Riga, via South Egremont, Mount Washington, Bashbish, Copake Flats, near Millerton, Lakeville,	48
North Egremont, Prospect Lake, turn to right at J. L. Millard's, top of mountain, return via Ox Bow summit, Baldwin Hill,	14

FROM SHEFFIELD.

	Miles
Sage's Ravine,	6
Twin Lakes, East Side,	7
Twin Lakes, between lakes,	8
Babes' Hill,	6
Salisbury, Ct.,	10
Lakeville, Ct.,	12
Millerton, N. Y.,	16
Canaan, Ct.,	6
Canaan Camp Meeting Grounds,	8
Ashley Falls,	4
New Marlboro,	8
Mill River,	6
Campbell's Falls,	9
Norfolk, Ct.,	14
Winsted, Ct.,	23
Falls Village, Ct.,	11
Clayton,	6
Clayton, via East road,	7
Clayton, via East road, return via Mill River,	16
Bashbish, via Guilder Hollow,	14
Bashbish, via Sage's Ravine,	12
The Dome,	14
South Egremont,	5
Lake Buel,	7
Lake Buel, return via Great Barrington,	19
Under the Mountain, Chapinville, return via Cooper Hill,	15
Wetaug, over South End Ashley Mountain to Twin Lakes, return,	16
Tipping Rock, via Mill River, return via Southfield, New Marlboro,	17
Guilder Hollow, via "Bowwow," return Under Mountain,	14
Mossy Glen,	4
Sunset Hill,	3
White's Hill,	11
Prospect Lake,	8
Ice Gulf,	5
Spurr Lake,	3
Six round drives over 4 roads to cross roads towards Great Barrington,	7 to 12

For drives to Great Barrington, see Great Barrington

FROM SOUTH EGREMONT.

	Miles.		Miles.
Prospect Lake,	3½	Green River Village,	7
White's Hill,	6	North Egremont, Prospect Lake, turn to the right at J. L. Millard's, top of mountain, return via summit of Ox Bow, under mountain road,	11
North Egremont,	3		
North Egremont, return via Baldwin Hill,	7		
Sage's Ravine,	8	Sheffield,	5
Hillsdale, N. Y.,	6	Sheffield, via under mountain road, return,	14
Twin Lakes, between the lakes,	11		
Twin Lakes, East Side,	12	Guilder Hollow, Jug End, Frank Curtis's, return,	7
Salisbury, Ct.,	12		

The Great Barrington drives can nearly all be made from South Egremont; for distance add or subtract 4 or 8 miles, where necessary.

FROM ADAMS.

	Miles.		Miles.
North Adams,	5	The Afternoon and Sunset drive, via North Savoy, through Florida, with a view of the Deerfield valley, returning via North Adams and back to Adams,	20
North Adams by one route, return the other,	10		
Cheshire,	10		
Cheshire, east road, return via west side of valley,	12	New Ashford, via Cheshire and then over the hills,	10
Williamstown, via the Notch road,	7		
Williamstown, via North Adams,	10	Continue this drive through New Ashford, South Williamstown and Williamstown and back via the Notch road,	25
Williamstown, via Notch road, return via North Adams and east road,	17		
Pittsfield, either via Cheshire and the Glass Works, or keeping west of the reservoir through Lanesboro,	15	West Cummington,	12
		Cummington,	15
Go out by one of the routes to Pittsfield, and return the other,	30	Greylock Hall in Williamstown,	12
		Lanesboro, via Cheshire,	10
Savoy, (fine twilight drive),	7	To Cross Road north of Howlands, via west road, return on east road,	4
North Savoy, via North Hoosac street,	4	Windsor Hill,	8
Stamford, Vt.,	10	Stafford's Hill,	4

FROM NORTH ADAMS.

	Miles.		Miles.
Williamstown, either by Greylock Village or Blackinton,	6	Hartwellville, Vt., via Stamford, Vt.,	12
Adams, either the east or west road,	5	Readsboro City, Vt., via Hartwellville, Vt., and Stamford, Vt.,	17
Adams, via east road, return west road,	10	West Summit of Hoosac or Florida Mountain, over Tunnel,	4
Summit of Greylock, via The Notch,	8	Central Shaft of Tunnel,	5
Adams, via the Notch road,	8	East Summit of Florida Mountain, over Tunnel,	7
Stamford, Vt., three routes. This drive north through North Eagle street; or via Weslyan Hill road, or through the Union, or the Beaver,	5	Hoosac Tunnel Station and Jenks & Rice's Hotel,	9
		Pittsfield,	20

FROM NORTH ADAMS.—(Continued.)

	Miles.		Miles.
To the Cascade, in The Notch, . .	2½	Pittsfield, via east road, leaving out Adams village to Cheshire, then on east side of reservoir to Glass Works and the Junction, return via Lanesboro, over hill on west side of reservoir, through Cheshire, then on west road to Adams, Zylonite, ...	40
Natural Bridge, ...	1		
Readsboro, Vt., to east end of Tunnel, return over the Hoosac range via Florida, ...	33		
Sadawga Springs, Vt., via Stamford, Hartwellville and Readsboro City,	21		
Jacksonville, Vt., via Readsboro City,	24		
Wilmington, Vt., ...	27	Pittsfield, via South Williamstown and Lanesboro, ...	26
Bennington, Vt., via Pownal, . .	20		
West Portal of the Hoosac Tunnel, or the West Shaft, ...	2	Pittsfield, via South Williamstown, Lanesboro, return via Cheshire, .	46
West Portal of Tunnel, along the base of the mountain, return to village through Main street, . .	4	Lanesboro, ...	15
		Cheshire, ...	10
		South Williamstown, . . .	9
Go east from the village to the "Five Roads," or "Five Points," north through Clarksburg, along base of mountain, return via the Beaver and the Union, ...	8	Greylock Hall, following the river all the way, ...	7
		Greylock Hall, return via Williamstown village, ...	13

FROM WILLIAMSTOWN.

	Miles.		Miles.
Berlin Mountain, ...	5	For a day's driving one of these routes is taken out and the other back, .	45
Petersburg Mountain, . . .	5		
(The "Snow Hole," is two miles beyond Petersburg Mountain.)		North Pownal, Vt., ...	8
		Hoosac Corners, ...	14
Mason's Hill, return, ...	6	Hoosac Falls, N. Y., ...	17
Bennington, Vt., via Pownal, . .	14	Stamford, Vt., via North Adams, .	10
North Adams, either by Greylock Village, or by Blackinton, . .	6	East end of Hoosac Tunnel, . .	19
		Central Shaft of the Hoosac Tunnel,	8½
To the Notch, above and east of North Adams, ...	7	Notch road to Adams, . . .	7
The Cascade, in the Notch, . .	4½	Same route out, return through the valley via North Adams, . . .	18
Summit of Greylock, via new road of the Park Association, . . .	9	Adams, via North Adams, . . .	11
		New Ashford, ...	8
South Williamstown, three roads, .	4½	Bald Mountain, near Greylock, .	7
South Williamstown, via the "Oblong,"	9	To "The Hopper,"	5
		To the Notch, returning via Braytonville and Blackinton, . . .	9
Around the "Oblong" (Short), . .	2		
Lebanon Springs, via Hancock, .	20	Northwest Hill, return via Pownal,	9
Mount Lebanon Shaker Village, .	22	Macomber Hill, turning to the left a mile from Berlin Mountain, . .	9
Over Potter Mountain, Lanesboro, return via New Ashford, South Williamstown, ...	32		
		To the "White Oaks," on the east side of the river, going northeast and returning via the Professor Hopkins chapel, ...	
Pittsfield, via New Ashford and Lanesboro, ...	20		

FROM WILLIAMSTOWN.—(Continued.)

	Miles.		Miles.
Hancock, ...	13	Bennington, Vt., return via Pownal,	12
Pittsfield, via North Adams and		Mt. Anthony, via Pownal, . .	12
Hoosac Valley to Cheshire, . .	25	Mt. Anthony, via Bennington, Vt., .	16

FROM SALISBURY, CT.

	Miles.		Miles.
Around Twin Lakes, ...	11	Prospect Mountain, ...	2
Between Twin Lakes, return via Chapinville, ...	7	Sharon Village, same way out, return via Indian Lake, Old Ore Hill, Lakeville, ...	20
Between Twin Lakes, return via East road, ...	11	Sharon Village, same way out, over Sharon Mountain to Housatonic River at Cornwall Bridge, return via Lime Rock, ...	35
Between Twin Lakes, return via under mountain road, ...	8		
Around Twin Lakes, via under mountain road, ...	13	Sharon Village, same way out, South Amenia, Leedsville, Sharon Valley, return via Mudge Lake, . .	25
Sage's Ravine, ...	4½		
Sage's Ravine, return via between Twin Lakes, ...	10½	West Cornwall, via Lime Rock, return via Cream Hill, . . .	28
Canaan road to Frink's Hill, Knapp road Canaan Falls, return, . .	13	Cornwall Bridge, via west side of river, Cornwall Plains, Mohawk Mountain, Cream Hill, return, .	38
Canaan Falls, Lime Rock, return, .	12		
Around Lake Wononscopomuc, . .	7		
Around Lake Wononscopomuc, return via Rose Hill, ...	13	Bashbish, via Rossiter Hollow, Mount Riga, return via Copake, Rudd Pond, ...	37
Mount Riga, via Rossiter Hollow, return via Selleck Hill, . . .	10	The Dome, via Rossiter Hollow, Mount Riga, return via South Egremont, ...	41
Mount Riga, via Rossiter Hollow, return via Selleck Hill, Lincoln City, ...	11	The Dome, ...	17
Mount Riga, via Rossiter Hollow, return via West road, Lakeville, .	13	Bear Mountain, via Rossiter Hollow, Mount Riga, 1 mile beyond, path of half mile, ...	5
Over Selleck Hill, return via Lincoln City, ...	4	Bear Rock, ...	6
Sharon Village, via Lakeville, east side Lake Wononscopomuc, Town Hill, return via Mudge Lake, Lakeville, ...	17	Bear Rock, return via Mount Riga, .	19
		Winchell Hill, (3 miles west of Millerton), return via Bird Hill, . .	18
		Sheffield, ...	10

These drives are all made from Lakeville; for distance, add or subtract 1½ or 3 miles where necessary.

FROM CANAAN, CT.

	Miles.		Miles.
Dutcher's Bridge, east side Twin Lakes, return via Cooper Hill, Wetaug, ...	13	Norfolk, ...	7
		East Canaan, Clayton, return, . .	10
Dutcher's Bridge, between Twin Lakes, return via Cooper Hill, Wetaug, ...	15	East Canaan, Whiting River Fill, Clayton, return, ...	12
		Campbell's Falls, ...	7½
		The Dome, via South Egremont, .	20
Sage's Ravine, ...	9	Around Rattlesnake Hill, . . .	4

FROM CANAAN, CT.—(Continued.)

	Miles.		Miles.
Around Twin Lakes, through Chapinville,	18	Campbell's Falls, via East Canaan, Whiting River Fill, return via Clayton,	15
Dutcher's Bridge, west side river to Canaan Falls, return east side,	13	Sheffield,	6
		Salisbury,	9
There are 4 roads to Falls Village—west, east, west of railroad, under Canaan Mountain—affording 6 drives,	12 to 14	Canaan Mountain Pond, via Norfolk,	11
		Canaan Mountain Pond, return via South Canaan,	20

FROM NORFOLK, CT.

	Miles.		Miles.
Around Haystack Mountain,		Ivy Mountain, return via Cream Hill, Canaan,	40
Doolittle Pond,	4		
Canaan Mountain Pond,	4	Mohawk Mountain Tower,	18
Canaan Mountain Pond, return via South Canaan, Canaan,	20	Colebrook,	6
		Colebrook, return via North Colebrook, Doolittle Pond,	15
Winsted,	8		
Winsted, return via Grantville,	18	Canaan,	7
South Norfolk,	4	Canaan Mountain,	6
Winchester,	9	Campbell's Falls,	5
Winchester, return via Winsted,	20	Ashley Falls, via Campbell's Falls,	11
The 5 mile square drive southwest of the village,	5	Litchfield,	18
		Hartford,	35
Ivy Mountain Tower in Goshen,	10	Great Barrington,	18

Trips to Twin Lakes, Salisbury and Lakeville are made by cars.

Trips to the Dome, Bear Mountain, Sage's Ravine, Bashbish, are made by cars to Salisbury, where teams are got.

A HASTY TOUR THROUGH BERKSHIRE.

WITH SOME OF ITS MAIN FEATURES.

THE years of late show a marked increase in the number of tourists through Berkshire; including in the term, those who made a tour of the region with horse and carriage, or on foot, on horseback, or with bicycle. The tourist, however, has a very faint idea of the real Berkshire; it is only those who live here for a whole season, at least, who begin to have an appreciation of the region that is its due. No one should come here expecting to be startled by awful forms of nature. Berkshire has a few of these, but one must go elsewhere to find them abundant. The scenes here are beautiful and picturesque, interspersed with wildness, and to appreciate such scenes requires a more refined taste than to stand in awe of bold and imposing effects. But the tourist who does not hurry, and who will take excursions from the main lines of travel, will much enjoy his Berkshire journey. The remarkably fine condition of the roads are very favorable to agreeable travel in all ways, and the choice keeping at hotels will alone do much toward putting the traveler in good humor.

The Berkshire region is entered on the north through Bennington, Vt.; on the northeast over the Florida Mountains at the Hoosac Tunnel; on the east up the Westfield River to Pittsfield, or from Westfield or Springfield over the hills to Lenox, Stockbridge, Great Barrington or Sheffield; on the southeast, through Winsted, Ct., to the outpost at Norfolk; on the south by the Housatonic River valley in Connecticut; on the southwest through Millerton, N. Y.; on the west to the south end of the county through Hillsdale, N. Y., to the middle through Chatham, N. Y., and to the north end through Hoosac Falls, N. Y., on the northwest. The terminus of the tour through the region should be Salisbury or Norfolk in Connecticut on the south, and Williamstown or North Adams on the north. In the following outline, village attractions, and others that take but little time or may be seen in passing, are not mentioned, and only such principal matters are referred to as a tourist would most like to see, with not time enough to see all. A reading of the town articles may discover other objects of interest.

Beginning at the south end, no one should neglect to visit Salisbury and see the lake at Lakeville, the Twin Lakes, Washinee and Washining, get some of the views from the mountain tops and enjoy some of the beautiful drives of the region. Sage's Ravine lies near the state line on the way to Sheffield and, near by, a steep road goes up the mountain to Bear Rock, about a mile from the main road. After a sufficient stay in Sheffield, the east road to Great Barrington should be taken. Here several days can well be utilized. One should walk to East Rock, Belcher's Cave, Berkshire Heights south of the pine grove. Among the drives that must be taken are those to White's Hill, to Lake Buel and Ice Gulf, to Monument Mountain, and an excursion of two days should be made to Mount Washington, one day for the Dome, and one for Bashbish, going to one of the mountain boarding houses for food and lodging.

At Stockbridge one should walk to Ice Glen and Laura's Rest, and take several of the charming rides of the neighborhood, including the one to "Fernside," one around Lake Mahkeenac and "the new drive" through Lake Averic, near Fuary's quarries, along the base of the mountain, and the West Stockbridge road back. The Lenox visit must be largely devoted to drives, including, on the way, the old county road from Stockbridge to Lenox, a visit to "Highlawn Farm," if the traveler is a lover of horses, a ride to the top of Bald Head Mountain, one through "Cliffwood" park, a visit to the glass works at Lenox Furnace, and other rides over the principal roads of the town. It is well to go to Pittsfield over the east road along the base of the mountain, taking in Tory Glen and Roaring Brook on the way, or through Richmond, ascending on the way, Perry's Peak. Pittsfield has some beautiful drives that would more than take the time that can probably be spared for them. One ride may be to Wahconah Falls in the edge of Windsor, near Dalton, ten miles, returning by the way of the farm of Z. Crane, Jr., in the north part of Pittsfield. If Sunday finds the tourist in Stockbridge, Lenox, Pittsfield, or Cheshire, he will want to visit the Lebanon Shakers, and see their religious observances. Interesting drives are to Wizard's Glen, four miles off, Roaring Brook and Tory's Glen, not far off on the side of Washington Mountain, a ride over Potter Mountain, nine miles away, to Perry's Peak, nine miles, and the glass works at Berkshire Village, six miles off. From

Pittsfield the traveler will pass through Lanesboro, seeing the Balanced Rock in that town, and proceed to Williamstown, where he will be greatly interested in village perfection, and in examining the scenery from several favorable places. At North Adams the Hoosac Tunnel, the magnificent prospect from Florida Mountain, and the Natural Bridge, a mile northeast of the village will take a day, and from North Adams a carriage road leads to the top of Greylock, the outlook from which no one must omit seeing. The order of this tour will vary a little according to the point of beginning, in what respect the map will show. If the tourist's exit is on the northwest, the order will be Lanesboro, Adams, North Adams and Williamstown, instead of the order mentioned, which was intended for a northeast exit.

This tour embraces some of the leading features of the region, and will give the traveler some idea of what it really is. An allowance of the usual vacation time of two weeks for the journey will be very inadequate, though it will be better than not seeing the country at all. Three weeks will do better, and a month should be taken. If the time is short, it would be better to do merely as much of a small part of the county as possible, and do it thoroughly. That a three-weeks' allowance is none too much for only a mere skeleton of a tour within the region, appears when the time is thus allotted: Salisbury, 3 days; Great Barrington, 3; Mount Washington, 2; Stockbridge, 3; Lenox, 3; Pittsfield, 3; Williamstown, 2; North Adams, 2; total: 21 days. To force the journey in two weeks this allowance may be made: Salisbury, 2; Great Barrington, 2; Mount Washington, 2; Stockbridge, 2; Lenox 2; Pittsfield, 2; Williamstown, 1; North Adams, 1; total: 14 days. But instead of doing this, the tourist should better cover less territory and see no more than he can become thoroughly acquainted with. Tours are sometimes made by traveling only on straight roads from either Norfolk, Canaan or Salisbury, through Sheffield, Great Barrington, Stockbridge, Lenox, Pittsfield, Lanesboro, Williamstown and North Adams. In such a course, the tourist is assured, he will get nothing more than an introduction to Berkshire, and will fail to see ninety-nine hundredths of what will be spread before him if he beholds even no more than is suggested in this article.

The only time that is open to many people to make a tour is in some part of July or August, months that are too hot for such an undertaking with the most comfort, and, if the summer be hot and dry a time when Berkshire is not at its best. In early June, when apple trees are in bloom, Berkshire is incomparably lovely, and then, when the hours of daylight are long and the heat is not too great, is a good time for the tour. The roads, however, may not be in quite as good condition as later, but they will be good at their worst. Like a belle of fashion, Berkshire changes her garb with great frequency, and the tourist can see the country in any way he pleases, if he will pick the suitable time of year. But, if he cannot come in June and can come in the middle of September or a little later, by all means let him come at the latter time, when he will behold the brilliant foliage and find temperature most suitable for traveling.

BERKSHIRE PROSE AND POETRY.

THE BEAUTY AND MAJESTY OF BERKSHIRE.

Thou who would'st see the lovely and the wild
Mingled in harmony on Nature's face,
Ascend our rocky mountains. Let thy foot
Fail not with weariness, for on their tops
The beauty and the majesty of earth,
Spread wide beneath, shall make thee to forget
The steep and toilsome way. There, as thou stand'st,
The haunts of men below thee, and around
The mountain summits, thy expanding heart
Shall feel a kindred with that loftier world
To which thou art translated, and partake
The enlargement of thy vision. Thou shalt look
Upon the green and rolling forest tops,
And down into the secrets of the glens,
And streams, that with their bordering thickets strive
To hide their windings. Thou shalt gaze at once,
Here on white villages, and tilth, and herds,
And swarming roads, and there on solitudes
That only hear the torrent, and the wind,
And eagle's shriek.
—*Bryant's Monument Mountain.*

SUNRISE SEEN FROM A BERKSHIRE HILL.

Along the pathway, tangles of white morning glories crept over hedges of thistles and daisies, while meadow veronica rose up dewily fresh in the field grasses, filling the cool morning breeze with sweetest perfume. Over us a few stars lingered in the soft gray heavens, and far over the deep dark eastern hills and beyond the blue range of the Green Mountain chain, the horizon was flushed with rosy gold which deepened into salmon pink as the sun came up from his bath of blue gray mountain mists. Then all the east grew rosy as he left the glowing heaven and curtained himself under falls of soft dove tinted clouds. Not many moments did these somber hued garments enfold him; they quickly changed to the delicate hue of peach blossoms and the billowy edges of their soft gray folds, floating in a light of liquid pearl caught up a fringe of gold and flashed the splendors of day dawn up to the zenith. Through cloud rifts the sun shown over the land. The vapors floated around the nearer mountains, and valleys were tinged with the pinky salmon light of the mountain rim, the tips of the pine forests caught the glow and glittered like walls of emerald set in gold, the bending heads of the rye fields reflected the radiance and rustled in ripples of red gold light; the eastern heaven burned in splendor of opal and lit its signal fire on every mountain height, heralding to the quiet valleys the dawn of another day.—"*Octavia Hensel.*"

BERKSHIRE IN AUTUMN FOLIAGE.

The scenery which a few weeks ago stood in summer green now seemed enchanted. The Housatonic was the same. The skies were the same. The mountain forms were unchanged. But they had blossomed into resplendent colors from top to base. It was strange to see such huge mountains, that are images of firmness and majesty, now tricked out with fairy pomp, as if all the spirits of the air had reveled there and hung their glowing scarfs on every leaf and bough. * * * One who breaks off in the summer and returns in autumn to the hills needs almost to come to a new acquaintance with the most familiar things. It is another world; or it is the old world a-masquerading. * * * But these holiday hills! Have the evening clouds, suffused with sunset, dropped down and become fixed into solid forms? Have the rainbows that followed autumn storms faded upon the mountains and left their mantles there? I stand alone upon the peaceful summit of this hill and turn in every direction. The east is all aglow; the blue north flushes all her hills with radiance; the west stands in burnished armor; the southern hills buckle the zone of the horizon together with emeralds and rubies, such as were never set in the fabled girdle of the gods! Of gazing there cannot be enough. The hunger of the eye grows by feeding.

But in vain do the evergreens give solemn examples to the merry leaves which frolic with every breeze that runs sweet riot in the glowing shades. Gay leaves will not be counseled, but will die bright and laughing. But both together—the transfigured leaves of deciduous trees and the calm unchangeableness of evergreens—how more beautiful are they than either alone! The solemn pine brings color to the cheek of the bushes, and the scarlet and golden maples rest gracefully upon the dark foliage of the million fingered pine. All summer long these leaves have wrought their tasks. Now hath come their play spell. Nature gives them a jubilee. It is a concert of colors for the eye. What a mighty charm of colors do the trees roll down the valleys, up the hillsides, and over the mountains!

When the Year, having wrought and finished her solid structures, unbends and consecrates the glad October month to fancy, then all hues that were before scattered in lurking flowers, in clouds, upon plumed birds, and burnished insects, are left loose like a flock and poured abroad in the wild magnificence of Divine bounty. The earth lifts up its head crowned as no monarch was ever crowned and the seasons go forth toward winter, chanting toward God a hymn of praise.—*Henry Ward Beecher.*

BERKSHIRE STIMULUS TO LITERARY WORK.

The repose and beauty of the scenery of Berkshire, its stimulating climate, its ease of access and its quiet, render it a favorable residence for literary persons, and we suggest to them that, if they desire to write their novels and poems and histories in the briefest possible time, and with the least fatigue, they should come hither.—*Rev. T. T. Munger.*

A BERKSHIRE SUNSET FROM A HILL-TOP.

The Sun hung low over the Catskills, flooding with gold the lakelike expanse of the Hudson as seen over the woodlands on the west. The sunset was one of those peculiar green and gold cloud effects, seldom seen, except at sea, but the great earth waves of the billowy mountains well recalled the waves of ocean, and the evening mists rising from the valleys of the plains, gleamed with the silver sheen of distant waters. Broad bands of sky, where salmon and primrose clouds floated like islands above the blue mirage of mountain and gold of river, lay along the western heaven; but, far above, the deepening blue light of evening spread up to the zenith, bearing on its azure shield the silver crescent of the moon. Then suddenly an orange hue filled all the sky, and rose in intensity of splendor to scarlet and gold; the mountains became gray and steel color beneath the great crimson ball of the sun, slowly sinking to the depths of the mountain billows. Down, down, down, till just a rim of light trembled on the crest of the mountains, then fell into a bath of crimson and glory.—" *Octavia Hensel.*"

The Nature of Country Enjoyment.

The fullest enjoyment of the country does not arise from strong excitements acting in straight lines; not from august mountains, wide panoramas, awful gorges, nor from anything that runs in upon you with strong stimulations. All these things have their place; but they are occasional. They are the sub-base and come in as the mighty undertone upon which soft and various melodies float. A thousand daily little things make their offering of pleasure to those who know how to be pleased.—*Henry Ward Beecher.*

Monument Mountain.

There is a precipice
That seems a fragment of some mighty wall,
Built by the hand that fashioned the old world,
To separate its nations, and thrown down
When the flood drowned them. To the north, a path
Conducts you up the narrow battlement.
Steep is the western side, shaggy and wild
With mossy trees and pinnacles of flint,
And many a hanging crag. But, to the east,
Sheer to the vale go down the bare old cliffs,—
Huge pillars, that in middle heaven upbear
Their weather-beaten capitals, here dark
With moss the growth of centuries, and there
Of chalky whiteness where the thunderbolt
Has splintered them. It is a fearful thing
To stand upon the beetling verge, and see
Where storm and lightning, from that huge gray wall,
Have tumbled down vast blocks, and at the base
Dashed them in fragments, and to lay thine ear
Over the dizzy depth, and hear the sound
Of winds, that struggle with the woods below,
Come up like ocean murmurs. But the scene
Is lovely round; a beautiful river there
Wanders amid the fresh and fertile meads,
The paradise he made unto himself,
Mining the soil for ages. On each side
The fields swell upward to the hills; beyond,
Above the hills, in the blue distance, rise
The mountain columns with which earth props heaven.
—*William Cullen Bryant.*

Country and City Life Contrasted.

It is no advantage to live in a great city, where poverty degrades and failure brings despair. The fields are lovelier than paved streets, and the great forests than walls of brick. Oaks and elms are more poetic than steeples and chimneys. In the country is the idea of home. There you see the rising and setting sun; you become acquainted with the stars and clouds. The constellations are your friends. Your hear the rain on the roof and listen to the rhythmic sighing of the winds. You are thrilled by the resurrection called Spring, touched and saddened by Autumn, the grace and poetry of death. Every field is a picture, a landscape; every landscape a poem; every flower a tender thought; and every forest a fairy-land. In the country you preserve your identity your personality. There you are an aggregation of atoms, but in the city you are only an atom of an aggregation.—*Robert G. Ingersoll.*

Green River.

Yet pure its waters—its shallows are bright
With colored pebbles and sparkles of light,
And clear the depths where its eddies play,
And dimples deepen and whirl away,
And the plane-tree's speckled arms o'ershoot
The swifter current that mines its root,
Through whose shifting leaves, as you walk the hill,
The quivering glimmer of sun and rill
With a sudden flash on the eye is thrown,
Like the ray that streams from the diamond stone.
Oh, loveliest there the spring days come,
With blossoms and birds and wild bees' hum;
The flowers of summer are fairest there,
And freshest the breath of the summer air;
And sweetest the golden autumn day
In silence and sunshine glides away.
—*William Cullen Bryant.*

BERKSHIRE'S HILLS AND HOMES.

Between where Hudson's waters flow
   Adown from gathering streams,
And where the clear Connecticut,
   In lengthened beauty gleams—
Where run bright rills, and stand high rocks,—
   Where health and beauty comes,
And peace and happiness abides,
   Rest Berkshire's Hills and Homes.

The Hoosac winds its tortuous course,
   The Housatonic sweeps
Through fields of living loveliness,
   As on its course it keeps.
Old Saddleback stands proudly by,
   Among Taconic's peaks,
And rugged mountain Monument
   Of Indian Legend speaks.

Mount Washington, with polished brow,
   Green in the Summer days,
Or white with winter's driving storms,
   Or with Autumn's flame ablaze,
Looms up across the southern sky,
   In native beauty dressed—
The home of Bash-Bish, weird and old,
   Anear the mountain's crest.

The winds come fresh from heaven's dome,
   Blue skies trend clear and bright,
Great clouds in turn swing gracefully,
   In majesty and might.
The hum of industry goes out,
   Upon the passing breeze,
And wealth and worth and weariness
   Bring competence and ease.

And still each streamlet runs its course,
   And still each mountain stands,
While Berkshire's sons and daughters roam
   Through home and foreign lands;
But though they roam, or though they rest,
   A thought spontaneous comes,
Of love and veneration for
   Our Berkshire Hills and Homes.

CLARK W. BRYAN.

BERKSHIRE'S NEXT DOOR NEIGHBORS.
SOME OF THE NEAREST ONES.

SALISBURY AND LAKEVILLE, CONN.

The distinctive Berkshire region extends southward into the northern part of Litchfield county, Ct., a few miles. In the northwest corner the town of Salisbury has marvelous beauties that do not pale under any comparison that can be made with them. The town is remarkable in having every variety of scenery within its limits, from the scenes of unbroken wildness to others that touch the last extremity of exquisite beauty. It is safe to say that there is no other town in the country that embraces greater varieties of natural scenery, and all of the very highest order of merit; and that there are none outside of this region that equal it. Salisbury is a country paradise, fit for the very gods themselves to revel in.

BARAK MATIFF AND PROSPECT MOUNTAINS.

Salisbury is singularly rich in mountain outlooks, from places, too, that are easily accessible and that are but short distances from the central villages of Salisbury and Lakeville. The Taconic Mountains here come to a bold, broad, abrupt end at the very margin of these villages, and afford the most indescribable views of Berkshire and Litchfield counties, and the Harlem and Hudson river valleys. The surface of the town away from the Taconics is thoroughly broken up by hills, and some mountains all conducive to making perfect landscapes. The narrow valley in which the picturesque village of Salisbury lies, is bounded on the east by the Watawanchu Mountain, a short range that rises distinct from the Taconics. The north end of this mountain, Barak Matiff, is seen from points far north in Berkshire, and consequently commands views of surprising beauty. People drive a mile to the foot and walk half a mile to the top. Mount Prospect is the highest elevation of this mountain and is often visited for its extensive and varied outlook. It is two miles east of the village of Salisbury, and one may ride to the summit, the last half mile over a private road. It is a favorite resort of people on the Housatonic valley side. Numerous and memorable walks can be made to places in the Watawanchu Mountain.

INDIAN CAVE AND THE POOL.

One half mile from the village across the fields is the Indian Cave, a wild place in the rocks; picnics are held in a neighboring grove, by which runs a mountain brook. A quarter of a mile beyond the cave is the Pool, a medicinal spring, that has much local celebrity for curing cutaneous diseases. The walk up the ravine to reach the spring is a most delightful one.

BABES' HILL.

Continuing with the elevation of the town, we find several on the east and northeast of Lake Washining, the upper one of the Twin Lakes. Babes' Hill is a little smooth conical mount overlooking the lake, easy of ascent, and surprising the climber with a much finer view than he will expect. Indeed, the view is nothing short of a masterpiece, the lake surrounded by darkly wooded shores, with its island, its glassy or rolling waters, the hills, forests, and cleared fields on all sides, and with the dark background of the Taconics to the westward. It is a transformation scene in fairy land, and will put a spell on the observer that he will be loth to break, though it held him for hours.

TOM'S MOUNT AND ASHLEY MOUNTAIN.

Shortly back of Babes' Hill, and rising much higher, is Tom's Mount, commanding this same view from a changing outlook, and including a much more extensive field on the south, and particularly on the north and northwest in Berkshire. East of this mount is Ashley Mountain somewhat higher, largely wooded, but affording from many an outlook on all sides of its circular summit a sweep of views that have few equals for variety in all the Berkshire region. Reference is made to this mountain in the article on Sheffield in which town it is partly situated. A drive to these mounts and a tramp over them would make a rich half day's experience.

INDIAN RELICS.

On the Wetaug road running along the earthen base of Ashley Mountain, parallel with the Housatonic River, is the old Council Elm of the Indians, a quarter of a mile south of Robert Little's house. The old Wetaug burial ground of the Indians is situated on the bank of the river near this place. The wearing of the river at one time washed out many skeletons that crumbled to dust upon exposure and brought to light many Indian relics in the way of weapons, implements, and so on, a large number of which Mr. Little has in his possession.

INDIAN MOUNTAIN AND LAKE.

In the opposite corner of the town, the southwest is Indian Mountain, where the Moravians had a mission in early times. The prospect westward is very fine. On the west side of this mountain in New York state is Indian Pond, a beautiful sheet of water that is the resort of many people from Sharon, from neighboring towns in New York and, often of people from Salisbury.

BEAR MOUNTAIN.

The elevations of the Taconics in this town afford numerous outlets of inexpressible delight. The highest one, Bear Mountain, is the loftiest mountain in Connecticut, being 2,350 feet above the ocean. On the top of this mountain, Robbins Battell of Norfolk has erected a stone monument 20 feet high, on which he has planted an iron post extending 15 feet higher, and on top of the post is a gilded globe 2½ feet in diameter, visible for a long distance, so that the top of the globe is about 2,290 feet above the ocean. People go to this mountain via Mount Riga taking a foot path, the last half mile.

BALD PEAK.

Bald Peak, three miles from Salisbury village, is easily reached by driving to within 100 rods of the top and walking the remainder of the distance.

LION'S HEAD.

Lion's Head is a breast on the eastern side of the Taconics, two miles from Salisbury village, the last half mile being a pathway. It is frequently resorted to, for the view is extensive in Salisbury and beyond and in Berkshire, and one of extreme beauty. A precipice, on one side of the summit gives the top the appearance of a lion's head, it is fancied.

THE COBBLE.

On the border of the north end of the village of Salisbury is a rocky knoll about 100 feet high called the Cobble, from the top of which the outlook is fine. It is of queer formation, rough, and somewhat wooded. The walk requires but ten minutes.

HEAVENLY LAKES.

But the strongest feature of Salisbury is its lakes. It may be said without reservation that in all the Berkshire region there is not another town so rich in lake scenery as this one. If the tourist would touch the highest exaltation of his æsthetic emotions let him come to this town and behold the lakes and their environments, and even if he be in search of lakes that shall convince him of their pre-eminent beauty, he will abide in Salisbury, satisfied that further search would be useless. They are worth a volume of description and enthusiasm, but the gap bebetween the words and their object would be too great. These lakes are simply heavenly.

TWIN LAKES.

The beautiful and the picturesque find their highest forms in the scenes in which the Twin Lakes have a place. A wordy description would fall so far short of doing them half justice that the attempt is too hopeless to be made. Washining the eastern lake and decidedly the most lovely, is nearly round, and about a mile and a half across. A long wooded island of 40 acres breaks its surface. A part of the east shore is like an ocean beach, with its sand and pebbles, and the other shores embrace every variety of description. The water is a clear green, fed almost exclusively by springs in the bed of the lake, which is very deep. Woodland embraces the lake on nearly every side, the hills rise around the bold Tom's Mount almost overhanging the water, and further off stand the mountains, with The Dome and the chain of the Taconics stretching along the whole western horizon. This lake is a famous camping resort and in August as many as 250 to 300 people may sometimes be found camping on the shores. The soft music that floats across the water upon the air of evening, the glitter of the lights, the illuminating moon disclosing the faint outlines of natural objects, and the rippling of her light from the surface of the water, make a night scene that the fancies of the fairies never conceived. Accommodations in the way of boats, horse feeding, and so on, may be had on the east side, which is the best place to go for a day's visit; but various accommodations may be had on the west side.

The west lake, Washinee, is connected with the other by a narrow stream about 50 yards long, flowing water enough to float a boat. The lake is long and curving and ends in a romantic outlet at Chapinville. Its shores are not resorted to for camping, very much, and it is inferior in appearance to the other lake, still it is beautiful beyond the common lot of lakes and affords delightful rowing. The names of these lakes are Indian; Washining, it is said, meaning "Laughing Water," according to the standard phrase, and Washinee "Smiling Water," to express inferior charms. Henry Ward Beecher wrote of them : " For more beautiful sheets of water and more beautiful sites upon which to look at them, one may search for without finding."

The Central N. E. & Western R. R. runs over portions of both lakes and has a station between them. It has been noticed that boulders in Lake Washinee and in North Pond on Mount Riga have changed their resting places and approached the shore. The explanation is that of water expansion when frozen, the ice carrying the imbedded boulders with it. The formation of the famous walled lake of Iowa is thus accounted for. In the woods a short distance from Washinee is a natural cave of considerable extent. It has been explored, but the passage ways are so small that there is no pleasure in crawling through them.

LAKE WONONSCOPOMUC.

A Lake of great beauty, also, is that at Lakeville, Lake Wononscopomuc (get the rhythm of the syllables and it is easy enough.) It is a large round lake, surrounded by groves and washing its northern shore close to the houses of Lakeville and at the base of the south end of the Taconics. The waters are of a clear blue, and have no inlet so that the lake is spring fed. It is a great resort in summer for the town's people and visitors who are spending the season there. All kinds of aquatic sport are feasible and are indulged in to a great extent. The beaches are fine and some camping is done on its shores. On the east side of the lake was an old Indian Council ground.

LAKE WONONPAKOK.

A quarter of a mile south of Wononscopomuc is Wononpakok, a picturesque lake embraced by woodland and field, with a margin that is bold and beachlike, in places. People ride to the south end, two or three miles from Lakeville, when they want to go out upon the lake.

NORTH POND AND ROUND POND.

Such is the wide variety of Salisbury's scenery that we may now pass from lakes embowered in beauty to those that lie in an unbroken wilderness. On Mount Riga are two lakes only four and four and a half miles from Salisbury village. The best one, North Pond, is a large lake in whose environment, as one stands on the margin, is no sign of civilization. The forest crowds down upon the water on all sides, the shores are very irregular and rocky, cliffs rise about the lake and project into it. There is a rough and rocky, wooded island of a few acres in one end and in the other end are clusters of small islands. This lake is about 1,500 feet above Salisbury, the village itself being 690 feet above the ocean. The place is the resort of camping parties, who have here, a step from civilization, a lake that seems to be in the Adirondack wilderness. Half a mile south of North Pond is Round Pond, a wild, rocky, picturesque lake with the old village of Mount Riga at its lower side.

SAGE'S RAVINE.

Salisbury is the home of wild scenery—of the cataract, the water-fall, ravines, glens, precipices, forest covered and rock strewn hills and mountains. Sage's Ravine, more particularly mentioned in the article on Sheffield, lies partly in this town, four miles north of Salisbury village.

ROSSITER HOLLOW AND CASCADES.

Rossiter Hollow and Cascades, two miles from the village on the road up to Mountain Riga, are noted for wildness. Here in a ravine two miles long the water plunges down numerous cascades among boulders and amid the most picturesque scenes.

SELLECK HILL.

From Selleck Hill, a mile and a half from the villages of Salisbury and Lakeville, at the "Broadview Farm" of Judge D. J. Warner of Salisbury is an outlook that challenges the most formidable comparison. The most beautiful and extensive views are had without leaving the carriage, and the road is most of it delightfully shady.

CANAAN FALLS.

As the Housatonic River, which is the eastern boundary, passes the the town, it descends at the famous Canaan Falls a distance of 70 feet. These are the greatest falls of this river from its source to the sound. This cataract, in volume of water, in height, in form, and in general effect, is a very notable one. It is seen, but not well, from the car window as one rides along the Housatonic Road. In the spring freshet of 1837 a man was swept over these falls and lived to tell of it. Salisbury has many other natural features that would be notable anywhere else, but here they are not particularly thought of, amid the prolific work of nature in which they are surpassed.

SALISBURY VILLAGE.

Salisbury has five post-offices and eight or nine villages. Salisbury village lies snug and quiet at the base of the Taconics and is a delightful spot in which to spend the summer and autumn. It is on the Central New England & Western R. R., three and a half hours from New York. The Maple Shade Hotel accommodates about 30 people, and "Lawn Cottage" near the center, about the same number. Boarders can find good entertainment at Mr. J. G. Landon's, and at a few other houses, and

CANAAN FALLS.

there are two or three houses in the village that could be hired furnished for the summer.

In the rear of "Lawn Cottage" is a handsome grove of primitive chestnut, oak and hemlock of some 28 acres, cut by a winding ravine through which is a path leading to Grove Spring. In this grove is a remarkable boulder that is often visited. Resting on the brow of a hill surrounded by large primitive timber of various kinds is a huge rock of a formation similar to the mountain ledges, about 15 feet high and 20 feet square. It rests on a smooth limestone ledge, and at an apparent angle of 45 degrees, and it looks as if a child could send it crashing down the slope by merely pushing it. It is commonly known as Rostrum Rock Grove; Rock Spring and ravine are within 5 minutes' walk of both hotels and are greatly resorted to by native and visitors. The grove is not enclosed. Just beyond is Clark's Knoll, 20 minutes' walk, an abrupt rise of 150 feet above the village from which a wide view of mountain ranges and lakes is obtained.

LAKEVILLE.

Lakeville is a busy village on the Central N. E. & Western R. R. on the slope of the Taconics where they end on the south. Its location is a truly delightful one, commanding a prospect of singular beauty and picturesqueness. At the foot of the slope is Lake Wononscopomuc, with all its offerings of enjoyment. The Wononsco House has its full quota of guests every summer and autumn, and entertains them off the top shelf under capable and efficient management. There are several boarding houses in and near the village. Words cannot express the beauties of the southerly view from this village, and without attempting to do so, we must be content to advise a visit to the place. A gentleman who has travelled far and wide, who has a quick appreciation of natural beauties, and whose name is known all over the United States and in Europe, came to this village with his wife to spend the honeymoon, selecting it as the most delightful place he knew of.

A fine drive or walk near Lakeville is around the lake, a distance of $3\frac{1}{4}$ miles. A near resort is the hill on the north side of the road, a mile and a half west of the village center. The view from this hill is so unusually fine that Henry Ward Beecher, early in the '50's, wanted to buy it for a site for a house in which he expected to live in the summer, but he was prevented from doing so. Rose Hill, on the road to Lime Rock, affords a fine view, and a ride or a walk across Rose Hill, down Wells

Hill, and a return by the old turnpike, is delightful, the distance being three miles. A very enjoyable walk is north to Selleck Hill, two miles out; and another is to Lincoln City and return via Burton Brook path, the whole trip being one mile.

OTHER VILLAGES.

Chapinville is a small village in the north part of the town, on the Central N. E. & Western R. R., where boarders are taken. At Lime Rock, near the Housatonic Railroad, there is a post-office village and one at Ore Hill, near the New York state line on the Central N. E. & Western R. R. On Town Hill, a little southeast of Lake Wononscopomuc was the first village in the town, and still seen there is the old stone Montgomery house, built by the Livingstons, over 100 years ago, when they ranged into Massachusetts and Connecticut.

THE DRIVES.

From the natural composition of the town, one may gain a faint idea of the transcendant delights of the drives. A list of the leading ones will be found in the proper place in this volume, but a hundred more could be mentioned. Henry Ward Beecher writes of the town that "the rides in all this neighborhood are very fine, and a week at Salisbury will be apt to tempt you back, again and again." The roads in the town cover about 100 miles in total length and are kept in the best state of repair. The visitor will be surprised to find how much there is to be seen in town upon short drives or walks, a feature peculiar to Salisbury. One-half mile from the village of Salisbury one finds himself in the extremest wildness, and at short distances he becomes elevated high above the country below, or stands upon the shores of the loveliest lakes. In the table of drives the distances mentioned are from Salisbury village. Lakeville is but a mile and a half away and the distances for that village will be shortened or lengthened, a mile and a half or three miles, as the case may demand.

COUNTRY HOMES.

Several city people have come to Salisbury to establish country homes. Jonathan and Nathaniel C. Scoville, both prominent men in Buffalo, N. Y., and both natives of this town, acquired a large estate in Chapinville in 1883, where they have large new buildings with finely laid out grounds. Isaac E. Garvey of New York has bought a place on the hill north of Lake Washining; Edward Rogers of Philadelphia has bought the island in that lake, and William C. Witter of New York has bought a place in Lakeville, where he spends the summer. There are numerous sites for country homes that can be bought in the town.

The Iron Industry.

Places of great interest in the town are the iron mines. The Davis Ore Bed is half way between the villages of Salisbury and Lakeville, and a short walk from either one. This ore bed supplied ore to the first iron furnace erected in Connecticut, built at Lime Rock about 1734. The other iron mine in town is the Old Ore Hill Bed in the west part of the town, two miles from Lakeville, which was worked in the last century. Numerous other iron ore beds have been opened in town at various times, but are not now worked. The Lime Rock iron furnace mentioned is still in operation in new buildings owned by the Barnum-Richardson Company, of which W. H. Barnum was long the head. It is the only survivor of several other iron furnaces that have been in the town. Much of the iron ore mined goes to ten or a dozen furnaces in the Housatonic valley. The Salisbury iron is classed with the best in the country and has long been of great use to the nation. In the Revolution the Lime Rock furnace was taken possession of by the Colonies, and large quantities of cannon, shot and shells were made from the town's ore. John Jay and Gouverneur Morris were often here superintending the work. The "Constellation" and the "Constitution,"—"Old Iron Sides,"—were both armed with cannon made here. In the Rebellion Oliver Ames's works at Canaan Falls made large numbers of cannon for the government. The old furnace at Mount Riga did famous work in its day. The manufacture of Bessemer steel was introduced into this country by a Salisbury engineer, Alexander L. Holley, who learned the process in England.

Many Distinguished Natives.

An astonishingly large number of men, most of them natives of this town and all of them living here for a considerable time, have become distinguished. The state of Vermont owes some of its best blood to Salisbury; among the rest, the Evarts family. Ethan Allen, the hero of Ticonderoga, and some of the famous "Green Mountain Boys," also migrated from this town, where Ethan was an owner of the first blast furnace in town, and in the state, erected in 1762. The Western Reserve, or "New Connecticut," in Ohio, got many of its best immigrants from Salisbury. Caleb Bingham, a prominent man in Boston, and compiler of that old school reader, the National Preceptor, was born in this town. Of the men who went to Vermont, Thomas Chittenden was governor, with the exception of one year, from 1778 to 1797; Ira Allen was state treasurer for many years, and Jonas Galusha was governor.

Martin Chittenden, governor of that state was a native of this town; Nathaniel Chipman, chief justice of the Vermont supreme court, was a native; chief justice Ambrose Spencer of New York, was another, and his son, John C. Spencer, was a brilliant lawyer and Secretary of War under President Tyler. Still another native was General Peter B. Porter, who was Secretary of War under part of John Quincy Adams's adminstration. Among other natives, Josiah S. Johnson was United States Senator from Louisiana; Chester Averill was a professor in Union College, Alexander H. Holley, but recently deceased, was governor of Connecticut; Samuel Church was chief justice of the Connecticut supreme court; Theron B. Strong, was a judge of the supreme court and of the court of appeals in New York, and Orville L. Holley, author, editor and lawyer, was for several years Surveyor-General of New York. John M. Holley was a talented member of Congress from western New York; John H. Hubbard was attorney-general of Connecticut for several years; Roger Averill was lieutenant-governor for several years, Judson S. Landon is now a judge of the New York supreme court; the Rev. Peter M. Bartlett is or was president of Marysville College in Tennessee, and the Rev. Alexander Bartlett was or is professor in the same. Albert E. Church became professor of mathematics in the West Point Military Academy, and published several mathematical works; the Rev. Isaac Bird was for years a missionary in Palestine, at Beirut, and at Mount Lebanon; Bishop E. S. Janes received a large portion of his education in town; William H. Barnum, lived long at Lime Rock and represented the state in the United States Senate, was a member of the House nine years, was chairman of the democratic national committee in 1876, that conducted for Samuel J. Tilden the most notable and able political campaign in the history of the country. The list is becoming tiresome, but is not exhausted. Among natives of the town there have been three United State Senators, eight Congressmen, three eminent chief justices, several judges of less note, four governors, two lieutenant-governors, two presidents and several professors in colleges, several military and naval officers, several lawyers and clergymen of high repute, and others whose offices were high, some of whom have been mentioned by name. This is a remarkable list for a town that never had 4,000 people.

Salisbury lies tucked away in a corner of the state where city people will find a most delightful resting place, with country enjoyments. It seems here as if the natural attractions of a whole state had been crowded into one town, so abundant are they on every hand and in every part of the town. The primitive wildness is unmarred, the beauty is exquisite, the picturesque is that of perfection, and all is where it can be readily enjoyed. Words, at the best, cannot do justice to Salisbury, and the limits of this article have allowed only a brief mention, and then only of the main points of interest. The visitor will discover a thousand more.

NORFOLK, CONN.

Norfolk is one of the towns of the Berkshire region in the bordering land of Connecticut. It conforms to the rule of dissimilarity that prevails among all these towns, a feature that is found more prominent among them than among the towns of any other region in the country. This is a hill town that has attained great popularity among the people who go into the country in the summer and autumn seasons and has made a good beginning as a location for country homes for city people. The wild and picturesque nature of the town, its high degree of healthfulness, its many points of lookout, its lakes and drives and its easy accessibility make it a favorite with a great many people of high social standing, who come here for congenial association with their fellows and an appreciative contact with nature's harmonies. The wild, rugged surface of the town draws forth much admiration from visitors, who find here many striking, picturesque touches of creative art, and rejoice in the exhilarating air to find country living so pleasurable.

The elevation of the habitable part of this town ranges from 1,200 to 1,400 feet above the ocean and the elevation of Norfolk village is 1,250 feet at the church. The highest point reached by a railroad in the state is here where the highest railway elevation is 1,236 feet. Here, amid the hills and mountains and the dry, bracing and somewhat rarified air, and the pure water, the germs of malaria are deprived of their nourishment, and, if they are ever brought this way, they at once die a speedy death. The summer temperature is low and the visitor finds much comfort in living here. He is fed from excellent dairies that are the pride of the region, where, as is well known to those who have given the matter attention, the grass of the hills makes better butter and milk than valley grass.

PUBLIC SPIRIT.

Norfolk village has an appearance that shows no ill keeping and neglect, but on the other hand, lives in an air of watchful regard for its material aspect and for the welfare of its people. There are several people in the village who have long taken special pains to see to this.

Judge Robbins Battell, a native of the town, whose grandfather, the Rev. Ammi R. Robbins, was the first settled clergyman in the town, beginning in 1761, has always taken a prominent part in village and town improvement, and, though doing business in New York, has ever been proud to maintain a home here for permanent residence. Judge Battell maintains a fine home where he has a collection of paintings, principally landscapes, by American painters, that hardly has a rival anywhere. All the best painters are represented and by their best work. The picture room is kindly opened to the public at certain regular times each week. Several years ago Judge Battell put in the Congregational church a chime of four bells which are connected with the clock and are made to strike the quarter hour. In many improvements, Judge Battell has had the active and ardent co-operation of his sister, Miss Anna B. Battell, and of Joseph B. Eldridge and his family, who have a delightful home in the village. A green or open park has been laid out where the streets make a large triangle, and set with large evergreens, beneath the shade of which visitors take refuge from the noonday sun. Here, during a week in the summer when the most people are in town, through the procurement of the Battells, a band of high class musicians from New York gives a public concert every morning and evening, the selections being such classical music as that of Beethoven and Schubert, and some of the musicians being from Thomas's and Damrosch's orchestra. The constantly active public spirit of the Battells and the Eldridges appears in the beautiful cemetery, in the fine roads, in a free public reading room where there is a good supply of the newspapers and the periodical literature of the day, in the village Hall Association which built a handsome structure in 1885, containing a hall for meetings and places for stores, and in numerous other ways.

Walks near the Village.

The natural attractions of the town are so many that it is only by traversing almost every acre that they can all be found. Numerous delightful walks and short drives may be had near the village. At no place within four miles of the village does the railroad cross a road at grade. Several charming drives will be found mentioned in the table of drives. Coming toward the village on the road from near Bigelow Pond, two miles east, the view is fine toward the west; and two miles north of the village the views are extremely attractive from all the roads in the vicinity of Haystack Mountain on its north and northeast. A pleasant walk is to Buttermilk Falls, on the western edge of the village, where the

Blackberry River makes a long plunge down the rocks. The ledge, near Judge Battell's house is much resorted to for the decidedly picturesque view down the valley toward Canaan, particularly about sunset, when the beauties of the scene are much enhanced. A water tower, built here has a private observatory on top. The walk to the cemetery one-half mile north of the village, is a fine one, and, indeed, good walks may be had in all quarters.

DUTTON HILL.

There are three easily accessible summits in the town, commanding wide, varied and charming views. The nearest is Dutton Hill, whose top is a mile from the village on the south. The top is clear of woods and an elevated platform has been built, from which the outlook, south, west and northwest is of a most impressive character. The elevation is 1,632 feet.

HAYSTACK MOUNTAIN.

The walk is easy to the summit of this conical-shaped mountain, a mile and a half north of the village, whose elevation is 1,680 feet. The magnificent outlook is the best in town, embracing, as it does, all the hills toward the Connecticut River, extending even 15 miles east of Hartford to the Bolton range; including the Talcott Mountain Tower, Ivy Mountain, and Mohawk Mountain toward the south; several valleys, including the picturesque Blackberry River valley leading to Canaan, and a long sweep of the Housatonic valley from Great Barrington to Kent, about 40 miles; the western horizon is the Taconic range, with glimpses beyond, and Bear Mountain in Salisbury, the highest land in Connecticut, stands up prominently; on the north the view extends through nearly all Berkshire, the northernmost point being the top of Greylock. A circular tower, 30 feet high and supported by stone arches, has been built by Judge Battell to get an outlook above the woods that cover the top of the mountain. A new road leading to this tower has been made, so that one may drive to the summit, if he does not care to walk. This place is a favorite with all visitors.

BALD MOUNTAIN.

Elevated 1,770 feet, Bald Mountain, in the northwest part of the town, four miles from the village, is the highest mountain in town. The view is extensive and very fine. People drive to within less than half a mile of the top and walk the remainder of the way over a path.

OTHER OUTLOOKS.

Moses Hill on the Goshen road, two miles out from the village affords a fine view. It is but ten minutes' walk from the road. Stillman Hill, two miles east of the village, with a five minutes' walk, exposes excellent views toward the east.

CANAAN MOUNTAIN.

The favorite out-of-town drive is that to Canaan Mountain, about six miles distant. Here one comes suddenly to the brink of the steep mountain and so striking is the effect that it seems as if half the world were spread out below. More particular reference to this mountain will be found in the article on Canaan.

THE LAKES.

Norfolk has several charming mountain lakes of very clear water that form part of picturesque landscapes and afford places for aquatic sports. Doolittle Pond, four miles northeast of the village, is the largest lake in town, being about a mile long. The water is surrounded by woods and wilderness, with cliffs rising on the west. A little north of this is Benedict Pond, also with a wild environment.

Tobey Pond, a mile and a half southwest of the village, is the resort of camping and boating parties. The neighboring hills and the fine woods around make the lake a choice object to the visitor.

The Canaan Mountain Pond is four miles from Norfolk village and is 300 feet higher. Boats may be got here and much enjoyment be had.

The Reservoir is an artificial lake a mile long three miles north from the village. The woods in the vicinity are magnificent, and the drive around the lake is most delightful.

Near the state line, five miles toward the north, are Campbell's Falls, a place much resorted to. For more particular reference see the New Marlboro article.

THE SUMMER VISITORS.

The accommodations for summer and autumn guests in Norfolk village and vicinity are sufficient for 600 to 800, which is the number that is commonly found here at one time at the favorite time of the season. Boarders are taken at about 20 houses and at the village hotel—the Stevens House—where about seventy-five find good entertainment at once. The influence of the residents and the constitution of the place have brought in a fine class of guests. A few of the people who have been in the habit of coming here are Chief Justice John Sedgwick and William Dowd, both of New York; Senator Joseph R. Hawley, the Rev. Dr. Nathaniel Burton, the Rev. Dr. Gage, Judge Chamberlain, Mrs. Isabella Beecher Hooker, the Rev. Dr. Horace Bushnell,—when he was living,—and

John Cole, all of Hartford; Prof. Gibbs and Prof. Thomas A. Thatcher's family, both Yale professors. "The Hillhurst," of which A. E. McLean is proprietor, is a new and elegant hotel built in 1887, by Hon. Robbins Battell, and has accommodations, second to none, for 250 guests. In distance Norfolk is but 35 miles from Hartford, and in time but one hour and three quarters by the Central N. E. & Western Railroad.

COUNTRY HOMES.

A movement among city people toward establishing country homes here began some time ago. Frederick Shepherd of Brooklyn, a native of this town, has taken his father's old place in the village to which he comes every summer. The place that Judge Sedgwick used to own, two miles north of the village, was sold to Captain Isaac Mallory of New Haven, who now lives here permanently. The family of Captain John Dewell, a deceased native, comes from New Haven every summer to occupy their country home in West Norfolk, two miles from Norfolk village. Several years ago Miss Hill of Hartford built a house on the edge of the village, which she sold to Robert Geer of Brooklyn, a native of the town, who comes here every summer and at other times during the year, the house being occupied by his parents. There are many fine locations for country homes in the village and town, yet unoccupied.

The Robbins school, established here in 1884, affords excellent means of education to the children of those people who make the town their residence. The present principal, H. W. Carter, with assistants, fits pupils for college and makes a good home for boarding pupils. No boarders are taken but boys, although girls are among the day pupils. There is a handsome, well appointed school house.

The winter attractions of Norfolk are marvelously beautiful, as one may judge from what he can see from a car window, some days, in riding over the Central N. E. & Western R. R. When there is rain in the lowlands, there is sleet or an ice storm in this town, and the appearance of the rain or ice as it freezes on the trees is a decidedly striking sight. The long slender, elastic white birches may be seen bending their tops to earth under the heavy weight of glittering ice, the trees of the forests are all coated with crystal, and myriads of diamonds sparkle on the evergreen boughs. If the sleet turns into a damp snow that freezes as it falls, the evergreens present the appearance of frosted silver in the exposed places, making contrasts of white and green in graceful curvatures that are exceedingly beautiful. Norfolk, all in all, is a most engaging town in its natural and social features, and has become one of the principal mountain resorts in Connecticut.

CANAAN, CONN.

THE town of North Canaan, Conn., is generally called Canaan, which is the name of its post-office and principal village. Though the area of the town is rather small, it embraces that same variety of scenery that characterizes the whole Berkshire region. The leading features only can be mentioned, but it should be noted that woven among them are many things that the visitor will find of interest. Summer guests are taken at the hotel in this village, the Warner House and at several private houses in the village, in East Canaan, Canaan Valley, and the neighboring country. Canaan village lies in the beautiful valley of the Housatonic River at a place where the valley is contracting to a narrow width. Mountains and hills surround it, some of them being quite near. East Canaan 2¼ miles from Canaan, is a small village in a fine valley, through which flows the Blackberry River after coming down from the elevated town of Norfolk. Extending from this valley to the northward is the Canaan valley, in which is a small village of the same name, a short distance from Canaan and East Canaan. The Central N. E. & Western Railroad runs east and west through Canaan and East Canaan, and the Housatonic Road crosses that one at Canaan.

CANAAN MOUNTAIN.

There is a mountain outlook near Canaan village that rivals anything of the kind that can be found in Berkshire from common heights. This is Canaan Mountain, whose Indian name, less commonly known, is Wangum Mountain. Its point or angle where visitors go is a mile and a half southeast of Canaan by road, and a path of 50 rods, or one mile in a walk across the fields. People drive from East Canaan to the very top. This mountain is conspicuous in all south views from the south half of Berkshire and from Greylock, and hence it commands a marvelously extensive and beautiful sweep of prospect, embracing all this and the memorable town of Salisbury, including the Twin Lakes, on the west, while Sharon is on the southwest and the narrowing Housatonic valley is on the south. The view immediately below this mountain, admirably exposed at the point where the mountain forms a right angle, is like that from a balloon. Twenty miles of the Housatonic River are here visible, including the hidden places. This is a place of frequent resort for picnics and sightseeing. Under the bluff at the point of the mountain is Sentinel Rock, which is a cube of 30 feet dimensions, a huge mass to the top of which one may climb by a ladder. A few rods south of the point is House Rock, which is 60 feet high on the upper side, and under the cover of which 100 men could easily find shelter. A ladder leads to the top. In this mountain there are many ravines, fissures, caves, and other works of nature that will keep the visitor long interested. A view of this mountain from the valley below, is in *Picturesque America*.

THE CANAAN MOUNTAIN POND,

Is a lake a mile long, with a bluff on the west side and with woods on nearly every side. It is an attractive place that is the object of many excursions. People ride to Norfolk, 7 miles, from which place the lake is 4 miles distant, and return via South Canaan, the return being 9 miles, but down a steep road.

TWIN LAKES.

Across the river on the west, in Salisbury, are the Ashley Mountain, Tom's Mount, Babes' Hill and Twin Lakes, that are described in the article on Salisbury. They are but 2 to 3 miles from Canaan, and, with all their attractions, seem to be as much a part of Canaan as of Salisbury.

DELIGHTFUL DRIVES.

There are many delightful drives in this town, a few of which are mentioned in the table of drives. One road goes over Road Hill, 2 miles northeast of Canaan village, and from the summit of the hill the views along the Housatonic valley are very fine. Williams Hill, half a mile from the village is the object of a very pleasing walk. Campbell's Falls, mentioned more particularly in the article on New Marlboro, are 7¼ miles off and are the place of many picnics and most agreeable excursions.

PINE GROVE CAMP GROUNDS.

The grounds of the Canaan Pine Grove Camp Meeting Association of the Poughkeepsie District are situated 2 miles south of Canaan village, between the Housatonic Railroad and the river. They embrace about 35 acres, having many attractive features of hill, woodland and view, and were put to their present use in 1860 for the first time, and permanently in 1871, since which time the annual meeting, beginning usually the last week in August, on the Monday nearest the 20th, and ending a week afterwards, has drawn many thousands of attendants. A Sunday during camp meeting will find 10,000 people here. The Association has a large eating and lodging house and many other buildings that are put to various uses, among them being several cottages that are rented to people who attend camp meeting. Besides these, a large number of cottages are owned by those who have built them on land leased from the

Association. It has become the practice of many of these people, in July and August previous to camp meeting time, to occupy their cottages as a place of summer resort. This number is constantly increasing; numbering about 25 families in July, and about 50 in August, previous to the week of the meeting. They have a post-office on the grounds and telephone connection with Canaan. Following is a list of those who have cottages on the grounds:

Salisbury, Ct.: J. McArthur, A. T. Parselles; Lime Rock, Ct.: Nelson A. McNeil, Sidney Ensign; Canaan, Ct.: Mrs. Nelson M. Brown, Charles Emmons, J. S. Corbit, Mary Owens; Falls Village, Conn.: Mrs. George W. Stevens, Edward Ward; Goshen, Conn.: E. S. Richards; Winsted, Conn.: S. A. Granger, Mrs. Abel Snow, A. Waters, Emory L. Mead; Sharon, Conn.: Mrs. Harrison B. St. John; Sharon Valley, Conn.: Fitch Landon; Kent, Conn.: Alfred Chapman, George R. Bull; New Milford, Conn.: John Flynn, S. C. Ferris; Kensington, Conn.: Mrs. Mary McAllister; Bridgeport, Conn.: Mrs. John White, Walter Nichols; Cornwall Bridge, Conn.: Charles Hall; New Haven, Conn.: Mrs. Mary J. Hoppen, the Rev. A. H. Wyatt; Sheffield, Mass.: Cyrus French; Great Barrington, Mass.: Ward Lewis, S. E. Forest, George W. Anderson; Housatonic, Mass.: F. R. Warfield; Worcester, Mass.: Mrs. F. M. Olin; Stockbridge, Mass.: Mrs. William Rathburn; New York, N. Y.: Miss Mary Clark, the Rev. William C. Smith, the Rev. A. K. Sanford, Secretary of the Association, 357 West 24th street; Bangall, N. Y.: the Rev. George B. Clark, Nathan C. Sackett; Lake Mahopac, N. Y.: the Rev. J. W. Macomber; Poughkeepsie, N. Y.: Mrs. G. H. Adriance; Lagrangeville, N. Y.: The Rev. Robert Kay; Otego, N. Y.: The Rev. A. Nash; Pawling, N. Y.: The Rev. A. B. Corbin; East Chatham, N. Y.: Mrs. C. K. Jones, Miss Hester A. Cady; Dover, N. Y.: Mrs. Sarah A. Hoag; Peckskill, N. Y.: The Rev. James H. Haight, George W. Robertson; Hillsdale, N. Y.: Miss Flavia M. Bristol; Prattsville, N. Y.: The Rev. B. H. Burch; Pine Plains, N. Y.: Mrs. W. S. Eno, Ann Eliza Dussance; Matteawan, N. Y.: John F. Tallardy. Address wanting: Mrs. Charles Sanford, E. B. Atwell, and the Rev. J. R. Vandewater, Florida.

NEW LEBANON, N. Y.

THE rugged Taconics, with their many interesting peaks and steeps, divide the Berkshire valley from another of charming beauty over in the state of New York, called by many the gem of the valleys in all that region. There New Lebanon is situated. The valley stretches for many miles north and south of the center— as far north as Petersburg, up near the Pownals, and south down to Chatham. The Wynomanock Valley, it may be called, from the river of that name, flowing through it. New Lebanon's eastern boundary is the Taconics; and it lays claim to their grandeur as well as Berkshire.

The village of New Lebanon is about the center of the town, and is the birthplace of Samuel J. Tilden, where the Tilden family still makes its home, and relatives of the distinguished statesman live. Mount Lebanon is a mile further south and a little east, and is the Shaker settlement of several families and the resort on Sunday in summer of those who wish to attend the peculiar ceremonies of their sect. People drive for miles to attend their "public meetings"—from Williamstown, from Pittsfield by scores, from Lenox, from Stockbridge, from "Fernside," and in short from nearly all over Berkshire. Their community is also an interesting place to visit at any time and here is the home of the seer of their sect, the well-known Elder Frederick W. Evans, whose fame is almost world-wide in connection with Shakerism.

LEBANON SPRINGS.

North of New Lebanon, a mile or more, is the pretty little village of Lebanon Springs. The village proper is down on the flat, as it may be termed. Up on the hillside, a pretty steep ascent and yet reached by a good road, with many glens and wild places along the way, for half a mile, is Columbia Hall, one of the old time, as it is perhaps among the oldest, resorts. It dates its establishment before the days of the railroad, when the stages were loaded with tourists; and aristocracy, foreign guests, presidents and statesmen by the score have sought its retreat and enjoyed its alluring rest and quietude. It stands on an eminence overlooking the valley south and west for miles, and the scene, as one stands looking from the balcony or the heights farther up the hill, is simply enchanting. The Columbia Springs are in the hotel grounds and, possessing medicinal virtues, mainly of sulphur and iron, their healing properties are much sought, both for bathing and for drinking purposes. The temperature of the springs is the same all the year round, and the flow is very large. The hotel has accommodations for about 400 guests and is now the property of Mr Phillips, a hotel proprietor in Philadelphia. In the village is the Fields Hotel, a famous hostelry, a hotel for many years and also quite a resort. There are also several cottagers and summer residents in the village, for whom the slopes, which abound on the eastern border of the valley, are pleasant and inviting spots.

The views hereabouts are unsurpassed in all the region. At any point back of the Columbia Hall, going east, is a continual opening of new views and a cause for repeated ejaculations of delight as some new vision of beauty greets the eye. There are many beautiful drives in Lebanon. The valley itself is a treat; the roads are well-kept and there is hardly a hill to slacken a trot for miles. To the east towards Pittsfield is another drive which baffles a pen picture; a favorite drive is to leave the Hall as it is called, go directly east to Pittsfield, 7 miles, then return through Bakersville, the Hancock Shakers, over the mountain, again west through the Mount Lebanon Shaker community, and then north again home, a distance of about 16 miles. A coaching party is almost of daily occurrence from Lebanon Springs to Pittsfield, and telephonic communication makes Lenox and in fact all Berkshire, or even Albany or Troy, literally within speaking distance.

The Harlem Extension Railroad passes through this valley, running from Chatham, N. Y., to Bennington Vt., and there are frequent trains, in summer especially.

CUMMINGTON.

THE rugged, yet charming town of Cummington, in Hampshire county, borders on Berkshire, adjoining Windsor and Peru, and Berkshire has a very neighborly feeling for it. Sequestered among the picturesque summits of the Green Mountains, this town has become a warmly appreciated resort in the summer and early autumn and attracts many people hither. The pure water, the mountain air, the array of the works of nature on every hand, and the restful repose of the place, have been enjoyed by many visitors. The village is on the north branch of the Westfield River and is approached by stages from Hinsdale and from Northampton. The town has given birth to two distinguished citizens: —William Cullen Bryant, the poet and editor, who left the town after graduation at College, to gain a world wide fame, though he had already written "Thanatopsis;" and Senator Henry L. Dawes of Pittsfield, who has been many years a Representative or Senator in Congress, where his services have been of a most conspicuous nature. Mr Bryant established a public library in the village in a pretty little building. Summer guests are hospitably entertained at some of the farm houses of the town and carry away many pleasant memories of their well spent outing.

HILLSDALE, N. Y.

THE hamlet of Hillsdale, N. Y., is favorably situated for the reception of summer guests. Accommodations can be found at private houses and at the Mount Washington House, which was built particularly for summer business and has had considerable success. Many fine drives and natural attractions lie in the neighboring region—Copake Lake, four miles off, where all sorts of aquatic sports are indulged in, White's Hill, near by, The Dome, a short and easy drive, Bashbish and many places in the Housatonic valley.

STAMFORD, VT.

THE valley to the northeast, from North Adams, and on through Clarksburg, terminates in the town of Stamford, Vt., five miles distant from North Adams. Stamford village is a pretty little hamlet, and its famous Paradise Hotel, about a mile farther on, has a great reputation for trout suppers and has otherwise a well appointed table and fine surroundings. It is the great out-dining place of northern Berkshire. The hotel was for years kept by Col. Wilmarth, of a prominent family in Berkshire, and the old landlord died as one of the leading men of the town. A. F. Wilmarth, now of North Adams and for many years a prominent officer of the Home Insurance Company of New York, is of that stock.

In the Green Mountains is Wiley Mountain, which, though not easily accessible, has nevertheless a fine look-off, and is about 1,000 feet above the village. Farther south is another peak, which can be reached by another road through Clarksburg.

The topography of the town is such that there are but few drives in its borders, a peculiarity of many other northern Berkshire towns, where the hills are close together and there are no broad valleys and far away stretches as in southern Berkshire and the central part. A crazy road, as the villagers call it, is that along the west hills northwest, and leading on towards Bennington. The street through the village is the main stage road away over the mountain to Hartwellville, thence to Readsboro, Sadwaga, and thence to Jacksonville, or to Whitingham. Leaving Stamford village to the west and then south, there is also a very pleasant road on through Clarksburg and to North Adams through Eagle street. Or this west road can be continued to Pownal over the high spur of the mountain there, or turning south, through what in other years was known as the Peak neighborhood, North Adams is reached via Houghtonville and the west part of Clarksburg. Turning east a short distance beyond the Paradise House, we enter what is called "The Basin," a valley of some magnitude under the ragged edge of the Green Mountains.

There have a great many men gone out from this town in the different walks of life. It was here that many of the Green Mountain boys were mustered, and the town is full of historic interest, which we cannot stop to glean. The Wilmarths were an old family; the Houghtons, of which A. C. Houghton, of the Arnold Print Works at North Adams, and his brother, Andrew, a Boston merchant, are fair specimens of self-made manhood, and J. C. Houghton, of the firm of Houghton & Wilmarth, carrying on the largest wood acid works in the country in the little village—quite a curious industry to visit. The Millards were a prominent family; Dr. H. J. Millard of North Adams, and his brother, N. L. Millard, the shoe manufacturer, and Col. Millard, of Binghamton, N. Y., a member of the present Congress from that city, are excellent representatives. D. C. Stroud, a hotel-keeper of some reputation, in New York State, is a native of Stamford; the Copelands of Pittsfield, the Wilmarths, and many others have gone out from their old native town and made their mark in the world. Stamford is not a summer resort in that sense and there are no summer residents or homes in the town for them. But as a resort for rare sport in fishing or a quiet day's rest, there are few places that equal it.

CAMPING IN BERKSHIRE.

THE writer will yield to none in his ardent affection for Berkshire, and the manner in which THE BOOK OF BERKSHIRE celebrates her manifold claims on public attention will be very grateful to every son of the old county. But "faithful are the wounds of a friend." There is just a suspicion awakened in the thought of those who love her best that Berkshire is, year by year, yielding herself more and more to that vexing element, fashionable society. Grander and more luxurious palaces, intrusive livery, and tiresome dances for the serene twilights and glorious nights—hops, too, under stifling roofs, when the moon illumines and stars glimmer over velvety lawns and bounteous old trees—these are tendencies to be noted in the north, the center and south of Berkshire.

The pity of it! A summer life worth having does not perpetuate conventionalities. It is apprehension that this present drift may for a time overshadow some other and more desirable phases of Berkshire life that leads the writer to add a word in recognition of a simpler aspect of summer living.

But let this characterization be understood. These tendencies have not hardened into set conditions. Perhaps it was too much to expect that the character which Berkshire derived from Hawthorne, Holmes, Miss Sedgwick, Fanny Kemble Butler and Henry Ward Beecher would tinge and refine peculiarly and always the summer life of the county. We might be satisfied that it has colored and unpretentiously, almost imperceptibly, elevated its tone for so many years.

The new day has made Berkshire the autumn capital for those who affect Newport during the hotter months, but the old life remains strong and healthful enough to still assert its claims over the newer and more pretentious fashions of this transplanted city life. There are earnest workers who make sensible resters, and the ripe culture that this fruitful region has sent out comes back to her with each all too brief vacation season; others quite as distinguished and fully as loyal have found out her simple, sweet ways of living; and it will require many long years and an extended multiplication of great hotels to rob Berkshire of all her deserved prestige in things genuine and helpful.

Nature "mothers" best those children of men who study her moods, and seek her society by relaxing the artificial conditions that are the product of what we call "high civilization." She delights in the free life of the camp, and to those who seek it she grants the largest measure of recuperation. To such as go out of houses and stereotyped ways for annual communion with nature, Berkshire yields her choicest benediction—and there are many who understand this through the experience of over a score of years. There is much systematic study of the woods and fields of Berkshire—more now, surely, than at any previous time in her history—and we will only trace this appreciation of nature back to the late Prof. Albert Hopkins of Williamstown.

Over a quarter of a century ago he organized the Alpine club, which, through several sets of young people, lived to tramp over this land of "delicious surprises," and to know intimately all its best aspects and revelations, bold and shy. He was a rare interpreter of nature, a very seer of the woods; the prophet David in dignity and delicacy of soul, whom we always imagined he must resemble in personal appearance; and the impetus and character which he gave to this perfect life of the woods has never been lost in Northern Berkshire. Each year, Williamstown sends its camping party to the heights of Bald Mountain, southeast of the village, and to that loftier summit of privilege, old Greylock, now made easy of access from the valley of the Hoosac.

The stranger can scarcely go amiss in picking out a camping spot in Berkshire, and the native or old resident needs no instruction. The choice lies between mountain and pond,—but where hill, wood and water can be combined, the widest conditions of beauty are compassed. Fishing parties have been attracted to Lanesboro pond since the Indians left its banks. The lakes about Pittsfield, Onota and Pontoosuc, are much frequented. "Apple Tree Point" and "Point of Pines" at the latter lake are favorite spots for picnic parties. Lake Queechy, near Canaan, N. Y., is a very beautiful body of water. The Otis ponds draw camping parties from Berkshire, Hampden county, and the borders of Connecticut. Berry pond on the top of West mountain is attractive to Pittsfield people. The south of the county is richest of all in localities that woo the dwellers in tents, with Lake Buel for Great Barrington, Stockbridge Bowl, Laurel Lake at Lee, Bear Cliff in Mount Washington, —and, last and most wonderful, Bashbish falls, a little over the New York border.

The finest lake town in the region is Salisbury, Conn.,—a town adjoining Berkshire on its southern borders—whose eight lakes all offer delightful camping places. There is sometimes as much camping on Washining, the upper one of the beautiful Twin Lakes, as in all Berkshire, the number of campers sometimes numbering 200. But, on this account, and because of many day visitors, it would be avoided by many. The Connecticut Western Railroad has a station between the lakes, so that all supplies and baggage can easily be brought to camp. Bread and various farm supplies, including ice, can be got in the neighborhood. The nearest groceries, post-offices, etc., are at Chapinville, two or three miles distant, and at Canaan, three miles, on the railway. The margin of the lake is a forest in many places suitable for camping. On the adjoining lake, Washinee, camping has not been allowed.

Lake Wononscopomuc, on the north side of which lies Lakeville, has some camping parties in marginal groves. One of the wildest and most secluded camping places in all that region is North Pond on Mount Riga, 4½ miles from Salisbury village. There are no boats on the lake, but they might be taken from Lakeville, 4 miles distant. Farm houses are within 2 miles.

Mount Washington has a dozen camping sites on every square mile, by some brook, or lake, in a canyon or on elevated ground. The same may be said of half the whole Berkshire region. The greatest abundance of lakes, however, is found in the southern part. On Long Lake in Great Barrington, at the base of the south end of Tom Ball Mountain, a man can deceive himself into thinking that he is in the Adirondacks, and nearly as well on the Otis reservoir. With 50 or more lakes in the Berkshire region, and hundreds of suitable camping places on streams, it is not necessary to catalogue places well known to each locality—and the accessories of camping do not vary much. There should not be too much "roughing it," and the pleasure of this natural way of living is enhanced by experienced attention to details. Not only blankets, rubber and woolen, with those personal conveniences that come without the telling are necessary, but the trained cook with a modern cooking stove and a full accompaniment of crockery, skillets and pans should be provided. In other words, let the provision tent be furnished with all that the careful housewife would desire,—and then the machinery of life goes on in these new surroundings in the old way.

The delights of camping? That is not a theme to be treated in half a page of formal glorification. You will live out of doors, sleep on the fragrant spruce boughs under the transparent tent roof, lazily loaf in "hammock grove," and, by means of frequent walks compassing noble scenery, cultivate the most enormous appetites. Each day will be rounded out by a magnificent camp fire, about which the well trained quartette are inspired as no where else—particularly in rendering the slave songs, whose rude pathos seems singularly to chord with the picturesque surroundings ; and in the towering blaze each will see for himself shapes and thoughts innumerable. During all the day the cloud and shadow effects upon the sea of woods or expanse of water spread ever changing pictures that the cleverest artist cannot steal. Each shifting of the weather, too, brings its delight of color, odor and grouping—as after the rain, upon the sunset background the trees, with their shining burdens, sparkle with lustrous gems,—for we see old Mother Earth at home!

COACHING IN BERKSHIRE.

OF recent years the plan of doing Berkshire on wheels has grown in popularity, and is certainly a most delightful way of seeing the sights in the Berkshire Hills. Coaching parties are now quite the proper thing, and scores of gay parties visit the county every season, and take in the beauties of the region from that charming vantage point, the roof of a coach drawn by four or six horses. It is more than likely that coaching was brought into popularity in this region, by the Lenox people who ride all over Berkshire on their handsome "drags." Many coaching parties come from Springfield, Worcester, Hartford, and other places in Massachusetts and Connecticut, while others come from more distant points. Most of them traverse the entire county, and a favorite route is to start from Williamstown and drive to Pittsfield via South Williamstown, New Ashford, and Lanesboro. From Pittsfield they drive to Lenox, then to Lee, Stockbridge, Great Barrington and Sheffield, thus getting glimpses of the ever-changing views along the entire route. The fine hotels at Williamstown, North Adams, Dalton, Pittsfield, Lenox, Stockbridge, Great Barrington, Egremont and Sheffield, add largely to the pleasure of such a trip as the tourist is assured of the very best accommodations. A very popular plan for these coaching parties is to spend from three days to a fortnight at each of the popular stopping places, and make daily trips to the interesting places in the immediate neighborhood. In this way all the sights of the county are seen, and at the same time the exhilarating rides from place to place are more enjoyable because less continuous and therefore not so tiresome. Coaching is probably only in its infancy in Berkshire, however, and in time to come it is almost certain to be much more general, and will bring to its Hills and Homes scores of people who would probably never come under any other circumstances. Certainly no place in the country is more attractive for coaching, as the fine roads, the excellent hotels and the magnificent scenery, furnish all that can be desired in this style of touring.

BERKSHIRE SUMMER GUESTS.

CAPACITY, ACCOMMODATIONS AND LOCATIONS, IN DETAIL.

Supplementing the established Hotels and Boarding Houses, accommodations for summer guests are had in private families in nearly every town in Berkshire County. As near a complete list of all these as can be gathered by a painstaking inquiry, is here given.

ASHLEY FALLS.

George G. Peck, E. S. Conklin, F. F. Cooper.

BECKET.

Claflin Hotel, William A. Schlesinger, Proprietor; accommodations for 60; terms, $10 to $14 per week; one-quarter mile from Boston & Albany Railroad station; transportation, free.

Milton J. Alderman, Delos H. Hatch, S. C. Pomeroy, Mrs. Anna Collins, Jarvis Norcott, William E. Higley, Mrs. F. E. Rogers.

BECKET CENTER.

Mrs. M. J. Hennessey, Mrs. Calvin Geer, Mrs. Clinker.

BERKSHIRE.

George W. Farnum, H. W. Reed.

BRIGGSVILLE.

George W. Weld.

CHESHIRE.

West Brook Cottage, Mrs. N. W. Mason; accommodations for 20; terms, $7 to $8 per week; half mile from Boston & Albany Railroad station; transportation, 25 cents each. .

F. C. Brown, W. A. Pomeroy, Mrs. N. W. Mason, Mrs. D. Wood.

CURTISVILLE.

John M. Cooper, J. W. Ford.

DALTON.

Irving House, F. L. Bourne, Proprietor; accommodations for 75; terms per week, $14 to $18; half mile from Boston & Albany Railroad station.

Elmwood Cottages, William B. Clark, Proprietor; accommodations for 40; terms, $10 to $15 per week; transportation to and from station, free.

Chamberlin's Eagle Hotel, J. C. Chamberlin, Proprietor; 14 rooms; $7 to $10 per week, or $2 per day; 150 rods from Boston & Albany Railroad station; transportation, free. Established in 1800, and has always been kept as a hotel.

Mrs. John S. Barton.

EAST LEE.

Mrs. H. Oakley.

FLORIDA.

I. N. Barnett.

GLENDALE.

Private house on high ground on main road to Great Barrington, Stockbridge, Lenox, etc., Mrs. G. N. Spoore; accommodations for 7 or 8; terms, $5 to $6 per week; near Housatonic Railway station and post-office.

GREAT BARRINGTON.

Berkshire House, Caleb Ticknor, Proprietor; accommodations for 100; terms, $10.50 per week, upwards; two minutes walk from Housatonic Railroad station.

Collins House, Alfred Peck, Proprietor; accommodations for 65; terms, $8 to $12 per week; half mile from Housatonic Railroad station.

Miller House, W. B. Loveland, Proprietor; accommodations for 20; terms. $10 per week; transportation free.

Miss Sarah Moore, Mrs. M. D. Sexton,
Mrs. J. F. Sanford, G. W. Lester,
Mrs. Isaac H. Rice, Seth L. Sheldon,
W. M. Merrill, C. K. Brown,
Mrs. S. Whitwell, Mrs. McDonald,
H. C. Woodin, Miss Pierce,
E. L. Tuller, W. H. Leslie.
John Gibson,

HARTSVILLE.

Mrs. May Stevens, Francis Brochu.

HINSDALE.

Belmont House, S. J. Warner, Proprietor.

Mrs. Mary Axtell, Mrs. T. A. Frissell,
Mrs. E. B. Tracy, Miss J. L. Clark,
Mrs. C. C. Robinson, Mrs. E. W. Clark.

HOOSAC TUNNEL.

Rice's Hotel, Jenks & Rice, Proprietors; one-half mile from east portal of the Tunnel, at the junction of the Fitchburg and Hoosac Tunnel & Wilmington Railroads; accommodations for 60; terms, $10 to $15 per week, and $2.50 per day; two minutes' walk from Fitchburg Railroad station; baggage transported free.

George N. Thatcher, R. B. Tower.

HOUSATONIC.

Wm. I. Van Deusen, Mrs. A. E. Smith.
Mrs. Thomas W. Barnes,

LANESBORO.

"Brookside Farm," J. A. Royce. Proprietor; Farm House with accommodations for 20; terms, $7 to $9 per week; public stage from Boston & Albany and Housatonic Railroad station, Pittsfield, at 2.30 p. m., daily; six and one-half miles to house; or private conveyance and terms on application.

Jesse C. Pratt, William S. Royce,
Mrs. E. A. Sherman, H. A. Reed,
John Gordon, George Hallis,
F. D. Deming, George Farnam,
Mrs. Frank Nourse, Mrs. Livermore.

LEE.

Golden Hill Boarding House, A. C. Swift, Proprietor; $8 a week, children half price; one mile from Housatonic Railroad and post-office, and one-half mile from Laurel Lake; plenty of fresh milk, cream, fruit, etc.

Private House, J. M. Howk; accommodations for 10; prices on application; half a mile from station; cost of transportation, 25 cents.

Mrs. L. C. Bosworth, A. C. Swift,
E. A. Bradley, F. K. Kinckley,
D. P. Bradley, Mrs. A. P. Bassett,
James H. Wood, Mrs. R. A. Webster.

LENOX.

Curtis's Hotel, William O. and William D. Curtis, Proprietors; accommodations for 250; terms on application; two and one-half miles from Housatonic Railroad station; transportation, 25 cents.

Mrs. J. H. Curtis, Miss G. M. Seeley,
James Clifford, Mrs. J. S. Ross,
Mrs. H. S. Tucker, Mrs. L. Flint,
Geo. C. Thompson, Mrs. F. Washburn,
C. Batolany. Bellevieu Hotel.

LENOX DALE.

Geo. C. Thompson, Henry Sedgwick,
A. J. Taintor, S. C. Swift.

MILL RIVER.

Mrs. William Huntley.

MONTEREY.

Prospect Hill Farm, Henry Woods, Proprietor; accommodations for 20; terms,

$7 to $9 per week; near Stockbridge and Great Barrington; best of city references.

Lake Farm, M. S. Bidwell, Proprietor.
The Pines, Henry Clapp, Proprietor.
Edward Edmonds, D. C. Tryon,
Horace Purdy, W. E. Brewer.
John Townsend,

MOUNT WASHINGTON.
(Alandar P. O.)

Hotel Alandar, F. S. Weaver, Proprietor; accommodations for 40 to 50; terms, $7 to $12 per week; open June to October; 1,000 feet above the Housatonic Valley; five and one-half miles from Copake Iron Works station, Harlem Railroad.

Taconic Farm, H. F. Keith, Proprietor; accommodates 15; terms, $7 to $15 per week; three miles from Harlem Railroad station; transportation from 50 to 75 cents.

O. C. Whitbeck, Frank B. Schutt,
Ira L. Patterson, Isaac Spurr,
William H. Weaver, Linus Melius.

NEW ASHFORD.
R. J. Smith.

NEW MARLBOROUGH.

South Berkshire House, Wells & Jenks, Proprietors.
Woodlawn, A. J. Wood, Proprietor.
Mrs. J. G. Voorhees.

NORTH ADAMS.

Kemp Park House, J. H. Melvin, Proprietor; accommodations for 20; terms, $1 per day, to families; one-half mile from station; transportation free, on notice. A large grove adjoining for accommodation of picnics and private parties, with use of flying horses, swings and dancing pavilion; prices given on application.

Wilson House, F. E. Swift, Proprietor.
Richmond House, L. L. Scott, Proprietor.
J. H. Melvin, Park Avenue.
Mrs. John Crossett, 12 Church Street.
Mrs. William Holbrooks, Church Place.
Mrs. A. B. Harrison, West Main Street.

NORTH EGREMONT.

Farm House, W. H. May, Proprietor; ample grounds and shade; terms, $5 to $10 per week; twenty minutes' drive from station at Great Barrington; five minutes' walk from post-office, stores, church, telephone and telegraph office; short drives to Mount Everett, Monument Mountain, Lake Buell, Twin Lakes, the Housatonic, Konkapot, Green River, etc., in which excellent trout, bass and pickerel fishing may be found in their season.

Old-Fashioned Farm House, Mrs. B. E. Stoddard, Proprietor; situated on Baldwin Hill; six rooms; families preferred; terms moderate; one-half mile from post-office and church; one mile from Prospect Lake; delightful scenery; five miles from Great Barrington station of Housatonic Railroad.

S. B. Dewey, L. M. Joyner.
F. M. Olmsted,

OTIS.

H. A. Day, J. B. Clark.

PERU.

Mrs. S. B. French, E. Shumway,
Mrs. H. Parks, Austin Stowell.
Henry Barlow,

PITTSFIELD.

Maplewood, E. W. Plumb, Proprietor; accommodations for 300; terms on application; free transportation from Boston & Albany and Housatonic Railroad station.

American House, Plumb & Clark, Proprietors; accommodations for 60; terms on application; transportation from Boston & Albany and Housatonic Railroad stations, free.

Burbank Hotel, R. E. Burbank, Proprietor; accommodations for 100; terms on application; adjoining Housatonic and Boston & Albany Railroad stations.

Mrs. W. H. Nichols, F. M. Strong,
Mrs. M. Backus, South Street.
Mrs. Hubbard, Grand Avenue.
Mrs. Kate P. Stevens.

RICHMOND.

M. J. Sherrill,	Frank Barnes, Jr.,
M. M. Groat,	M. Sharp,
W. H. Nichols,	C. H. Nichols.
C. P. Lovelace,	

ROCK DALE MILLS.

Mrs. Thomas W. Barnes.

SANDISFIELD.

Mrs. Maria D. Butler, Mrs. Olcott Cone.

SHEFFIELD.

Conway House, J. E. Conway, Proprietor; accommodations for 60; terms, $14 to $21 per week; three minutes' walk from Housatonic Railroad station.

Farm House, Mrs. Walter Briggs; accommodations for 10; $6 per week; one mile from Housatonic Railroad station; transportation, 25 cents.

J. M. Bacon,	Henry Spurr,
Harvey Roys,	George Peck,
J. H. Field,	Cyrus French.
Milo Knickerbocker,	George Cook.

SOUTH EGREMONT.

Mount Everett House, W. B. Peck, Proprietor; accommodations for 75; terms, $10 to $12 per week, $2 per day; four miles from Housatonic Railroad station at Great Barrington, six miles from Harlem Railroad station at Hillsdale, N. Y.; transportation to railroad station, $1.

Mrs. Almon Smith, Mrs. V. L. Wilcox,
William Fee, Mrs. Elwin R. Peck,
Miss Sarah Williams, C. Williams.

SOUTHFIELD.

I. R. Baldwin,	William E. Rasson,
A. C. Hunt,	J. B. Haskell.

SOUTH SANDISFIELD.

Sportsmen parties, etc., are entertained by

Mrs. Lyman Gaylord, Mrs. J. C. Smith.
Mrs. Daniel Webster.

SOUTH WILLIAMSTOWN.

Sabin House, Thomas Sabin, Proprietor; accommodations for 15; terms on application; four miles from Williams College, five miles from Fitchburg Railroad station; two mail stages a day; stable connected with hotel.

STOCKBRIDGE.

Stockbridge House, C. H. Plumb, Proprietor; accommodations for 100; terms, $15 to $21 per week; half mile from Housatonic Railroad station; transportation, 25 cents.

Farm House, G. Irving Bradley, Proprietor; high location; tennis; accommodations for 15; terms on application; horses to let; two miles from Housatonic Railroad station.

Edwards Hall, Mrs. Mary A. Ward, Proprietress.

C. H. Willis,	S. P. Lincoln,
George T. Bradley,	John P. Sayles,
Mrs. A. M. Goodrich,	T. B. Patterson,
Miss Louise Stafford,	Anson Buck.

TYRINGHAM.

Fernside, J. Jones, M. D., Proprietor.
L. B. Moore.

WEST BECKET.
Curtis A. Andrews.

WEST STOCKBRIDGE.
Mrs. E. Hinman, M. E. Sprague,
Mrs. H. K. Kent, P. Seals.

WILLIAMSTOWN.
The Greylock, F. K. McLaughlin, Manager; accommodations for 175; terms on application; one and a half miles from Fitchburg Railroad station; transportation to and from station, 25 cents, including trunk.

Taconic Inn, F. K. McLaughlin, Manager; accommodations for 100; terms on application; (open all the year;) steam heat and open fire places; one and a half miles from the Fitchburg Railroad station; transportation to and from station, 25 cents, including trunk.

Misses E. and C. Bardwell,
Chauncy Hickox, Mrs. Wheeler,
Mrs. Daniel White, Mrs. S. B. Kellogg.

WINDSOR.
H. C. Cleveland, G. W. Converse,
Edward Hume, Jud Converse,
James Cornell, Ward D. White.
H. Ward Ford,

ZYLONITE.
Lyman Fields, Harry Donohue.

INDEX.

	PAGE.		PAGE.
ADAMS,	176	HANCOCK,	210
ALFORD,	204	HASTY TOUR,	257
BECKET,	206	HILLSDALE, N. Y.,	289
BERKSHIRE PROSE AND POETRY,	261	HINSDALE,	228
CANAAN, CT.,	284	LAKEVILLE, CT.,	275
CAMPING IN BERKSHIRE,	291	LANESBORO,	212
CHESHIRE,	231	LEE,	199
CLARKSBURG,	238	LENOX,	21
CLIMATE,	241	MONTEREY,	208
COACHING IN BERKSHIRE,	205	MOUNT WASHINGTON,	153
CUMMINGTON, HAMPSHIRE CO.,	288	NEW ASHFORD,	235
DALTON,	216	NEW LEBANON, N. Y.,	286
DRIVES—	248	NEW MARLBORO,	194
Adams,	253	NORFOLK, CT.,	279
Canaan, Ct.,	255	NORTH ADAMS,	167
Great Barrington,	231	OTIS,	203
Lenox,	240	PERU,	229
Norfolk, Ct.,	256	PITTSFIELD,	105
North Adams,	253	POPULATION,	242
Pittsfield,	248	PREFATORY,	5
Salisbury, Ct.,	255	RICHMOND,	209
Sheffield,	252	SALISBURY, CT.,	268
South Egremont,	253	SANDISFIELD,	203
Stockbridge,	250	SAVOY,	234
Williamstown,	254	SHEFFIELD,	141
EGREMONT—	149	STAMFORD, VT.,	289
South,	149	STOCKBRIDGE,	51
North,	151	TOPOGRAPHY,	243
ELEVATIONS,	245	TYRINGHAM,	190
FLORIDA,	236	WASHINGTON,	215
FUTURE OF BERKSHIRE,	19	WEST STOCKBRIDGE,	205
GENERAL SURVEY,	7	WILD FLOWERS AND PLANTS,	239
GREAT BARRINGTON,	77	WILLIAMSTOWN,	129
GREYLOCK PARK,	181	WINDSOR,	230
ACCOMMODATIONS FOR SUMMER GUESTS,			296

INDEX TO ILLUSTRATIONS.

FRONTISPIECE, GREYLOCK.

Bashbish Lower Falls, Mount Washington, . . .	159
"Bonanza" Artesian Well, Dalton, ...	224
Bryant House, Great Barrington, . . .	88
Canaan Falls, . . .	274
Chime of Bells Tower, Stockbridge, ...	68
Claflin House, Becket, . .	207
Congregational Church, Dalton, ...	227
Dome of the Taconics, Mount Washington, . . .	4
Fernside, Tyringham, . .	191
Gibson's Landing, Lake Buel,	196
Great Barrington, from the Northwest, ...	76
Hopkins Memorial, Williamstown, ...	137
Hopkins-Searle Mansion, the South View, Great Barrington, ...	79
Initial "A," Lanesboro, .	212
Initial "A," Pittsfield, .	105
Initial "B," Berkshire, .	7
Initial "I," Lenox, . .	21
Initial "N," Stockbridge, .	51
Initial "O," Great Barrington, ...	77
Initial "T," A Hasty Tour, .	257
Initial "T," Mount Washington, ...	153
Initial "W," Williamstown, .	129
Monument Mountain, Great Barrington, . .	90
"Old Berkshire Mills" Flowing Artesian Well, Dalton,	225
Old Court House, Lenox, now Sedgwick Hall, . . .	45
Old Indian Burial Ground, Stockbridge, . . .	62
Park Square, Pittsfield, .	127
Sheffield Elm, . . .	142
Sky Farm Cottage, Mount Washington, . . .	156
Soldiers' Monument, Pittsfield, ...	104
Stockbridge Bowl, . .	72
Swiss Chalet, Mount Weston,	226
Wahconah Falls, Dalton, .	221
Williamstown, Main Street,	130
Group of Pictures, .	14
1. Lake Garfield, Monterey.	
2. Congregational Church, Lenox.	
3. Ancient House, South Egremont.	
4. Sage's Ravine, Mount Washington.	
5. Plantain Pond, Mount Washington.	
Group of Pictures, . .	112
1. Wonderful Birch Tree, Lanesboro.	
2. Wahconah Falls, Windsor.	
3. Pontoosuc Lake, Pittsfield.	
4. Onota Lake, Pittsfield.	
Group of Pictures, . .	125
1. The Berkshire County Court House, Pittsfield.	
2, 4. Flowing Artesian Wells, Dalton.	
3. Lenox Club House.	
5. Crane Library, Dalton.	
Group of Pictures, . .	166
1. Campbell's Falls, New Marlboro.	
2. Hotel, Bashbish Falls.	
3. Eastern Portal, Hoosac Tunnel.	
4. Natural Bridge, at North Adams.	
5. Upper Bashbish Falls.	

THE CLAFLIN HOTEL,

BECKET,
BERKSHIRE COUNTY, MASS.

APPLY FOR CIRCULAR.

WILLIAM A. SCHLESINGER, PROPRIETOR.

THE REPUBLICAN BUILDING,
Corner Main Street and Harrison Avenue, Springfield, Mass.

THE SPRINGFIELD REPUBLICAN,
THE LEADING NEW ENGLAND NEWSPAPER.

ESTABLISHED IN 1824 BY SAMUEL BOWLES.

DAILY, $8.   **SUNDAY, $2.**   **WEEKLY, $1.**

The Republican devotes special attention to THE NEWS OF BERKSHIRE, and has long been THE FAVORITE DAILY JOURNAL among the people of the county.

THE DAILY REPUBLICAN reaches Pittsfield BEFORE 6 A. M., and THE SUNDAY REPUBLICAN BY 8 A. M. Both editions are promptly distributed by regular trains, or special expresses, North and South through the county, and are sold by local agents in the principal towns, or sent by mail to subscribers in the smaller places.

THE WEEKLY REPUBLICAN is a 12-page news and family paper of the first quality, able, interesting, varied, newsy and reliable.

THE SPRINGFIELD REPUBLICAN is recognized as the most effective advertising medium in Western Massachusetts. Send for rates.

Sample copies free.   Address,

THE REPUBLICAN, SPRINGFIELD, MASS.

SEND FOR CIRCULAR 1890.

BERKSHIRE HOUSE

15th SEASON.

C. TICKNOR, Proprietor.

Southern Berkshire Resort. Matchless Surroundings and Drives. Gunning, Fishing, Boating, convenient distance. Entire absence of Mosquitoes and Malaria. House provides for Hundred Guests. Excellent Sanitary Provision, Mountain Spring Water, Electric Light, Gas, Complete Sewerage, Etc., and has connected the

BERKSHIRE STABLES,

WILLIAM W. NORTON, Proprietor,

Where the most modern and complete provision for riding can be secured. Well-selected Horses, with easy, comfortable carriages, for safe driving, particularly considered. Space for Transient and Boarding horses ample.

GREAT BARRINGTON, MASS.

PITTSFIELD, BERKSHIRE CO., MASS.

ARTHUR W. PLUMB, Proprietor.

ONE OF THE MOST ATTRACTIVE RESORTS IN THE BERKSHIRE HILLS.

A large recreation room for the guests, containing Bowling Alleys, Dancing Floor, Stage for Amateur Theatricals, Concerts, etc.

All amateur photographers and tourists are cordially invited to use our dark room, for changing plates, developing, etc.

For further information, please address as above.

OPEN FROM JUNE 1st TO NOVEMBER 1st.

J. M. WATERMAN,
Livery Boarding and Sale
STABLES.

Main Street, WILLIAMSTOWN, MASS.
Opp. Methodist Church.

Good horses and carriages furnished at short notice, on reasonable terms. Coaches to and from all the trains.

VILLAGE PROPERTY
For Sale and to Rent.

A. C. COLLINS,
ATTORNEY AT LAW,
Commissioner of Deeds for the State of New York.

OFFICE.
Summer Building, - Main Street,
GREAT BARRINGTON, MASS.

SAMUEL BRIDGES, AMERICAN AND BERKSHIRE HOUSE STABLES.

ALL KINDS OF SINGLE AND DOUBLE CARRIAGES.
Prompt attention given to all orders.
Connected by telephone.

PITTSFIELD, MASS.

GOOD HOUSEKEEPING, $2.50 a year, published Fortnightly at Springfield, Mass., is the best home magazine in the country.—*Janesville, Wis., Signal.*

DALTON.

Old Berkshire Mills,
(ESTABLISHED 1801,)

Linen Ledger and Extra Superfine

WRITING PAPER,

Possesses every requisite for Books of Record, where Delicate and Permanent Color, Ease in Engrossing upon its pages, and Great Durability in Long and Hard Service are essential. Every blank book maker can furnish this paper, and the manufacturers will pay for any book rejected for fault in the Linen Ledger Paper. The Flat and Folded Papers made by this Company commend themselves as unexcelled for Correspondence—business or pleasure—and for legal blanks and important documents.

Tourists and visitors in the County, are always welcome to inspect the works.

OLD BERKSHIRE MILLS CO., Manuf'rs.

JOHN D. CARSON, Treas.   W. MURRAY CRANE, Prest.

CURTIS' HOTEL, LENOX, MASS.

OPEN ALL THE YEAR.

BROOKSIDE FARM.
Summer Board.

Accommodates from 15 to 20 guests from early June to October. 1890 is the 13th Season. Location is pleasant and healthy, with pure air and water, good roads, fine drives and rambles. At upper end of Housatonic valley, 6½ miles north of Pittsfield, and 1,800 feet above sea-level. Terms reasonable. Address, **J. A. ROYCE,**
Lanesboro, Mass.

J. H. FLAGG,
LIVERY, BOARDING AND SALE
STABLES,
57 Main Street,
North Adams, Mass.

Good Horses and Carriages furnished at short notice on reasonable terms. Hacks to and from all trains. Mountain wagons, especially adapted for taking parties to Greylock.

MAPLEWOOD
Livery, Boarding and Feed Stable,
No. 12 1-2 West Street,
GEORGE R. BARBER, Proprietor,
Pittsfield, Mass.

MASSASOIT HOUSE,
SPRINGFIELD, MASS.
W. H. CHAPIN.

BERKSHIRE VIEWS.

Complete list constantly on hand. Nothing but the highest grade of workmanship. RECOMMENDS from the leading residents of Lenox, Stockbridge, Pittsfield, Great Barrington and other places of note among the Berkshire Hills. Interiors, Exteriors Architectural and Landscape views. Also instantaneous photos of Animals made as quick as a flash. We always guarantee our work satisfactory. **A. M. COSTELLO,**
Berkshire Photographer.
Studio, Great Barrington Mass.
One door north of Post-office.

The Best Family Magazine.

GOOD HOUSEKEEPING is as near perfection as capital and skill can approach.—*Lowell, Mass., Vox Populi.*
GOOD HOUSEKEEPING is a veritable encyclopedia of useful household knowledge.—*Portland, Me., Globe.*
SUBSCRIBE WHEN? NOW.
GOOD HOUSEKEEPING,
Springfield, Mass.
PUBLISHED FORTNIGHTLY, $2.50 A YEAR.
All newsdealers sell it or will take subscriptions for it.

AMERICAN HOUSE,

PITTSFIELD, MASS.

Open all the Year. ——————————
———————— ———————— Completely Renovated.

Newly, Elegantly, and Comfortably Furnished. Modern Improvements and First-class in all respects.

PLUMB & CLARK, Proprietors.

Mt. EVERETT HOUSE,

Located in the village of

SOUTH EGREMONT (Berkshire Co.), MASS.

Four miles from Great Barrington Station, on the Housatonic Railroad, and Six miles from Hillsdale, N. Y., on the Harlem Railroad.

Livery attached, with good stabling for private horses. Telephone (free to guests) connects with Depot, Telegraph and Doctors' Offices, Drug Stores, Hotels, Etc.

W. B. PECK, Prop.

THE GREYLOCK,
WILLIAMSTOWN, MASS.
OPEN JUNE TO OCTOBER.

THE TACONIC INN,
WILLIAMSTOWN, MASS.
OPEN THE YEAR AROUND.

STEAM HEAT AND OPEN FIRES.

For Terms, etc., address,

F. K. McLAUGHLIN,
MANAGER.

COLLINS HOUSE,
GREAT BARRINGTON, MASS.

Eligibly situated within easy reach of the Post-Office, Telegraph and Railway Station.

GOOD LIVERY STABLE CONNECTED WITH THE HOUSE.

ALFRED PECK, *Proprietor*.

MILLER HOUSE,

W. B. LOVELAND, AGENT,　　　GREAT BARRINGTON, MASS.

The Edison Electric Light has been introduced, and the house has recently been renovated and put in first-class order for the accommodation of the public.

GOOD LIVERY CONNECTED WITH THE HOUSE.

CHAS. H. BERRY,
Livery, Sale and Boarding
STABLE,
82 Main St., No. Adams, Mass.

**DO YOU TAKE
GOOD HOUSEKEEPING?**

LOUIS H. REGNIER,
Dealer in
DRY GOODS, BOOTS AND SHOES.
Specialty of Fine Custom Made Shoes.
Also Newsdealer and Stationer.
Fine Line of Cigars and all kinds of Tobacco.

WALKER ST., LENOX, MASS.

BARDEN STATIONERY CO.

MAKERS OF

HIGH GRADE CORRESPONDENCE PAPERS

UNDER THE FOLLOWING BRANDS:

"GREYLOCK ALL LINEN,"

"BARDEN'S HAND-MADE LINEN,"

"WESTBROOK LINEN."

FACTORY AT

ADAMS, MASS.

Great Barrington Baggage Express.

Baggage Express Wagons to the railway station of the Housatonic railroad on the arrival of every train.
Baggage called for in any part of the town and delivered promptly.
Harnesses of all kinds for Sale or Made to Order.
Repairing of all kinds Neatly and Promptly Done.

RAILROAD STREET.   E. D. HUMPHREY, Prop.

JACK METCALF, Foreman.

MAIN ST., NEAR R. R. DEPOT.   TERMS, $2.50 PER DAY.

HOTEL WARWICK,
SPRINGFIELD, MASS.

ELEVATOR AND ALL MODERN CONVENIENCES.   GEO. E. BARR,
OFFICE ON GROUND FLOOR.   127 ROOMS.   PROPRIETOR.

HOTEL VENDOME, BOSTON.
COMMONWEALTH AVENUE.
C. H. GREENLEAF & CO., Props.

UNSURPASSED by any hotel in the country for the beauty of its surroundings, the excellence of its accommodations, and the high order of its patronage. Most desirable for families and tourists.

With a hundred feet of park running through its center, and the finest and costliest residences of the city facing upon it, Commonwealth avenue, Boston, is justly famed as the most beautiful boulevard of America. It is appropriate that here should be found one of the largest and handsomest hotels in the country. The VENDOME, whose elegance, spaciousness and unusual excellence make it most desirable for transient visitors and tourists, and a peculiarly attractive residence for ladies and families.

The proprietors, Messrs. C. H. Greenleaf & Co., also have the celebrated Profile House, which needs little mention here; its name is so familiar to every one, that to speak of the White Mountains is to think of Franconia Notch and "The Profile," of summer rest and enjoyment, amid magnificent scenery and luxurious surroundings.

IF you want to sell goods to a paper-maker, paper dealer, manufacturing stationer, retail stationer, printer, lithographer, engraver, bookbinder, or a manufacturer of printers' or bookbinders' supplies, advertise in THE PAPER WORLD. It is acknowledged to have more merit than all the other paper trade journals put together.

CLARK W. BRYAN & Co., Publishers, Springfield, Mass.

COOLEY'S HOTEL,

J. M. COOLEY & CO., Proprietors.

211 Main Street,   SPRINGFIELD, MASS.
Near Boston & Albany Railroad Depot.

NEW YORK & NEW ENGLAND RAILROAD.

TRAINS BETWEEN BOSTON AND NEW YORK,

| Leave Either City, | 12.00 M. | Arrive at the Other | 6.30 P. M. |
| " " " | 3.00 P. M. | " " " | 9.00 P. M. |

The Shortest Line. Always on Time.
Dining Cars. New Parlor Cars and Coaches.

THE 3.00 P. M. TRAIN RUNS DAILY, INCLUDING SUNDAYS.

Office, 322 Washington Street, **BOSTON.**   Grand Central Station, **NEW YORK.**
Depot, Foot of Summer Street,   353 Broadway,

CHARLES HOWARD, Gen. Manager.   A. C. KENDALL, Gen. Pass. Agent.
June, 1890.

CONWAY ✠ HOUSE.
Open all the year. Good Livery attached.
J. E. CONWAY, PROP., SHEFFIELD, MASS.

DALTON, MASS.,

MANUFACTURERS OF

Bond, Bank Note, Parchment

PAPER

Onion Skin, Legal Cap, etc.

At these Mills the Bank Note Papers used by the National Banks of the United States, and the Paper used by the U. S. Government for their Legal Tender and Bonds is made.

Paper for the Currency and Bonds of other Governments is also made here.

Extra Fine Papers,

MANUFACTURED BY

Z. & W. M. CRANE,

DALTON, MASS., U. S. A.

This Trade Mark on every box.

Trade Mark on our "DISTAFF" brand.

THESE GOODS, WHICH ARE ACKNOWLEDGED TO EQUAL THE FINEST FOREIGN MANUFACTURES, ARE PRESENTED IN THE FOLLOWING STYLES AND QUALITIES:

SUPERFINE QUALITY.

In handsome light Blue Boxes, containing one-quarter of a ream of Note Paper each, and bearing in blue letters description of contents.

In separate Boxes of uniform size, are one-eighth of a thousand Envelopes, corresponding in tint and quality to the paper.

EXTRA SUPERFINE QUALITY.

In attractive Lavender-Colored Boxes, containing one-fourth ream of Extra Fine Paper each, with contents printed in red. Corresponding to this, in like Boxes, are Envelopes to match.

All this Stationery may be relied on to be according to representation. It is suited to the tastes of the most select trade.

SOLD BY ALL BOOKSELLERS AND STATIONERS.

Our Papers are Supplied in Fine Wedding Stationery, Visiting Cards, and other Specialties by

GEO. B. HURD & CO., 77 and 79 Beekman Street,

NEW YORK.

FAMOUS FOR HALF A CENTURY.
RECENTLY ENLARGED AND GREATLY IMPROVED, FURNISHING FIRST-CLASS ACCOMMODATIONS FOR FIVE HUNDRED GUESTS.

Pleasure Parties, Ladies and Families Visiting the East, will find the UNITED STATES combining all the conveniences and substantial comforts of a pleasant home, free alike from extravagant show, or still more extravagant charges, while its very convenient location directly opposite the **Boston & Albany**, and only three blocks from **Old Colony and Fall River, New York and New England**, and **Providence and Stonington Stations**. Six Hundred Horse Cars pass three sides of the Hotel, bringing it in direct and close connection with every **Northern and Eastern Railway Station and Steamboat** as well as the thousand attractions of **City, Seashore, and Suburbs, Unequalled by any Hotel in Boston**. Thus making a most convenient point to stop on arriving in the city, saving all carriage fares, and, for those who desire to spend a day or week in shopping, or visiting the thousand objects of art and interest, a most central, desirable, and convenient location, being only two minutes' walk from all the great fashionable **Retail Establishments, Theatres, Objects of Interest, and Places of Amusement.**

       TILLY HAYNES,   ·   ·   ·   ·   **Resident Proprietor.**

HOUSATONIC RAILROAD,

The Only Route to

GREAT BARRINGTON, STOCKBRIDGE, LENOX, PITTSFIELD,

And all the

Famous Summer Resorts in the Berkshire Hills.

Fast Limited Express Trains Between New York City (Grand Central Depot), Sheffield, Great Barrington, Stockbridge, Lee, Lenox, Pittsfield and North Adams.

Dep. New York (Grand Central Depot, via N. Y. N. H. & H. R. R.), *4.00 p. m.

Due Sheffield, 7.35 p. m.; Great Barrington, 7.48 p. m.; Stockbridge, 8.07 p. m.; Lee, 8.18 p. m.; Lenox, 8.25 p. m.; Pittsfield, 8.40 p. m.

Dep. North Adams, *3.05 p. m.; Pittsfield, 4.10 p. m.; Lenox, 4.21 p. m.; Lee, 4.29 p. m.; Stockbridge, 4.40 p. m.; Great Barrington, 4.58 p. m.; Sheffield, 5.07 p. m.

Due New York (Grand Central Depot), 9.00 p. m.

Limited Express Trains are composed of Elegant New Drawing-Room Cars and Coaches, built expressly for the Berkshire Hills travel.

*Daily (Except Sunday).

WILLIAM H. STEVENSON,
   Vice-President and General Manager.
    A. W. PERRIN, General Passenger Agent.

SPRINGFIELD
FIRE AND MARINE
INSURANCE COMPANY,
OF SPRINGFIELD, MASS.
Annual Statement, January 1st, 1890.
CAPITAL, 1,500,000 DOLLARS.

ASSETS.

United States 6 per cent Currency Reg. Bonds,	$125,000.00
Water Company Bonds,	166,000.00
Railroad Bonds,	336,880.00
Railroad Stocks,	1,327,350.00
Bank Stocks,	660,630.00
Real Estate owned by the Company,	110,853.00
Cash on hand, in Banks, and in hands of Agents, in course of transmission,	323,066.32
Loans on Mortgage of Real Estate,	301,500.00
Loans secured by R. R. and Bank Stocks,	26,500.00
Accrued Interest, Rents and other dues,	33,203.62
	$3,410,982.91

LIABILITIES.

Capital Stock all paid up,	$1,500,000.00	
Outstanding Losses,	186,716.25	
Re-Insurance Fund,	1,174,546.51	
All other Claims,	29,210.52	**$2,890,473.28**
Surplus over all Liabilities,		**$520,509.66**
Surplus as regards Policy Holders,		**$2,020,509.66**

J. N. DUNHAM, President.
SANFORD J. HALL, Secretary.　　　　ANDREW J. WRIGHT, Treasurer.

	AGENTS.	
Wellington & Bixby,	"	Adams.
John C. Wheeler,	"	Great Barrington.
M. H. Pease & Co.,	"	Lee.
Geo. F. Miller,	"	North Adams.
Wilson & Read,	"	Pittsfield.
Clarence M. Smith,	"	Williamstown.

STOCKBRIDGE HOUSE.

✻ STOCKBRIDGE, MASS.

C. H. PLUMB,
Proprietor.

HURLBUT PAPER MFG. CO.
ESTABLISHED IN 1822.

HURLBUT PAPER MFG. CO.,

SOUTH LEE, MASS.,

MANUFACTURERS OF

French Linen.

Oriental Linen.

Queen Anne Linen.

Fernside Linen.

IN BOXES, WITH ENVELOPES TO MATCH.

Also Bond, Ledger, Wedding and Extra Superfine Papers.

BOLTON

Best Record for Longest Time in Coldest Climates.

HOT WATER

Most Durable and Economical, Cleanly and Safe.

HEATER.

Its Vertical Circulation renders its action prompt and rapid.
Its Fire Surface is the Largest in proportion to Grate Surface.
No bolted, flanged or packed joints; therefore cannot leak.
Its brick casing entirely prevents loss of heat in cellar.
Wrought Iron; therefore cannot crack.

10° Below and Blowing a Gale.

J. H. MOCKETT, JR., Gen'l Manager N. W. Mutual Life Ins. Co., Lincoln, Neb., writes:

January 14, 1890.

Gentlemen: No difficulty in keeping up an even heat in any weather which we have had this winter.

The thermometer registered 10 degrees below zero last night, with the wind blowing a gale. The house is in an exposed location, no storm doors or windows, and it was easy to keep the temperature at 73 degrees all over the house.

I am certain that the Bolton Boiler is the best apparatus for heating, both in mild and severe weather, I have ever seen.

DETROIT
HEATING AND LIGHTING
COMPANY.

421 Wight St., Detroit, Mich.

42 Pearl St., Boston.
88 Lake St., Chicago.
508 N. 4th St., St. Louis.
Send for Illustrated Books.

COMBINATION
GAS MACHINE.

Best Independent Gas Apparatus
For Country and Suburban Residences, Hotels, Churches, Schools, Stores, etc.
Over 20 Years in Use, with Never an Accident.
Average cost of gas, ½ cent per hour per burner.

AMERICAN
EXPRESS COMPANY

Transacts a general express business to and from all points on the

BOSTON AND ALBANY,   **FITCHBURG,**
N. Y. C. & H. R. R. R.,

and also upon 40,000 miles of additional railroad, with 6000 agencies extending throughout 22 States and Canada; also forwarders to and from Europe by the fastest mail and passenger steamers crossing the Atlantic.

Special Exclusive Express Train Service, carrying no passengers, but making the fastest possible time. The Special American Express Trains from the eastern to the western cities continue to run as usual, departing from New York at 8 and 9 p. m. and from Boston at 3 and 7 p. m.

Order and Commission Department, through which orders for goods or household supplies may be filled at any place reached by the Company. Promptness and careful exection of such orders assured, with no charge for such extra service.

Express Money Order System, by which the public are supplied with a cheap and convenient method for the transmission of money with absolute security. Orders are payable at 15,000 places in the United States, Canada and Europe, and are practically good everywhere. Travelers, whether at home or abroad, will find in these Orders a most convenient way to carry funds with absolute safety, and a simple plan of indentification.

RATES FOR EXPRESS MONEY ORDERS.

PAYABLE IN U. S. AND CANADA:		PAYABLE IN EUROPE:	
For not over $5 00, - - -	5 Cents.	For not over $10 00, - - -	10 Cents.
For not over 10 00, - - -	8 Cents.	For not over 20 00, - - -	18 Cents.
For not over 20 00, - - -	10 Cents.	For not over 30 00, - - -	25 Cents.
For not over 30 00, - - -	12 Cents.	For not over 40 00, - - -	35 Cents.
For not over 40 00, - - -	15 Cents.	For not over 50 00, - - -	45 Cents.
For not over 50 00, - - -	20 Cents.		

For Amounts Exceeding $50 00 at same Rates.

Telegraphic Transfer Department, through which money can be transmitted by wire between all of the Company's 6000 agencies with great promptness at the following rates in addition to cost of telegraph service: $100 or less, one per cent. (no charge less than fifty cents); over $100 to $200, $1.25; over $200 to $300, $1.50; over $300 to $400, $1.75; over $400 to $500, $2.00. For rates for larger sums apply to agents.

European Department: Merchandise and Passengers' Baggage from Europe carried IN BOND from New York and Boston, without Customs examination, to Inland Ports of the United States WITHOUT CHARGE for CUSTOM HOUSE BROKERAGE or CARTAGE service, when carried by this Company.

Baggage accompanying returning European travelers can be carried under the above arrangement—also to Canada. The Uniformed Agent of the Company will meet steamers arriving at New York, prepared to give receipts and otherwise assist passengers in making shipments.

LIVERY STABLES. D. J. PRATT'S DALTON, MASS.

We have two first-class liverys in connection with the Irving House, the IRVING HOUSE LIVERY, one of the modern stables of the county, and the UPPER STABLE, situated at the corner of Main Street and Weston Avenue. Our stables contain all the latest styles of vehicles, including fine Berlin Coaches and five Glass Landaus, Six and Four-in-Hand Tally-hoes, Four, Three and Two-Seaters of the best kind. Single Turn-outs of all descriptions.

Our horses are selected especially for the wants of Summer Guests, are all good roaders and safe; a number of fine Saddlers have been added since last season. We are fully equipped in every department and are confident that we shall be able to please our patrons for the season of 1890.

Carriages meet all trains arriving at the Boston & Albany depot.

D. J. PRATT, Proprietor.

IRVING HOUSE
DALTON, Berkshire Co., MASS.

THIS House is situated in the center of the famous Berkshire Hills. Drives and scenery unsurpassed. Electric lights, and all modern improvements. Spacious lawn.

F. L. BOURNE, PROP.

Elmwood Cottages.
BERKSHIRE HILLS, DALTON, MASS.

These are two good spacious cottages, finely located in the flourishing town of Dalton, Mass., on the Boston and Albany railroad, five miles east of Pittsfield, and easy of access from all points.

The buildings are two and one-half stories high; all handsomely furnished throughout; large rooms, hot and cold water, bath-rooms, range, cement floor to cellar, perfect drainage, and with every appliance and convenience for a first-class summer home.

They may be rented from May 1st to Nov. 1st, or later, if desired. For terms, apply to
WILLIAM B. CLARK,
Dalton, Berkshire Co., Mass.

WRITE FOR SAMPLES of something or other. Take us at our word, and bother us as much as you like. You can't do it enough to do us the good we are after.

FORBES & WALLACE, Springfield, Mass.

COLTON'S SELECT FLAVORS

PERFECTLY PURE Extracts of Choicest Fruits. **THE BEST.** Unequaled Strength for All. Thousands of Gross Sold.
Winning Friends Everywhere. **EVERY FAMILY** Should Know Their Delicious Flavors.
Dealers Treble Sales with Them. Ask Your Grocer or Dealer for Them.

6 BOOKS for $1.75, sent postpaid by CLARK W. BRYAN & Co., Publishers Good Housekeeping, Springfield, Mass. Perfect Bread, Key to Cooking, Lessons in Candy Making, Six Cups of Coffee, Dainty Desserts for Dainty Diners, In the Sick Room.

Chamberlin's Eagle Hotel.

First-class Livery Stable in connection with the hotel. J. C. CHAMBERLIN, Proprietor, Cor. Main and Depot Streets, DALTON, MASS.

IT matters not whether you are a paper-maker or a paper manufacturer, whether you run a printing-office or set type in the same, whether you are a lithographer, engraver, bookbinder, clerk in a stationery store, or proprietor of the same, sell ink or manufacture it, run an amateur office in your back garret or a big metropolitan printing-office, you should take THE PAPER WORLD. It is $2 a year, and is published by CLARK W. BRYAN & Co., Springfield, Mass.

THE "BABCOCK" BUCKBOARD.

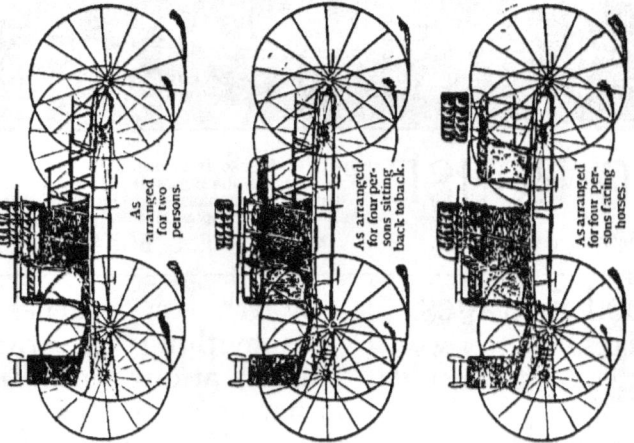

H. H. BABCOCK COMPANY, WATERTOWN, N. Y. Salesrooms in New York City, 406-412 Broome Street.

G. W. PLATT, DRUGGIST AND APOTHECARY, GRAT BARRINGTON, MASS.

A thorough knowledge of business, honest dealing and accuracy.

DRUGS, MEDICINES AND CHEMICALS.

Choice Confectionery, Imported Cigars, Pure Wines, Liquors and Mineral Waters at Lowest Prices.

ORDERS TAKEN FOR CUT FLOWERS.

GREAT BARRINGTON, MASS.

If you intend spending the summer at or near this beautiful place,

REMEMBER YOU CAN FIND AT **LILLIE & SIMMONS'**

A FIRST-CLASS DRUG STORE.

Anything usually to be found in the finest city stores. Prescriptions a specialty at any hour. DON'T FORGET.

No. 3 BERKSHIRE HOUSE BLOCK, - - - GREAT BARRINGTON, MASS.

F. T. WHITING & SON, APOTHECARIES. 1847.—1890.

Fancy Goods in all varieties we keep a very complete stock of, and can show anything useful in that line. Also Foreign and Domestic Cigars we carry a very large stock of. Then our

DRUG AND PATENT MEDICINE LINE

Is larger than is often found in the country. HUYLER'S CONFECTIONERY.

GREAT BARRINGTON, MASS.

COLLINS HOUSE AND MILLER HOUSE STABLES
LIVERY AND BOARDING

GREAT BARRINGTON, MASS.

First-class Teams furnished with experienced drivers. Orders left at Lillie & Simmons' Drug Store will have prompt attention, by Telephone.

GEORGE A. TULLER.

AMID THE BERKSHIRE HILLS.
Four Hours from New York.
Great Barrington, Mass.,

Where Bryant dwelt during his early life, and visitors in the succeeding years find a source of inspiration and pleasure, in natural and cultivated conditions for summer sojourn or year-round life. There is an increasing demand for best sites and summer residence property, inside, and farm homes outside, for reasons, namely: Great Barrington is without a peer in all New England, and in varied attractions. Convenient to the principal cities, no malaria, no mosquitoes nor hot nights in summer, or blasting wind-storms or fogs at any season. Mountains and lakes, grand view-points and cascades, fishing and shooting are all within drive of an hour or two, with roads superb. The town has 5,000 population. Has soft and pure water supply. Sewerage system throughout the village. Its main street shaded one and a half miles by large elms. Electric light system for the streets. Incandescent light system and gas for interior use. Substantial public buildings. Five excellent churches. Mahaiwe National Bank and a Savings Institution. Public schools of high order. Sedgwick Institute for boys, private. Housatonic Hall for girls, private. Hotels Berkshire, Collins, Miller, all good. Trout Hatchery Club (half million capacity). Out-and-Indoor Club (village improvement). Newspapers, the Berkshire *Courier* and the Berkshire *News*.

The prevailing order, free library, expensive residences, buildings and grounds, miles of concrete walks, superior building stone, hydrant and steam fire protection, rare sanitary conditions, enhance the interest and pride of citizens who have organized THE BERKSHIRE HILLS ASSOCIATION, the secretary of which will cheerfully reply to inquiries concerning lease or sale of property, boarding-houses, etc.

WESLEYAN ACADEMY,

WILBRAHAM, MASS.

This is one of the half-dozen best Classical and Preparatory Schools in New England. It is open to both sexes, and furnishes rare advantages, not only for fitting students for all the colleges of the country, but also for academic and industrial science studies and for commercial and ornamental branches.

The situation is one of the most beautiful that can well be imagined. It is entirely rural, in a quiet village, with no places of demoralizing resort. The grounds are ample and tastefully laid out. The buildings are capacious, neat, and every way convenient. The facilities, both for the enjoyment and the improvement of the students, are seldom equalled.

SEVEN COURSES OF STUDY.

1. The Common English. 2. Commercial Course. 3. Preparatory Course, of four years, fitting Gentlemen for any of the New England Colleges, and Ladies for Middletown, Vassar, Smith, and Wellesley. 4. An Academic Course, comprising a generous range of studies for those not designing to enter College. 5. An Industrial Science Course, a new and most promising feature of the Institution. 6. A Course in Music, of an unusually high character. 7. A Course in Art, affording excellent facilities for study and culture.

SEND FOR CATALOGUE TO

GEO. M. STEELE,

PRINCIPAL.

WILBRAHAM, MASS.

CRANE'S FINE STATIONERY AT MILL PRICES.

GEORGE BLATCHFORD,
12 North Street, Pittsfield, Mass.

BOOKS, STATIONERY AND ENGRAVING. CARD AND INVITATION ENGRAVING AND PRINTING. CRESTS, MONOGRAMS, Etc., Etc. SEND FOR SAMPLE BOOK OF FINE PAPERS.

John L. Russell, Livery, Pittsfield, Mass.

CLARK W. BRYAN & COMPANY,
39, 41 and 43 Lyman Street., - - - Springfield, Mass

PUBLISHERS, PRINTERS AND BINDERS.

ALL KINDS OF MERCANTILE, MANUFACTURING, CATALOGUE AND COUNTING-ROOM WORK.

ALL IMPURE
AND
OFFENSIVE ODORS
ABSOLUTELY
REMOVED.

EDITORIAL ROOMS,
GOOD HOUSEKEEPING,
 THE PAPER WORLD,
  LIBRARY BULLETIN.

SPRINGFIELD, MASS., April 5, 1890.
THE SHERMAN "KING" VAPORIZER CO., Chicopee Falls, Mass.

Gentlemen:—I have used your Vaporizer for an aggravated case of catarrh, with excellent results. In the mid-winter of 1888-1889, I first tried the Vaporizer and soon found myself free from catarrh, from which I had suffered for several years, especially in cold weather. I have since used the Vaporizer during the past winter —one of the worst seasons known for catarrhal complaints—and have been entirely free from catarrh, the first winter season for many years.   Yours truly,

CLARK W. BRYAN.

SELF-ACTING.

Each Vaporizer sold charged for use. No care except to replenish once in two months, at expense of 4 to 8 cents, according to size. Three sizes, $3.50, $5.00, $8.00. Illustrated pamphlet free to all. Address,

SHERMAN "KING" VAPORIZER CO.,
CHICOPEE FALLS, MASS.

BOSTON, NEW YORK, PHILADELPHIA, CHICAGO, OR COLUMBUS, O.

F. M. PEASE, PHARMACIST, 14 Main St., Lee, Mass., Established 1860. Physicians' Prescriptions Receive Special Attention. All Clerks Registered. Fine Toilet Requisites, Chamois, Sponges. Good Goods at Fair Prices.

NOW READY.

Massachusetts in the War.

1861–1865.

By JAMES L. BOWEN.

With an Introduction by HON. HENRY L. DAWES.

Massachusetts in the War, from the publishers' standpoint, is a fine specimen of modern book-making, and the completed work must take a high place in its class, for its mechanical as well as its literary merit. In one magnificent volume of 1,050 large 8vo pages, richly illustrated with portraits, is given a graphic and comprehensive summary of the doings of the Commonwealth and of her soldiers and statesmen during the four years of civil war.

The Historical Narrative, with which the book opens, covers about 100 pages, and touches carefully every important phase of the struggle as it was presented to the State in its relation to the general government.

The Histories of Organizations form the body of the work, covering 773 pages. In this compass the story is fully told of 71 regiments, 16 batteries of light artillery, 3 battalions and 33 separate companies. The narrative of each is complete, starting with its organization, giving the original roster of officers, field, staff and line; following the command through all its wanderings; narrating its part and stating its loss in every action in which it was engaged; and completing the record with its muster out and the return of its members to civil life.

General Officers from Massachusetts, whether serving with the volunteer forces or in the regular army, are treated individually, and carefully prepared sketches are given of the military service of 122 officers attaining to the rank of Brevet Brigadier General or higher grade.

The portraits comprise a fine frontispiece of Governor Andrew, with handsome half-page pictures of Senators Sumner, Wilson, and Dawes, the author, and 57 of the general officers.

The Statistical Table presents in compact form for instant reference, the principal facts regarding each organization, and there is a very full and valuable index.

Price.—The book will be sold at the low price of $4.50, in fine and attractive cloth binding; leather back and corners, cloth sides, $5.00; the same with marbled paper sides, $5.00; full library, $5.00; full leather, $6.00.

CLARK W. BRYAN & CO., Publishers.
SPRINGFIELD, MASS.

Grand Prize Gold Medal Awarded.

MEDAL OF HONOR AND PERFECTION RECOMMENDED, PARIS, 1878.

THE HIGHEST AND ONLY AWARD WAS GIVEN

BYRON WESTON

—— FOR ——

LEDGER AND RECORD PAPER,

Which has received *the highest premium and medal* over all others from

Adelaide,	Gold	Franklin Institute,	Silver
American Institute,	Bronze	Louisville,	Silver
American Institute,	Silver	Calcutta Exposition,	Silver
Mass Charitable,	Silver	New England Society,	Silver
Mass. Charitable,	Improvement	St. Louis,	Silver
Paris,	Gold	New Zealand,	Gold
Cincinnati,	Silver	New York,	Superiority
Atlanta,	Gold	Sydney, Australia,	Silver
Centennial,	Bronze	Southern Exposition,	Bronze
American Institute,	Progress		

Its principal advantages are as follows :

    1. It contains more LINEN than any other Ledger Paper, has a longer fibre, and is consequently tougher.
    2. Having a harder and better body, and being more thoroughly sized, the ink spreads less after making an erasure.
    3. It is more uniform in Weight, Color and Finish.
    4. It never cockles if properly bound.
    5. Its non-chemical action upon ink is such that it both writes and rules up better.
    For proof of the above, refer to a large number of Stationers, Bookbinders, Bookkeepers and Recorders, who have given it, after a severe test, the preference over all others.
    This paper is DOUBLE-SIZED, and will stand any climate, or the most acid of fluid inks.
    Each sheet is water-marked with name and date, "BYRON WESTON'S LINEN RECORD, 1890."

In ordering Books, specify this brand of Paper to be used.

The Berkshire Life
INSURANCE COMPANY,
OF PITTSFIELD, MASS.

It issues one of the plainest and most liberal policy contracts extant.

It has ample solid assets, and a large and substantial surplus.

It has offices in the principal Cities and Towns in the North, East and West.

For circulars and pamphlets apply to any of its Agents or to the Home Office.

WILLIAM R. PLUNKETT, PRESIDENT.
JAMES M. BARKER, VICE-PRESIDENT.
JAMES W. HULL, SECRETARY.

HAMER & STONE, General Agents for Western Massachusetts.
OFFICE, COMPANY'S BUILDING, PITTSFIELD.

Those interested in the Berkshire Hills will be furnished with fine maps free on application.

www.ingramcontent.com/pod-product-compliance
Lightning Source LLC
Chambersburg PA
CBHW021154230426
43667CB00006B/389